Reading
Price Charts
Bar by Bar

Founded in 1807, John Wiley & Sons is the oldest independent publishing company in the United States. With offices in North America, Europe, Australia and Asia, Wiley is globally committed to developing and marketing print and electronic products and services for our customers' professional and personal knowledge and understanding.

The Wiley Trading series features books by traders who have survived the market's ever changing temperament and have prospered—some by reinventing systems, others by getting back to basics. Whether a novice trader, professional or somewhere in-between, these books will provide the advice and strategies needed to prosper today and well into the future.

For a list of available titles, visit our Web site at www.WileyFinance.com.

Reading Price Charts Bar by Bar

The Technical Analysis of Price Action for the Serious Trader

AL BROOKS

WILEY

John Wiley & Sons, Inc.

Published by John Wiley & Sons, Inc., Hoboken, New Jersey.
Published simultaneously in Canada.

All charts were created using TradeStation. © TradeStation Technologies, 2001–2008. All rights reserved. No investment or trading advice, recommendation or opinion is being given or intended.

For general information on our other products and services or for technical support, please contact our Customer Care Department within the United States at (800) 762-2974, outside the United States at (317) 572-3993 or fax (317) 572-4002.

Wiley also publishes its books in a variety of electronic formats. Some content that appears in print may not be available in electronic books. For more information about Wiley products, visit our web site at www.wiley.com.

Library of Congress Cataloging-in-Publication Data:

Brooks, Al, 1952–
  Reading price charts bar by bar : the technical analysis of price action for the serious trader / Al Brooks.
      p. cm. – (Wiley trading series)
  Includes index.
  ISBN 978-0-470-44395-8 (cloth)
  1. Stocks–Prices–Charts, diagrams, etc.   2. Financial futures–Charts, diagrams, etc.
3. Investment analysis.   I. Title.
  HG4638.B76 2009
  332.63'2042–dc22

                                                                    2008042575

Printed and bound by CPI Group (UK) Ltd, Croydon, CR0 4YY

C9780470443958_181023

This book is dedicated to my three loving, talented, and beautiful daughters, Meegan, Skylar, and Tess, who have provided me with the greatest joy of my life. I love all of you very, very much and think of you with a smile and pride throughout every day.

Contents

Preface

M y goals in writing this book are to describe my understanding of why the trades in Figure P.1 offer great risk-reward ratios, and to present ways to profit from setups like these in both stocks and futures trading. The most important message that I can deliver is to focus on the absolute best trades, avoid the absolute worst setups, and work on increasing the number of shares that you are trading. I freely recognize that every one of my reasons behind each setup is just my opinion and my reasoning about why a trade works might be completely wrong. However, that is irrelevant. What is important is that reading price action is a very effective way to trade, and I have thought a lot about why certain things happen the way that they do. I am comfortable with my explanations, and they give me confidence when I place a trade, but they are irrelevant to

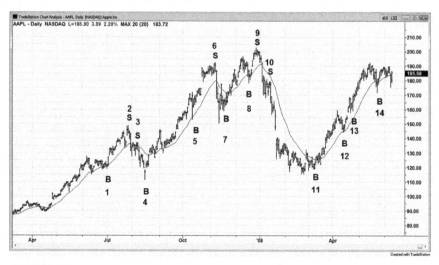

FIGURE P.1 AAPL, Daily Chart through June 10, 2008 (This chart with trendlines added is also in the final chapter, along with the explanations behind each trade.)

my placing trades, so it is not important to me that they are right. Just as I can reverse my opinion about the direction of the market in an instant, I can also reverse my opinion about why a particular pattern works if I come across a reason that is more logical or if I discover a flaw in my logic. I am providing the opinions because they appear to make sense, and they may help readers become more comfortable trading certain setups and because they may be intellectually stimulating, but they are not needed for any price action trades.

The book is a comprehensive guide to understanding price action and is directed toward sophisticated traders and market professionals. However, the concepts are useful to traders at all levels. It uses many of the standard techniques described by Edwards and Magee and many others, but will focus more on individual bars to demonstrate how the information they provide can significantly enhance the risk-reward ratio of trading. Most books point out three or four trades on a chart, which implies that everything else on the chart is incomprehensible, meaningless, or risky. I believe that there is something to be learned from every tick that takes place during the day and that there are far more great trades on every chart than just the few obvious ones, but to see them, you have to understand price action, and you cannot dismiss any bars as unimportant. I learned from performing thousands of operations through a microscope that some of the most important things can be very small.

I read charts bar by bar and look for any information that each bar is telling me. They are all important. At the end of every bar, most traders ask themselves, "What just took place?" With most bars, they conclude that it is just too confusing to understand and choose to wait for a pattern that they recognize. It is as if they believe that the bar did not exist, or they dismiss it as just institutional program activity that is not tradable by an individual trader. They do not feel as though they are part of the market at these times, but these times constitute the vast majority of the day. Yet, if they look at the volume, all of those bars that they are ignoring have as much volume as the bars they are using for the bases for their trades. Clearly, a lot of trading is taking place, but they don't understand how that can be, and essentially they pretend that it does not exist. But that is denying reality. There is always trading taking place, and as a trader you owe it to yourself to understand why it's taking place and to figure out a way to make money off it. Learning what the market is telling you is very time consuming and difficult, but it gives you the foundation that you need to be a successful trader.

Unlike most books on candle charts where the majority of readers feel compelled to memorize patterns, this book will provide a rationale for why particular patterns are reliable setups for traders. Some of the terms used have specific meaning to market technicians but different meanings to traders and I am writing this entirely from a trader's perspective. I am certain that many traders already understand everything in this book, but likely wouldn't describe price action in the same way that I do. There are no secrets among successful traders, and they all know common setups, and many have their own names for each one. All of them are buying and selling pretty much at the same time, catching the same swings, and each has his own reasons for getting into a trade. Many trade price action intuitively without ever feeling a need to articulate why a certain setup works. I hope that they enjoy reading my understanding of and perspective on price action and that this gives them some insights that will improve their already successful trading.

The goal for most traders is to maximize trading profits through a style that is compatible with their personalities. Without that compatibility, I believe that it is virtually impossible to trade profitably long term. Many traders wonder how long it will take them to be successful and are willing to lose money for some period of time, even a few years. However, it took me over 10 years to be able to trade successfully. Each of us has many considerations and distractions, so the time will vary, but a trader has to work though most obstacles before becoming consistently profitable. I had several major problems that had to be corrected, including raising three wonderful daughters who always filled my mind with thoughts of them and what I needed to be doing as their father. That was solved as they got older and more independent. Then it took me a long time to accept many personality traits as real and unchangeable (or at least I concluded that I was unwilling to change them). And finally there was the issue of confidence. I have always been confident to the point of arrogant in so many things that those who know me would be surprised that this was difficult for me. However, deep inside I believed that I really would never come up with a consistently profitable approach that I would enjoy employing for many years. Instead, I bought many systems, wrote and tested countless indicators and systems, read many books and magazines, went to seminars, hired tutors, joined chat rooms, and talked with people who presented themselves as successful traders, but I never saw their account statements and suspect that most could teach but few if any could trade. Usually in trading, those who know don't talk, and those who talk don't know.

This was all extremely helpful because it showed all of the things that I needed to avoid before becoming successful. Any nontrader who looks at a chart will invariably conclude that trading has to be extremely easy, and that is part of the appeal. At the end of the day, anyone can look at any chart and see very clear entry and exit points. However, it is much more difficult to do in real time. There is a natural tendency to want to buy the exact low and never have the trade come back. If it does, a novice will take the loss to avoid a bigger loss, resulting in a series of losing trades that will ultimately bust his account. Using wide stops solves that to some extent, but invariably a trader will soon hit a few big losses that will put him into the red and make him too scared to continue using that approach.

Why do so many business schools continue to recommend Edwards and Magee when their book is essentially simplistic, largely using trend-lines, breakouts, and pullbacks as the basis for trading? They do so because the system works, and it always has, and it always will. Now that just about all traders have computers with access to intraday data, many of those techniques can be adapted to day trading. Also, candle charts give additional information about who is controlling the market, which results in a more timely entry with smaller risk. Edwards and Magee's focus is on the overall trend. I use those same basic techniques but pay much closer attention to the individual bars on the chart to improve the risk-reward ratio, and I devote considerable attention to intraday charts.

It seemed obvious to me that if one could simply read the charts well enough to be able to enter at the exact times that the move would take off and not come back, then that trader would have a huge advantage. He would have a high winning percentage and the few losses would be small. I decided that this would be my starting point, and what I discovered was that nothing had to be added. In fact, any additions are distractions that result in lower profitability. This sounds so obvious and easy that it is difficult for most people to believe.

I am a day trader who relies entirely on price action on the intraday Emini S&P 500 Futures (the "Emini") charts, and I believe that reading price action well is an invaluable skill for all traders. Beginners often instead have a deep-seated belief that something more is required, that maybe some complex mathematical formula that very few use would give them just the edge that they need. Goldman Sachs is so rich and sophisticated that they must have a supercomputer and high-powered software that gives them an advantage that insures that all the individual traders are doomed to failure. They start looking at all kinds of indicators and playing with the inputs to customize the indicators to make them just right. Every indicator works some of the time, but for me, they obfuscate instead of elucidate. In fact, without even looking at a chart, you can place a buy order and have a 50 percent chance of being right!

I am not dismissing indicators and systems out of ignorance of their subtleties. I have spent over 10,000 hours writing and testing indicators and systems over the years, and that probably is far more experience than most. This extensive experience with indicators and systems was an essential part of my becoming a successful trader. Indicators work well for many traders, but the best success comes once a trader finds an approach that is compatible with his personality. My single biggest problem with indicators and systems is that I never fully trusted them. At every setup, I saw exceptions that needed to be tested. I always wanted every last penny out of the market and was never satisfied with a return from a system if I could incorporate a new twist that would make it better. I am simply too controlling, compulsive, restless, observant, and untrusting to make money long term off indicators or automated systems, but I am at the extreme in many ways, and most people don't have these same issues.

Many traders, especially beginners, are drawn to indicators, hoping that an indicator will show them when to enter a trade. What they don't realize is that the vast majority of indicators are based on simple price action, and when I am placing trades, I simply cannot think fast enough to process what several indicators might be telling me. Also, oscillators tend to make traders look for reversals and focus less on price charts. These can be effective tools on most days when the market has two or three reversals lasting an hour or more. The problem comes when the market is trending strongly. If you focus too much on your indicators, you will see that they are forming divergences all day long, and you may find yourself repeatedly entering Countertrend and losing money. By the time you come to accept that the market is trending, you will not have enough time left in the day to recoup your losses. Instead, if you were simply looking at a bar or candle chart, you would see that the market is clearly trending, and you would not be tempted by indicators to look for trend reversals. The most common successful reversals first break a trendline with strong momentum and then pullback to test the extreme, and if a trader focuses too much on divergences, she will often overlook this fundamental fact. A divergence in the absence of a Countertrend momentum surge that breaks a trendline is a losing strategy. Wait for the trendline break, and then see if the test of the old extreme reverses or if the old trend resumes. You do not need an indicator to tell you that a strong reversal here is a high-probability trade, at least for a scalp, and there will almost certainly be a divergence, so why complicate your thinking by adding the indicator to your calculus?

Some pundits recommend a combination of time frames, indicators, wave counting, and Fibonacci retracements and extensions, but when it comes time to place the trade, they will only do it if there is a good price action setup. Also, when they see a good price action setup, they start looking for indicators that show divergences or different time frames for moving average tests or wave counts or Fibonacci setups to confirm what is in front of them. In reality, they are price action traders who are trading exclusively off price action on only one chart but don't feel comfortable admitting it. They are complicating their trading to the point that they certainly are missing many, many trades because their overanalysis takes too much time to place their orders, and they are forced to wait for the next setup. The logic just isn't there for making the simple so complicated. Obviously adding any information can lead to better decision making, and many people may be able to process lots of inputs when deciding whether to place a trade. Ignoring data because of a simplistic ideology alone is foolish. The goal is to make money, and a trader should do everything he can to maximize his profits. I simply cannot process multiple indicators and time frames well in the time needed to place my orders accurately, and I find that carefully reading a single chart is far more profitable for me. Also, if I rely on indicators, I find that I get lazy in my price action reading and often miss the obvious. Price action is far more important than any other information, and if you sacrifice some of what it is telling you to gain information from something else, you are likely making a bad decision.

There are countless ways to make money trading stocks and Eminis, but all require movement (well, except for shorting options). If you learn to read the charts, you will catch a great number of these profitable trades every day without ever knowing why some institution started the trend and without ever knowing what any indicator is showing. You don't need their software or analysts because they will show you what they are doing. All you have to do is piggy-back onto their trades, and you will make a profit. Price action will tell you what they are doing and allow you an early entry with a tight stop.

I have found that I consistently make far more money by minimizing what I have to consider when placing a trade. All I need is a single chart on my laptop computer with no indicators except a 20-bar exponential moving average, which does not require too much analysis and clarifies many good setups each day. I sometimes trade even without the moving average, but it provides enough setups that it is usually worth having on the chart. Volume on 1-minute charts is also sometimes minimally useful when looking for a sign that a trend reversal might be imminent, but I never look at it because I trade mostly off the 5-minute chart (rarely I will take an early 5-minute With Trend entry off the 1-minute chart). An unusually large 1-minute volume spike often comes near the end of a bear trend, and the next new swing low or two often provide profitable long scalps. However, this is simply an observation; it is far too unreliable to be a part of your trading and should be ignored. Volume spikes also sometimes occur on daily charts when a selloff is overdone.

Even traders who base their trades on a collection of indicators routinely look at price action when placing their entries and exits. Who wouldn't feel better about buying a divergence if there was also a strong reversal bar at the low? However, charts provide far more information about who is in control of the market than most traders realize. Almost every bar offers important clues as to where the market is going, and a trader who dismisses any activity as noise is passing up many profitable trades each day.

As a trader, I see everything in shades of gray and am constantly thinking in terms of probabilities. If a pattern is setting up and it is not perfect but it is reasonably similar to a reliable setup, it will likely behave similarly as well. Close is usually close enough. If something resembles a textbook setup, the trade will likely unfold similarly to the trade from the textbook setup. This is the art of trading, and it takes years to become good at trading in the gray zone. Everyone wants concrete, clear rules, or indicators, and chat rooms, newsletters, hotlines, or tutors that will tell them when exactly to get in to minimize risk and maximize profit, but none of it works in the long run. You have to take responsibility for your decisions, but you first have to learn how to make them, and that means that you have to get used to operating in the gray fog. Nothing is ever as clear as black and white, and I have been doing this long enough to appreciate that anything, no matter how unlikely, can and will happen. It's like quantum physics. Every conceivable event has a probability, and so do events that you have yet to consider. It is not emotional, and the reasons why something happens are irrelevant. Watching to see if the Feds cut rates today is a waste of time because there is both a bullish and bearish interpretation of anything that they do. What is key is to see what the market does, not what the Fed does. Never watch the news during the trading day. If you want to know what a news event means, the chart in front of you will tell you. If a pundit on CNBC announces that a report was bearish and the market goes up, are you going to look to short? Only look at the chart, and it will tell you what you need to know. The chart is what will give you money or take money from you, so it is the only thing that you should ever consider when trading. If you are on the floor, you can't even trust what your best friend is doing. He might be offering a lot of orange juice calls but secretly having a broker looking to buy 10 times as many below the market. Your friend is just trying to create a panic to drive the market down so he can load up through a surrogate at a much better price.

There is one other problem with the news. Invariably when the market makes a huge move, the reporters will find some confident, convincing expert who predicted it and interview him, leading the viewers to believe that this pundit has an uncanny ability to predict the market, despite the untold reality that this same pundit has been wrong in his last 10 predictions. The pundit then makes some future prediction, and the naïve viewer will attach significance to it and let it affect his trading. What the viewer may not realize is that some pundits are bullish 100 percent of the time and others are bearish 100 percent of the time, and still others just swing for the fences all of the time and make outrageous predictions. The reporter just rushes to the one who is consistent with the day's news, which is totally useless to a trader. In fact it is destructive because it can influence his trading and make him question and deviate from his own methods. So, if you really must watch TV during the trading day, I recommend cartoons or foreign language shows, so there will be no chance that the show will influence your trading.

Friends and colleagues freely offer opinions for you to ignore. Occasionally traders will tell me that they have a great setup and want to discuss it with me. I invariably get them angry at me when I tell them that I am not interested. They immediately perceive me as selfish, stubborn, and close-minded, and when it comes to trading, I am all of that and probably much more. The skills that make you money are generally seen as flaws to the lay person. Why do I no longer read books or articles about trading, or talk to other traders about their ideas? As I said, the chart tells me all that I need to know, and any other information is a distraction. Several people have been offended by my attitude, but I think it in part comes from me turning down what they are presenting as something helpful to me when in reality they are making an offering, hoping that I will reciprocate with some tutoring. They become frustrated and angry when I tell them that I don't want to hear about anyone else's trading techniques. I tell them that I haven't even mastered my own and probably never will, but I am confident that I will make far more money perfecting what I already know than trying to incorporate non-price action approaches into my trading. I ask them if James Galway offered a beautiful flute to Yo Yo Mah and insisted that Yo Yo start learning the flute because Galway makes so much money by playing his flute, should Mah accept the offer? Clearly not. Mah should continue to become better and better at the cello and by doing so he will make far more money than if he also started playing the flute. I am no Galway or Mah, but the concept is the same. Price action is the only instrument that I want to play and I strongly believe that I will make far more money by mastering it than by incorporating ideas from other successful traders.

Yesterday, Costco's earnings were up 32 percent on the quarter and above analysts' expectations. It gapped up on the open, tested the gap on the first bar and then ran up over a dollar in twenty minutes. (See Figure P.2.) It then drifted down to test yesterday's close. It had two rallies that broke bear trendlines, and both failed. This created a Double Top (Bars 2 and 3) Bear Flag or Triple Top (Bars 1, 2, and 3) and the market then plunged three dollars, below the prior day's low. If you were unaware of the report, you would have shorted at the failed bear trendline breaks at Bars 2 and 3 and you would have sold more on the Breakout Pullback at Bar 4. You would have reversed to long on the Bar 5 big reversal bar, which was the second attempt to reverse the breakout below yesterday's low and a climactic reversal of the breakout of the bottom of the steep bear trend channel line. Alternatively, you could have bought the open because of the bullish report, and then worried about why the stock was collapsing instead of soaring the way that TV analysts predicted, and you likely would have sold out your long on the second plunge down to Bar 5.

Any trend that covers a lot of points in very few bars, meaning that there is some combination of large bars and bars with very little overlap,

FIGURE P.2 Should You Buy Based on a Great Earnings Report or Short Based on Price Action?

will eventually have a pullback. These trends have such strong momentum that the odds favor a test of the trend's extreme after the pullback and usually the extreme will be exceeded, as long as the pullback does not become a new trend and extend beyond the start of the prior trend. In general, the odds that a pullback will get back to the prior trend's extreme fall substantially if the pullback retraces 75 percent or more. For a pullback in a bear, at that point, a trader is better to think of the pullback as a new bull trend rather than a pullback in an old bear. Bar 6 was about a 70 percent pullback and then the market tested the climactic bear low on the open of the next day.

The only thing that is as it seems is the chart. If you cannot figure out what it is telling you, do not trade. Wait for clarity. It will always come. But once it is there, you must place the trade and assume the risk and follow your plan. Do not dial down to a 1-minute chart and tighten your stop because you will lose. The problem with the 1-minute chart is that it tempts you by offering lots of entries. However, you will not be able to take them all and you will instead cherry-pick, which will lead to the death of your account; you will invariably pick too many bad cherries. The best trades often happen too fast for you to place your orders and that means you will be choosing among the less desirable trades and will lose more often. When you enter on a 5-minute chart, your trade is based on your analysis of the 5-minute chart without any idea of what the 1-minute looks like. You must therefore rely on your 5-minute stops and targets, and just accept the reality that the 1-minute chart will move against you and hit a 1-minute stop frequently. If you watch the 1-minute chart, you will not be devoting your full attention to the 5-minute chart and I will take your money from your account and put it in my account. If you want to compete, you must minimize all distractions and all inputs other than what is on the chart in front of you, and trust that if you do, you will make a lot of money. It will seem unreal but it is very real. Never question it. Just keep things simple and follow your simple rules. It is extremely difficult to consistently do something simple, but in my opinion, it is the best way to trade. Ultimately, as a trader understands price action better and better, trading becomes much less stressful and actually pretty boring, but much more profitable.

Although I never gamble because the odds are against me and I never want to bet against math, there are some similarities with gambling, especially in the minds of those who don't trade. For example, some traders use simple game theory and increase the size of a trade after one or more losing trades. Blackjack card counters are very similar to trading range traders. The card counter is trying to determine when the math has gone too far in one direction. In particular, he wants to know then the remaining cards in the deck are likely overweighed with face cards. When his count indicates that this is likely, he places a trade (bet) based on the probability that a disproportionate number of face cards will be coming up, increasing his odds of winning. A trading range trader is looking for times when he thinks the market has gone too far in one direction and then he places his trade in the opposite direction (a fade).

One unfortunate reality is that there are aspects of trading that are very similar to gambling—the most important one is that many losing games win often enough to make you believe that you will be able to find a way to win at them in the long run. You are fighting relentless, unstoppable math and you will go broke trying to beat it. The most obvious example is trading off the 1-minute chart. Since it looks the same as the 5-minute and since you can make many winning trades day trading it, it is logical to conclude that you can use it as your primary chart. However, too many of the best trades happen too fast to catch and you will find yourself left with the second-tier trades. Over time, you will either go broke or make substantially less than you would off the 5-minute chart.

One unfortunate comparison is from non-traders who assume that all day traders, and all market traders for that matter, are addicted gamblers and therefore have a mental illness. I suspect that many are in that they are doing it more for excitement than for profit and are willing to make low probability bets and lose large sums of money because of the huge rush they feel when they occasionally win. However, most successful traders are essentially investors, just like an investor who buys commercial real estate or a small business. The only real differences from any other type of investing are that the time frame is shorter and the leverage is greater.

One final point about gambling. Monte Carlo techniques work well in theory but not in practice because of the conflict between math and emotion. If you double (or even triple) your position size and reverse at each loss, you will theoretically make money. Although four losers in a row is rare on the 5-minute Emini chart (especially if you avoid trading in small sideways trading ranges in the middle of the day's range), they will happen, and so will six, seven, or more, even though I can't remember ever seeing that. In any case, if you are comfortable trading ten contracts and you decide to double and reverse with each loser, but begin with one contract, four consecutive losers would require sixteen contracts and it is unlikely that you would place a trade that is larger than your comfort zone following four losers. Also, if you like trading ten contracts, you will not be satisfied with the profit from trading one contract, which is what you would end up trading most of the time.

Lay people are also concerned about the risk of crashes and because of that risk, they again associate trading with gambling. Crashes are very rare on daily charts (but common on intraday charts). They are afraid of their inability to function effectively during extremely emotional events. Although the term "crash" is generally reserved for daily charts and applied to bear markets of about 20 percent or more happening in a short time frame, like in 1927 and 1987, it is more useful to think of it as just a simple and common chart pattern because that removes the emotion and helps a trader follow his rules. If you remove the time and price axes from a chart and focus simply on the price action, there are market movements that occur on intraday charts that are indistinguishable from the patterns in a classic crash. If you can get passed the emotion, you can make money off crashes because with all charts, they display tradable price action.

Figure P.3 (from TradeStation) shows how markets can crash in any timeframe. The one on the left is a daily chart of GE during the 1987 crash, the middle is a 5-minute chart of COST after a very strong earnings report, and the one on the right is a 1-minute Emini chart. Although the term "crash" is used almost exclusively to refer to a 20 percent or more selloff over a short time on a daily chart and was widely used only twice in past hundred years, a price action trader looks for shape and the same crash pattern is common on intraday charts. Since crashes are so common intraday, there is no need to apply the term because from a trading perspective, they are just a bear swing with tradable price action.

Most traders only consider price action when trading divergences and trend pullbacks. They like to see a strong close on a large reversal bar, but in reality this is a fairly rare occurrence. The most useful tools for understanding price action are trendlines and trend channel lines, prior highs and lows, breakouts and failed breakouts, the size of bodies and tails on candles, and relationships between the current bar to the prior several bars. In

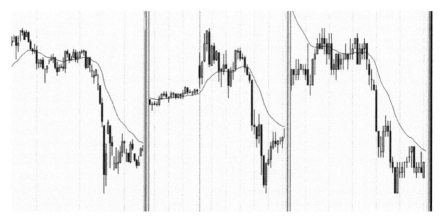

FIGURE P.3 Market Crashes Look the Same on All Timeframes

particular, how the open, high, low, and close of the current bar compare
to the action of the prior several bars tells a lot about what will happen
next. Most of the observations in this book are directly related to placing
trades, but a few have to do with simple curious price action tendencies
without sufficient dependability to be the basis for a trade.

I personally rely mainly on candle charts for Emini trading and bar
charts for stock trading, but most signals are also visible on any type of
chart and many are even evident on simple line charts. I will focus primarily on 5-minute candle charts to illustrate basic principles but will also
thoroughly discuss daily and weekly charts as well. Additionally, I place intraday swing trades on several stocks each day and make occasional option
purchases based on daily charts, and will discuss how using price action
alone can be the basis for this type of trading.

Most of the charts in the book demonstrate many different concepts
and I indicated key price action observations on most. Because of this,
almost any chart could be on any page, but I placed them in the section where I thought they best illustrated a point. Many charts reference
setups that are described later in the book, but when they are clear examples of important setups, I point them out, which should be helpful on a second read through the book. Also, almost every pattern that you see during
the day can be placed into several categories in this book. Don't waste
time deciding if a reversal is unfolding as a Double Bottom Pullback or a
Spike and Trading Range low or a simple Higher Low. You are a trader,
not a file clerk. When you see a reversal pattern, just take the trade and
don't labor over which name most accurately applies. Also, not all chapters are created equal. Some are essential to your success whereas others
are included for completeness. If you are a beginner, focus on Chapter 15

because it describes the best trades, and then refer back to the appropriate earlier chapters to learn more. Don't spend a lot of time on concepts like Magnets and Measured Moves, because that is not where the money is. They are included simply because they demonstrate aspects of price action, but do not offer reliable trading patterns.

Since I trade in California, all of the charts are in Pacific Standard Time. All of the charts were created with TradeStation.

CHAPTER 1

Price Action

For a trader, the fundamental issue that confronts him repeatedly throughout the day is the decision of whether the market is trending or not trending. If it is trending, he assumes that the trend will continue, and he will look to enter in the direction of the trend ("With Trend"). If it is not trending, he will look to enter in the opposite direction of the most recent move ("fade" or "Countertrend"). A trend can be as short as a single bar (on a smaller time frame, there can be a strong trend contained within that bar) or, on a 5-minute chart, it can last a day or more. How does he make this decision? By reading the price action on the chart in front of him.

The most useful definition of price action for a trader is also the simplest: it is any change in price on any chart type or time frame. The smallest unit of change is the tick, which has a different value for each market. Incidentally, a tick has two meanings. It is the smallest unit of change in price that a market can make, and it is also every trade that takes place (so if you buy, your order will appear on the Time and Sales table, and your fill, no matter how large or small, is one tick). Since price is changing with every tick (trade) during the day, each price change becomes an example of price action. There is no universally accepted definition of price action, and since you need to always try to be aware of even the seemingly least significant piece of information that the market is offering, you must have a very broad definition. You cannot dismiss anything because very often something that initially appears minor leads to a great trade. The broadest definition includes any representation of price movement during the course of trading. This includes any financial instrument, on any type of chart, in any time frame.

The definition alone does not tell you anything about placing a trade because every bar is a potential signal both for a short and a long trade. There are traders out there who will be looking to short the next tick, believing that the market won't go one tick higher, and others who will buy it believing that the market will likely not go one tick lower. One side will be right, and the other will be wrong. If the buyers are wrong and the market goes one tick lower and then another and then another, they will begin to entertain the prospect that their belief is wrong. At some point, they will have to sell their position at a loss, making them new sellers and no longer buyers, and this will drive the market down further. Sellers will continue to enter the market, either as new shorts or as longs forced to liquidate, until some point when more buyers come in. These buyers will be a combination of new buyers, profit-taking shorts, and new shorts who now have a loss and will have to buy to cover their positions. The market will continue up until the process reverses once again.

Everything is relative, and everything can change into the exact opposite in an instant, even without any movement in price. It might be that you suddenly see a trendline seven ticks above the high of the current bar and instead of looking to short, you now are looking to buy for a test of the trendline. Trading through the rearview mirror is a sure way to lose money. You have to keep looking ahead, not worrying about the mistakes you just made. They have absolutely no bearing on the next tick, so you must ignore them and just keep reassessing the price action and not your profit and loss (P&L) on the day.

Each tick changes the price action of every time frame chart from a tick chart or 1-minute chart through a monthly chart, and on all charts, whether the chart is based on time, volume, the number of ticks, point and figure, or anything else. Obviously, a single tick move is usually meaningless on a monthly chart (unless, for example, it is a one tick breakout of some chart point that immediately reverses), but it becomes increasingly more useful on smaller time frame charts. This is obviously true because if the average bar today on a 1-minute Emini chart is three ticks tall, then a one tick move is 33 percent of the size of the average bar, and that can represent a significant move.

The most useful aspect of price action is watching what happens after the market moves beyond (breaks out beyond) prior bars or trendlines on the chart. For example, if the market goes above a significant prior high and each subsequent bar forms a low that is above the prior bar's low and a high that is above the prior bar's high, then this price action indicates that the market will likely be higher on some subsequent bar, even if it pulls back for a few bars near term. On the other hand, if the market breaks out to the upside, and then the next bar is a small inside bar (its high is not higher than that of the large breakout bar), and then the following bar has a low that is below this small bar, the odds of a failed breakout and a reversal back down increase considerably.

Over time, fundamentals control the price of a stock, and that price is set by institutional traders (like mutual funds, banks, brokerage houses, insurance companies, pension funds, hedge funds, and so on), who are by far the biggest volume players. Price action is the movement that takes place along the way as institutions probe for value. When they feel that the price is too high, they will exit or even short, and when they feel it is too low (a good value), they will go long or take profits on their shorts. Although conspiracy theorists will never believe it, institutions do not have secret meetings to vote on what the price should be in an attempt to steal money from unsuspecting, well-intentioned individual traders. Their voting is essentially independent and secret, and comes in the form of their buying and selling, but the results are displayed on price charts. In the short run, an institution can manipulate the price of a stock, especially if it is thinly traded. However, they would make relatively much less money doing that compared to what they could make in other forms of trading, making the concern of manipulation of negligible importance, especially in stocks and markets where huge volume is traded, like the Eminis, major stocks, debt instruments, and currencies.

Why does price move up one tick? It is because there is more volume being bid at the current price than being offered, and a number of those buyers are willing to pay even more than the current price if necessary. This is sometimes described as the market having more buyers than sellers, or as the buyers being in control, or as buying pressure. Once all of those buy orders that can possibly be filled are filled at the current price (the last price traded), the remaining buyers will have to decide whether they are willing to buy at one tick higher. If they are, they will continue to bid at the higher price. This higher price will make all market participants re-evaluate their perspective on the market. If there continues to be more volume being bid than offered, price will continue to move up since there are an insufficient number of contracts being offered by sellers at the last price to fill the requests to buy by buyers. At some point, buyers will start offering some of their contracts as they take partial profits. Also, sellers will perceive the current price as a good value for a short and offer to sell more than buyers want to buy. Once there are more contracts being offered by sellers (either buyers who are looking to cover some or all of their long contracts or by new sellers who are attempting to short), all of the buy orders will be filled at the current price, but some sellers will be unable to find enough buyers. The bid will move down a tick. If there are sellers willing to sell at this lower price, this will become the new last price.

Since most markets are driven by institutional orders, it is reasonable to wonder whether the institutions are basing their entries on price action, or whether their actions are causing the price action. The reality is that institutions are not all watching AAPL or SPY tick by tick and then starting a buy program when they see a two-legged pullback on a 1-minute chart. They have a huge number of orders to be filled during the day and are working to fill them at the best price. Price action is just one of many considerations, and some firms will rely more on it, and others will rely on it less or not at all. Many firms have mathematical models and programs that determine when and how much to buy and sell, and all firms continue to receive new orders from clients all day long.

The price action that traders see during the day is the result of institutional activity and much less the cause of the activity. When a profitable setup unfolds, there will be a confluence of unknowable influences taking place during the trade that results in the trade being profitable or a loser. The setup is the actual first phase of a move that is already underway and a price action entry lets a trader just jump onto the wave early on. As more price action unfolds, more traders will enter in the direction of the move, generating momentum on the charts, causing additional traders to enter. Traders, including institutions, place their bids and offers for every imaginable reason, and the reasons are largely irrelevant. However, one reason that is relevant, because it is evident to smart price action traders, is to benefit from trapped traders. If you know that protective stops are located at one tick below a bar and will result in losses to traders who just bought, then you should get short on a stop at that same price to make a profit off the trapped traders as they are forced out.

Since institutional activity controls the move and their volume is so huge and they place most of their trades with the intention of holding them for hours to months, most will not be looking to scalp and instead they will defend their original entry. If Vanguard or Fidelity have to buy stock for one of their mutual funds, their clients will want the fund to own stock at the end of the day. Clients do not buy mutual funds with the expectation that the funds will day trade and end up in all cash by the close. The funds have to own stock, which means they have to buy and hold, not buy and scalp. For example, after their initial buy, they will likely have much more to buy and will use any small pullback to add on. If there is none, they will continue to buy as the market rises.

Some beginner traders wonder who is buying as the market is going straight up and also wonder why anyone would buy at the market instead of waiting for a pullback. The answer is simple. It is institutions working to fill all of their orders at the best possible price, and they will buy in many pieces as the market continues up. A lot of this trading is being done by institutional computer programs, and it will end after the programs are complete. If a trade fails, it is far more likely the result of the trader misreading the price action than it is of an institution changing its mind or taking a couple ticks of profit within minutes of initiating a program.

The only importance of realizing that institutions are responsible for price action is that it makes placing trades based on price action more reliable. Most institutions are not going to be day trading in and out, making the market reverse after every one of your entries. Your price action entry is just a piggyback trade on their activity, but, unlike them, you are scalping all or part of your trade.

There are some firms that day trade substantial volume. However, for their trades to be profitable the market has to move many ticks in their direction, and a price action trader will see the earliest parts of the move, allowing her to get in early and be confident that the odds of a successful scalp are high. That firm cannot have the market go 15 ticks against them if they are trying to scalp 4 or 8 ticks. As such, they will enter only when they feel that the risk of an adverse move is small. If you read their activity on the charts, you should likewise be confident in your trade, but always have a stop in the market in case your read is wrong.

Also, since often the entry bar extreme is tested to the tick and the stops are not run, there must be institutional size volume protecting the stops, and they are doing so based on price action. In the 5-minute Emini, there are certain price action events that change the perspective of smart traders. For example, if a High 2 long pullback fails, smart traders will assume that the market will likely have two more legs down. If you are an institutional trader and you bought that High 2, you do not want it to fail, and you will buy more all the way down to one tick above that key protective stop price. That institution is using price action to support their long.

The big legs are essentially unstoppable, but the small price action is fine-tuned by some institutional traders who are watching every tick. Sometimes when there is a 5-tick long failure setting up and the price just keeps hitting 5 ticks but not 6 where you can scalp 4 ticks out of your long, there will suddenly be a trade of 250 Emini contracts, and the price does not tick down. In general, anything over 100 contracts should be considered institutional in today's Emini market. Even if it is just a large individual trader, he likely has the insight of an institution, and since he is trading institutional volume, he is indistinguishable from an institution. Since the price is still hanging at 5 ticks, almost certainly that 250 lot order was an institutional buy. This is because if institutions were selling in a market filled with nervous longs, the market would fall quickly. When the institutions start buying when the market is up 5 ticks, they expect it to go more than just 1 tick higher and usually within a minute or so the price will surge through 6 ticks and swing up for at least many more. The institutions were buying at the high, which means that they think the market will go higher and they will likely buy more as it goes up. Also, since 4-tick scalps work so often, it is likely that there is institutional scalping that exerts a great influence over most scalps during the day.

Traders pay close attention to the seconds before key time frames close, especially 3-, 5-, 15-, and 60-minute bars. This is also true on key volumes for volume bar charts. For example, if many traders follow the 10,000 shares per bar chart for the Ten Year Note futures contract, then when the bar is about to close (it closes on the first trade of any size that results in at least 10,000 shares traded since the start of the bar, so the bar is rarely ever exactly 10,000 shares), there may be a flurry of activity to influence the final appearance of the bar. One side might want to demonstrate a willingness to make the bar appear more bullish or bearish. In simplest terms, a strong bull trend bar means that the bulls owned the bar. It is very common in strong trends for a reversal bar to totally reverse its appearance in the final few seconds before a 5-minute bar closes. For example, in a strong bear, there might be a High 2 long setting up with a very strong bull reversal bar. Then, with 5 seconds remaining before the bar closes, the price plummets, and the bar closes on its low, trapping lots of front running longs who expected a bull trend reversal bar. When trading Countertrend against a strong trend, it is imperative to wait for the signal bar to close before you place your order, and then only enter on a stop at 1 tick beyond the bar in the direction of your trade (if you are buying, buy at 1 tick above the high of the prior bar on a stop).

What is the best way to learn how to read price action? It is to print out charts and then look for every profitable trade. If you are a scalper looking for 50 cents in AAPL or $2 in GOOG on the 5-minute chart, then find every move during the day where that amount of profit was possible. After several weeks, you will begin to see a few patterns that would allow you to make those trades while risking about the same amount. If the risk is the same as the reward, you have to win much more than 50 percent of the time to make the trade worthwhile. However, lots of patterns have a 70 percent or better success rate, and many trades allow you to move up your stop from below the signal bar extreme to below the entry bar extreme while waiting for your profit target to be reached, reducing your risk. Also, you should be trying to enter trades that have a good chance of running well past your profit target, and you should therefore only take partial profits. In fact, initially you should only focus on those entries. Move your stop to breakeven and then let the remainder run. You will likely have at least a couple of trades each week that run to four or more times your initial target before setting up a reverse entry pattern.

Fibonacci retracements and extensions are a part of price action, but since most are just approximations and most fail, do not use them for trading. If one is good, it will be associated with a chart pattern that is reliable and tradable on its own, independent of the Fibonacci measurement or any indicators. Elliott Wave Theory is also a type of price action analysis, but for most traders it is not tradable. The waves are usually not clear until many, many bars after the ideal entry point, and with so many opposite interpretations at every instant, it requires far too much thought and uncertainty for most active day traders.

Should you be concerned that making the information in this book available will create lots of great price action traders, all doing the same thing at the same time, thereby removing the late entrants needed to drive the market to your price target? No, because the institutions control the market, and they already have the smartest traders in the world, and those traders already know everything in this book, at least intuitively. The reason that the patterns that we all see unfold as they do is because that is the appearance that occurs in an efficient market with countless traders placing orders for thousands of different reasons, but with the controlling volume being traded based on sound logic. That is just what it looks like, and it has forever. The same patterns unfold on all time frames in all markets around the world and it would simply be impossible for all of it to be manipulated instantaneously on so many different levels.

If everyone suddenly became a price action scalper, the smaller patterns might change a little for a while, but over time, the efficient market will win out, and the votes by all traders will get distilled into standard price action patterns because that is the inescapable result of countless people behaving logically. Also, the reality is that it is very difficult to trade, and although basing trades on price action is a sound approach, it is still very difficult to do real time. There just won't be enough traders doing it well enough, all at the same time, to have any significant influence over time on the patterns. Just look at Edwards and Magee. The best traders in the world have been using those ideas for decades and they continue to work, again for the same reason . . . charts look they way they do because that is the unchangeable fingerprint of an efficient market filled with a huge number of smart people using a huge number of approaches and time frames, all trying to make the most money that they can.

TREND BARS AND DOJI BARS

The market is either trending on the chart in front of you, or it is not. When it is not, it is in some kind of trading range, which is composed of trends on smaller time frames. On the level of an individual bar, it is either a trend bar or a trading range bar. Either the bulls or bears are in control of the bar, or they are largely in equilibrium (a one bar trading range).

For a trader, it is most useful to think of all bars as being either trend bars or nontrend (trading range) bars. Since the latter is an awkward term and most are similar to dojis, it is simpler to refer to all nontrend bars as dojis (doji bars) (see Figure 1.1). If the body appears tiny or nonexistent on the chart, the bar is a doji, and neither the bulls nor bears controlled the bar, and the bar is essentially a one bar trading range. On a 5-minute Emini chart, a doji body is only a tick or two large. However, on a daily or weekly Google chart, the body can be 100 ticks ($1) or more and still have the same significance as a perfect doji, and therefore it makes sense to refer to it as a doji. The determination is relative and subjective, and it depends on the market and the time frame.

If there is a body, then the close trended away from the open, and the bar is a trend bar. Obviously, if the bar is large and the body is small, there was not much trending strength. Also, within the bar (as seen on a smaller time frame), there may have been several swings of largely sideways movement, but this is irrelevant because you should focus on only one chart. Larger bodies in general indicate more strength, but an extremely large body after a protracted move or a breakout can represent an exhaustive end of a trend, and no trade should be taken until more price action unfolds. A series of strong trend bars is the sign of a healthy trend and will usually be followed by a further extreme, even if a pullback immediately ensues.

An ideal trend bar is one with a moderate-size body, indicating that the market trended away from the open of the bar by the time the bar closed. The minimum is a close above the open in a bull trend bar, indicated by a white candle body in this book. The bulls can demonstrate stronger control

FIGURE 1.1 Examples of Dojis

by having the body be about the size or larger than that of the median body size over the past 5 or 10 bars. Additional signs of strength include the open being on or near the low, the close on or near the high, the close at or above the closes and highs of several prior bars, the high above the high of one or more prior bars, and the tails being small. If the bar is very large, it might represent exhaustion or a one bar false breakout that is trapping new bulls, only to reverse down in the next bar or two. The opposite is true for bear trend bars.

Everything is relative and subject to constant reassessment even to the point of totally changing your opinion about the direction of the market. Yes, every bar is either a trend bar or a doji bar, and a doji bar means that the bulls and bears are in balance. However, sometimes a series of dojis can mean that a trend is in effect. For example, if there is a series of dojis, each with a higher close and most with a high above the high of the prior bar and a low above the low of the prior bar, the market is displaying trending closes, highs, and lows, so a trend is in effect (see Figure 1.2).

For trading purposes, it is useful to think of all bars are either trend bars or dojis (or nontrend bars, shown in Figure 1.1 with a "D"), and the labeling is loose. One bar with a small body could be a doji in one area of price action but a small trend bar in another. The only purpose for the distinction is to help you quickly assess whether one side is in control of the bar or if bulls and bears are at a stalemate. Several of the bars in Figure 1.1 could arguably be thought of as both trend bars and dojis.

The 5-minute chart on the right of Figure 1.2 had four dojis in a row, starting at Bar 1, each With Trending closes, highs and lows. The 15-minute

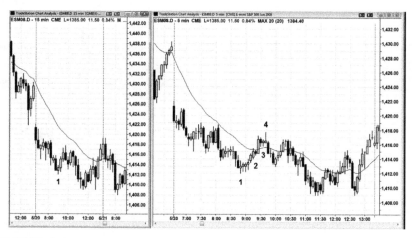

FIGURE 1.2 Trending Doji Bars

chart on the left of Figure 1.2 shows that they created a bull reversal bar at what was then a new swing low and a bear trend channel line overshoot (not drawn). Individual dojis mean that neither the bulls nor the bears are controlling the market, but trending dojis indicate a trend.

Bar 4 was a doji, which is a one-bar trading range, but it still can be a good setup bar, depending on context. Here, it was a Failed Final Flag (an ii flag) and an EMA Gap Bar short setup, and therefore a reliable signal.

Just like dojis don't always mean the market is trendless, a trend bar does not always mean that the market is trending. Bar 1 in Figure 1.3 is a strong bull trend bar that broke out of a line of dojis. However, there was no follow through. The next bar extended one tick above the trend bar and then closed on its low. The longs exited at one tick below this bear pause bar and new shorts sold there as well, viewing this as a failed bull breakout. No one was interested in buying without more bullish price action, and this caused the market to drop. The bulls tried to protect the low of the bull breakout bar by forming a small bull trend bar (Bar 2 was a setup for a Breakout Pullback long but it was never triggered), but the market fell

FIGURE 1.3 Trend Bars Do Not Always Indicate a Trend

though its low, and these new early bulls exited again there, and more new shorts came in. At this point, after the bulls failed in two attempts, they would not be willing to buy without substantial price action in their favor, and both they and the bears would be looking for at least two legs down.

BAR BASICS: SIGNAL BARS, ENTRY BARS, SETUPS, AND CANDLE PATTERNS

Traders look for setups all day long. A setup is a chart pattern composed of one or more bars that leads a trader to believe that an order can be placed that has a good chance of resulting in a profitable trade. In practice, every bar on the chart is a setup because the next bar always can be the start of a strong move in either direction. If the trade is in the direction of the recent or prevailing trend, it is a "With Trend," and if it is in the opposite direction, it is a Countertrend setup. For example, if the recent trend is up and you buy, the setup was a With Trend setup. If instead you shorted, the setup that you used as the basis for your trade was a Countertrend setup, and your short was a Countertrend trade.

A signal bar is always labeled in hindsight, after the bar has closed and after a trade is entered. As soon as your entry order is filled, the prior bar becomes a signal bar instead of just a setup bar, and the current bar is the entry bar. A beginner trader should only enter when the signal bar is also a trend bar in the direction of his trade. For example, if he is shorting, he should restrict himself to signal bars that are bear trend bars, because then the market has already demonstrated selling pressure, and the odds of follow-through are higher than if the signal bar had a close above its open. Similarly, when a beginner is looking to buy, he should only buy when the signal bar has a close above its open.

Almost every bar is a potential signal bar, but the majority never lead to an entry, and therefore do not become signal bars. As a day trader, you will place many orders that never get filled. It is usually best to enter on a stop at one tick above or below the prior bar, and if the stop is not hit, cancel the order and look for a new location for an order. For stocks, it is often better to place the entry stop at a couple of ticks beyond the potential signal bar because one tick traps are common, where the market breaks out by only one tick and then reverses, trapping all of the traders who just entered on stops.

If the entry stop order is hit, you based the trade in part on the prior bar, so that bar is called the signal bar (it gave you a signal that you needed to place an order). Often a bar can be a setup bar in both directions, and you will place entry stops beyond both extremes and will enter in the direction of either bar breakout.

Much has been written about candle patterns, and it feels as if their unusual Japanese names must mean that they have some mystical power and that they are derived from special ancient wisdom. This is just what novice traders are looking for ... the power of the gods telling them what to do, instead of relying on their own hard work. For a trader, the single most important issue is determining whether the market is trending or in a trading range. When it comes to analyzing an individual bar, the issue is also whether it is trending or not. If either the bulls or bears are in control, the candle has a body and is a trend bar. If they are in a state of equilibrium and the body is small or nonexistent, it is a doji. Many candle traders use the term "wick" to refer to the lines that usually extend above and below the bodies, presumably to be consistent with the concept of candles. Others call them "shadows." Since all of us are constantly looking for reversal bars and reversal bars look more like tadpoles or small fish, a "tail" is a more accurate descriptive term.

You should only think of bars in terms of price action and not a collection of meaningless and misleading candle names (misleading to the extent that they convey imagery of a mystical power). Each bar or candle is only important in relation to price action, and the vast majority of candle patterns are not helpful most of the time because they occur in price action where they have no high-probability predictive value. Therefore, it will complicate your trading by giving you too much to think about, and they take your mind off the trend.

Figure 1.4 shows a break above the bear trendline and then a two-legged selloff to a Lower Low below yesterday's low. The first leg was

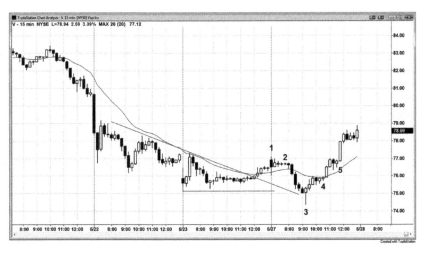

FIGURE 1.4   15-minute Chart of Visa with a Perfect Trend Reversal

completed by the iii ending at Bar 2. Bar 3 was a strong bull reversal bar that reversed both yesterday's low and a test of the bear trendline, setting up a possible long. A buy stop at one tick above this bar would have been filled, and then Bar 3 becomes a signal bar (instead of just a setup bar), and the bar in which the trade was entered becomes the entry bar.

Bar 4 is an entry bar off of an ii setup for a second leg up.

Bar 5 is an entry bar off of an inside bar Breakout Pullback (the market barely broke above the Bar 2 iii). The bodies of the two pause bars are each inside bodies, so this setup effectively was the same as an ii pattern. Bars 4 and 5 are also High 1 longs.

SIGNAL BARS: REVERSAL BARS

The market can trend up or down after any bar, and therefore every bar is a setup bar. A setup bar becomes a signal bar only if a trade is entered on the next bar (the entry bar). A setup bar in and of itself is not a reason to enter a trade. It has to be viewed in relation to the bars before it, and it can only lead to a trade if it is part of a continuation or reversal pattern.

Since it is always wisest to be trading with the trend, a trade is most likely to succeed if the signal bar is a strong trend bar in the direction of the trade. Even though you are entering after only a one-bar trend, you expecting more trending in your direction. Waiting to enter on a stop beyond the signal bar requires the market to be going even more in your direction, increasing your odds of success. However, a trend bar that is in the opposite direction can also be a reasonable signal bar, depending on other price action on the chart. In general, signal bars that are doji bars or trend bars in the opposite direction of your trade have a greater chance of failure since the side of the market that you need to be in control has not yet asserted itself. It is always better to get into a market after the correct side (bulls or bears) have taken control of at least the signal bar. That trend bar will give traders much more confidence to enter, use looser stops, and trade more volume, all of which increase the chances that their scalper's target will be reached. However, a doji bar can be an excellent signal bar, depending on context.

The best known signal bar is the reversal bar, and the best bull reversal bars have more than one of the following:

- An open near or below the close of the prior bar and a close above the open and above the prior bar's close
- A lower tail that is about one-third to one-half the height of the bar and a small or nonexistent upper tail
- Not much overlap with the prior bar or bars

The best bear reversal bars have:

- An open near or above the close of the prior bar and a close below the open and below the prior bar's close
- An upper tail that is about one-third to one-half the height of the bar and a small or nonexistent lower tail
- Not much overlap with the prior bar or bars

Reversal bars can have characteristics that indicate strength. The most familiar bull reversal bar has a bull body (it closes well above its open) and a moderate tail at the bottom. This indicates that the market traded down and then rallied into the close of the bar, showing that the bulls won the bar and were aggressive right up to the final tick. A reversal bar alone is not enough of a reason to take a trade. It has to be viewed in the context of the prior price action.

When considering a Countertrend trade in a strong trend, you must wait for a trendline to be broken and then a strong reversal bar to form on the test of the extreme, or else the chances of a profitable trade are too small. Also, do not enter on a 1-minute reversal bar since the majority of them fail and become With Trend setups. The loss might be small, but if you lose four ticks on five trades, you will never get back to being profitable on the day (you will bleed to death from a thousand paper cuts).

Why is that test of the extreme important? For example, at the end of a bear market, buyers took control and the market rallied. When the market comes back down to the area of that final low, it is testing to see whether the buyers will again aggressively come in around that price or if they will be overwhelmed by sellers who are trying again to push prices below that earlier low. If the sellers fail on this second attempt to drive the market down, it will likely go up, at least for a while. Whenever the market tries to do something twice and fails, it usually then tries the opposite. This is why double tops and bottoms work and why traders will not develop conviction in a reversal until the old trend extreme was tested.

If a reversal bar largely overlaps one or more of the prior bars or if the tail extends beyond the prior bars by only a couple of ticks, it might just be part of a trading range. If so, there is nothing to reverse because the market is sideways and not trending. In this case, it should not be used as a signal bar, and it even might turn into a setup in the opposite direction if enough traders are trapped. Even if the bar has the shape of a perfect bull reversal bar, since no bears were trapped, there will likely be no follow-through buying, and a new long will spend several bars hoping that the market will come back to his entry price so he can get out at breakeven. This is pent-up selling pressure.

If the body is tiny so that the bar is a doji, but the bar is large, it should not be used as a basis for a trade. A large doji is basically a one bar trading range, and it is not wise to buy at the top of a trading range in a bear or sell the low of a trading range in a bull. It is better to wait for a second signal.

If a bull reversal bar has a large tail at the top or a bear reversal bar has a large tail at the bottom, the Countertrend traders lost conviction going into the close of the bar, and the Countertrend trade should only be taken if the body looks reasonably strong and the price action is supportive (like a second entry).

If the reversal bar is much smaller than the last several bars, especially if it has a small body, it lacks Countertrend strength and is a riskier signal bar. However, if the bar has a strong body and is in the right context, the risk of the trade is small (one tick beyond the other side of the small bar).

In a strong trend, it is common to see a reversal bar forming and then seconds before the bar closes, the reversal fails. For example, in a bear, you could see a strong bull reversal bar with a big down tail, a last price (the bar hasn't closed yet) well above its open and above the close of the prior bar, and the low of the bar overshooting a bear trend channel line, but then in the final few seconds before the bar closes, the price collapses and the bar closes on its low. Instead of a bull reversal bar off the trend channel line overshoot, the market formed a strong bear trend bar, and all of the traders who entered early in anticipation of a strong bull reversal are now trapped and will help drive the market down further as they are forced to cover at a loss.

A big bull reversal bar with a small body also has to be considered in the context of the prior price action. The large lower tail indicates that the selling was rejected and the buyers controlled the bar. However, if the bar overlaps the prior bar or bars excessively, then it might just represent a trading range on a smaller time frame, and the close at the top of the bar might simply be a close near the top of the range, destined to be followed by more selling as the 1-minute bulls take profit. In this situation, you need additional price action before entering a Countertrend trade. You don't want to be buying at the top of a flag in a bear or selling at the bottom of a bull flag.

In Figure 1.5, Reversal Bar 1 largely overlaps the four prior bars, indicating a two-sided market so there was nothing to reverse. This is not a long setup bar.

Reversal Bar 2 is an excellent bear signal bar because it reverses the breakout of Reversal Bar 1 (there are trapped longs here off that bull reversal bar breakout) and it also reverses a breakout above the bear trendline down from the high of the day. The trapped longs will be forced to reverse to sellers as they exit.

FIGURE 1.5 Reversal Bars in Sideways Markets Must Be Analyzed in Context

When the market is in a trading range in a downswing, it is forming a bear flag. Smart traders will look to sell near the high, and they would only buy near the low if the setup was strong. As trite as the saying is, "Buy low, sell high" remains one of the best guiding principles for traders.

Reversal bars with big tails and small bodies must be evaluated in the context of the prior price action. Reversal Bar 1 in Figure 1.6 was a breakout below a prior major swing low in a very oversold market (it reversed up from a breakout below the steep trend channel line of the prior eight bars). Profit takers would want to cover their shorts and wait for the excess to be worked off with time and price before they would be eager to sell again. It was a doji bar and therefore a possible bear flag, and traders need a second signal before going long. Two bars later, the market broke below a small bar (a one bar bear flag) but this bear breakout failed on the next bar, trapping shorts and giving longs the second signal that they need for at least a scalp up.

FIGURE 1.6 Reversal Bars with Small Bodies Must Be Analyzed in Context

Reversal Bar 2 overlapped about 50 percent of the prior bar and several of the bars before it, and it did not spike below a prior low. It likely just represents a trading range on the 1-minute chart, and no trades should be taken until more price action unfolds.

Although a classic reversal bar is one of the most reliable signal bars, most reversals occur in their absence. There are many other bar patterns that yield reliable signals. In almost all cases, the signal bar is stronger if it is a trend bar in the direction of your trade. For example, if you are looking to buy a possible bear reversal, the odds of a successful trade are significantly increased if the signal bar has a close well above its open.

SIGNAL BARS: OTHER TYPES

Remember, a signal bar is a setup bar that led to an entry. However, not all trades are worth taking, and just because a stop was triggered and turned the prior bar into a signal bar, that does not make the trade worthwhile (for example, many signals in Barb Wire are best avoided). All signal bars are meaningless in the absence of price action that indicates that a reversal (trend reversal or reversal at the end of a pullback) is likely.

Besides a classic reversal bar, other common signal bars (some are two bar patterns) include:

Small Bars
- Inside bar
- ii or iii pattern (two or three increasingly smaller inside bars in a row)
- Small bar near the high or low of a big bar (trend bar or outside bar) or trading range (especially if there is a body in the direction of your trade indicating that your side has taken control)

Note that doji bars are rarely good signal bars because they are one bar trading ranges, and when the market is in a trading range, you should not be looking to buy above the high or go short below the low. They can be decent signal bars if they occur near the high or low of a trading range day, or if they are a With Trend setup in a strong trend. In a trading range, it can be fine to sell below a doji if the doji is at the high of the range, especially if it is a second entry. The bigger trading range trumps the tiny trading range represented by the doji bar, so selling below the doji bar is also selling at the top of a large trading range, which is usually a good trade.

Other Types of Signal Bars
- Outside bar (see next section)
- Double Bottom Twin: consecutive bars in a strong bear with identical lows and preferably small or nonexistent bottom tails (a type of bear flag)
- Double Top Twin: consecutive bars in a strong bull with identical highs and preferably small or nonexistent top tails (a type of bull flag)
- Opposite Twins: Up Down Twin Top and Down Up Twin Bottom (consecutive trend bars in opposite directions with small tails and nearly identical highs and lows)
- Reversal bar failure (for instance, buy above a bear reversal bar in a strong bull)
- Shaved bar (no tail at one or both of its extremes) in a strong trend
- Exhaustion Bar (huge trend bar)

There are many types of small bars and many different situations in which they occur, and all represent a lack of enthusiasm from both the bulls and bears. Each has to be evaluated in context. A small bar is a much better setup if it has a body in the direction of your trade (a small reversal bar), indicating that your side owns the bar. If the small bar has no body, it is usually better to wait for a second entry, since the probability of a successful trade is much less and the chance of a whipsaw is too great.

An inside bar does not have to be totally inside (high below the prior bar's high and a low above the prior bar's low). One or both of its extremes can be identical to that of the prior bar. In general, it forms a more reliable signal when it is a small bar and when its close is in the direction of the trade you want to take (it is always better to have bull setup bars when you are looking to buy and bear bars when you are looking to sell).

When an inside bar occurs after a big trend breakout bar, it could be simply a pause by the trend traders or a loss of conviction that will lead to a reversal (failed breakout). A reversal is more likely when the small bar is an inside bar and if it is a trend bar in the opposite direction of the large breakout bar. A With Trend inside bar increases the chance that the breakout move will continue, especially if the market had been trending in that direction earlier in the day (for example, if this might be the start of the second leg that you were expecting).

Small inside bars after breakout trend bars are somewhat emotional because a trader will consider entering in either direction on a stop and will have to process a lot of information quickly. For example, if there is a bull breakout during a down day, he will often place an order to buy at one tick above the high of the inside bar and a second order to sell at one tick below its low. Once one order is filled, the other order becomes the protective stop. If he was filled on a breakout failure (that is, on the sell order), he should consider doubling the size of the buy stop order, in case the failed breakout becomes a Breakout Pullback (a failed failure is usually a reliable trade). On the other hand, if he was first filled on the buy (With Trend) order, he usually should not reverse on his protective stop, but he might if the day had been a bear trend day. Once there has been a second or third bar without a failure, a failure that then occurs has a higher chance of simply setting up a Breakout Pullback entry rather than a tradable failure. In general, good traders make quick subjective decisions based on many subtle factors, and if the process feels too confusing or emotional, it is better to not place an order, especially complicated orders like a pair of breakout orders or an order to reverse. A trader cannot invest too much emotion in a confusing trade because he will likely be less ready to take a clear trade that may soon follow.

An inside bar after a swing move might mark the end of the swing, especially if its close is against the trend and other factors are in play, like a trendline, trend channel line overshoot, a High or Low 2, or a new swing high in a trading range. Also, any small bar, whether or not it is an inside bar, near an extreme of any large bar (trend bar, doji, or outside bar) can set up a reversal, especially if the small bar is a small reversal bar. In general, traders should be looking to buy low and sell high. In a trading range (a trading range day or a trading range in a trend day), the only small bar entries should be fades at the extremes. For example, if a small bar is a swing high or follows a bear trendline test or bull trend channel line overshoot and reversal, only look for a short entry. If it is a swing low, only look for a buy.

In a trend (even one during a trading range day), a small bar can setup an entry in either direction. For example, if there is a strong bull move and no prior bull trendline break, an inside bar near the high of a large bull trend bar or a small bar that extends above the high of the trend bar should only be viewed as a buy setup. If it is an inside bar, especially if it is a bull trend bar, it is a great long setup. If it is simply a small bar that extends above the high of the bull trend bar, it might be a safe long setup if the trend is strong enough. In general, it would be better to wait for a pullback, unless the small bar was a bear reversal bar, in which case it could trap bears, and it might make sense to buy on a stop at one tick above its high.

An ii pattern is an inside bar that follows a larger inside bar. It is two in a row with the second being inside the first and of the same size or smaller (an iii is even stronger, with three in a row). After a protracted move, especially if there has been a trendline break, a With Trend breakout from an ii pattern is often just a scalp and has a good chance of reversing before or after the profit target is reached (a Failed Final Flag). However, a Countertrend breakout (or a reversal from a Failed Final Flag) often leads to a large reversal. The pattern often develops in a final flag because it finally indicates balance between the bulls and the bears; the strength of the weaker side has caught up to that of the stronger side, at least temporarily. As such, if the With Trend side takes control, the odds are high that the Countertrend side will try to take it back after the With Trend breakout. The stop on an ii pattern is beyond the opposite side of both bars (not just the second bar, which technically is the signal bar), but sometimes you can use a smaller stop (beyond the second of the two bars instead of beyond both bars) if the bars are relatively large. After the entry bar closes, tighten the stop, and consider reversing at one tick beyond the entry bar. Keep looking to reverse on any failure in the next several bars since failures are common soon after ii breakouts, especially if the pattern forms in the middle of the day's range.

A 5-minute ii pattern is often a 1-minute Double Bottom/Top Pullback, which is a reversal pattern and might explain why a small ii can lead to a large Countertrend move.

When there is a strong bull, there will sometimes be two consecutive bars with identical highs, and usually with small tails at the tops of the two bars. This is a Double Top Twin buy setup and is a Double Top on the 1-minute chart. Place a stop to go long at one tick above the high of the bars because you will be buying a failed Double Top, and there will be protective stops there from traders who shorted it, adding fuel to the move. Likewise, in a strong bear, look to short on a stop at one tick below a Double Bottom Twin sell setup.

Up Down and a Down Up Twins setups go by several names, and each is an overlapping pair of trend bars with opposite directions and bodies of about the same size (Opposite Twins). In an Up Down setup, the first bar is a bull trend bar, and the second is a bear trend bar, and this combination is a sell setup if the market is not in a trading range. A Down Up Twin is a bear trend bar and then a bull trend bar and forms a buy setup. They are each basically a two bar reversal pattern and they correspond to a 10-minute reversal bar (just imagine how the two 5-minute bars would look when combined into a single 10-minute bar).

When a trend bar in a strong trend has a shaved body (no tail) at one or both ends, it indicates that the market is one-sided and strong. However, a shaved top on a 5-minute bull trend bar in a runaway bull is stronger than a shaved bottom, because the extreme strength is right into the close of the bar, and it is more likely to continue than strength that occurred five minutes earlier. Therefore, a shaved top is a good setup for a long, but it is often impossible to place a buy stop order because the next bar will already be above the high before you can place your order. If the bar has a one tick tail at its high or a shaved bottom, it is still strong, but in general, that alone would not be reason enough to buy above its high. Also, the bar has to be analyzed in context. If the bar is in a trading range, it would be foolish to buy above its high because trading ranges tend to test the extremes repeatedly, and you should not be buying near the high when the odds of the bar being a test are greater than the odds of the bar being a successful breakout.

Similarly, a bear trend bar with a shaved bottom in a runaway bear is a setup to short at one tick below its low.

Not all small bars are good fade setups. There is one particular situation where they should not be used as signal bars, and that is when the bar is a small doji (small, relative to the recent bars), especially if there is no body, it is near the EMA and occurring approximately between 9 A.M. and 11:00 A.M. PST in a Barb Wire pattern. These have a very high failure rate and always require more price action before placing a trade.

Although most large trend bars that are With Trend in a trend are strong, if a bar is unusually large, it often represents a climactic exhaustion. For example, in a bull, it often means that the last buyers bought. If there are no more buyers, the market will go down. Any standard reversal setup can serve as a signal bar, but a second entry with a strong reversal bar is always the safest setup when trading Countertrend.

Big trend bars on breakouts often fail on the next bar, trapping traders into the wrong side of the market. This is especially common on quiet trading range days.

FIGURE 1.7   A Small Bar Can Be a With Trend or Countertrend Setup

In a trend, a small bar on a pullback is only a With Trend setup. In Figure 1.7, Bars 1, 2, 4, and 6 were small bars in pullbacks, and the only trade they offer is a short on a stop at one tick below the low. Even though they are mostly doji bars, they are With Trend and therefore reasonable shorts.

A small bar can also setup a Countertrend trade in a trend if it occurs at a swing low and there are other reasons for trading Countertrend, like a prior trendline break. Bar 3 was a swing low, a reversal up from a Low 2 short, and the second leg down of a second leg down, making it a High 4 long setup. Bar 5 was a High 2 after a strong move up to Bar 4 (it broke a trendline), making a second leg up likely. It was also at the low of a trading range.

The only time that you would sell a small bar at a low is in a bear. Bar 8 is not particularly small, but it was an inside bar, which functions like a small bar, and it was a bear trend bar, making it a safe short at the low of the day. It was also a Breakout Pullback short setup and a Microtrendline (Low 1) short.

In Figure 1.8, Bar 1 is a failed bear reversal bar long setup in GS. The small bear reversal bar formed after the large bull trend bar broke out of a trading range on a bull trend day (most bars are above the rising EMA). Early shorts entered on the reversal bar before it triggered a short signal (the next bar did not trade one tick below its low), and these overly eager shorts were now trapped. There was likely a 1-minute reversal pattern that trapped shorts into one of the many small losing 1-minute Countertrend

FIGURE 1.8 Failed Reversal Bars Are Often Setups in the Opposite Direction

trades that occur all day long in strong trends and just eat away at your account, small piece by small piece. They would exit at one tick above the bear reversal bar, which is where and why smart traders went long. A reversal bar alone is not enough reason to enter, even if it is in an area where a reversal might reasonably take place. Here, it appeared to be setting up a failed trading range breakout but the short entry below the bar was never triggered, and it therefore set up an entry in the opposite direction.

In Figure 1.9, Bar 3 is a huge trend bar that collapsed below the low of the open and through a bear trend channel line and was followed by a bull inside bar with a shaved top, meaning that buyers were aggressively buying it right into its close. This is a great setup for at least a two-legged rally. It was also the bottom of a Spike and Channel Bear Trend, and the reversal should test the Bar 2 start of the channel, which is did.

The failed Bar 4 reversal bar was a great long entry on the Bar 5 outside bar in this strong bull (a failed Low 2 top in a strong bull). The Low 2 trapped naïve traders who sold under the reversal bar, but they failed

FIGURE 1.9 Strong Trend Bars Can Indicate the End of a Trend (Exhaustion, Capitulation)

to wait for a prior demonstration of bearish strength. You cannot sell in a strong bull if there has not been a prior bull trendline break.

Note that none of the dojis before and after Bar 1 are good signal bars because they are in the middle of the day's range and next to a flat EMA.

In Figure 1.10, POT gapped below yesterday's low and reversed up beyond the EMA. The market yesterday broke a few bear trend lines,

FIGURE 1.10 Countertrend Trades Need a Prior Trendline Break

indicating that there was a reasonable chance for a tradable long, if there is a good buy setup and a good signal bar. Both are needed.

Bar 3 was a clear long, reversing up from below yesterday's low with a strong bull reversal bar. The rally up from Bar 2 broke the bear trendline of the prior hour or so (the line is not shown).

The Bar 4 EMA Gap Bar short was followed by a possible High 2 long at Bar 6, except that there was no signal bar. Bar 5 was a bear trend bar and not a bull signal bar, which is needed when you are buying in a bear trend. The trendline from Bars 4 to 6 allowed for the creation of the trend channel line attached to the Bar 5 low.

Bar 7 took out the high of the prior bar but that bar had a bear close. A pullback after a probe below a trend channel line is not reason enough to buy. You need a bull signal bar.

Bar 8 was a small bull inside bar after a larger bull inside bar, and that bar followed a second probe below the trend channel line. This might also be a Higher Low test of the Bar 3 low of the bear trend. The rally to Bar 4 broke all bear trendlines, so you should be looking to buy a test of the Bar 3 low, and the Bar 8 ii bull inside bar was a great long setup.

An aggressive trader could have bought the Double Bottom Pullback reversal in GS above the Bar 5 ii in Figure 1.11, but there was not yet a trendline break in the small bear down from Bar 4.

There was a second entry above the Bar 6 ii setup. This flag drifted far enough to break a small trendline down from Bar 4, plus it was a second entry.

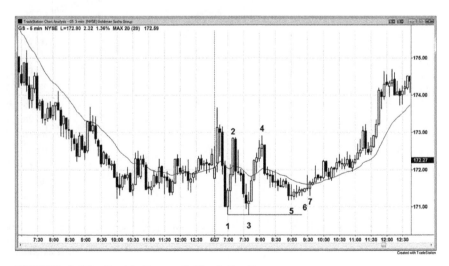

FIGURE 1.11 Double Bottom Pullback Buy Setup

Bar 7 set up a third entry on the failed failure (the market failed on the upside breakout and this failed on the downside on the next bar), which is a very reliable Breakout Pullback long setup and a Microtrendline High 1 buy.

Double Bottom Pullbacks have a pullback that typically extends more than 50 percent and often almost the entire way to the Double Bottom. This Double Bottom was exact to the tick. The Higher Low often forms a rounded bottom, and traditional stock traders would describe it as an area of accumulation. The name is irrelevant; what is important is that the market failed to put in a Lower Low on this second attempt down (Bar 3 was the first), so if it can't go down, the bears will step aside, and the market will probe up (in search of sellers willing to sell at a higher price). Instead of finding sellers, the market found buyers willing to buy at the higher price.

FIGURE 1.12 Failed Final Flag Buy Setup

The Bar 2 signal bar in Figure 1.12 was a tiny bar (11 cents in a $185 stock), but if you look at a line chart of the closes, the small Higher Low was clear at point 2. The High 2 from two bars earlier did not have a good prior trendline break, so it was not an ideal Lower Low, Failed Final Flag long entry. Bar 2 is a second entry and a small Higher Low, which is a good setup with minimal risk. Also, it is almost an ii pattern, and close is close enough in trading.

The High 1 at Bar 1 was not a good entry since there was no bull trend bar, which is needed to reverse a strong bear. Also, it followed five bear bodies so there was not yet any up momentum prior to the setup, and this is always needed when looking to buy a bear.

On the 5-minute chart on the right of Figure 1.13, there were two ii patterns (the first is an iii). As you can see from the 1-minute chart on the left, the first one was a Double Bottom Pullback buy pattern, and the second was a failed Low 2.

In both cases, the bull trend bar at the end of the ii was a great setup for a long entry. Even though small bars have less directional significance, it is always better to have the final one being a trend bar in the direction of your intended entry.

In Figure 1.14, Bar 1 was a Double Bottom Twin setup (consecutive bars with identical lows, in a strong bear). Sell at one tick below its low.

FIGURE 1.13 An ii Buy Setup Is Often a Double Bottom Pullback on a Smaller Time frame

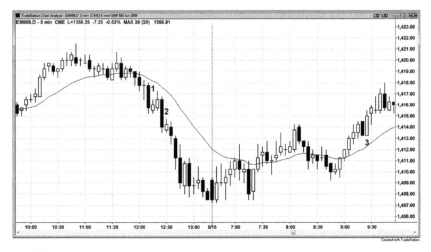

FIGURE 1.14   Double Bottom Twin Sell Setup

You could also sell below the two bar Breakout Pullback setup on the next bar, giving you an earlier entry. This was also a Microtrendline Low 1 short.

Bar 2 was another example.

Bar 3 was a Double Top Twin setup for a long trade, and it was also a Microtrendline long (a High 1).

LEH had a Down Up Twin Bar reversal on a test of the bear trend channel line in Figure 1.15. The selloff was climactic because it was

FIGURE 1.15   Up Down Twin Buy Setup

unsustainable behavior. Sixteen of the prior 17 bars all had a high that was below the high of the bar before. A climax is usually followed by a two-legged correction that lasts for many bars (at least an hour on a 5-minute chart).

In Figure 1.16, Bar 4 was an Up Down Twin Bar reversal on a break above yesterday's high and a bull trend channel line, and after the breakout of a small flag (Bar 3).

Bar 1 was not a good Down Up Twin buy setup because there was too much down momentum in the prior two bear trend bars on their breakout from the Lower High. It was followed by another Down Up Twin buy setup (back to back happens occasionally), but four overlapping bars is a bear flag and you cannot buy at the top of a trading range in a bear. These patterns are only Countertrend signals if there is a reason to expect a reversal; the first pause after a strong breakout is a breakout pullback, and it is usually followed by more trending.

Bar 2 was a good short because there were trapped bulls who bought above the back to back Down Up Twin reversals, and because it ended a two-legged pullback to the EMA in a bear (the two up legs were the two bull trend bars separated by a bear trend bar in the bear flag).

Bar 2 resembles the second bar of an Up Down Twin sell setup, but its close and low were too far below the low of the prior bar; besides, traders were already short before the close of the bar, based on the bear M2S (Low 2 Short at the Moving Average).

FIGURE 1.16 Up Down Twin Sell Setup

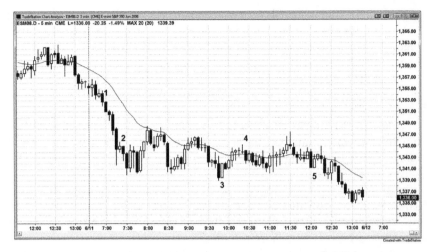

FIGURE 1.17 Shaved Tops and Bottoms Indicate Conviction and Urgency

A bar with no tail at either end in the middle of a strong trend is a sign of strength, and traders should enter With Trend on its breakout. In Figure 1.17, Bar 1 had no tail at both its high and low, indicating severe selling pressure (they sold it from start to finish), so it was likely that there would be more selling to come. Traders have to be fast in placing their sell stop orders because the market is moving fast.

Bar 2 had a shaved top in a bear, but since the market was not in free fall at this point, that was not the reason for a short. However, it was a short entry based on taking out the low of a small inside bar in a bear (a Low 1).

Bar 3 was a bull trend bar with a shaved top and bottom, but it was not in a bull trend, and therefore it does not function as a buy setup. However, there was still a buy on the next bar because it was a High 2, and a Down Up Twin reversal at a Lower Low, which was also a failed breakout of a trading range. The first EMA pullback broke the bear trend line so the move down to Bar 3 was a two-legged Lower Low, which is usually good for at least a scalp.

Bars 4 and 5 were not shaved bar sell setups because they were not in a free fall bear.

AAPL demonstrates many common signal bars on this 5-minute chart (Figure 1.18). Bar 1 is a doji with a tiny body and was the third overlapping bar (Barb Wire). It would be foolish to buy above its high because you would be buying the top of a bear flag (Barb Wire below the EMA), despite the tempting doji bar that will make many candle worshipers enter into a bad long trade.

FIGURE 1.18 A Variety of Good Setups

Bar 2 was a good reversal bar with a long tail that went far below the low of the prior bar and reversed up, and it had a decent-size bull body. The tail at the top showed some weakness, but this was erased by the trend bars that followed it. It was a High 2 long Opening Reversal at a new swing low and a trend channel line breakout (not shown, but it could be drawn across the lows of the prior three bars).

Bar 3 was an outside up bar and a Microtrendline long after a pause bar that followed the breakout to a new high of the day. Outside bars in new trends often trap traders out of great trades because they happen so quickly. Many traders don't have enough time to reverse their perspective fast enough from bearish to bullish, and then they have to chase the market up.

Bar 4 was a bear doji at a new high, but the up momentum is so strong and the reversal bar was so weak that a short could be considered only on a second entry.

Bar 5 was a bull outside up bar that tested the EMA and the breakout from the opening range, and it was the First Pullback in a strong up move and a High 1 long. Bar 6 was a relatively small bear reversal bar and a second entry short after taking out the Bar 4 swing high and yesterday's high. It was also the second leg up from the Bar 5 First Pullback and from the Bar 2 low, and second legs are often reversals. Also, it was a Low 4 and a Wedge shaped, Three Pushes Up from the Bar 3 low that started the bull breakout above the opening range. With this many factors operating, a trader should expect at least two legs down.

Bar 7 was an ii short at a time when you were expecting two legs down and more of a test of the EMA than what happened on the prior test at Bar 5. It was a small piece of Barb Wire, but the risk was small. The bar after the small entry bar extended above the entry bar but not above either of the ii bars where the protective stop would be. Normally you would tighten the protective stop after the entry bar closes, but when the entry bar is small and it only ran for a few cents, you should give it more room and risk to beyond the high of the ii bars. This is Barb Wire, and it is prone to run stops, so if you are going to take the short, you have to give it a little room. The ii breakout reverses back up a couple bars later, which is expected when an ii is in the middle of the day's range. Also, the market completed its goals of two legs down and a penetration of the EMA. The traders who went long on the High 2 above Bar 7 were immediately trapped by the large outside down bar, and astute traders would go short below the Bar 7 low. The new longs who were trapped and panicked would sell out their losing longs below Bar 7, creating a high probability short.

Bar 8 was a Lower High second entry short after two legs up and a trendline break (the pullback from Bar 6). This is a possible trend reversal and you have to take it seriously. Even though it is a doji, which is a one bar trading range and you should not be shorting below a trading range, it is at the top of a large trading range, and it is a second entry. Also, back-to-back dojis and three sideways bars in a row at a possible turning point is similar to an ii pattern (two bars with small bodies), and therefore become an acceptable short setup.

Bar 9 was a Down Up Twin Bar reversal (which, if you think about it, is a reversal bar on a 10-minute chart), after a new swing low and test of the Bar 5 low (an attempt to form a Double Bottom Bull Flag). It is also a second leg down from the Bar 6 high.

Bar 10 is a Breakout Pullback and a Double Bottom Twin short, which is a pair of consecutive bars with the same low in a strong bear.

Bar 11 is a bull reversal bar after a third push down, but the prior bar was a big doji, and Bar 11 had a large bear tail and small body, and it largely overlapped the two prior bars. This is not a strong reversal but does show some sign of bullish strength. The odds of a trading range are greater than the odds of a significant reversal.

Bar 1 in Figure 1.19 is a break below a bull reversal bar (failed reversal bar) in a strong bear and is a great short because the early bulls who bought will be trapped and forced to sell at one or more ticks below its low.

A doji is a one bar trading range, and selling below a small bar at the top of a trading range is always a good trade, especially in a strong bear, as

FIGURE 1.19 A Reversal Bar Can Be a with Trend Setup Instead of a Countertrend Setup

was the case with Bars 2 and 3, both of which followed large dojis. Bar 3 was also a Low 2 in a bear.

Bar 1 in Figure 1.20 is a Down Up Twin buy reversal after taking out the low of the open, and it was a Higher Low.

Bar 2 is a small bear reversal bar at the high of a large bull trend bar, and it tested the EMA. It failed to reverse the market and set up a buy at one tick above its high for a second leg up (it marked the end of the one bar first leg).

Bar 3 was an bear inside bar after a break of a bull trend channel line and yesterday's high, setting up a short of the Wedge.

Bar 4 was a doji bar after two other dojis, and a bar with a tiny body is not a good setup bar when the lows, highs, and closes are trending up. The needed second entry setup came two bars later, completing the Lower High that followed a trendline break.

Bar 5 is a one tick failed breakout of the top of an ii, setting up a Failed Final Flag, which was reversed by the Bar 6 reversal bar. This also reversed a breakout to a new low of the day, and formed a Double Bottom Bull Flag with Bar 1, and it was a Five Tick Failed Breakout.

FIGURE 1.20   Detailed Analysis of Many Setups

Bar 7 was a doji bar that set up a M2B (a High 2 above the EMA) and a Higher Low long after the bull leg from Bar 6. Even though it had a small body, it was a second entry and was With Trend.

Bar 8 was an inside bear trend bar that was the end of the second leg up and a test of the high of the day. It also was after a trend channel line breakout. However, the momentum up from Bar 7 was strong, so it is better to wait for a second entry, which came with the Bar 10 outside down bar and failed bull reversal bar. The move up from Bar 7 was strong so many longs bought the small (especially compared to the two bear trend bars that came before it) bull reversal bar (Bar 9 was a High 1), but were immediately trapped by the Bar 10 outside bar down. The bears seized control of the market, so there should be two legs down from here. An outside bar that traps traders usually leads to two more legs.

Bar 11 was technically a High 3, but should be expected to behave like a High 2, since the Bar 10 outside bar bull trap should be considered the start of the downswing (not the Bar 6 actual swing high).

Bar 11 was a bull inside bar (ioi) and the second attempt to reverse the breakout below Bar 7, and it reversed the trendline break. It was an EMA Gap 2 Bar on a nontrend day and a High 2 after the Bar 10 bear outside bar that trapped longs.

Bar 1 in Figure 1.21 was a big bull trend bar, but there was so much momentum leading up to it that only a second entry short (Bar 2) could be considered.

FIGURE 1.21 Good and Bad Setups

Bar 3 was a bear trend bar, but the next two bars were small doji bars so there was no long setup. Small dojis are rarely ever good Countertrend entry bars, and it is almost always better to wait for another setup.

Bar 5 was a good bull reversal bar after a bear trend bar in a bear and also Three Pushes Down from the rally following the Bar 4 low (there was also a trend channel line breakout and reversal, from the line that could be drawn starting at Bar 4). This was an acceptable long scalp. Bar 6 was a large bear trend bar with a big bottom tail after a collapse at the end of the bear. It was also an overshoot of several bear trend channel lines (not shown). With four large bear trend bars in a row, only a second entry long can be considered, which came on the Bar 7 outside up bar. The Bar 7 low was a small Higher Low, which is the start of the second leg up.

Bar 1 in Figure 1.22 was a relatively small bar after a big bear trend bar broke out of a large flag (a failed breakout setup), and it was an exact test of the earlier low. On a trading range day with Bar 1 setting up these two reversals, it was a reasonable long setup.

Bar 2 followed a large bull trend bar breakout of a Tight Trading Range and formed a Higher High (nine bars earlier). It was a bear reversal bar that setup a failed breakout short that led to a strong bear into the close (the market closed 30 points lower, but this is not shown because it would shrink this bull trend bar to the point of looking unremarkable instead of how it appeared in real time).

FIGURE 1.22 Failed Breakouts

OUTSIDE BARS

If the high of the current bar is above the high of the previous bar and the low is below the low of the previous bar, then the current bar is an outside bar. Outside bars are complicated to read, and there are many subtleties in their analysis. The increased size of the bar means that bulls and bears are willing to be more aggressive, but if the close is near the middle, it is essentially a one bar long trading range. At other times, they can act as reversal bars or trend bars. Traders must pay attention to the context in which they occur.

Traditional technical analysis teaches that outside bars are setup bars for a breakout in either direction, and you should put an entry stop above and below. Once filled, double the size of the unfilled stop and make it a reversal order. However, it is almost always unwise to enter on a breakout of a 5-minute outside bar, especially if the outside bar is large (a breakout of a 1-minute outside bar is often a good trade) because of the greater risk that the distant stop entails. If for some rare reason you did enter on the breakout of an outside bar and the protective stop is too large, consider using a money stop (like two points in the Emini) or trading fewer contracts. Since an outside bar is a one bar trading range and it is better to not buy at the top of a sideways market or sell below it, it is almost always imprudent to enter on a breakout of the bar.

Sometimes you have to enter on an outside bar (not on its breakout) because you know that traders are trapped. This is especially true after a strong move. If an outside bar occurs as the second entry in a strong reversal from a trendline break or trend channel line overshoot, it can be an excellent entry bar. For example, if the market just sold off below a swing low for the second time and reversed up from a trend channel line overshoot, you are likely looking to buy, and you keep moving a buy stop order to one tick above the prior bar's high until you get filled. Sometimes the fill will be on an outside up bar. This is usually a good reversal trade, and it is due to strong buyers and not just anxious trading range traders getting in and then quickly getting out in a panic once they realized that they made the mistake of buying near the high of an outside bar in a trading range.

If an outside bar is in the middle of a trading range, it is meaningless and should not be used to generate trades, unless it is followed by a small bar near the high or low of the outside bar, setting up a fade. An outside bar in a trading range just reaffirms what everyone already knows . . . that both sides are balanced and both will sell near the top of the range and buy near the bottom, expecting a move toward the opposite end of the outside bar. If the market instead breaks out in the other direction, just let it go and look to fade a failed breakout of the outside bar, which commonly happens within a few bars. Otherwise, just wait for a pullback (a failed failure of the breakout becomes a Breakout Pullback).

If the bar after the outside bar is an inside bar, then this is an ioi pattern (inside-outside-inside) and can be a setup for an entry in the direction of the breakout of the inside bar. However, only take the entry if there is a reason to believe that the market could move far enough to hit your profit target. For example, if the ioi is at a new swing high, a downside breakout could be a good short since it is likely a second entry (the low of the outside bar will probably be the first entry). If it is in Barb Wire, especially if the inside bar is large and in the center of the outside bar, it is usually better to wait for a stronger setup.

When a With Trend outside bar occurs in the first leg of a trend reversal and the prior trend was strong, it functions like a strong trend bar and not a trading range type of bar. It usually leads to two legs after the outside bar because the outside bar is an attempted With Trend entry that failed. Everyone suddenly agrees about the new direction, and therefore the move will have so much momentum and extend so far that it will likely get tested after a pullback, creating a second leg. The outside bar will act as the start of the trend rather than the actual old trend extreme. For example, if the beginning of the bar triggers a Low 1 (or Low 2) short in a bear rally, but by the end of the bar, the bar has become an outside up bar that ran the protective stops on the shorts and then closed on its high, this bar will have formed a Higher Low in the new bull. This failure puts everyone in agreement that the new trend is strong, and once everyone agrees, the first leg up will likely require a test in the form of a second leg up. This failure, and not the actual bear low, is the start of the up leg, so there should be two legs up from here. This will appear as three legs up on the chart, but functionally, it is two legs up from the outside bar low, which is the point where it became clear that the bulls seized control.

Why is the move often strong? The Low 1 enticed the old bears to short. Then the entry bar will quickly reverse to an outside bar up, trapping the bears in and trapping the bulls out. Invariably, the market will trend up hard for many more bars as everyone realizes that the market has reversed and they are trying to figure out how to position themselves. The bears are hoping for a dip so they can exit with a smaller loss and the bulls want the same dip so they can buy more with limited risk. When everyone wants the same thing, it will not happen because both sides will start buying even two or three tick pullbacks, preventing a two to three bar pullback from developing until the trend has gone very far. A smart price action trader will be aware of this possibility at the outset, and if she is looking for a two-legged extended up move, she will watch the first Low 1 and Low 2 carefully and anticipate its failure. She will place her entry orders just above the high of the prior bar, even if it means entering on an outside bar up (especially if it is the entry bar for the shorts).

The single most important thing to remember about outside bars is that whenever a trader is uncertain about what to do, the best decision is to wait for more price action to develop.

A strong trend that goes sideways midday often has a second leg later in the day. This is a Trend Resumption move in Figure 1.23. Note that outside bar breakouts in a strong trend usually result in a two-legged move. Bar 1 is an outside bar, and smart traders would have orders to go short at one tick below its low because the enthusiastic longs will exit there and not look to buy until more support develops.

Bar 2 was the second leg down (the first leg was the High 1 outside bar two bars earlier). After a two-legged move from a breakout, the market will usually try to correct.

Bar 5 was an outside down bar but the market was basically sideways with lots of overlapping bars, so it is not a reliable setup for a breakout entry. The inside bar that followed it (ioi) was too large to use as a breakout signal, because you would be either selling at the bottom of a trading range or buying at the top, and you only want to buy low or sell high.

Outside bars are tricky because both the bulls and bears were in control at some point during the bar, so the movement over the next few bars can have further reversals. Bar 1 in Figure 1.24 is an outside bar that formed an inside-outside-inside (ioi) pattern. The Bar 2 breakout of the inside bar following Bar 1 failed, which is common. Bar 2 would have been a terrible long because the inside setup bar was too large and it would have forced

FIGURE 1.23 Strong Trends Often Go Sideways in the Middle of the Day and Then Resume

FIGURE 1.24 Outside Bars Can Be Tricky to Read

the trader to buy near the high of the range. A small failure bar is a great entry because the risk is small. The short down from Bar 2 broke below the outside bar, triggering longs to exit and resulting in two small legs down to Bar 4. This was also a failure of the reversal up from the bear trend channel line.

Bar 4 is almost an outside up bar, and in trading if something is almost a reliable pattern, it will likely yield the reliable result. Bar 4 was the second bull bar in the second leg, and the second attempt to reverse the low of the day, and so it was a great setup for a long.

Bar 5 is an outside bar followed by a small inside bar near its high. Again, this yields a great short with minimal risk. Once the market ran the stops below the outside bar, traders would expect two legs down, because bulls were trapped into longs on the strong bull trend outside bar. This time, the two legs formed dojis (Bars 8 and 9) and a small Double Bottom, which was not the down momentum that traders were expecting. This loss of down momentum was followed by the Bar 10 Double Bottom Pullback long and a failed Low 2 short, so there are trapped shorts. Bar 9 was also a High 2 long on the pullback from the bull up from Bar 4, forming a Higher Low on the day after a protracted rally following the break of the bear trendline. This High 2 is reason enough to buy.

In Figure 1.25 Bar 2 was an outside bar up that trapped traders who shorted the Low 1.

The next bar was a bear reversal bar at the high of the outside bar, setting up a great short fade. Even on days like this with a sideways open, the

FIGURE 1.25 Outside Bars

moves on the open are usually good enough to provide at least a scalper's profit. Trading the upside breakout of the Bar 1 bear trend bar by the outside bar on a big gap down opening is a good bet, since the market will try to close the gap and now you also have trapped bears. The odds of success were increased by the Bar 2 entry bar breaking below the inside before breaking above. That downside move trapped more shorts since it was the second attempt down (the first bar of the day was the first attempt).

The Bar 4 outside bar was part of Barb Wire, and the next bar was not a small bar that could be faded. In fact, it was an even larger outside bar, trapping both the longs and shorts who entered on the Bar 4 outside bar as it broke above and below its prior bar.

The bar after Bar 5 was a great setup. It was a small bar near the low of the outside bar, making it a low risk long. It was also a High 2 and a Higher Low.

Bar 6 was a bear reversal bar and a Low 2 bar near the high of an outside bar and a good short.

Bar 7 broke to a swing high and reversed down as an outside bar. The next bar was a small bar near the low, but there was no reversal above its high, and so there was no long entry. The two bars before Bar 8 also tried to trigger the long, but they too failed to hit the entry stop above that small inside bar that followed Bar 7. Even though this is Barb Wire, it is a possible short after so many failed attempts to hit the buy stops. Also, a down move would create a second leg down from the Bar 7 high, and this was a great day for second legs. Bar 8 was also something of a Microtrendline short.

The selloff to Bar 3 in Figure 1.26 broke a major trendline, alerting traders to short a test of the Bar 2 high. Bar 3 was an outside bar that was a reversal bar and an entry bar.

Bar 4 was a large bull trend bar (climactic) that formed a Higher High, and it was followed by a strong bear inside bar that was the signal for the short. Traders were expecting two legs down from such a strong setup. As such, smart traders will be watching for the formation of a High 1 and then a High 2 and readying themselves to short more if these long setups fail and trap the bulls.

Bar 5 was a short setup for a failed High 1, and Bar 6 was a great bull trap. It was a failed High 2 and the long entry bar reversed into an outside bar down, trapping longs in and bears out. This outside bar acted like a bear trend bar and not just an outside bar. Because it is an outside bar, the entry bar and its failure happen within a minute or two of each other, not giving traders enough time to process the information. Within a bar or two, they realize that the market, in fact, has become a bear trend and the longs are hoping for a two- or three-bar pullback to exit with a smaller loss and the bears are hoping for the same rally to allow for a short entry with a smaller

FIGURE 1.26 An Outside Bar Is a Good With Trend Entry Bar at the End of a Two-Legged Pullback

risk. What happens is that both sides start selling every two- or three-tick pullback, so a two- or three-bar rally does not come until the market has gone a long way.

Note that the High 2 long was a terrible setup because five of the six prior bars were bear bars and the other bar was a doji. A High 2 alone is not a setup, especially after a climax top and possible major reversal down. There first has to be earlier strength, usually in the form of a High 1 leg that breaks a trendline or at least an earlier strong bull trend bar.

THE IMPORTANCE OF THE CLOSE OF THE BAR

A bar usually assumes something similar to its final appearance seconds to a minute or more before the bar closes. If you enter before the bar closes, you might occasionally make a tick or so more on your trade. However, once or twice every day, the signal that you thought was going to happen does not and you will lose about eight ticks. That means that you need about eight early entries to work as planned for every one that does not, and that simply won't happen. You can enter early With Trend in a strong trend, and you will likely be fine. However, when there is a strong trend, you have so much confidence in the signal that there is no downside to waiting for the bar to close and then entering on a stop beyond the bar. You cannot be deciding on every bar if an early entry is appropriate because you have too many other important decisions to make. If you add that to your list of things to think about, you will likely end up missing many good trades every day and forgo far more in missed opportunities than you could gain on an occasional early entry.

This holds true for all time frames. For example, look at a daily chart, and you will see many bars that opened near the low but closed in the middle. Each one of those bars was a strong bull trend bar with a last price on the high at some point during the day. If you bought under the assumption that the bar was going to close on its high and bought near the high and instead it closed in the middle, you would realize your mistake. You are carrying home a trade that you never would have entered at the end of the day.

There are two common problems that regularly occur on the 5-minute chart. The most costly is when you try to pick a bottom in a strong trend. Typically you will see a Lower Low after a trendline break, and traders will be hoping for a strong reversal bar, especially if there is also a bear trend channel line overshoot. The bar sets up nicely and is a strong bull reversal bar by the third minute or so. The price is hanging near the high of the bar for a couple of minutes, attracting more and more Countertrend traders who want to get in early so that their stop will be smaller (their stop will be below the bar), but then with five seconds remaining before the bar closes, the price collapses, and the bar closes on its low. All of those early longs who were trying to risk a tick or two less end up losing two points or more. These longs let themselves get trapped into a bad trade.

The other common problem is getting trapped out of a good trade. For example, if you just bought and your trade has had three to five ticks of open profit but the market just can't hit six, allowing you to scalp out with four ticks of profit, you start to become nervous. You look at the 3- or 5-minute chart with about 10 seconds before its bar closes, and it is a strong bear reversal bar. You then move your protective stop up to one tick below that bar, and just before the bar closes the market drops and hits your stop only to pop up several ticks in the final two seconds of the bar. Then, within the first 30 seconds of the next bar, the market quickly goes up to 6 ticks where smart traders took partial profits while you are sitting on the sidelines. Good entry, good plan, bad discipline. You just let yourself get trapped out of a good trade. If you had followed your plan and relied on your initial stop until the entry bar closed, you would have secured your profit.

There is one other point about bar closes. Pay very close attention to the close of every bar, especially for the entry bar and the bar or two later. If the entry bar is six ticks tall, you would much prefer seeing the body suddenly increase from a two-tick trend bar to a four-tick trend bar in the final seconds of the bar. You will then likely reduce the number of contracts that you will scalp out. This is true for the next couple of bars as well. If there are strong closes, you should be more willing to swing more contracts and hold them for more points than if these bars had weak closes.

The 5-minute Emini in Figure 1.27 has been in a strong bear for weeks, and it is now starting to have bigger pullbacks and each new Lower Low is being bought, leading to profitable Countertrend trades. The bulls are more confident, and the bears are becoming more willing to take profits. The thumbnail on the left is a 3-minute chart, and the one on the right is a close-up of the 5-minute chart.

Bar 5 broke above a trendline, and Bar 8 exceeded another by a fraction of a tick.

Bar 10 was an ii, and if you look at the bodies alone, it was an iiii (four inside bars in a row, each smaller than the prior!), which could lead to a great Failed Final Flag and then a two-legged rally and probably a gap bar above the EMA (it happened at Bar 12), which will likely be exceeded after a pullback to a Higher Low (maybe the Bar 13 test of the trendline).

Bar 11 was a strong bull reversal bar and a second attempt to reverse up from a Lower Low (the iiii was the first). This is a very high probability long, but the stop would have to be beneath its low, three points below the entry price. This is more than what is typically required in the Emini (normally two points works for most trades), but that is what the price action shows is needed. If you are nervous, just trade half-size, but you must take a strong setup like this one and plan on swinging half.

FIGURE 1.27 A Strong Bear, But They Are Starting to Buy New Lows

This is a perfect example of a common problem that traders face when they try to reduce risk by watching a smaller time frame chart. There was also a 3-minute reversal bar at Bar 11, but the stop below the entry bar was hit by a bear trend bar with shaved tops and bottoms, indicating very strong sellers. At this point, it would be very difficult to reconcile that with the 5-minute chart where the stop had not been hit. The large size of the stop required on the 5-minute chart would make traders more willing to exit early and take a loss. If a trader was also watching the 3-minute chart, he almost certainly would have exited with a loss, and he would have been trapped out of the market by that strong bear trend bar. The next bar on the 3-minute chart was a very strong outside bull trend bar, indicating that the bulls were violently asserting themselves in creating a Higher Low, but most of the weak hands who were stopped out would likely be so scared that they would not take the entry and instead wait for a pullback.

Stop runs on the 3-minute chart are very common at important reversals, and smart traders look at them as great opportunities because they trap weak longs out of the market, forcing them to chase the market up. It is always better to just watch and trade off one chart because sometimes things happen too quickly for a trader to think fast enough to place his orders if he is watching two charts and trying to reconcile the inconsistencies.

EXCHANGE TRADED FUNDS (ETFs) AND INVERSE CHARTS

Sometimes the price action becomes clearer if you change something about the chart. You can switch to a bar or line chart or a chart based on volume or ticks, or a higher or lower time frame or simply print the chart. Several ETFs are also helpful. For example, the SPY is almost identical in appearance to the Emini chart and sometimes has clearer price action.

Also, it can be helpful to consider the chart from an opposite perspective. If you are seeing a bull flag but something doesn't seem quite right, consider looking at the SDS, which is an ETF that is based on the inverse of the SPY (but with twice the leverage). If you look at it, you might discover that the bull flag that you were seeing on the Emini and SPY might now look like a rounding bottom on the SDS. If it does, you would be wise not to buy the Emini flag and instead wait for more price action to unfold (like waiting for the breakout and then shorting if it fails). Sometimes patterns are clearer on other stock index futures, like the Emini Nasdaq-100, or its ETF, the QQQQ, or its double inverse, the QID, but it is usually not worth looking at these and it is better to stick with the Emini and sometimes the SDS.

FIGURE 1.28 The SDS Is Essentially the Inverse of the Emini, and It Can Help You Decide on an Emini Setup

The top chart of the Emini in Figure 1.28 is essentially identical to that of the SPY in the middle chart, but the price action on the SPY is sometimes easier to read. The bottom chart is the SDS, which is an ETF that is the inverse of the SPY (with twice the leverage). Sometimes the SDS chart will make you reconsider your read of the Emini chart.

SECOND ENTRIES

Bottoms on the daily chart usually require a second reversal off the low to convince enough traders to trade the market as a possible new bull. This second entry is almost always more likely to result in a profitable trade than is a first entry. The sellers are making a second attempt to drive the price down and if the market fails in two attempts to do something, it usually will attempt to do the opposite.

If the second entry on any time frame is letting you in at a better price than the first, be suspicious that it might be a trap. Most good second entries are at the same price or worse. A second entry trader is someone entering late, trying to minimize risk, and the market usually makes you pay a little more for that additional information. If it is charging you less, it might be setting you up to steal your money in a failed High/Low 2.

Traders looking for second entries are more aggressive and confident, and will often enter on smaller time frame charts. This usually results in traders on the 5-minute charts entering after many other traders have already entered, making the entry a little worse. If the market is letting you in at a better price, you should suspect that you are missing something and consider not taking the trade. Most of the time, a good fill equals a bad trade (and a bad fill equals a good trade!).

If you are fading a move, buying a pullback in a bull, for example, and the move had about four strong trend bars or two or three large trend bars, there is too much momentum for you to be placing an order in the opposite direction. It is better to wait for an entry, then don't take it, and then wait for a second pullback bar and then enter on the market's second attempt to reverse.

Since second entries in good setups usually succeed, if one fails, assume that you are reading the market incorrectly and do not take a third entry unless it is a Wedge (a failed trend channel line breakout).

There were many second entry trades today in Figure 1.29, and all but one were at the same price or a worse price than the first entry. Look at the

FIGURE 1.29 Second Entries Are Usually Great Signals

Bar 10 long. The market is letting you buy at one tick better than the traders who bought at Bar 9. In general, the "Good fill, bad trade" maxim applies. Whenever the market is offering you a bargain, assume that you are reading the chart incorrectly, and usually it is better not to take the trade.

Bar 1 in Figure 1.30 was a Low 1 short at a new high on the day, but it followed five bull trend bars, which is too much upward momentum to be looking to sell. Smart traders would wait to see if the bulls would fail in a second attempt to rally before going short, and this happened on the second short entry at Bar 2.

Bar 3 was a first entry long on a new low of the day, but after six bars without a bullish close, it makes more sense to wait for a second long entry, which occurred on Bar 4. In general, four or more trend bars against your intended direction means that a second entry is usually preferable.

Bar 5 was a High 2, but it followed four bear trend bars, which is too much down momentum. A second entry never developed, so smart traders averted a loss by waiting, although going long on a reversal out of an ii flag (7 bars earlier) after a long move is usually a good trade.

The Bar 7 ii was a possible Failed Final Flag. Traders could have gone long on Bar 8, but the prior reversal bar had too much overlap with the bar before it and the move down from Bar 6 was too strong. Bar 9 offered a second entry, following the prior bar's attempt to sell off.

Bar 10 was a Low 1 following two earlier bear bars since the Bar 8 low, but there were six bars with higher lows, indication too much bullish strength. There was a second entry at the Bar 11 bear reversal bar.

FIGURE 1.30 When the Market Is Strong, Wait for a Second Entry Before Fading

LATE AND MISSED ENTRIES

If you look at any chart and think that, if you had taken the original entry, you would still be holding the swing portion of your trade, then you need to enter at the market. However, you should only enter with the number of shares or contracts that you would still be holding had you taken the original entry, and you should use the same trailing stop. For example, if you see a strong trend underway in GS, and had you taken the original entry with 300 shares and you now would only be holding 100 shares with your protective stop at $1.50 away, you should buy 100 shares at the market and place a $1.50 protective stop. Logically, buying a swing size portion now or holding a swing position from an earlier entry doesn't make a difference. Although it might be easier emotionally to think of the trade with the open profit as risking someone else's money, that is not the reality. It is *your* money, and what you are risking is no different from buying now and risking the same $1.50. A trader knows this and will place the trade without hesitation. If he does not, then he simply does not believe that he would still be holding any shares had he entered earlier, or he needs to work on this emotional issue.

In Figure 1.31 GS ended in a strong bear yesterday that might have bottomed before the close when the rally into the close broke the bear trendline. There was a second long entry at Bar 1 following a strong bull trend bar and a High 2.

FIGURE 1.31 It's Never Too Late to Enter a Strong Trend

Today's open sold off for three bars to test the EMA and yesterday's close and then reversed up for an Opening Reversal and a Higher Low after a two-legged sideways correction.

If a trader had missed the long and saw this chart around Bar 4 after a series of bull bars, he would probably be wishing that he had caught the open so that he would at least have the swing portion of his position still working. If he normally trades 300 shares and he would normally only have 100 left around Bar 4 with a breakeven stop from the Bar 3 entry that he missed, he should buy 100 shares at the market and use that stop at the high of the Bar 3 signal bar (maybe 10 cents below the high, since GS often runs stops). He should also look for pauses and pullbacks to add on. After adding on at the High 2 after Bar 6, he could move the stop for the entire position to one tick below the Bar 6 signal bar and then trail it up.

Entering late and using the original stop is absolutely identical to being long the swing portion of the original position, using the same protective stop.

CHAPTER 2

Trendlines and Trend Channels

B oth trendlines and trend channel lines are straight lines that are parallel to the trend but on opposite sides of the trend, forming a channel that contains the price action. Trendlines most often set up With Trend trades, and trend channel lines are most helpful finding tradable reversals. Curved lines are too subjective and therefore require too much thought when you are trying to place trades quickly.

TRENDLINES

A trendline is most helpful when looking for entries in the direction of the trend on pullbacks and in the opposite direction after the trendline is broken. Trendlines can be drawn using swing points or best fit techniques such as linear regression calculations or simply quickly drawing a best approximation. They also can be drawn as a parallel of a trend channel line and then dragged to the trendline side of the bars, but this approach is rarely needed since any signals generated are usually also based on more common types of price action analysis. Sometimes the best fit trendline is drawn just using the candle bodies and ignoring the tails; this is common in Wedge patterns, which often do not have a Wedge shape. Most of the time it is not necessary to actually draw a line since the lines are usually obvious. If you do draw a line, you usually can erase it moments after you verify that the market has tested it.

Once a trend has been established by a series of trending highs and lows, the most profitable trades are in the direction of the trendline until the trendline is broken. Every time the market pulls back to the area around the trendline, even if it undershoots or overshoots the trendline, look for a reversal off of the trendline and then enter in the direction of the trend. Even after a trendline breaks, if it has been in effect for a couple of hours or more, the chances are high that the trend extreme will get tested after a pullback. The test can be followed by the trend continuing, the trend reversing, or the market entering a trading range. The single most important point about a trendline break is that it is the first sign that the market is no longer being controlled by just one side (buyers or sellers) and the chances of further two sided trading is now much greater. After every trendline break, there will be a new swing point upon which to base a new line. Typically, each successive line has a smaller slope, indicating that the trend is losing momentum. At some point, trendlines in the opposite direction will become more important as control of the market switches from the bears to the bulls or vice versa.

The strength of the trendline break provides an indication of the strength of the Countertrend traders. The bigger and faster the Countertrend move, the more likely that a reversal will occur after the market comes back to test the trend's extreme (for example, after a Lower High or a Higher High in the test of the high of the bull).

It is helpful to consider a gap opening and any large trend bar to effectively be breakouts and each one should be treated as if it is a one-bar trend, since breakouts commonly fail and you need to be prepared to fade them if there is a setup. Any sideways movement over the next few bars will break the trend. Usually, those bars will be setting up a flag and then be followed by a With Trend move out of the flag, but sometimes the breakout will fail and the market will reverse. Since the sideways bars "broke" the trendline, you can look to fade the trend if there is a good signal bar.

Which trendlines are valid in Figure 2.1? Every one of them that you can see has the potential to generate a trade. Look for every swing point that you can find and see if there is an earlier one that can be connected with a trendline, and then extend the line to the right and see how price responds when it penetrates or touches the line. Notice how each successive trendline tends to become flatter until some point when trendlines in the opposite direction become more important.

In actual practice, when you see a possible trendline and you are not certain how far it is from the current bar, draw it to see if the market has hit it and then quickly erase the line. You don't want lines on your chart for more than a few seconds when trading because you don't want distractions. You need to focus on the bars and see how they behave once near the line, and not focus on the line.

As a trend progresses, Countertrend moves break the trendlines, and usually the breakouts fail, setting up With Trend entries. Each breakout

FIGURE 2.1 All Trendlines Are Important

failure becomes the second point for the creation of a new, longer trendline with a shallower slope. Eventually failed breakouts fail, creating Breakout Pullbacks, and these allow for the drawing of trendlines in the opposite direction. After the major trendline is broken, the trendlines in the opposite direction become more important, and at that point the trend has likely reversed.

A trendline can be drawn from a trend channel line, but this rarely provides trades that are not already apparent using other more common price action analysis.

Here in Figure 2.2, a bear trend channel line from Bars 1 to 4 is used to create a parallel, and the parallel is dragged to the opposite side of the price and anchored at the Bar 2 high (because this then contains all of the prices between the Bars 1 and 4 beginning and end of the trend channel line).

Bar 6 is a second attempt to reverse the break above that line and therefore a good short setup.

The trendline is almost indistinguishable from the trendline created from the highs of Bars 2 and 5 and so adds nothing to a trader looking for a short. It is shown only for completeness.

Bar 6 was also a failed overshoot of the Bars 3 and 5 trend channel line, making the Bar 6 short an example of a Dueling Lines trade (trendline and trend channel lines intersecting and in opposite directions).

The trend channel line from Bars 2 and 3 in Figure 2.3 can be moved and anchored to Bar 1 to create a trendline that can give an idea of where a

FIGURE 2.2 A Trendline Drawn from a Trend Channel Line

FIGURE 2.3 A Trendline Created as a Parallel of a Trend Channel Line

tradable bounce might occur. A two-legged pullback overshot the trendline and reversed up on the 1-minute Emini.

Bar 2 is a big bar and should be considered to be a one-bar trend. Any sideways movement will break the trendline but usually will set up a flag, as it did here. However, reversals are common and can be traded if there is a good signal bar.

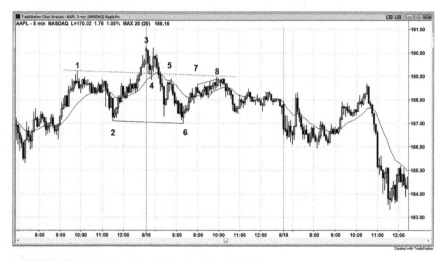

FIGURE 2.4   A Trend Channel Line Can Sometimes Approximate the Height of the Right Shoulder

When a possible Head and Shoulders pattern is setting up, a trend channel line drawn across the neckline (Bars 2 and 6 in Figure 2.4) and dragged to the left shoulder (Bar 1) sometimes gives an approximation of where the right shoulder should form (Bar 8). This is of minor importance since the most recent bars are always much more important in deciding where to enter. This chart is included only for completeness. Independent of any Head and Shoulders pattern, a trader would short the Bar 8 Lower High because it was a Double Top Bear Flag with Bar 5, a small Wedge, and the top of a Spike and Channel rally from the Bar 6 low.

MICRO TRENDLINES: SMALL, STEEP TRENDLINES IN STRONG TRENDS

A Micro Trendline is a trendline on any time frame that is drawn across from 2 to about 10 bars where most of the bars touch or are close to the trendline, and then one of the bars has a false breakout through the trendline. This false breakout sets up a With Trend entry and is the most reliable type of a High 1 long in a bull or a Low 1 short in a bear. These are tiny (usually just one or two bars long) but strong bull and bear flags. If it fails within a bar or two, then there is usually a Countertrend trade, which effectively becomes a Breakout Pullback entry and a Failed Final Flag. The vast majority of Micro Trendline false breakouts are 1 minute High/Low 1 and 2 pullbacks, but if you follow the 1 minute chart you will likely lose money because you will not be able to take all the trades and you will invariably pick too many bad cherries. When a trend is strong with no bar pullbacks and you are eager to get in, you can look at a 1-minute chart for a High/Low 2 pullback, but it is just as easy to enter on a 5- or 3-minute Micro Trendline failed breakout. Any poke through it is also likely a 1-minute pullback, so enter on the failed breakout (in a bull, enter at one tick above the bar that dips below the trendline). Small, steep trendlines, even drawn using two consecutive bars, often provide setups for With Trend trades. If the trend is steep, sometimes a small Pullback Bar or a pause bar can penetrate a tiny trendline and when it does, it can become a signal bar for a With Trend entry. Some of the penetrations are smaller than one tick in the Eminis, but are still valid.

If the Breakout Pullback entry fails, for example in a falling market with a bear Micro Trendline, then look at the size of the bodies of the bars. If the bars are trend bars, then this second failure (the failed breakout and then the failed breakout Pullback), the odds are high that the market is giving you a tradable Low 2 short. If the bars have more of a doji look, then the market will likely enter Barb Wire, but the odds still favor a downside breakout. If you are not certain, then wait because it is likely that most traders will not be certain and Barb Wire is likely.

Micro Trendlines can be used to create Micro Trend Channel Lines, which also can set up a reversal of a failed breakout. The Micro Trend Channel Line is usually created as a parallel of a Micro Trendline. However, sometimes as the Micro Trendline is forming, the opposite ends of the bars are also all close to a Micro Trendline that can be drawn after the first two or three bars of the leg form.

Finally, when a Micro Trendline contains a very tight channel for an extended period, like about ten bars, the odds increase substantially that the breakout failure will fail and become a Breakout Pullback reversal that should be good for at least a scalp. This is especially true when it develops after an extended trend move.

Micro trendlines can generate many scalps during the day, especially on the 1-minute chart, which is seldom worth trading. The chart on the left in Figure 2.5 is a 1-minute Emini chart, and the numbers correspond to the same bars on the 5-minute chart on the right. Both show that failed breakouts from tiny trendlines can result in profitable fades. There are other trades on the 1-minute chart that are not shown because the purpose of

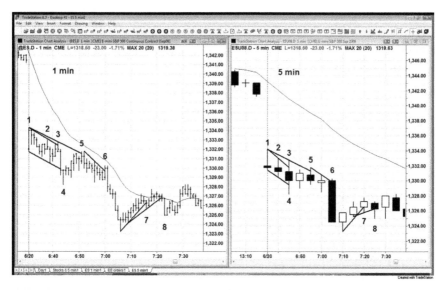

FIGURE 2.5   Micro Trendlines Can Create Great Entries

this figure is only to show how 5-minute Micro Trendlines correspond to more obvious, longer trendlines on the 1-minute chart, so if you can read the 5-minute chart, you do not have to additionally look at the 1-minute chart to place your orders. Many of these trades could have been profitable scalps on the 1-minute chart.

Note that several breaks of Micro Trendlines on the 5-minute chart are easy to overlook and are less than one tick in size. For example, Bars 3, 5, 6, and 7 are failed Micro Trendline breaks on the 5-minute chart that would be invisible to most traders, but the one at Bar 5 is particularly significant and led to a good short scalp. It was the second failed attempt to break above a bear trendline (Bar 3 was the first).

Price action trading works even at the tiniest level. Note how Bar 8 on the 1-minute chart was a Higher High Breakout Test long setup and that although the market came down to test the Bar 8 signal bar low two bars after entry, the protective stop below the signal bar would not have been hit. Also note that there was also an even smaller "major reversal" in this segment of the 1-minute chart. There was a tiny bull trend, indicated by the bull Micro Trendline up from the low of the chart, then a break of the trendline at Bar 7, and then a Higher High test of the tiny bull trend extreme. Since the pattern is so small, the "trend reversal" down to Bar 8 was just a scalp, as should be expected.

Even trendlines created using just two or three consecutive bars in a steep trend can setup With Trend entries when there is a small break that immediately reverses. Each new break becomes the second point in a longer, flatter trendline until eventually trendlines in the opposite direction become more important, and at that point the trend has reversed.

Bar 1 in Figure 2.6 dipped below a three-bar trendline and reversed up, creating a long entry at one tick above the prior bar.

Bar 2 dipped below a six-bar trendline. Traders would place a buy stop above its high. When not filled, they would move the stop to the high of the next bar and would be filled on Bar 3. Incidentally, the bar before Bar 2 was a possible short setup based on a Micro Trend Channel Line (not shown) that is a parallel of the three-bar Micro Trendline leading up to Bar 1. The upward momentum was too strong for a short without a second entry but this illustrates how Micro Trend Channel Lines can set up countertrend trades. Bar 4 was a small inside bar that extended below a two-bar trendline (the penetration is not shown). The buy is on a stop at one tick above the high of the small inside bar.

Bar 5 broke the major trendline of the day (any trendline lasting about an hour or so is more significant), so traders would be thinking that a two-legged pullback was more likely. After the break above the bear trendline on the bar following Bar 5, a short would be triggered on the Bar 6 Lower High. When bars are small doji bars like those following Bar 5, it is usually best to wait for bigger trend bars before taking more trades, but these trendline reversals still led to profitable scalps of 30 to 50 cents in Amazon.

FIGURE 2.6 Micro Trendlines Can Be Just Two or Three Bars Long

FIGURE 2.7   Micro Trendlines in Strong Trends

Small trendlines in strong trends, even when drawn using adjacent bars, often have failure tests (failed breakouts) that set up good With Trend entries. Many of these are High/Low 2 setups on 1-minute charts, but you don't need to look at the 1-minute when you see the false breakouts on the 5-minute chart, as seen in Figure 2.7.

When trading, you do not have to actually draw the trendlines on the chart very often because most are visible without the help of the lines.

The 1-minute Emini provided entries on trendline tests and trend channel overshoots and reversals all day long. Many of the penetrations in Figure 2.8 were less than one tick but still meaningful. The lines shown are just some of the ones that could be drawn on this chart, and there are many others.

Each successive trendline gets shallower until trendlines in the other direction dominate the price action.

In Figure 2.9, there were many Micro Trendline and Channel trades today (only four are shown), a very unusual day where the Dow was down over 700 points but rallied into the close to make back half of the loss.

Bar 5 is a Micro Trend Channel reversal where the channel line was a parallel of the Bars 1 to 4 Micro Trendline. You could also have drawn the channel line using the lows (the lows of the bars after Bar 1 and Bar 3).

FIGURE 2.8   Trendline Tests and Trend Channel Overshoots and Reversals

There was a great ii setup where both bars had bull closes, which is always desirable when fading a strong bear.

Bars 7 and 9 were Micro Trendline false breakout short scalps (Low 1 setups) and both were quickly followed by buy scalps as the failure failed, creating effectively a Breakout Pullback buy (even though both were Lower Lows) and a Failed Final Flag (the breakout from the one bar bear flags of Bars 7 and 9).

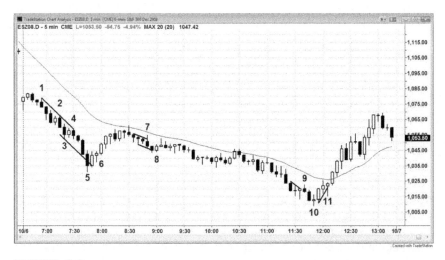

FIGURE 2.9

The rally from Bar 5 tested the EMA and broke a trendline so buyers were looking for a second entry long on a test of the Bar 5 low. Here, it was a Lower Low and Bar 10 was a second attempt to rally after taking out the Bar 5 low. This Lower Low was too far below the Bar 5 low and too long after the rally that broke the trendline (an extension of that from Bars 1 to 4) to be ideal, but it was still a second entry with a signal bar with an up close, and a failed failure of a Micro Trendline break.

Incidentally, note that although not drawn, there is a bull Micro Trendline up from the Bar 5 low and the small bear trend bar 6 bars later broke it. This was followed by a Higher High test of the extreme of this small bull and then a trend reversal down (off the EMA in a bear). The price action involved is the same as for a major trend reversal: a trend, a trendline break, a test of the trend's extreme as the market once again tries to push above that price area, and then a reversal as the market fails in this second attempt. When the market tries to do something twice and fails, it usually then tries to do the opposite.

Bar 11 was a classic trap to get you out of a strong rally. If you exited, you must buy again on the High 1 above the Bar 11 Micro Trendline false breakout.

Many of the bars today had a range of over 6 to 8 points. It would be prudent to reduce your position size to half or less, and increase your stop to 4 points and your profit target to 2 points. Otherwise, it was just another well-behaved price action day.

HORIZONTAL LINES: SWING POINTS AND OTHER KEY PRICE LEVELS

On most days, which are trading range days, horizontal lines across swing highs and lows often serve as barriers that result in failed breakouts and then reversals. Expect swing high breakouts to fail and form Higher Highs, and swing low breakouts to fail and form Lower Lows. Sometimes the failure fails, and the market makes a second more extreme Higher High or Lower Low. A fade of a second Higher High or Lower Low setup is even more likely to be successful because many of them are variants of Three Push patterns.

On trend days, horizontal lines should generally only be used to enter on pullbacks, like with the Double Top Bear Flag or a Double Bottom Bull Flag patterns. Once there has been a clear trendline break, a failed test of the extreme can be a good reversal setup, especially if there is a strong reversal bar and a second entry (a High/Low 2).

Most days are not strong trend days, and on these days traders should be looking at all prior swing highs and lows for failed tests and reversal

FIGURE 2.10 Horizontal Trendline Failed Breakouts

entries. High/Low 2 entries are the best. A second Higher High or Lower Low is a more extreme point on a trading range day where the middle of the day acts like a magnet, and a further extreme is therefore more likely to yield a scalper's profit. For example, Bar 5 in Figure 2.10 is a second Higher High over Bar 2 (and Three Pushes up from Bar 3).

Bar 9 is a Lower Low below the open of the day (and the seventh point of an Expanding Triangle Bottom).

Bar 13 is a large Double Bottom Pullback (there were multiple bottoms to choose from for labeling the Double Bottom, and Bars 3 and 9 might be the best).

Bar 15 is a Double Top Bear Flag. When it failed, the market became noticeably more bullish.

Bar 17 is a second Lower Low below Bar 14 and a Lower Low below Bar 16.

Both days were strong trend days in Figure 2.11 with one extreme near the open and then no EMA pullback for over two hours (2HM days). On strong trend days, only consider fading swing highs in bulls and swing lows in bears if there was first a good trendline break. Acceptable Countertrend entries were at Bars 4, 8, and 12. However, since these are Countertrend and there was only minimal Countertrend momentum on the trendline breaks, these trades should only be scalps. Do not take them if they are distracting you from the With Trend entries, where you should swing much of your position.

Bars 1 and 5 formed a Double Bottom Bull Flag, and Bar 9 was part of a Double Top Bear Flag.

FIGURE 2.11 Only Trade Countertrend If There Was First a Trendline Break

Both Bars 5 and 13 gave great With Trend entries (EMA Gap bars, 11:30 traps) based on swing fades (Bar 5 was a swing low breakout fade, and Bar 13 is a swing high breakout fade).

TREND CHANNEL LINES

Trend channel lines are on the opposite side of the price action from a trendline and have the same general slope. In a bull, a trendline is below the lows and a trend channel line is above the highs, and both are rising up and to the right. A trend channel line is a useful tool to fade a trend that has gone too far, too fast. Look for an overshoot that reverses, especially if it is a second reversal of the overshoot.

Usually when there is a trend, you can find a trendline and a trend channel line that contain it. The market will eventually break out of the channel in either direction. Most trend channel line overshoots reverse back into the channel but sometimes one will continue and this results in a steeper trend. Also, most trendline breaks fail but they generate a new swing point that creates a new, less steep trendline, indicating that the trend may have become weaker. Eventually, there will be a trendline break that extends so far beyond the trendline and has so much momentum that the pullback from this surge will fail to exceed the prior trend extreme. This swing point (a Higher Low in a new bull or a Lower High in a new bear) can be used to draw a trendline for the incipient trend, using the end of the old trend as the first point of the trendline. As the new trend develops, its trendlines and trend channel lines represent what is taking place better than the lines from the old trend and they become the focus of your trading. Since most trendline and trend channel line breakouts fail, entering on the breakouts is a losing strategy. It is far more profitable to look to enter on the failure, but if the breakout extends far, then you should wait for a pullback and then enter in the direction of the breakout.

A trend channel line can be a parallel to a trendline and dragged to the opposite side of the price action, it can be drawn across spikes on that opposite side, or it can be a best fit line, like a regression line or visually drawing a best fit line. In a bull, a trendline is drawn across two lows. If that trendline is used to form a trend channel line, then drag it to the opposite side of the trend. You want it to contain (be above) the highs of all of the bars located in between the two bars used to create the trendline, so drag it to the high of whatever bar that will leave it touching that bar alone. Occasionally you will get a better sense of the trend if you anchor the line to a bar that is outside of the two bars. Always do whatever best highlights the trend.

Alternatively, a trend channel line can be useful when created on its own. In a bear swing, a trendline will be downward sloping and above the highs. The trend channel line will have a similar slope, but draw it between any two swing lows in the bear swing. It is most useful if it contains (is below) all of the other bars in the swing, so choose the bars that will give that result.

Trend channel line overshoots are closely related to Wedges and should be viewed and traded as if they are one and the same. Most Wedges have failed trend channel breakouts as the trigger for a reversal trade, and most trend channel overshoots and reversals are also Wedge reversals, although the Wedge may not be obvious or have a perfect Wedge shape. The Wedges are less obvious and less likely to be present when the trend channel line is constructed as a parallel of a trendline, but Wedges are still often present.

Why do so many reversals occur after trend channel line overshoots when everyone knows that it commonly leads to a reversal? Won't early entrants prevent the line from ever being reached? Common wisdom is that novice traders on the wrong side hold their losing positions until they cannot stand any more pain, and then suddenly all of them exit at once, creating a blow-off or a parabolic climax. However, that is not a meaningful component of a reversal in a huge market like the Eminis. Smart traders won't trade Countertrend until either there is a pullback from a strong trendline break or there is a reversal from a trend channel line overshoot. For example, in a bull, smart money will keep buying until they drive the price above the bull trend channel line, and then they will take profits.

There may be a couple of failures along the way and then a longer and steeper line comes into play, but eventually the market will agree on which line is the final one. At the same time as the profit takers are taking profits, many will reverse, and many others who were already flat will initiate shorts. Other smart traders will wait for a reversal on the charts and there will be traders entering on reversals on all types of charts (1- to 5-minute, and volume charts and tick chart of any size).

Once they believe that the top is in, this smart money won't be looking to buy any longer. They are short, and many of these traders will hold through a new high, despite an open loss on their current position, believing that the top is in or close to in. In fact, many will add on above the high, both to get a better average price for their shorts and to help push the market down. The big players are only thinking short and won't be scared out except by the rare occurrence of a failed second entry or a huge failure (for example, maybe three points above their entry). There are no buyers left so the market only has one way to go.

Look at the volume at key turning points. It's huge. The only logical way that can happen is if institutions are exiting in one direction and entering in the other, and other institutions are taking the opposite side as part of a hedge in another market (stocks, options, bonds, currencies, and so on). They perceive that their risk-reward ratio is better by buying futures at the high or selling them at the low and offsetting the risk in another market. Nothing else makes sense. You know that the volume is not from small individual traders being squeezed out of shorts and buying at the high. There are plenty of stupid people out there, but if you were to pool all of their buys at the high, it is still small compared to the institutional volume.

The reversal at an overshoot happens because it is such an entrenched part of institutional trading psyche that it has to happen. Even if an institution does not look at charts, it will have some other criterion that tells them that the market has gone too far and it is time to exit or reverse, and this will invariably coincide with what price action traders are seeing. Remember, price action is the inescapable footprint of what is happening to price as a huge number of smart people are independently trying to make the most money that they can in the market. In a big market, it cannot be manipulated and will always be basically the same.

One final observation is that the slope of the final flag of a trend often provides an approximation of the slope of the new trend. This has limited value to a trader because there will be other much more important factors involved in the decision leading up to placing a trade, but it is an interesting observation.

Extend them to the right and watch how the price acts when it penetrates the channel line.

FIGURE 2.12 Trend Channel Lines Point in the Direction of Trends, But Are on the Opposite Side of the Trend from Trendlines

Trend channel lines are commonly drawn in one of two ways. First, as a parallel line (dashed line in Figure 2.12) of a trendline (solid line) and then dragged to the opposite side of the action, placed to touch a swing point located between the two bars used to create the trendline. Choose the point that will result in all of the bars between the trend and channel lines being contained between the lines. The second type (dotted line) of trend channel line is drawn across swing points and is independent of any trendline. You can also simply draw a best fit, but these are usually not helpful in trading.

The slope of the final flag of the bull in Figure 2.13 provided direction for the subsequent bear. A linear regression trendline drawn between Bars 1 and 2 became a rough bear trend channel line for the selloff that extended into the next day. It is possible that it contributed to the buying at Bar 7, but Bar 7 was a buy simply based on the trendline break and the second attempt to reverse the breakout below the low of the open. It is usually far better to place orders based on the most recent price action if it provides a justification for a trade than to look back 30 or more bars.

The trendline from Bars 2 and 3 in Figure 2.14 was used to create a parallel that was dragged to Bar 1 and extended to the right. This trend channel line (dotted) was not penetrated by Bar 5. Also, it was anchored to Bar 1, which is not in between Bars 2 and 3, the bars used to create the original trendline. However, traders should always be looking at every possibility. Had there been a penetration and reversal, the chances of a two-legged rally off the Bar 5 low would be improved.

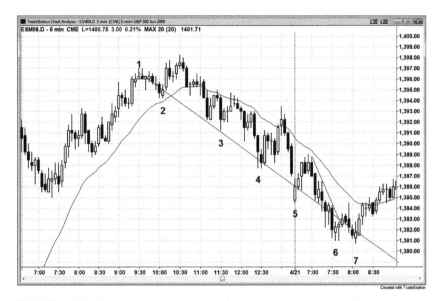

FIGURE 2.13   The Slope of Final Flag Often Dictates the Slope of the New Trend

The simple trend channel line using Bars 1 and 5 was penetrated by Bar 6, but this is not an ideal trend channel line to use as a basis for a Countertrend trade since Bars 1 and 5 were far apart and Bars 5 and 6 were close together. Trendlines work best when they are tested by a third leg, and here Bars 5 and 6 were essentially still part of the same leg (Three Pushes Down,

FIGURE 2.14   A Variant of Trend Channel Line

Bars 4, 5, and 6). The trade was still worth taking because Bar 6 was small, so the risk reward ratio was good. This is also a Shrinking Stair pattern down, which indicates waning bearish momentum and supports a long.

DUELING LINES: INTERSECTING TRENDLINE AND TREND CHANNEL LINE

When a longer trendline is tested and the test occurs at a shorter-term trend channel line of opposite slope, look to enter in the direction of the trend if the test is successful (failed breakout and reversal). The trend channel line test indicates that the correction is over and the location is perfect, since it is a test of a longer trendline.

A bear trend channel line drawn from Bars 3 and 5 in Figure 2.15 offered support at Bar 6. Bar 3 was a swing low in a bull, and Bar 5 appeared to be a swing low in a new bear. However, the move down to Bar 6 was just a large two-legged correction in the bull market. There were Dueling Lines at Bar 6 (a bull trendline and a bear trend channel line of opposite slope), and the market reversed up at the intersection, as is common. Since the move down to Bar 6 was steep, it is reasonable to wait for the second entry at the Bar 7 Higher Low, buying on a stop at one tick over its high.

FIGURE 2.15 All Swing Points Should Be Considered When Drawing Trendlines and Trend Channel Lines, Even Those from a Prior Trend

FIGURE 2.16 Dueling Lines

A bear trend channel line could also have been based on a trendline drawn across the two swing highs that followed the Bar 4 high, and then anchored to Bar 5. The goal is to look at the overall shape and then choose any trend channel line that contains the price action. Then, watch how the market reacts after penetrating the line.

Bar 4 in Figure 2.16 tested the bear trendline and as it did, there was an overshoot of a smaller bull trend channel line (from Bars 3 to 4), resulting in a short scalp off the Dueling Lines pattern. There was a second entry at the Bar 6 nominal Higher High.

CHAPTER 3

Trends

W hy is it important to recognize the existence of a trend? Because then most of your trades should be in that direction and you must try to take every With Trend entry and rarely take Countertrend entries. The earlier you see the trend, the more money you stand to make. Focusing on the Countertrend setups will likely make you miss the much more profitable but often scarier With Trend entries. The With Trend entries are scary because the market always looks overdone and it's hard to imagine that selling near the low of an overdone bear or buying near the high of an overdone bull could ever be profitable. However, that is exactly why it is! The market draws in Countertrend traders, and if you enter where they exit at a loss, they will drive the market in your direction, even though the market looks so overextended. This chapter describes many common trend patterns that you should look for every day. If you see one setting up within the first hour or two of the day, there will likely be several high probability With Trend trades that you can then make. You need to decide many times every day if the day resembles any of the types of trends described later in this chapter, and if it does, force yourself to take the With Trend trades.

A trend is a series of price changes that are mostly either up (a bull trend or a bull) or down (a bear trend or a bear). A trend can be as short as a single bar (remember, a trend bar is made up of a trend on a smaller time frame) or longer than all of the bars on your screen. Trends are loosely classified into four overlapping and often interchangeable categories: trend, swing, pullback, and leg. The distinctions are just guidelines because each of the three smaller versions is a different version on different time frames.

For example, a pullback in a bull on a 60-minute chart might be a strong bear trend on a 1-minute chart. Also, each category will contain one or more of the smaller versions. A trend might be made of 10 swings, each containing 1 to 4 pullbacks, and each pullback might have 1 to 4 legs. Also, every up and downswing of any size is commonly referred to a leg, so the distinctions are not very important, but each term carries a subtle distinction with it.

At its simplest, a trend is present when the chart on your computer screen starts at one of the two left-hand corners and ends at the diagonally opposite corner of the screen with no huge fluctuation in between. For example, if the bars on the left are near the lower left corner of your monitor and the bars on the right are near the upper right-hand corner and there are not many large upswings and downswings in the middle of your screen, then this is a bull trend. A chart only shows one or two trends.

If more than two trends are present on a chart, it is preferable to describe the trends by using one of the other three classifications because the two-sided action creates different trading opportunities. Both swings and legs are smaller trends, and there are at least two on the chart. The term *swing* is used when there are two or more smaller trends on the chart, even though the overall chart might be sideways.

A leg is any smaller trend that is part of a larger trend, and it can be a pullback (a Countertrend move), a swing in a trend or in a sideways market, or a With Trend move that occurs between any two pullbacks within a trend.

A pullback is a temporary Countertrend move and is part of a trend, swing, or leg. For example, a bull pullback is a sideways to downward move in a bull trend, swing, or leg that will be followed by at least a test of the prior high. Any bar or series of bars that represents any pause or loss of momentum is a pullback, even if there is no actual backward movement. This includes a single inside bar, which obviously does not extend below the low or above the high of the prior bar. When it is a single bar, the bar is called a Pause Bar or a Pullback Bar. These one-bar pullbacks are made up of a series of small swings on a smaller time frame chart. However, you might have to go all of the way down to a 1-minute or a 100 tick or smaller chart to see them. This is a waste of time for a trader, but it is helpful to be aware of the reality because it provides a rationale for considering placing a trade.

Within any trend, there are a number of smaller opposite trends, some lasting for only one or two bars, and all of them should be considered as likely to fail and therefore setups for trades in the direction of the larger trend. In a bull, the swings should be trending upward, meaning that each pullback should be above the prior pullback, and it should result in a new high (trending highs and lows, or trending swings). All moves with strong momentum usually have at least a test of the extreme following a pullback (all strong moves usually have at least two legs, even if the second one falls short and reverses).

All trends, no matter how small, must first break a trendline from the prior trend or trading range and then have trending swings (such as a series of Higher Highs and Lows in a bull). Absent either of these, there is no trend. The best risk reward ratio occurs when you enter on the First Pullback after a trendline break, before there is a clearly established trend. As a possible trend day is unfolding, traders should look for signs of strength, each of which increases the odds that the trend will continue.

The trend continues until after it breaks its trendline, and then it continues some more. You should not be trading countertrend until the market has enough strength to break the trendline. However, even then, you should not be entering countertrend until the market first goes back to test the extreme of the trend. This means that even after a trendline break, you should still be looking for With Trend trades because there should be a test of the old extreme. Sometimes there is so much strength on the trendline break that there should not be much of a test of the trend extreme, but this is the exception and not the rule.

If you find yourself drawing many trend channel lines or looking at a 1-minute chart, then you are too eager to find a reversal and are likely missing lots of great With Trend trades. You are in denial and are losing money because of it. Also, since most trend channel line overshoots and reversals are minor in a strong trend and fail, you will be trading lots of losers and wondering why these patterns are failing when they are supposed to be so good. Wait for a trendline break on the 5-minute chart before looking for a countertrend trade and look at all those minor trend channel line overshoots as With Trend setups, and enter where the losers are exiting on their protective stops. You will be much happier, relaxed, and richer, and you will be entertained by how well they work when intuitively they should not because the market appears to have gone much too far without a correction.

Whenever you find yourself waiting a long time for a great reversal, you are oblivious to the trend that is in front of you. When a trend is that strong that it cannot get anywhere near a trendline but you feel it has gone much too far, and you think that entering With Trend near the extreme is risky, you are missing the most reliable trades that exist. All minor pullbacks, even a single, small inside bar, are great With Trend entries.

After a substantial decline in a bear market on the daily chart, people begin to become very concerned about the money that they've lost and they do not want to lose any more money. This makes them sell, regardless of the fundamentals. There was an added problem in the bear of 2008. Baby Boomers were on the verge of retiring and were shocked by what they saw as comfortable nest eggs quickly falling 40 percent in value. So what will they do? They will continue to sell every rally as they try to preserve what they have left. Also, all that money that they are taking out of the market will never return to lift prices again. They will take their money at all the "Thank you, God" points along the way. This will be just below the prior swing high, where they exit and promise God that they will never buy again in return for him letting them recoup some of their losses. This creates a series of lower highs and lows until the last bear has sold. Once that happens, the market will then be able to rally above the prior swing high.

The result of people selling regardless of fundamentals is that the market often falls in huge bear trend days, dropping much further than what the fundamentals warrant, and often there is a huge plunge in the final 30 minutes as funds are forced to sell because of redemption orders. There will be vicious rallies along the way as people become convinced that the bottom is in and they panic to get back long. Also, because the trend is so clearly down, there will be many who are short and will cover aggressively, resulting in huge bull trend bars on the daily chart, but still in a bear market. The end result is a collection of very large range days once the bear is well underway. The huge ranges offer great price action day trading opportunities but you might have to increase your stop size and therefore reduce your position size. While people following the daily charts are selling at the low and buying at the high of each trap (every strong short covering rally), trading off emotion more than reason, a good price action trader can do very well just looking for standard price action setups.

This kind of mentality is not restricted to unsophisticated investors. In the fall of 2008, most hedge funds were down on the year and their sophisticated investors aggressively pulled their money out as the market continued to sell off. The hedge funds had to continue to liquidate on every small rally to meet redemptions and anticipated redemptions. This continued to drive the market down, independent of fundamentals, and just like with less sophisticated investors, the selling will continue until all that's left are positions that investors will hold until they fall to zero. Also, for many hedge fund managers a big part of their income is incentive-based. For example, every quarter that the fund closes at a new high, they might take 20 percent of that profit above the old equity high. If the fund instead is down 30 percent on the year, it will need to earn about 50 percent to get up to that incentive level again. Rather than working for free for several years, it might make more sense to close the fund and start over with a new fund. However, when they close the fund, they have to liquidate and since there is no incentive for them, they can liquidate at any price, no matter how low. This adds to selling that is independent of the intrinsic value of stocks. If they have a one billion dollar fund, their new fund is starting from scratch and it will take a few years before they have enough equity and own as much stock as they did in the old fund, so buying by the new funds don't immediately lift the market.

When the volatility reaches an extreme, the end of the bear is often near as traders give up responding to the whipsaws and decide that there is nothing left that they will sell at any price. When there are no more sellers and the market is overdone on the basis of fundamentals, a good rally should follow. And just how far can a big name stock fall in a bear? Much farther than you might think, even for the bluest of the blue chips. CSCO lost 90 percent of its value in three years after the tech wreck of 2000, and AAPL lost 85 percent of its value in the six years after 1991. GM lost 95 percent in the eight years after 2001. So don't be eager to buy just because a stock is down a Fibonacci 38, 50, or even 62 percent. Wait until there is a price action setup, and it must include a prior break of the bear trendline.

Incidentally, what caused the 2008 Crash? The housing bubble burst more than two years earlier and the credit crunch was well-known for more than a year, but the market began its crash when the world realized that Barack Obama was actually going to be the next president. The concern was that he would increase regulations on business and increase their labor costs, and both would reduce earnings. The world panicked in its adjustment to this new perceived reality and collapse in search of the new appropriate value for stocks given a less capitalistic America. It most likely overreacted and Obama will almost certainly not be as bad for the economy as people fear. He may even turn out to be great, but there is no way to know at this point. Since the market is technically overdone, it will likely go sideways for many months as it gives Obama a chance to reveal his hand. However, the fall was so sharp that it will probably be years before the old highs are surpassed, and it is possible that the market will drift down for several years. The odds still favor a trading range because that is the most common state of the market, especially after a violent move.

TWO LEGS

A break of a trendline creates a new leg. If there is a trend, even a small one, any pullback that breaks any trendline defines that trend as a leg, and the pullback as another leg. Any time there is a new trend or any capitulation of one side, there will usually be at least a two-legged move. This can occur in a pullback in a trend, a breakout, a major reversal, or any time that enough traders believe that the move has sufficient strength to warrant a second attempt to test whether or not a protracted trend will develop. Both the bulls and bears will be in agreement that the momentum is strong enough that a test will be needed before they develop a strong conviction one way or the other. If the second attempt fails (a reversal pattern forms), then the market will usually attempt to do the opposite.

Some complex two-legged moves take place over several hours and, if viewed on a higher time frame chart, would appear clear and simple. However, any time a trader diverts his attention away from his trading chart, he increases the chances that he will miss important 5-minute trades. To be checking the higher time frame charts for the one signal a day that they might provide simply is not a sound financial decision.

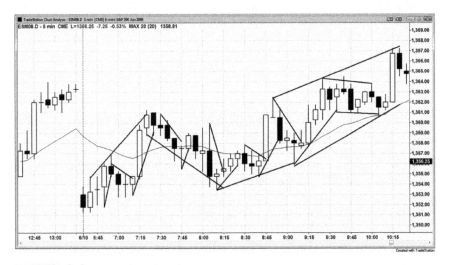

FIGURE 3.1   Examples of Legs

Every trendline break and every pullback in Figure 3.1 is a leg, and each larger leg is made of smaller legs. The term is very general and simply means that the direction of movement has changed, using any criterion that you choose to determine that the change exists.

SIGNS OF STRENGTH

There are many characteristics of strong trends. The most obvious one is that they run from one corner of your chart to the diagonally opposite corner with only small pullbacks. However, in the earlier stages of a trend, there are signs that indicate that the move is strong and likely to last. The more of these signs that are present, the more you should focus on With Trend entries. You should start to look at Countertrend setups only as great

With Trend setups, with you entering on a stop exactly where those Countertrend traders will be forced to exit with a loss.

One interesting phenomenon in trend days is that on many of the days, the best reversal bars and the biggest trend bars tend to be Countertrend, trapping traders into the wrong direction. Also, the lack of great With Trend signal bars makes traders question the entries, forcing them to chase the market and enter late.

Finally, once you realize that the market is in a strong trend, you don't need a setup to enter. You can enter any time all day long at the market if you wish with a relatively small stop. The only purpose of a setup is to minimize the risk.

Here are some characteristics of that are commonly found in strong trends:

- Big gap opening.
- Trending highs and lows (swings).
- No Climaxes and not many large bars (not even large trend bars). Often, the largest trend bars are Countertrend, trapping traders into looking for Countertrend trades and missing With Trend trades (the Countertrend setups almost always look better than the With Trend setups).
- No significant trend channel line overshoots, and the minor ones result in only sideways corrections.
- Failed Wedges.
- 2HM.
- Few if any profitable Countertrend trades.
- Small pullbacks (if the Emini's average range is 12 points, the pullbacks will all likely be less than 3 or 4 points). You find yourself waiting through countless bars for a good With Trend Pullback, and one never comes, yet the market slowly continues to trend.
- Sideways corrections after trendline breaks.
- Repeated High/Low 2 and M2B and M2S With Trend entries.
- No two consecutive trend bar closes on the opposite side of the EMA.
- Bars with no tails or small tails in either direction.

With a trend in runaway mode, there will likely be no pullbacks for many bars, and the bars will be good-size trend bars with mostly small tails. Since you want to keep scalping more as the trend continues while still holding onto the swing portion of your position, consider looking at the 3-minute chart. It often has more pause bars (Countertrend inside bars and one-bar pullbacks) that allow for With Trend entries. The 1-minute chart also has With Trend entries, but it also has some countertrend setups, which can be confusing when you are trying to only trade With Trend. This, along with the speed of the reading required, can create too much stress during a runaway trend and can interfere with your ability to trade effectively. Since you need to be making sure that you catch every With Trend entry, it is best to trade only off the 3- or 5-minute charts in a runaway trend.

The 5-minute Emini in Figure 3.2 gapped up 11 points, which is huge, and the first bar was a bull trend bar. Large gaps that don't reverse early usually mark the start of a strong trend for the day and the day often closes at or near the high (or low, in a bear). Also, the market did not test the EMA for over two hours (a 2HM pattern), another sign of strength. Notice how there was not much emotional behavior (big bars, climaxes, big swings). Quiet markets with lots of small bars, many of which are dojis, often lead to the biggest trends.

On days like this, the institutions have a huge amount to buy, and they want lower prices, but when the lower prices don't come, they have to fill their orders in pieces all day long, at increasingly higher prices. Even though they see the trend day unfolding and expect that they will likely have to be buying at higher prices all day long, they don't dump all of their

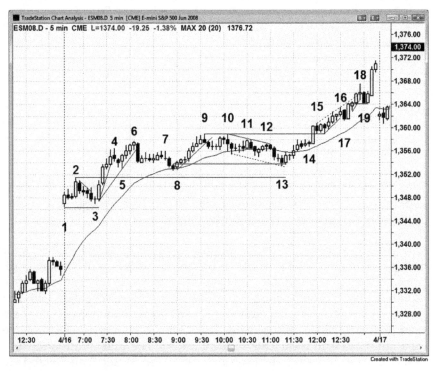

FIGURE 3.2 Signs of Strength in a Strong Bull Trend

buy orders onto the market at once because this could cause a climactic spike up and then possibly a reversal down below their average entry price. They are content filling their orders in manageable pieces all day long, understanding that they are buying higher and higher, but knowing that the market will likely go higher still. Also, strong days like this usually have higher prices over the next one to several days.

The market had a small two-leg move down to Bar 3. A bear trend bar and two dojis composed the first leg, and then a second leg made up of a bear trend bar with a large bear tail on top (the tail was the pullback that ended the first leg down) followed by a doji. This was a variant of a two-leg move and is certainly going to have two clear legs down on a smaller time frame chart, setting up a High 2 (variant). Buy at one tick above Bar 3. It is also a test of the gap, forming a Double Bottom Bull Flag (the opening gap is the flag pole). Since this is a possible trend day and as such could extend much further than most traders would ever suspect, smart traders will swing part or all of their positions.

Bar 5 is a High 1 Breakout Pullback after a strong move up (four bull trend bars), and a High 1 is always a good buy in a strong bull. The Bar 4 Low 1 break below the trendline and reversal from the new high is not a short, even for a scalp. After such a strong up move, smart traders would only be looking to buy and would only consider a short if there was a second entry.

Bar 6 is a Low 2, which is a second entry short. However, in the face of the strong bull trend, shorts would only scalp this trade. They would only swing it if there was first a prior strong down move that broke a substantial trendline (maybe 20 or more bars). If they short, they will be quick to exit and then they will look for a long setup for a swing trade. With Trend entries in a strong trend should be mostly swung, with only a small potion taken off as a scalp. If you find that you missed a With Trend entry, stop looking for Countertrend scalps and start trading only With Trend setups. During a trend day, you must try to catch every With Trend signal because that is where the source of the most consistent money is.

Since the Bar 6 entry bar was a strong bear trend bar, there is a chance for two legs down. Bar 7 is an entry bar for a Low 2 short into the second leg down, but after a six-bar Tight Trading Range, any breakout in either direction would likely fail after not going very far.

Bar 8 is a two-legged pullback and the first to the EMA in a strong bull, which is a great buy. Whenever the market stays away from the EMA for two hours or more, the trend is very strong.

Bar 9 is a reversal at a new swing high, but there were no bear trend bars among the prior seven bars so no short can be taken unless a second entry forms.

Bar 10 is a second entry, but in a Tight Trading Range in a bull, any short is a scalp at best, and it is probably best to pass on this trade. Outside bars are less reliable, but you could consider taking the short for a scalp since second entries are so reliable. Three small dojis developed at the EMA. The odds are high that there will be a trend bar breakout and it will fail. Hold short and risk maybe four ticks. The Bar 11 bull trend bar breakout failed, as expected, allowing you to take your four-tick scalp profit on the next bar.

Bar 13 was a Breakout Test that extended one tick below the high of the signal bar that generated the strong move up from the Bar 8 long. The move down from Bars 9 to 13 was very weak and appears essentially sideways. The market struggled to get down to test the breakout, meaning the bears lacked conviction. Bar 13 also setup a High 4 entry just below the EMA and it was the first EMA Gap Bar of the day (a bar with a high below the EMA). It formed a Higher Low (higher than Bar 8) following a Higher High at Bar 9, and is part of trending bull swings. It is essentially a Double Bottom Bull Flag with Bar 8.

Bar 14 is a High 2 breakout.

Bar 15 was a bear trend bar for the first leg down, followed by a bull trend bar, and then a second bear trend bar, completing the two "down" legs (actually, a small, sideways two-legged correction or flag). High 2 Breakout Pullbacks are strong entries.

There was also a failed Wedge top (it broke down for only a single bar) at Bar 16, setting up a long above the Bar 17 failure.

Bar 18 broke above a bull trend channel line and gave a Low 2 short signal. However, on a strong trend day, smart bears will only short if there is first a strong bear leg that broke a trendline. Otherwise, they will view all short setups as buy setups. They will place orders to go long exactly where the weak shorts will have to cover (such as one tick above the highs of Bars 17 and 19).

Bar 19 was a one-bar trendline break that failed and therefore a buy setup.

One peculiarity of trend days is that often the best-looking reversal bars and trend bars are Countertrend, trapping traders into losing trades in the wrong direction (Bars 1–8 in Figure 3.3). Notice how there was not a single great bear reversal signal bar all day, yet this was a huge bear. Just look at the moving average ... the market could not put two consecutive closes above it until the gap bar at the top of the rally that began with Bar 8. This is a bear, and every buy should be viewed as a short entry setup. Just place your entry order exactly where the longs will have their protective stops, and let them drive the market down as they liquidate.

FIGURE 3.3 Trend Days Often Have Better Looking (but Less Profitable) Setups in the Countertrend Direction

COMMON TREND PATTERNS

In the following sections, there are descriptions of several common types of trend days. The names are meaningless because all that a trader needs to know is how to read the price action, which is the same for any pattern. However, the names allow for the organization of common patterns, and this makes it easier for traders to learn and anticipate important price action concepts. With all trend patterns, the only reason to apply names to them is because they are commonly recurring patterns and if you recognize one as it is unfolding, you should be focusing on trading With Trend only and be more confident about swinging a larger part of your trade. The setups will be the same as during trading range days, but you should be trying to take every With Trend entry, no matter how weak the setup looks, and you should only take Countertrend entries after a trendline break and only if there is a good reversal bar, and only if you are still able to take every With Trend signal. If you find that you are missing any With Trend entries, stop trading Countertrend and focus only on With Trend setups. On the Countertrend trades, you should scalp your entire position. Also, you should not find more than two or three Countertrend trades in the day, and if you do, you are spending too much time looking in the wrong direction and likely missing great With Trend swings. The stronger the trend, the more you need to be swinging With Trend and not scalping Countertrend.

In a very strong trend, all trades should be With Trend swings (scalping out part), and no trades should be Countertrend scalps, as tempting as they are.

Once you are familiar with these patterns, you will find that you can see them potentially setting up in the first 30 to 60 minutes. If you do, make sure to take every With Trend trade and swing part of your position. Sometimes you will get stopped out of the swing portion a couple times, but keep swinging a part because if the day becomes a trend day, a single swing can be as profitable as 10 scalps.

As a corollary, if you cannot see one of these patterns setting up, then assume that the day is a trading range day and look for entries in both directions. Also, a trend day can turn into a trading range day or a trend in the opposite direction at any time. When it happens, don't question it or be upset by it. Just accept it and trade it.

TREND FROM THE OPEN

This is usually the strongest form of trend pattern. The market forms one extreme in the first bar or two and then trends all day, closing at or near the opposite extreme. After the first couple bars of every day, especially if there is a large gap, you always have to consider the possibility that a Trend from the Open might be forming and you must look for swing entries. In the majority of cases, your breakeven stop will be hit, but there will be a sufficient number of times that it will not and you will make a large enough windfall profit to make this type of trading worthwhile.

There may be a small trading range for the first 30 minutes or so and then a breakout, but the open of the day will usually be very close to one extreme of the day (the low in a bull or the high in a bear). These days often open with large gaps, and then the market continues as a trend in either direction. In other words, a large gap down can lead to a Trend from the Open bull or bear.

This type of trend is so strong that there is usually follow-through in the first hour or two of the next day, so traders should be looking to enter With Trend on a pullback after the open. The pullback is often a higher time-frame, two-legged correction, like a pullback to the 15-minute EMA. However, most traders would find it easier to simply read only one chart when trading.

Whenever a trend is so strong that it never pulls back enough to make you feel comfortable, it is tempting to look at 1-minute charts to find entries with smaller risk. However, if it was just that easy, everyone would do it. The problem is that there will be countless stop runs on all 1-minute entries that will just kill you as the day goes on. You keep entering With Trend but your stop keeps getting hit by sharp, quick tails. If you want to make money, just stay with the 5-minute and take every tiny entry and you will be shocked at the end of the day to discover that all of those trades that looked like they couldn't possibly work because you were selling the low of the day in a bear or buying the high of a bull and because the 1-minute was so choppy in fact all worked.

In Figure 3.4 yesterday closed strongly above an earlier strong swing high. The first leg up was climactic, with many bull trend bars, very little overlap, and only small tails. However, the correction to Bar 3 broke a trendline and made a reversal after the next leg up more likely. Also, Bar 4 broke above a bull trend channel line and was followed by an inside bar (a possible signal bar, but the best bear signal bars usually have bear bodies).

Bar 5 was the first bar of the day, and it opened on its high tick. Most traders would not be nimble enough to sell below that inside bar, but it would be reasonable to sell a small position on the close of the bar. If you missed the first entry, you could look at a 1-minute chart for a small pullback (there were many) to short or simply wait for a 5-minute setup. When there is a Trend from the First Bar, selling the First Pullback is a high probability trade, even though it is hard to take since you are selling near the low of a big move down.

Bar 6 gave a Low 1 short and Bar 7 gave a Low 2 Breakout Pullback (after breaking below yesterday's low) and the trade continued down for about $5 more.

FIGURE 3.4 Bear Trend from the Open

Bar 8 was a reversal up from a second break below a bear trend channel line (drawn parallel to the Bars 6 and 7 trendline), so two legs up are likely. They ended with a M2S short at Bar 9.

The day turned into a Spike and Channel Bear and did not close near the low.

The day started as a bear Trend from the Open in Figure 3.5 after a one-bar rally to close the gap to yesterday's low (not shown). However, the Bar 4 Higher Low that followed the Bar 3 rally that broke the bear trendline led to a runaway bull. Bar 2 also reversed up after a trend channel line overshoot (the line is not shown).

Why are the best trends so difficult to trade? Because all of the With Trend entries look weak and there are many small pullbacks that trap traders out of the market. None of these pullbacks in Figure 3.6 would have hit a two-point money stop, which is usually the best stop to use in a strong trend, unless the average daily range is more than about 15 points. With so many small bars, price action stops get hit too often, and it makes more sense to rely on the original two-point stop. When the trend is strong, you need to do whatever you can to stay long.

With a large gap up on the open, the odds favored a trend day up or down. With no significant selling in the first several bars, there was a possibility of a bull Trend from the Open, so traders had to be looking long.

Bar 3 was a High 2 and a Low 2 that failed, but when there is was a Barb Wire pattern, you should be selective about entries and wait until one side is trapped or until there is a small bar near the high or low. Since this

FIGURE 3.5 A Bear Trend from the Open That Later Reversed Up

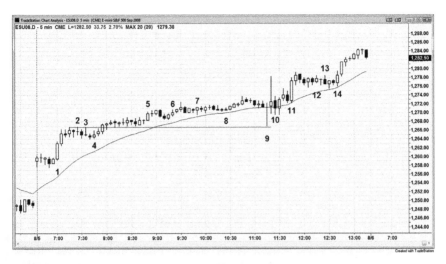

FIGURE 3.6 Strong Trends Can Be Difficult to Enter

is a possible Trend from the Open bull, you can only be looking to buy for the time being.

Bar 4 was a small bar near the low of a bull Barb Wire pattern, and it is a buy, even though it is a High 3. It is also a High 2 from the Bar 2 high. You cannot wait to see if a High 4 will develop when there is a strong trend.

Bars 1, 5, 8, 11, and 14 are all High 2 longs.

Bar 6 is a long since it is a failed Wedge short. Bears are trapped.

Bar 9 was the FOMC report (Federal Open Market Committee). It was a Breakout test of the high of Bars 2 and 3 and hit it the breakeven stop on longs from that breakout to the tick. Just like earlier in the day during the breakout above Bars 2 and 3, the market found aggressive buyers at the same price.

Notice something unusual about Bar 10. It is the first bar in five hours of trading that had a close below the EMA and is therefore likely to fail, setting up a buy.

Bars 3 and 13 were failed High 2 longs (Barb Wire), but when there is a strong trend, either rely on a 2-point stop or take the loss, but if you take the loss, you must buy again on the very next setup (Bars 4 and 14).

Bar 14 was a great bull trap that set up the rally into the close. It first gave a buy signal and then traded below the inside bar (you cannot tell from this chart but that is what happened . . . it first traded above the inside bar, then below it, and then above it again, all in Bar 14), running stops on traders who used a price action stop instead of a 2-point stop, and then it reversed back up. An outside bar that traps traders out of a trend often leads to a strong trend leg as traders are forced to chase the market up.

REVERSAL DAY

Some of the strongest trends begin in the middle of the day (not the first or last hour) and originate as trading range breakouts or trend reversals, usually attributed to some news item, but this is unimportant. In either case, the market can enter a runaway trend mode where it trends relentlessly with only minor pullbacks. There are large trend bars with little overlap and mostly small tails. You must enter quickly, even if the new trend looks climactic and overdone (and it is, but it will likely continue to get much more so!) and swing most of your position.

FIGURE 3.7 The 3-minute Chart Can Be Used to Find Additional With Trend Entries

In a runaway bull, there are more chances to buy on the 3-minute chart. Bars 1 and 2 in Figure 3.7, which were small countertrend inside bars on the 3-minute chart, were not clear signals on the 5-minute chart, but offered profitable High 1 long opportunities. The Bar 3 long was present on both charts.

TREND RESUMPTION DAY

On a Trend Resumption Day, there is a trend off the open and then sideways action that can last two to three hours, and finally a breakout and resumption of the original trend. The midday sideways action sometimes has three Countertrend lazy swings, and sometimes the third fails to surpass the second, forming a Head and Shoulders flag (most Head and Shoulders reversal patterns fail and become continuation patterns). Because the pattern often has Three Pushes instead of two, it traps traders out, thinking that this Countertrend action might in fact be a new trend. However, don't let yourself get trapped out, and be ready to enter when you see a good setup that will get you into the market in the same direction as the morning trend. The difficult part of this type of day is that the quiet midday sideways movement often leads traders to give up on the day when in fact they should view this as an opportunity. Just be ready to enter.

The market opened with a large gap up and then had a test of the low and a big rally up to Bar 3 in Figure 3.8. From there, it traded in a tight range for more than three hours, lulling traders into thinking that the good trading was done. Bar 6 reversed up from a poke below a bear trend channel line, and it also dipped one tick below the Bar 4 signal bar high. Finally, the signal bar was the first EMA Gap Bar of the day.

There were several other chances to get long. Bar 7 was a High 2 and a reversal up from a one-tick break of a bull Micro Trendline. Bar 8 was a High 2 variant (bear-bull-bear bars). Bars 9 and 10 were failed breaks below Micro Trendlines.

FIGURE 3.8 Don't Get Trapped Out of a Trend Resumption Day

TRENDING TRADING RANGE DAYS

Unlike other types of trend days when you want to trade almost exclusively With Trend, Trending Trading Range Days are made up of trading ranges, so you should trade each trading range like any other trading range, and don't hesitate to trade in both directions, fading the trading range extremes.

Some trend days are made of a series of two or more trading ranges separated by brief breakouts, and sometimes they may not be readily seen as trading ranges. However, on the daily chart, the day is clearly a trend day, opening near one end and closing near the other. The market breaks out of one range and then forms another. Sometimes even three or four can develop in a day. If the market later pulls back into a prior range, it often will retrace all the way to the other side of that range. The implication is that the market consolidates in a range after the breakout, which means that there will be two-sided trading that tests both the top and bottom of the range and possibly a breakout in either direction at some point. Because of this two-sided trading throughout the day, it is common for the day to reverse through at least one of the trading ranges in the final hour or two of the day. If the market reverses back into the prior range, it will likely test the Countertrend signal bars in the prior range. For example, if a bear trend reverses up, it will attempt to reach the high of prior failed bull signal bars.

Today may not look like a trend day, but as can be seen on the thumbnail of the daily chart (today is Bar 1 in Figure 3.9) it is, and it is made of

FIGURE 3.9   Trending Trading Ranges

FIGURE 3.10 Bear Trending Trading Range Day

a series of trending small trading ranges. These days frequently reverse in the final couple of hours and retrace at least the final trading range.

This is another Trending Trading Range day with the first trading range beginning yesterday. The thumbnail of the daily chart shows it is a bear trend day (Bar 1 in Figure 3.10).

The first hour in Figure 3.11 was contained in a 7-point range but the average range lately has been about 20 points. Traders were aware that the market could break out and run. Once the market broke out, it formed a higher range from Bars 4 to 6. It broke out to a third range, from Bars 9 to 8. When it broke out again, it failed at Bar 10 and retraced through the bottom of the third range and ultimately to the bottom of the second range.

The implication in the word "range" is that the market will test the low of the range at some point, although it could continue trading up. When a market retraces a strong move, the first target is always the earlier Countertrend entry points. Here, the closest bear entry point after the market broke out of the top range was the low of the closest bear signal bar, Bar 6. The market broke out of the top range and then broke into the next-lower range and took out that bear signal bar low on Bar 13.

The market gave a Breakout Pullback short entry after Bar 11 (and another after Bar 12). By the close, the market had tested the low of the Bar 3 lowest bear signal bar in the second range.

Although the day opened on its high and closed on its low in Figure 3.12 and arguably is a Trend from the Open bear, there was too much sideways

FIGURE 3.11 Bull Trending Trading Range Day with a Late Reversal Back Down into a Lower Trading Range

FIGURE 3.12 Bear Trending Trading Range Day

action during the first two hours for this to trade like one. A Trend from the Open trend day doesn't have tradable Countertrend swings, but a Trending Trading Range does and is a weaker, less predictable type of trend day. The initial trading range broke down into a lower range on Bar 4, creating a Trending Trading Range day.

Bar 9 tested back up into the earlier range, and Bar 11 tried again to rally but failed.

Bar 12 broke down into a third range, which did not have time to test up to the Bar 13 top of the range.

Incidentally, Bar 15 was a failed High 2 (a failed second attempt to reverse the breakout below Bar 7), which is a very high-probability short setup. The market made two attempts to reverse the new low of the day, and the second one failed on the bar after the Bar 15 long.

TIGHT CHANNELS AND SPIKE AND CHANNEL BULL OR BEAR

Sometimes the market trends in a tight channel with basically a trendline that is parallel to the trend channel line, and they are close together, forming a tight channel. There will often be frequent pullback bars, trapping countertrend traders who are entering before there has been a trendline break. They see the trend as weak, since there are few strong trend bars, lots of overlapping bars with relatively big tails and frequent pullback bars. All of these are signs of weakness, except for one thing ... the market is relentlessly moving slowly and very far in one direction without breaking a trendline. This is a very strong trend, even though the bars look weak. When it starts after a climax spike at the end of the prior trend, there is usually a small spike in the direction of this new trend, creating a Spike and Channel trend. Sometimes the spike is so small that it is nonexistent on the 5-minute chart, and the trend channel just develops after a climax in the prior trend. Whether or not there is a clear spike at the start, if you do not get in at the start, these trends are very difficult to enter later because there are no easy pullbacks and the trend looks weak. Unfortunately, they are often difficult to recognize until they are well underway and therefore are usually difficult to trade. Do not worry about failing to recognize the pattern until it has progressed for a couple hours. Just take the With Trend trades that you see from this point onward and simply accept the reality that some days are harder to read than others. Easier patterns will soon develop, so be patient and don't force yourself to take unclear trades in the meantime.

Some days have an early strong momentum move (a spike), and then the move continues in a less steep channel for the rest of the day. Usually the start of the channel is tested within a day or two, and the result can be a trading range or a trend in either direction. The important thing to realize is that the channel is tradable only in the With Trend direction because the channel is so tight that the pullbacks will not go far enough for a Countertrend trade to be profitable. You should be prepared to look for entries in the Countertrend direction after there is a breakout from the channel, since there is a good chance that the Countertrend move will extend all the way back to test the start of the channel. Also, once you recognize the pattern, do not take Countertrend High/Low 2 entries because invariably there will have been no prior trendline break, and the tightness of the channel makes Countertrend trading a losing strategy. Their failures are great With Trend setups.

After the strong rally was followed by a major bull trendline break at Bar 2 in Figure 3.13, the market tested the Bull extreme with a Three Push move that created a Double Top at Bar 3. A protracted (at least an hour) pullback of at least two legs should begin, and the market could reverse into a bear trend, which it did. Price Action traders would only be looking for shorts until there is a break of the bear trendline followed by a clear buy setup (such as a strong bull reversal bar).

The bear trend down from Bar 3 was in several tight trend channels, all of which would have been difficult emotionally to short. In the absence of a climactic top, bulls will be looking at the move as a bull pullback. They

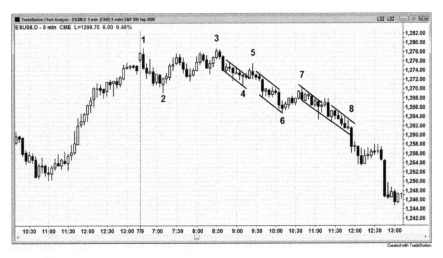

FIGURE 3.13 Tight Trend Channels

will start losing patience, and they will buy Fibonacci pullbacks, oversold oscillators, divergences, and EMA pullbacks on all time frames, even in the absence of a break of the bear trendline and a strong bull reversal bar. Price action traders will view the absence of a good bull pullback setup as a sign that the market had reversed into a bear, and they will short all Low 1 and 2 setups.

At Bar 8, the bulls finally capitulated, and the market collapsed below the bear trend channel line.

FIGURE 3.14   Bear Spike and Channel Day

The March 28 bear Spike and Channel day in Figure 3.14 began with a spike up that reversed into a spike down to Bar 3 where it attempted to form a Double Bottom Bull Flag. From there, it drifted down in a tight channel all day, with several good short entries near the EMA. The market broke above the channel on the next day and since the start of the channel usually gets tested, don't continue to only trade the short side after the reversal because there now should be good long entries as well as the market works its way back to the top of the channel at Bar 4, which it reached on the Bar 7 gap up opening.

IBM had several Spike and Channel days in Figure 3.15, and since the start of the channel often gets tested within a day or two, make sure to consider Countertrend setups on the next day. Each of the channel beginnings was tested (Bars 2, 5, and 8) except the last one (Bar 12). Bar 13 tried to begin the selloff to test Bar 12 but instead it quickly failed and reversed up strongly.

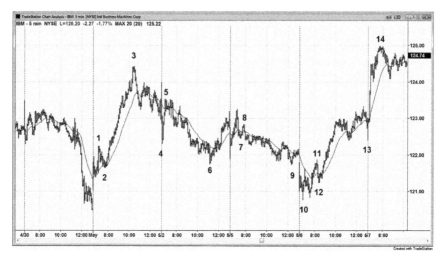

FIGURE 3.15 Several Spike and Channel Days

Sometimes a gap can be the spike, forming a Gap Spike and Channel day. The Bar 2 in Figure 3.16 start of the channel was tested on the next day (Bar 4). The bull flag from Bars 1 and 2 that led to the channel breakout functions like a Failed Final Flag but with a protracted breakout. Sometimes the failure leads to a major trend reversal.

FIGURE 3.16 Gap Spike and Channel Day

STAIRS: BROAD CHANNEL TREND

When a market has a series of three or more trending swings that resembles a mildly sloping trading range or channel, both the bulls and bears are active, but one side is exerting somewhat more control. Two-way trading is taking place so traders can look for entries in both directions. If the breakouts get smaller and smaller, then this is a Shrinking Stairs pattern and indicates waning momentum. It often leads to a two-legged reversal and a trend line break. Many Three Push Reversals qualify as Stairs or Shrinking Stairs Trends that failed and reversed (many others are Wedge-shaped instead of channel-shaped).

Alternatively, one stair might suddenly accelerate and break out of the trend channel in the With Trend direction. If it then reverses, this overshoot and reversal will likely result it at least a two-legged move. If it does not, the breakout will probably continue for at least a couple of more legs or at least the approximate height of the channel in an approximately Measured Move (the distance beyond the channel should be about the same as the distance within the channel).

Bar 7 in Figure 3.17 was the third push down and a Shrinking Stair (it extended less below Bar 5 than Bar 5 extended below Bar 3). The channel lines are just approximate and drawn to highlight that the market is trending down and in a channel. There is clearly two-sided trading, and traders should be buying the lows and selling the highs when they see appropriate setups.

FIGURE 3.17 Shrinking Stair in a Broad Channel Bear Trend

FIGURE 3.18 Stair-Type Bull Trend

By Bar 7 in Figure 3.18, the EURUSD Forex chart had three Higher Highs and Lows in a channel and therefore formed a Stair-type bull trend.

Bar 8 was a bull trend bar that broke out of the top of the channel, and it was followed by a bear reversal bar that never triggered a short. The breakout should extend to about a Measured Move up to a parallel line that

FIGURE 3.19 Shrinking Stairs in Bull Trend Stairs Day

is about the same distance from the middle line as the middle line is from the bottom line (an Andrew's Pitchfork move), which it did.

This is a bull trend Stairs pattern in Figure 3.19 with three or more trending Higher Highs and Lows contained in a roughly drawn channel. Bars 4, 6, and 8 formed Shrinking Stairs, representing waning bullish momentum and presaging the reversal.

After the Bar 9 breakout, there was a Lower High Breakout Pullback to Bar 10 that resulted in a Stair bear trend. Bar 10 was a rough Double Top Bear Flag with the high of the first pull back in the move down to Bar 9.

Bar 11 overshot the bear channel to the downside and led to a small two-legged reversal up.

CHAPTER 4

Pullbacks

I n the strictest sense, a pullback is a bar that moves against the trend enough to take out the prior bar's extreme. In a bull, a pullback is a move where a bar extends at least one tick below the low of the prior bar. However, a broader definition is more useful, and any pause (including an inside bar or an opposite trend bar) in a trend's momentum should be considered to be a pullback, even though there may only be sideways action and not an actual move backwards.

Since a pullback itself is a trend, even though it is usually small compared to the larger trend from which it is pulling back, like all trends it will commonly have at least two legs. Sometimes the legs are visible only on a smaller time frame chart, and other times they are large, and each leg breaks down into smaller legs, each of which also has two legs. Remember, the second leg is a second attempt to reverse the market and if it fails in its second attempt, the market will likely do the opposite . . . the trend will resume.

Any move that has two legs should be traded as if it is a pullback, even if it is With Trend (sometimes the final leg in a trend is a two-legged, With Trend move to a Higher High in a bull or a Lower Low in a bear). Two clear swings are generally referred to as an ABC correction, with the A and C legs being the two Countertrend swings while the B leg is the small leg in between. For example, after a swing high and then a selloff that falls through the bull trendline, if there is then a two-legged move to a new high, this should be looked at as a possible pullback in the new bear that broke the bull trendline, even though traditional chart interpretation says that the new high negates the bear and that you have to begin again looking for a bear reversal down.

What qualifies as two legs? You can create a line chart based on closes and often clearly see a two-legged move. If you are using bar or candle charts, the easiest two-legged move to see is one in which there is a Countertrend move, then a smaller With Trend move, and then a second Countertrend move (a textbook ABC pullback).

However, oftentimes the two legs are only clearly visible on a smaller time frame chart and have to be inferred on the chart that you are viewing. Since it is easier to use a single chart for trading than to be checking multiple charts all day long, a trader has an advantage if he can see the two legs on the chart in front of him, if only by inference.

In a bull market, when there is a series of bull trend bars, a bear trend bar can be assumed to be the first leg of a pullback, even if the low of the bar is above the low of the prior bar. If you examined a smaller time frame chart, a Countertrend leg would likely be evident. If the next bar has a With Trend close but a high below that of the bar that ended the bull swing, then this is the second leg. If there is then a bear bar or a bar with a low below the low of the prior bar, this will create the second leg down.

The more that has to be inferred, the less reliable is the pattern, since fewer traders will see it or have confidence in it. Traders will likely commit less capital and be quicker to exit.

Invariably, pullbacks are difficult entries because they so often follow what appears to be a climactic end to the trend and many traders will have an altered mindset, expecting either that the trend has reversed or that the market has entered a trading range. However, one of the hallmarks of a strong trend is that it keeps forming reversals all day and they all fail. The reversals trap With Trend traders out and Countertrend traders in. They work as great With Trend setups because they trap both sides and then there are many traders who will be chasing the market in the direction of the trend. For example, in a bull, those trapped bears will scramble to get out, and the bulls who thought that the top was in now will chase the market up. If you bought that High 2 near the EMA, these traders will provide the fuel for the move to your profit target.

There is an obvious point here. If the trend that is now pulling back ended in a climax like a trend channel line overshoot and reversal or in any significant trend reversal pattern, the trend has changed and you should not be looking to enter pullbacks in the old trend. It is over, at least for an hour or so and maybe for the rest of the day. So after a strong rally, if there is a Wedge top or a Lower High after a break of the bull trendline, you should now be looking for shorts and not pullbacks in the old bull.

FIRST PULLBACK SEQUENCE: BAR, MINOR TRENDLINE, EMA, EMA GAP, MAJOR TRENDLINE

There are many types of pullbacks that can occur in a trend, some shallow and others deep, and they can be classified and ranked in terms of their extent. The first time any one of them appears is a First Pullback for that type of pullback. Each subsequent pullback will be the first one of a larger variety, and each one will usually be followed by a test of the trend extreme since strong trend moves usually have at least two legs (each test is a second leg). Each type of "first" Countertrend move will therefore likely be followed by another leg in the trend.

Most of the First Pullbacks are minor and are still part of the larger trend's first leg. However, each pullback tends to be greater as the Countertrend traders become more willing to take positions and the With Trend traders become quicker to take profits. At some point, the Countertrend traders will overwhelm the With Trend traders, and the trend will reverse.

The first minor pullback in a strong trend is a one- or two-bar pullback (typically a High/Low 1 entry and it often is a Micro Trendline entry), which almost always is followed by a new extreme. The next pullback might be three to five bars long and will likely break a minor trendline and then be followed by another new extreme; it is often a High/Low 2 setup but can be another High/Low 1 in a strong trend. If the market went from one or two High/Low 1 entries and then a High/Low 2 entry, and it appeared to be setting up another High/Low 1, it is wise to wait. After a series of winning trades, you should be suspicious of renewed strength without first seeing a larger pullback, since this strength might be a trap setting up (like a Failed Final Flag). It is better to wait for more price action and miss a possible trap than to feel invincible and fearless because you fooled yourself into believing that you are playing with someone else's money. If you trade, it will likely become someone else's money.

If the trend is strong, it might stay away from the EMA for two hours or more, but once it hits the EMA, it will likely form another With Trend setup that will lead to another new extreme, or at least a test of the old extreme. At some point, there will be a pullback that not only goes beyond the EMA, but it will likely have an EMA Gap Bar and be followed by a test of the extreme and likely a new extreme. Eventually, there will be a Countertrend move that will break a major trendline (often, it is the pullback with the EMA Gap Bar) and will be followed by a test of the extreme, which may undershoot (Higher Low in a bear or Lower High in a bull) or overshoot (Lower Low in a bear or a Higher High in a bull) the old extreme, and then be followed by at least a two-legged Countertrend move, if not a trend reversal. Each pullback prior to the reversal is a With Trend entry, because each is a First Pullback of one type or another (bar, minor trendline, EMA, EMA Gap, major trendline) and any type of First Pullback is usually followed by at least a test of the extreme and usually a new extreme until after the major trendline is broken.

Although it is not worth the effort to pay attention to higher timeframe charts when trading on a 5-minute chart, it is likely that the larger 5-minute pullbacks end at 15, 30, or 60-minute, or even daily, weekly, or monthly chart points of significance like EMAs, breakout points, and trendlines. Also, there is often a tendency for the first pullback to the 15-minute EMA to be followed by a test of the trend extreme, and then a pullback to the 30 or 60-minute EMA, which be followed by another test of the extreme. With higher timeframe points of significance occurring relatively infrequently, spending time looking for tests of those points will be a distraction and cause traders to miss too many 5-minute signals.

If a trend is strong and you have made several profitable trades but now there are several sideways bars, be cautious about further entries because this is effectively a trading range and it could become a Failed Final Flag. In a bull, you can buy if there is a setup near the low of the range, but be careful buying a breakout of the high of the trading range because bears might be willing to sell a new high and bulls might be beginning to take profits at the high.

The same is true in a bear flag after a protracted down move. Sideways bars means that both buyers and sellers are active and you do not want to be shorting on a breakout of the low of the flag that could become a bear trap (a Failed Final Flag). However, if there is a short setup near the top of the flag, your risk is small and the trade is worthwhile.

In a trend there will always be pullbacks, and they tend to get larger as the trend progresses. However, until there is a reversal, each pullback should be followed by at least a test of the prior extreme (here, in a bear, the prior low of the day), and the test will usually create a new extreme.

Bar 3 in Figure 4.1 was a short after a two-bar pullback, which was the First Pullback in the bear that started on the reversal down from above yesterday's high. It was a Breakout Pullback following the breakout below yesterday's swing low.

Bar 4 was the first break of a trendline and the EMA, albeit by only a tick or so, and this Low 2 was followed by a new low.

Bar 5 was the second test of the EMA, and this time there were two closes above the EMA, but barely, and the pullback was followed by a new low.

Bar 8 broke a major trendline and formed the first EMA Gap Bar (a bar with a low above the EMA). The first gap bar is usually followed by a test of the low, but sometimes there is a second entry. The break of a major trendline might be the first leg of a new trend, but will usually be

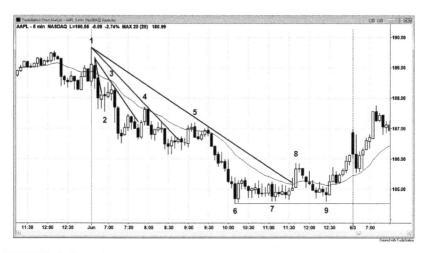

FIGURE 4.1 Each Pullback Tends to Be Larger Than the Prior Ones

followed by a test of the low that can overshoot or undershoot before a Countertrend move of at least two legs unfolds (here, in a bear, a rally).

The market formed a Double Bottom Bull Flag at Bars 7 and 9. Bar 9 dipped one tick below Bar 7, running stops, but it was not able to put in a new low. The bulls were defending their longs and were aggressively buying the dips (accumulation). The second leg up was completed the next day.

Although the bottom was at Bar 1 in Figure 4.2, the first strong bull surge began at Bar 3. There were several pullbacks to the 20-bar EMA that

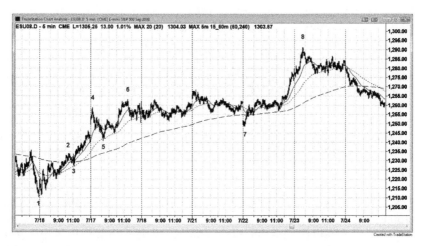

FIGURE 4.2 EMA Pullbacks in All Time Frames Usually Result in at Least a Test of the Trend Extreme

led to new highs on the move up from Bar 3. Bar 4 was a Trend Channel Line overshoot that led to a sharp correction to Bar 5, which tested the 15-minute 20-bar EMA (dashed line) and was then followed by a test of the trend high (Bar 6 was a Higher High).

The market gapped down to Bar 7, and although the market initially appeared bearish, the move down was the first pullback to the 60-minute 20-bar EMA (dashed line), and it was followed by the Bar 8 new high.

DOUBLE TOP BEAR FLAGS AND DOUBLE BOTTOM BULL FLAGS

After a strong move of one or more legs, and even after the first leg if the leg is strong, the market often goes sideways for a number of bars before the trend resumes. The sideways move can last for hours and have large swings, and it often begins and ends with spikes that have extremes that are very close in price (the second spike can slightly overshoot or undershoot the first one). The first spike acts as a magnet, pulling the market back to see if it is strong enough to prevent running the stops that are beyond the first spike. If it is, it becomes an excellent With Trend entry setup. In a bull trend, the two pullbacks form a Double Bottom Bull Flag. For example, in a Double Bottom Bull Flag, the first bottom found buyers. When the market comes back to that same price area and the buyers again overwhelm the sellers, the market has twice failed to go down and will therefore likely go up. In a bear, they form a Double Top Bear Flag. These patterns are similar to the deep pullback to the start of the channel after a Spike and Channel trend, and that pullback often becomes a Double Top/Bottom flag. Also, a Head and Shoulders continuation pattern is another variation.

These patterns are also frequently a right shoulder of a Head and Shoulders reversal pattern. Traders know that if that right shoulder fails, instead of a reversal (like a Higher Low in a new Bull or a Lower High in a new bear), the pattern becomes a continuation pattern. Therefore traders will defend their entry often to the exact tick. More commonly, the test slightly overshoots or undershoots, making the double top or bottom less than perfect, but still effective. If it holds, consensus forms, and the market will usually run.

A With Trend bull flag sets up a long entry on a buy stop order at one tick above the high of the second bottom bar, and the initial protective stop is one tick below the low of that signal bar. After the entry bar closes, the stop is moved to one tick below the entry bar. Although Double Tops and Double Bottoms are well-known reversal patterns, these flags are With

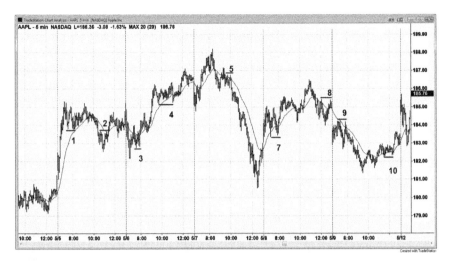

FIGURE 4.3 Double Top and Double Bottom Flags

Trend setups. By ending the pullback, they are reversing it, but it is better to think of them as With Trend patterns.

The Double Top Bear Flag at Bar 2 in Figure 4.3 failed and resulted in a tradable long (and became a small Head and Shoulders Bottom).

GS formed a Double Bottom Bull Flag with Bars 5 and 7 in Figure 4.4, even though there was a Higher High in between. Bar 5 was the last Higher

FIGURE 4.4 Double Top and Double Bottom Flags

Low of the bull, and Bar 7 was possibly the first swing low of a bear or trading range. In this situation, the market can form a Head and Shoulders Top
if Bar 6 is not exceeded by the rally off Bar 7. In any case, a Double Bottom
Bull Flag is a reliable setup for at least a scalp. Also, since most Head and
Shoulders Tops, like all tops, turn into failures and become continuation
patterns, it is always wise to keep buying in a bull. In a trend, most reversal
patterns fail and most continuation patterns succeed.

There was also a small Double Bottom Bull Flag after the Bar 3 Low
formed by the third and seventh bars that followed Bar 3.

Bars 2 and 3 and Bars 5 and 6 in Figure 4.5 formed Double Bottom Bull
Flags. Both Bars 3 and 6 slightly undershot their first legs, but patterns are
rarely perfect.

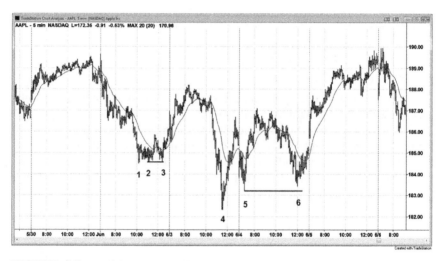

FIGURE 4.5   Double Bottom Bull Flags

When the Double Bottom forms right near the trend low, as it did with
Bars 2 and 3, the pattern is often a small Spike and Trading Range Bull
Reversal if the spike down was climactic enough. The Bar 1 spike down is
close enough for this to also be considered to be a Spike and Trading Range
Bull Reversal, but that is not important since the small Double Bottom Bull
Flag is reason enough to go long. Many patterns resemble one another and
often coexist. All you need to do is recognize one of the patterns because
by itself, it is a valid entry. Also, whenever a pattern resembles another
pattern, the two of them will usually unfold in a similar way.

Bars 3 and 4 in Figure 4.6 formed a small Double Bottom Bull Flag
after the sharp move up to Bar 2. It is also arguably a Spike and Bull Trading
Range buy set up but it is a little too high above the Bar 1 low, so the market

FIGURE 4.6 The Daily Chart of GS Is Forming Either a Head and Shoulders Bear Flag or a Possible Double Bottom Pullback

has likely already been recognized as a new bull, and a reversal up at this point adds little . . . traders already believe that the market has reversed to at least two legs up.

After the selloff to Bar 6, the Bar 2 high could turn into a left shoulder of the Head and Shoulders Bear Flag. If Bar 8 tests the Bar 6 low and is followed by a rally above Bar 7, the market will likely rally to test at least the Bar 5 high as is typical when a Head and Shoulders pattern fails.

If Bar 8 becomes a swing low that is above Bar 6, then it would be a long setup for a Double Bottom Pullback. On the other hand, if the market drops below the Bars 3, 4, and 6 lows, it will form a Head and Shoulders Bear Flag, and then the first target is the obvious magnet at the Bar 1 climactic low. Although a trader could short on the breakout below Bar 6, it is less risky to short a Breakout Pullback. The pullback can come before or after the actual breakout. If the market almost breaks out and then forms a pullback, it will likely behave as if the breakout had in fact occurred. Close is usually good enough. Since the market has been in a downtrend since November 2007 and there should be a second down leg after such a protracted move, the odds favor a downside breakout with a move below the Bar 1 low. The trading range from Bars 2 through 7 may end up being the middle of a Measured Move down, which would project to around 100, or a loss of 60 percent from the high. That is not a prediction; instead, it is just an academic observation of what could result from this of pattern.

Bar 4 in Figure 4.7 attempted to form a Double Bottom Bull Flag with the bar before Bar 3, and Bars 5 and 6 also tried to complete the base. Often

FIGURE 4.7 The Market Failed in Its Attempt to Form a Bear Spike and Trading Range Reversal after the Bar 2 Low

the market breaks below the first bottom by a tick or so, trapping bulls out and bears in, as was the case at Bar 5.

However, the market cannot fall below that low by even a tick, or traders will start to assume that the bears are taking control. Bar 6 was an exact test of the Bar 5 false breakout of the Bar 4 low, and it led to the Bar 7 breakout of the top of the range.

Once the market took out the Bar 6 low at Bar 8, the die was cast. A false breakout of the low (Bar 6) followed by a false breakout of the high (Bar 7) confirmed by the Bar 8 breakout of the low again made the smart shorts feel pretty good at this point. They would have shorted below the bear inside bar that followed the Bar 7 failed failed breakout. They would exit at breakeven on the small rally after Bar 8 but then would have taken the second entry short of the lower high at Bar 9, and then rode the market all the way down.

A failed Double Bottom Bull Flag can have one small breakout of the bottom, as at Bar 5, but that low must hold or else the bulls will stop buying, and the bears will become aggressive.

EMA AND GAP EMA PULLBACKS

A *gap* is a general term that simply means that there is a space between two points on the chart. For example, if today's open is above yesterday's close, there is a gap. If the open is above yesterday's high, there will be a gap on the daily chart. A broader use of the term opens up other trading opportunities. For example, if the high of a bar is below the EMA, then there is a gap between that bar and the EMA. In a bull market or sideways market, there is a good chance that the market will move to fill that gap above the bar that is below the EMA. Sometimes a bar will go above the high of the previous bar, but then within a bar or two, the pullback continues down again. If the market again goes above the high of a prior bar, this is an EMA Gap 2 Bar, or a second attempt to fill an EMA Gap in a bull, and the odds are excellent that there will be a tradable rally off this setup. Likewise, gaps above the EMA will tend to get filled in a bear or sideways market.

Bar 2 in Figure 4.8 was a second attempt to fill the gap below the EMA in a sideways market. The down momentum was strong, which arguably means that the market is not sideways today, but the EMA was basically flat because of yesterday's strong close.

Bars 3 and 8 were also second attempts (the first attempt can be simply a bull trend bar), or EMA Gap 2 Bar entries.

FIGURE 4.8 Gap EMA Pullbacks

Bars 6 and 9 were EMA Gap 2 Bar shorts. Once the market broke above Bar 9, there was then a bull trend because two attempts to go down failed (Bar 9 was a EMA Gap 2 Bar, which means that it was a second attempt).

2HM: IF AWAY FROM EMA FOR TWO OR MORE HOURS, THEN FADE EMA AND FIRST EMA GAP BAR

When the market stays on one side of the EMA without touching it for two hours or more, the trend is strong, but it may also be a sign of an overdone market that will soon reverse. The first touch is a high probability scalp for a test of the trend's extreme, but wait for a price action entry in case the market goes well beyond the EMA. There is nothing magical about two hours. It is just a guideline that is useful to remind you that a trend is strong. A trend can be extremely strong and still touch the EMA every 30 minutes, and a trend can be away from the EMA for four hours only to suddenly reverse into an opposite trend. Also, the two hours can be at any time during the day, not necessarily the first two hours.

Once you become aware that a 2HM is present, look to fade all touches of the EMA, but wait for a setup off the EMA, and enter on a stop. After one or more EMA tests, there will likely be a test that goes through the EMA and forms an EMA Gap Bar. Look to fade the first gap bar (in a bull, buy one tick above the high of the first bar where the high is below the EMA), especially if there is a second entry. Since you are trading With Trend, you should swing part of your position, because the market may run much further than you thought possible. EMA tests are particularly reliable in stocks and often provide great entries all day long.

Each EMA test tends to have more penetration of the EMA than the prior one, and at some point one will likely break a major trendline. Once that happens, the correction will probably have at least a second leg. For example, in a bear, the pullback after the trendline break usually forms a Higher Low and then runs above the high of the first leg.

The market did not test the EMA until 9:10 A.M. PST on the rally after the after Bar 3 low (Bar 2 in Figure 4.9 missed the EMA by one tick, but it was a good enough test to take the Low 2 short there). Always look for a With Trend entry for a test of the extreme. Bar 4 was an EMA Gap Bar and a failed ii breakout, and a short entry there yielded a scalper's profit but not a new low.

Because the rally to Bar 4 broke a minor trendline (from the Bar 2 top to the Bar 3 bottom) and only barely broke the major trendline (from Bars 1 and 2) before reversing, the Countertrend momentum was not impressive,

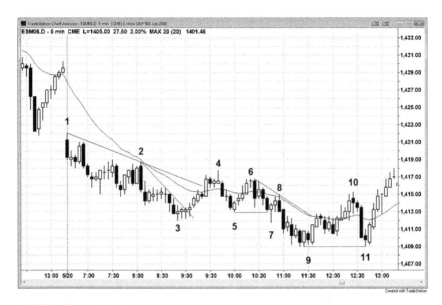

FIGURE 4.9 2HM Example 1

despite the string of small bull trend bars in the rally to Bar 4. Bar 5 tried to form a Higher Low and a new bull after the trendline break, but the rally failed. Some longs covered on the Bar 7 move to below Bar 5, but there was good buying, forming the Bar 7 reversal bar. The High 2 long above Bar 7 (the High 1 was above Bar 5 in this larger two-legged possible bull pullback) failed at the Bar 8 Breakout Pullback, and the market finally sank to a new low. The stop run below the Bar 7 low resulted in a bear trend bar as the second-chance longs were forced to sell out.

Despite the bear strength in the first half of the day, the bulls broke several bear trendlines and were finally able to move the market up after the stop run plunge down to Bar 11 that formed a Double Bottom (and a Failed Final Flag reversal). This was basically a bear Trending Trading Range Day, which often will rally above the final trading range by the end of the day, since trading ranges indicate two-sided trading, and the day would therefore be unlikely to close on its extreme.

RIMM did not touch the EMA in Figure 4.10 until three and a half hours into the day at Bar 5 on a three bear trend bar plunge. However, the 20 or so bull trend bars in the rally from Bars 1 to 2 with only one Pullback Bar is unusual behavior, and unusual behavior is not sustainable and therefore a form of a climax. It had a parabolic shape and there was a failed trend channel line breakout at Bar 2 (the line is not shown but there were a couple ways to draw one). After a climactic move, traders should not look

FIGURE 4.10   2HM Example 2

to enter With Trend on an EMA pullback unless the pullback has been long (at least an hour or so) and the setup is strong. The Tight Trading Range between Bars 5 and 7 is not a place to look for entries in either direction and could be the middle of the bear pullback, as is often the case after a climax where a two-legged correction should be expected. It could also be the start of a bear channel after the spike down to Bar 5 (a Spike and Channel Top reversal), although the high at Bar 4 was not as climactic as is typical in Spike and Channel reversals. You need to wait for a breakout of the Tight Trading Range where the breakout is by one or more strong trend bars, and then look to enter on a failed breakout or a Breakout Pullback. It is best to look to trade other stocks after a climax devolves into a Tight Trading Range, because the risk reward ratio is poor.

TREND DAY 11:30 STOP RUN PULLBACK TO TRAP YOU OUT

Very commonly on strong trend days there will be a strong Countertrend panic move that will scare people out of their positions and this normally happens between 11:00 and 11:30 A.M. PST, although it can come earlier or later. Once it is clear that your were fooled by a strong Countertrend move, the trend will have gone a long way back towards its old extreme, and you and the other greedy traders who were trapped out will chase it, making it go further. What causes the move? Institutions benefit from the spike because it allows them to add on at much better prices, expecting the trend to resume into the close. If you were an institutional trader who wanted to load up going into the close and you wanted to enter at much better prices and you know that if stops could be run on some rumor, you would be looking to contribute to any rumor in any way that you could. It doesn't matter what the rumor or news item is or whether some institution spread it to make some money. All that matters is that the stop run gives traders an opportunity to piggy-back on the institutions and make a profit off the failed trend reversal.

Here are two 2HM days in Figure 4.11, both with late stop runs. Bar 5 is the entry after the 11:25 PST stop run and it is also a Gap 2 long. Notice how strong the bear trend bar was with a large body and a close near its low. This will make all weak hands think that the market has turned into a bear. Smart traders will look at this as the great buying opportunity that it is.

Bar 10 is a 12:15 PST stop run short that is also an EMA Gap entry.

On both days, the EMA Gap fades developed after two or more tests of the EMA, which is to be expected. After the Countertrend traders were able to bring the market back to the EMA multiple times, they developed the confidence to press their bets, resulting in a break well beyond the EMA. However, the first such break usually fails, providing a great fade for the expected trend resumption.

FIGURE 4.11   Late Stop Run Pullback

FIGURE 4.12 11:30 PST Trap

On a bear Trend from the Open day followed by an inability to get above the EMA, traders were expecting an 11:30 A.M. PST trap, and it occurred today exactly on time. Bar 3 in Figure 4.12 was also the first EMA Gap Bar in a bear. Usually the trap is a strong Countertrend leg, getting hopeful longs to buy aggressively only to get forced into liquidation as the market quickly reverses back down. Today, however, the rally from Bar 2 was composed of large dojis and had a Barb Wire look, indicating that traders were nervous in both directions. If there was no conviction, then how could traders get trapped? Well, the bar before Bar 3 attempted to form a Double Top Bear Flag, and Bar 3 spoiled it by going above the Bar 1 high. This made many traders give up on the bear case, forcing the shorts to liquidate. So it was not so much trapping the bulls into the trade as it was trapping the bears out, but it is still a trap, and therefore there still was fuel for the short side. Those shorts all wanted back in, and they helped push the market down. The weakness of the down leg from Bar 3 is consistent with the weakness of the up leg from Bar 2, but the result was as expected . . . a close on the low of the day. This was a bear Trend Resumption day, but since the resumption started so late, it resulted in a smaller leg than the selloff at the open.

COUNTING THE LEGS OF A TREND

Trends often have two legs. If the momentum on the first leg (Countertrend, since the new trend is not yet confirmed) after the reversal is strong, both the bulls and bears will wonder if it will be the first of possibly many legs, creating a new trend. Because of this, both bulls and bears will expect that a test of the old trend's extreme will fail and the With Trend (with the old trend) traders will be quick to exit. For example, if there is a strong move up after a protracted bear and the up move goes above the EMA and above the last lower high of the bear, and there were many bull trend bars in this up move, both bulls and bears will assume that there will be a test of the low that will hold above the bear low. Once the momentum of this first up leg wanes, bulls will take partial or full profits, and bears will short, just in case the bears are able to maintain control of the market. The bears are not certain if their trend is over and will be willing to initiate new short positions. The market will work down since buyers will be reluctant to buy until there is more bullish price action. As bulls come back in on the pullback that is testing the low, the new bears will be quick to exit because they don't want to take a loss on the trade. The buying by the bears covering their shorts will add to the upward pressure. The market will then form a Higher Low. The bears will not consider shorting again unless this leg falters near the top of the first up leg (a possible Double Top Bear Flag). If it does, the new bulls will be quick to exit because they won't want a loss, and the bears will become more aggressive since they will sense that this second leg up has failed. Eventually, one side will win out. However, this kind of trading goes on all day long in all markets and creates a lot of two-legged moves.

The Bear from the Open down to Bar 6 occurred in two legs, and the second leg subdivided into two smaller legs. The move up to Bar 9 was also in two legs as was the move down to Bar 12 in Figure 4.13.

Bar 12 was a perfect Breakout Test of the start of the bull move. Its low exactly equaled the high of the Bar 6 signal bar, running the breakeven stops of the Bar 6 longs by one tick. Whenever there is a perfect or near-perfect Breakout Test, the odds are very high that the market will make an approximate Measured Move (expect the move up from the Bar 12 low to be equal in points to the move from Bars 6 to 9).

There was a two-legged move up to Bar 15, but when its high was surpassed, the market ran up quickly in a bull trend bar as the new shorts had to buy back their positions from the failed Low 2 off the Bar 15 short setup. Bar 9 formed a Double Top Bear Flag with Bar 3, and its failure on the rally up from Bar 16 also contributed to the bull breakout. The day was also a Head and Shoulders Bottom.

As with all patterns, they do not have to be exact.

Bars 1 and 4 in Figure 4.14 formed a common Double Bottom Bull Flag (the Bar 4 low was one penny higher). These flags are often seen in the First Pullback of a trend day.

Bars 3 and 5 formed a Double Top, but its high was exceeded three bars later, creating a failure. There was a Breakout Pullback at Bar 7 that led to a large up move.

FIGURE 4.13   Moves Often Occur in Two Legs

FIGURE 4.14   Double Tops and Bottoms in USO

There were several two- and three-bar Double Bottoms and Tops (Bars 2, 7, 8, and 11).

Bars 12 and 13 formed what is effectively a Double Top, but it doesn't matter what you call it. What matters is that you short it. Bar 13 was a slightly Higher High after the breaking of a small bull trendline up from Bar 11. Also, it was a second entry after Bar 12 reversed down following an overshoot of the trend channel line drawn across the Bar 9 high (the channel was a parallel of the bull trendline between Bars 6 and 10).

This is also a Spike and Channel Bull day and a Trend from the Open Bull.

AAPL is a well-behaved stock on the 5-minute chart. It formed a common Double Top Bear Flag at Bar 2 (one cent below the high of Bar 1 in Figure 4.15) and more than met the approximate target of twice the height of the trading range. Bar 2 was also the top of a two-legged move up to the EMA in a bear, forming a bear M2S (a Low 2 at the EMA, or a Moving average Short 2nd entry). Trends in many stocks are very respectful of the EMA, which means that the EMA provides opportunities all day long to enter in the direction of the trend with limited risk. Four bars after Bar 2, there was a Double Top Pullback short.

FIGURE 4.15 Double Top Bear Flag

HIGH/LOW 1, 2, 3, AND 4

A reliable sign that a pullback in a bull or in a trading range has ended is when the current bar's high extends at least one tick above the high of the prior bar. This leads to a useful concept of counting the number of attempts that this occurs. In a sideways or downward move in a bull trend or a trading range, the first bar whose high is above the high of the prior bar is a High 1, and this ends the first leg of the sideways or down move, although this leg may become a small leg in a larger pullback. If the market does not turn into a bull swing and instead continues sideways or down, label the next occurrence of a bar with a high above the high of the prior bar as a High 2, ending the second leg. There needs to be at least a tiny trendline break between the High 1 and the High 2 to indicate that the trend traders are still active. Without this, do not yet look to buy since the High 1 and High 2 are more likely to be just part of the same first leg down. In a strong upswing, the High 2 entry can be higher than that of the High 1, and in a strong downswing a Low 2 entry can be lower than that of the Low 1. Some pullbacks can continue to form a High 3 or a High 4. Beyond a High 4, it is likely that the market is no longer pulling back in a bull move and instead is in a bear swing. Wait for more price action to unfold before placing a trade.

When a bear trend or a sideways market is correcting sideways or up, the first bar with a low below the low of the prior bar is a Low 1, ending the first leg of the correction, which can be as short as that single bar. Subsequent occurrences are called Low 2, Low 3, and Low 4. If the Low 4 fails (a bar extends above the high of the Low 4), the price action indicates that the bears have lost control and either the market will become two-sided, with bulls and bears alternating control, or the bulls will gain control. In any case, the bears can best demonstrate that they have regained control by breaking a bull trendline with strong momentum.

As you are counting these pullbacks, you will often see the market continue its correction instead of reversing, in which case you have to change your perspective. If you think that you are in a trading range with simply a strong new high and then see a Low 2 above the old high (a sell setup), but instead of falling, the market continues up, you should begin to look for High 1 and 2 entries. It is likely that the bull strength is sufficient for you to be only trading longs. You should defer looking for Low 1 and 2 shorts until the bears demonstrate enough strength to make a tradable down move likely (like a trendline break followed by a failed test of the swing high).

Notice that in a sideways price action, it is common to see a High 1, High 2, Low 1, and Low 2 all present in the course of 10 bars or so, even though a High 2 is bullish and a Low 2 is bearish. Since the market is sideways, neither the bulls nor the bears are controlling the price action for more than a brief period, so it makes sense that each will try to wrest control, and as each tries to assert itself, bull or bear patterns will form.

There are variations on this numbering, but the goal is still to help spot two-legged corrections. For example, in a strong bull, a two-legged pullback can form and have just a High 1, but functionally be a two-legged pullback. If there is a bear close (or two), this can represent the first leg down even if the next bar does not extend above the high of the bear bar. If that next bar has a bull close but its high is still below the trend high, it then becomes the end of the first down leg if the next bar or so is again a bear trend bar. If the next bar extends below its low, look for a bar within the next few bars that extends above the high of its prior bar, ending the two legs down. View each bar as a potential signal bar, and place a buy stop at one tick above its high. Once filled, you now have a variant of a High 2. This entry bar is strictly speaking just a High 1 but treat it as a High 2. That bear bar at the start of the pullback was followed by a bar with a bull close. On a smaller time frame, this was almost certainly a small down leg followed by an up leg that became a Lower High, and then finally another push down to where the High 2 ended the second leg.

There is also a variation for a failed High/Low 4. If the signal bar for the High 4 or Low 4 is particularly small, especially if it is a doji, sometimes the entry bar will quickly reverse into an outside bar, running the protective stops of the traders who just entered. When the signal bar is small, it is often best to place your protective stop at more than 1 tick beyond the signal bar (maybe three ticks, but no more than a total of eight ticks from your entry in the Emini), to avoid a whipsaw, and still treat the pattern as valid even though technically, it failed, albeit by only a tick or so. Remember, everything is subjective, and a trader is always looking for something close to perfect, never expecting perfection because perfection is rare. Finally, complex corrections on the 5-minute chart often appear as simple High/Low 1 or 2 corrections on higher timeframe charts. It is not worth looking at the higher timeframe charts since the trades are evident on the 5-minute, and you risk distracting yourself looking for rare signals and missing too many 5-minute signals.

The most reliable High 1 and Low 1 entries occur when there is a false breakout of a Micro Trendline because Micro Trendlines are only present in the strongest segments of trends. The one- or two-bar false breakout that creates the High 1 pullback in a bull or Low 1 pullback in a bear is a high-probability With Trend scalp. The other time when you need to take these entries is when there is a strong move well beyond the EMA and then a High 1 pullback (in a bull) or a Low 1 pullback (in a bear) to the EMA, even without a Micro Trendline being present.

Trends have trending highs and lows. In a bull, each low is usually above the prior low (a Higher Low) and each high gets higher (a Higher High), and in bear trends, there are Lower Highs and Lower Lows. In general, the terms Higher High and Higher Low are reserved for situations in which a bull trend appears to be in place or in the process of developing, and a Lower Low, and a Lower High imply that a bear might be in effect. These terms imply that there will have been at least a minor trendline break so you are considering buying a Higher Low in a bull (a pullback) or a bear (countertrend but maybe a reversal) and selling a Lower High in a bull or a bear. When trading countertrend, you should scalp most or all of your position unless the reversal is strong.

In Figure 4.16, a High 1 (H1) occurs in a down or sideways leg of a bull move, and it is the first bar with a high above that of the prior bar. If there is then a high that is lower than the prior bar, the next occurrence of a Higher High is a High 2. A High 3 is the third occurrence and a High 4 is the fourth. Counting beyond four does not offer reliable trades since it is likely that the pullback has extended far enough to be considered a trend in the opposite direction.

Likewise, a Low 1 (L1) occurs in an down or sideways market, and a Low 2, 3, and 4 are comparable to their High 2, 3, and 4 counterparts.

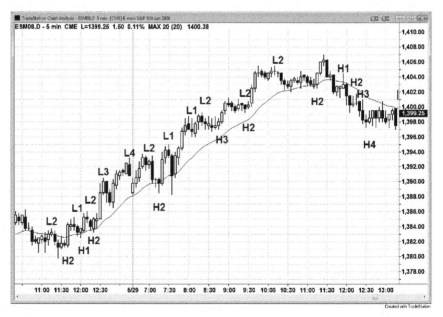

FIGURE 4.16 Bar Counting

Although many are labeled, when the market is clearly trending up, you should not be looking to sell most Low 1 and Low 2 setups.

Sometimes, a High 2 and Low 2 can occur in the same sideways market. There are many variations, but many of those meeting the basic definition are labeled on the chart.

This difficult day to count (but fairly easy to trade) shows many subtleties to counting the legs of pullbacks. When the first leg is steep and its correction is only a couple of bars long (to Bar 2 in Figure 4.17, above) and then a High 2 forms, again after only a bar or two (here, Bar 3), no significant trendline will be broken so you should not be looking to buy a High 2. Bars 1 and 2 set up Micro Trendline shorts, which indicate strong bearish momentum.

Even though there have been two attempts to go up, the first attempt was too weak. You always want a show of strength before your buy setup. Otherwise, assume that the market is still in its first leg down. If the bar after Bar 3 went above the Bar 3 high, it would still be a long entry, but the buy is always better if the rally after the first leg down (the High 1) shows more strength.

FIGURE 4.17 Bar Count Variations

The market sometimes drops again and forms a High 3 after penetrating a trend channel line and reversing up. This is a Wedge reversal (three legs and a failed breakout of a trend channel line). This occurred at Bar 4. Note that neither Bar 2 nor Bar 3 went above their prior bars, but they each effectively ended a small leg down. On a 1-minute chart, there was almost certainly a small corrective rally that formed these 5-minute bull trend bars.

Bar 4 was the end of the bear Wedge and set up a High 3 long on the next bar. Although you do not like to see your long entry bar turn into a bear trend bar, the stop below the entry bar was not hit.

All counts gain more significance when they follow a break of a longer and stronger trendline. If no meaningful trendline is broken on the prior leg (like Bar 2), then the next leg's reversal will not have much conviction (Bar 3), and you should wait for additional price action (like the Wedge bottom at Bar 4).

Bar 5 can be viewed as a Low 1 or as a Low 2, but when the chart is not clear, it doesn't matter what you call it because you must wait for a trendline break and clarity before shorting. Also, following a Wedge bottom, you should not be looking to sell until the market has made two legs up (here, the Low 4 at Bar 7 was as good as two legs up). Once the market went above Bar 5, there was now a failed Low 2 and this usually results in two more legs up.

Bar 6 strictly speaking is a Low 2, but since there was no meaningful bull trendline break at the Low 1, you would not be shorting it. However, you should be thinking of it as a Low 3 and expecting one more leg up. You would need more price action, like a second entry at the EMA, which developed at Bar 7. Bar 5 was just a huge doji and had no bearish conviction, so it does not represent an adequately strong Low 1 (in fact, it set up a failed Low 2 with the long entry on the next bar).

Bar 8 is a High 1, but again it occurred after a single small bar, so it does not have much predictive power and was a Micro Trendline short.

Bar 10 is a EMA Gap 2 Bar, which is the second attempt to rally from below the EMA in a flat or up market. The space between the high of these bars and the EMA is the gap in question. The first attempt was the bull trend Bar 9. Bar 4 earlier was also a EMA Gap 2 Bar buy.

Bar 10 is also a clear High 2 in a flat market, which is usually a good buy.

Bar 11 was a High 1 variant (a bull trend bar that did not extend above the prior bar). In these unclear cases, you need to see further price action before you know whether the bar will work as a High 1. Its Higher Low is constructive because it is a minor disruption of the downswing and therefore a sign of upward strength, although minimal. The leg down to Bar 10 did not break any significant bear trendlines (from Bar 7 down to Bar 10), so it had a lot of momentum. It is reasonable to assume that there will be a second leg down and a Lower Low or at least a test of the Bar 10 low.

Bar 12 was a bull reversal bar in a quiet day, and it was the new low of the day, making it a high probability trade for at least a scalp. At this point, you would not be expecting more down movement until after a tradable rally, so you would now call Bar 11 a High 1. But why bother? Because it makes a case for Bar 12 being a High 2, which is a second entry and therefore more likely to lead to a profitable long. If there was no traditional High 1 or a High 1 variant (here, a bull trend bar at Bar 11), the long at Bar 12 would be less certain, and you would likely scalp most or all of your contracts and then wait for more price action. However, under the scenario that unfolded, Bar 12 was likely to have at least two legs up so a trader would want to swing about half of her contracts. Also, Bar 12 was the end of a Measured Move (approximately) in a larger two-legged pullback, with the first leg ending at Bar 10, and the end of an even larger Measured Move from the high of the day with a first leg ending at Bar 4. Finally, Bar 12 was a reversal from a bear trend channel overshoot (not shown, but based a parallel drawn from the Bar 7 high to the swing high that followed Bar 10, and then dragged to the Bar 10 low).

Bar 14 was a Low 2, ending the second leg up. It was also a Double Top Bear Flag. There was a strong move down on the open with a corrective move up ending on the bar before Bar 7. Bar 14 is a test of that, creating a second failed attempt to run to the high of the day and a Double Top. On a trendless day and after a Double Top Bear Flag, you should look for two legs down. The first leg ended with the Bar 15 High 1, which was followed by two small legs up, ending with the bear M2S at Bar 16. It is Barb Wire, but the small bar at the high of the trading range is a good short.

The second leg ended with the High 2 at Bar 17, but Bar 17 was a bear trend bar following a bear trend bar, following a first leg down to Bar 15 that was very strong. It is still a valid buy, but the uncertainty as seen by the large tails resulted in a second chance entry at the Bar 18 High 2. This second entry developed because enough traders were sufficiently uncomfortable with the first entry to make them wait for a second setup. It is also an ii variant based on bodies only.

The Low 2 at Bar 19 was after strong upward momentum, but it is still a valid short. However, it resulted in a Five Tick Failure at Bar 20 (Bar 20 extended above the high of the prior bar after the move down from Bar 19 only reached five ticks and therefore left many shorts still trapped without a scalper's profit).

Bar 20 formed a failed Low 2, which traps lots of shorts and is a great entry, especially when the up momentum has been good. When it occurs, it usually results in two legs up and often ends in a Low 4. Because of this, buying the High 1 at Bar 21 was a great trade. Everyone knew that the momentum was strong and there was going to be a second leg up. It is possible for this leg down to develop a second leg down with a low below the low of Bar 21 (forming a High 2 buy setup), but the odds were against it. There was simply too much strength.

The bar counts are much more reliable if the legs are at least several bars long and break clear trendlines. For example, a bear Low 4 is not a good short if it occurs in a rally that is an up-sloping Tight Trading Range because there have been no clear trendline breaks.

The 5-minute Emini had two strong legs down in Figure 4.18 that ended in a one-tick false breakout at Bar 1. The market drifted sideways and upward in a tight channel and finally broke the trendline from the open. After two legs down and a broken trendline, two legs up are likely.

Bar 5 is a Low 4 short at the EMA, but this is not a strong short since the market has been largely sideways with lots of small dojis and there will probably be a Higher Low and there is not much room for the short to be profitable. However, if a trader relied on a protective stop above the signal bar, it would have resulted in a profitable scalp. Since a Higher Low and then a second leg up is likely, traders would be looking for a reason to buy.

The market was in a tight channel down from Bar 6 but then gave a High 4 buy after a test below the EMA (the High 1, 2, and 3 were Bars 6, 7, and 8). The market then rallied into the close to form the second leg up.

Trading when there is a Tight Trading Range is not particularly good. There are constant pullback bars and too much overlap. The patterns act as a huge magnet, making it difficult for the market to go very far in

FIGURE 4.18 Extended Moves Are Often Followed by Two-Legged Corrections

either direction until there has been a failed breakout (Bar 9 set up a failed downside breakout).

Any time there is a trendline breakout, the chances are high that there will be a second leg, because everyone now is aware of the possibility of a Higher Low/Lower High trend reversal. In general, avoid a With Trend entry until after the second attempt fails. For example, after a strong break of a bear trendline, it is better to focus on buying a Higher Low than to look for short setups until after the Higher Low is setting up a failure. However, if there is a lot of room to the old low, you can look to short that strong first up move, especially if it ends with the first gap bar above the EMA in the bear.

Whenever a High or Low 2 develops and one or more of the bars touches the EMA, especially in a strong trend, it is called an M2B (moving average, second entry, buy setup or entry) or an M2S (moving average, second entry, sell setup or entry). It is worth distinguishing from other High/Low 2 setups because it is particularly reliable (a two-legged pullback to the EMA in a trend is a great setup).

Bars 5, 6, and 8 were M2S entries in Figure 4.19. Bar 3 is a Low 2, but none of the bars of the setup touched the EMA. Bars 2 and 4 were M2B setups.

The bear Bar 8 M2S was immediately followed by the Bar 9 bull High 2 (but not a good bull M2B since it was largely below the EMA).

Although a High 2 and a Low 2 are common reversal setups, they should never be traded unless the prior High 1 or Low 1 broke a trendline.

FIGURE 4.19 M2B and M2S Setups

The break can occur from a Countertrend move or a sideways move, and the more bars and more momentum in the leg, the more the Countertrend strength, and the more likely that the High 2 or Low 2 Countertrend trade will be profitable.

On the left in Figure 4.20 is the 5-min Emini, and on the right is the 5-min SDS, an ETF that is the inverse of the SPY (an ETF that is comparable to the Emini) but twice the leverage. On the Emini chart, there is a High 2 at Bar 5 following a bull trendline break at Bar 1, and then the Higher High at Bar 3 tested the old trend high. This could be a trend reversal. The down momentum is strong, and the High 1 at Bar 4 was weak. It poked above the bull Micro Trendline from the Bar 3 high and immediately reversed down indicating that the bulls were weak. This was a much better Low 1 short. It would be unwise to buy the High 2 at Bar 5 unless it showed exceptional strength, for instance, if there were a strong bull reversal signal bar. Also, the signal bar was too large, forcing you to buy high in a weak market, and the signal bar was a doji bar that was almost entirely within the prior two bars (both were bear trend bars). When there are three or more bars with a lot of overlap and one or more is a doji (Barb Wire), it is best to wait for more price action before initiating a trade. The bulls and bears are in balance, and any breakout will likely fail (like the High 2 buy signal at Bar 5), and you certainly shouldn't be buying a breakout above its high, in particular in a bear leg, especially since most trading ranges are With Trend and the prior leg was down.

Whenever you are wondering if a signal is strong enough, it is helpful to study the chart from different perspectives: for instance, using a bar chart

FIGURE 4.20 An Inverse Chart Often Clarifies a Setup

or an inverse chart. In general, just the fact that you feel that you need further study should tell you that it is not a clear and strong signal and therefore you should not take the trade.

Even if you were tempted to buy the High 2 on the Emini chart, virtually no one would be looking to sell the Bar 5 Low 2 on the SDS chart on the right because the up momentum is so strong. Since these charts are essentially just the inverse of one another, if you would not buy on the SDS, you should not sell on the Emini.

Note that Bar 7 on the Emini was a High 4, which is usually a reliable buy signal. However, in the absence of any bullish strength in the High 1, 2, or 3, you cannot take the trade. A bar count alone is not sufficient. You need prior strength in the form of relatively strong move that broke at least a minor trendline.

Notice that earlier there was a strong bull and that Low 2 shorts were bad trades until after the market broke the bull trendline. There was not a strong down surge, but the market went sideways for about 10 bars, indicating that the bears were strong enough to hold the bulls at bay for a protracted period. This show of strength by the bears was necessary for a trader to feel confident to short the Failed Final Flag breakout to the Bar 3 new high of the day.

A failed Low 2 often ends up as a Low 4 short. Bar 2 was a failed Low 2 so two more legs up were to be expected. In Figure 4.21, a Low 4 ended the bear rally and another one ended the selloff to the low of the day. It does not matter that the Bar A High 1 occurred before the Low 4 of the prior leg.

FIGURE 4.21 Corrections Sometimes Have Four Legs and Not Two

Bar 1 was a Micro Trendline short that was good for a scalp. It reversed to a Breakout Pullback long on the next bar (the breakout above the Micro Trendline failed but the failure only lasted a couple bars and those bars became just a pullback from the break above the trendline).

VARIATIONS OF HIGH/LOW 2 SETUPS

The key to understanding the concept of High/Low 2 setups is to remember its intent. The idea is that the market will tend to make two attempts at anything, and in its attempt to correct, it frequently will try twice to reverse the trend. If it fails twice, it will likely do the opposite (the trend will resume). The advantage of buying a High 2 pullback in a bull is that there is very little thought involved, and it is easy to do. The difficulty comes when a correction has two attempts but does not form a clear High or Low 2. That is why it is necessary to look at variations . . . you can make money by trading two-legged pullbacks even when they don't offer a perfect High or Low 2 setup.

The most obvious two-legged move has two clear swings with an opposite swing in between that breaks a minor trendline. The pullback usually forms a High 2 pullback in a Bull or a Low 2 in a Bear (an ABC correction). However, there are less clear variations that provide just as reliable trades, so it is important to recognize these as well. Anytime that you see a correction where you can infer two legs, then you have found an acceptable pattern. However, the further from the ideal that it is, the less likely it will behave like the ideal. This uncertainty will make traders hesitant and therefore the pattern will be more likely to fail.

The Bar 2 doji in Figure 4.22 had a large tail on the top, which indicates that the market moved up and down within that bar. That up move was the end of the first leg down, and therefore Bar 3 should act like a High 2, which it did. Since there is a new low of the day and a third push down on the day (here, a Shrinking Stairs pattern, which indicates waning bear strength; it was also a Failed Final Flag reversal), you were looking to buy, despite the three bear trend bars. The implied High 2 at Bar 3 is the final component that gives you confidence to enter without further price action (such as waiting for a second entry). Anytime that you can infer two legs, the market will likely behave as if there were two legs.

Bars 3 and 4 in Figure 4.23 create a two-legged correction in a bull swing, even though the bar after Bar 3 was the end of the up leg. Because it was a two-legged correction, Bar 4 is a High 2 long entry. The sideways pattern with two bear bars separated by a bull bar created the two legs.

Bar 8 is a High 1 long because it followed a bear reversal bar that tried to end two legs up from the low of the day. There were trapped shorts who sold the Low 2 at Bar 6.

FIGURE 4.22 Bar Counting Variation: A Large Tail Can Be One of the Legs

Bar 10 is a High 2 long (Bar 8 was the High 1) because it followed two attempts to sell off at the high of the day (Bars 7 and 10). Two attempts down is the same as a two-legged correction, so it is a High 2 long setup. You could also look at it as High 1 but since the prior six bars were largely sideways, it is reasonable to look at it as part of one pattern with Bar 7 being the first leg down.

Bar 12 is a High 2 long setup because it is a second leg down (the first leg was the doji inside bar just before it).

FIGURE 4.23 Bar Counting Variation: Sideways Correction

All of this analysis is loose, but its objective is important. Traders need to see two-legged corrections because they set up excellent With Trend entries.

This chart in Figure 4.24 of the SPY demonstrates lots of variations in Low 2 setups, but if you think about each one, each is the logical end of a two-legged bear correction. Since the chart is clearly bearish (most of the bars are below the falling EMA), traders are looking for opportunities to enter shorts, so anything that resembles a Low 2 is good enough.

Bar 3 is a Low 1, and its high is taken out by Bar 4, making Bar 4 a second attempt up and a setup for the Low 2 short that triggered on the next bar.

Bar 6 was a Low 1 setup, and two bars later there was a bull trend bar, indicating an up leg. Bar 7 was the signal bar for the short on the following bar, even though it was lower than the Low 1. It was still a two-legged correction.

Bar 8 was a small bear trend bar inside bar in an upward correction, and it therefore constitutes a tiny correction, ending the first leg up. Bar 9 followed another bull trend bar (actually two), so it is the second attempt down and effectively a Low 2 short near the EMA.

Bar 11 is lower than Bar 10, so it is the start of the move up to Bar 12. Why is the bar after the Bar 12 top a Low 2? The low of the Bar 12 bull outside bar dipped below the prior bar just after Bar 12 opened, although

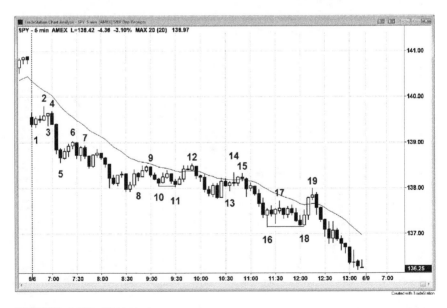

FIGURE 4.24 L2 Variations

you cannot tell from this chart, but you can tell for certain by looking at a 1-minute chart (not shown). This makes Bar 12 a Low 1. An outside bar breaks out of both sides of its prior bar, and you do not know which side it broke through first, although the direction of its body is usually reliable (for example, a bull body usually indicates that the upside breakout occurred second, since its direction is up into its close). The bar after Bar 12 broke below Bar 12, so it was the second time in this leg up from Bar 11 that a bar broke below the low of the prior bar and is therefore a Low 2 short at the EMA (an M2S).

Bar 13 is a clear Low 1. Once there was a second leg up (Bar 14 has a Higher High, and so it is clearly a small second leg), any bar that has a low below the prior bar is a Low 2 short. Bar 15 turned into a Low 2 short signal bar even though it is a small swing high that was below the high of the two legs up (it was a Lower High in what should be expected to be at least two legs down).

Bar 17 was a Low 2 setup even though this is Barb Wire because it was a small bar near the high.

Bar 18 is the end of a bear trend bar breakout from Barb Wire and a High 2.

Barb Wire often has back-to-back failures, and Bar 19 is therefore a good short (also, it is the first EMA Gap Bar in a bear and the second leg up from the Bar 16 low).

Sometimes a two-legged pullback has three legs, as is the case with most Wedge pullbacks. View the first leg as the sharp move up to Bar 2 in Figure 4.25 (here, most of it was a gap open). After a sharp move, there is

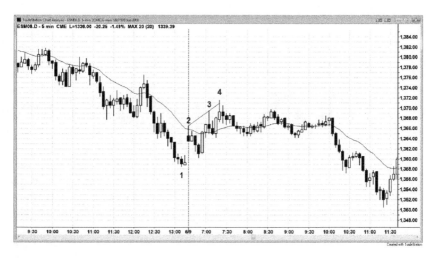

FIGURE 4.25 A Wedge Has Three Pushes But Is Often Two Legs

usually a two-legged move. The two legs, Bars 3 and 4, are subdivisions of the second leg up.

THREE PUSH PULLBACKS

Just as a Three Push pattern or perfect Wedge can end a trend, they can also end a pullback. A strong trend sometimes has a three-swing pullback midday that lasts a couple of hours and lacks much momentum. That third swing traps Countertrend traders, because most pullbacks have two legs, and a third leg is often a new trend.

A strong trend is often followed by a three-swing pullback that typically has low momentum. Bars 4, 6, and 8 in Figure 4.26 are the ends of the three pullbacks after the Bar 3 new low, and each was a bull trending swing (Higher Lows and Highs). Since there was no significant upward momentum, traders will short each new high.

FIGURE 4.26 Three Push Top

There was also an Expanding Triangle (Bars 1, 2, 3, 8, and 9). The long entry setup ended with inside bar after Bar 9, which completed the triangle bottom. However, the next day gapped up above the signal bar (in general it is better to only take an entry if the entry bar opens below the high of the signal bar and then trades through your buy stop), so there was no entry until the Bar 10 Breakout Pullback on the next day.

FIGURE 4.27 Three Pushes

This three swing pullback in Figure 4.27 in the QQQQ (a bear trend, followed by a Three Push rally, and then a test of the bear's low) unfolded over three days. Even though the upward momentum was good, it was actually minor compared to the size of the prior bear trend, whose low almost certainly would be tested. The test of the low occurred on the open of the third day.

The large gap up in AAPL in Figure 4.28 effectively is a steep bull leg (a bull spike). This was followed by three pullbacks, the third of which was a failure swing (it failed to go below the prior low). Since this pattern is often in the middle of a trend, traders should swing part or all of their longs from the Bar 3 entry, expecting approximately a Measured Move up. This is a variant of a Trend Resumption Day where here the first bull leg was the gap opening. Arguably, a failed third push is also a Head and Shoulders bull flag.

LEH had a huge reversal day at Bar 1 in Figure 4.29. Bar 8 was the end of a Wedge pullback (Bars 4, 6 or 7, and 8) and of a small Three Push pattern (Bars 6, 7, and 8). It was also a Double Top Bear Flag with Bar 2 (Bar 8 was 24 cents higher, but close enough on a daily chart).

FIGURE 4.28 Three Pushes and the Third Was a Failure Swing

A big down move followed by a big up move that retraces part of the bear is basically a doji-type move. Remember, a doji is a trading range, so until there is a series of higher lows and highs, this move up to Bar 2 should be considered the start of a trading range in a bear, which is a bear flag. The odds favor a downside breakout and this occurred following Bar 8.

FIGURE 4.29 Wedge Pullback

FIGURE 4.30 Wedge with Three Pushes but Two Legs

It ultimately failed in its test of the Bar 1 low and the company went out of business within a few months.

There was a two-legged correction up to Bar 6, and the first leg ended at Bar 5 in Figure 4.30. Bar 5 was a Wedge, but as is often the case, it is effectively two legs with the second one being made of two smaller legs (Bars 4 and 5). Bar 6 was a setup for a failed failed Wedge (the Wedge selloff after Bar 5 failed and reversed out the other side, above Bar 5, but that breakout also failed), and failed failures are great setups.

There was a second three-legged correction up from Bar 7. It doesn't matter if you see this as a triangle or as two legs, one from Bars 7 to 8 and the other from Bars 9 to 11 with the second leg being made of two smaller legs. Three-legged corrections are common in trends and sometimes they are really just two legs with the second leg having two smaller legs. When it gets this hard to think about it, stop thinking about anything other than the trend and the market's inability to get much above the EMA. Look for short entries, and don't worry too much about counting legs if those thoughts are giving you an excuse to avoid placing orders.

CHAPTER 5

Trading Ranges

I f the chart is composed of upswings and downswings across the entire screen, then neither the bulls nor the bears are dominant, and they are alternating control over the market. Each swing is a small trend that is potentially tradable, especially on a smaller time frame.

If the sideways price action has lasted for about 5 to 20 bars, then a trader has to be particularly careful because the bulls and bears are in very tight balance. Trading breakouts in this situation can be costly since every brief up move is sold aggressively by the bears, and the new bulls are quick to exit. This results in a tail at the top of the bar. Likewise, every sharp move down is quickly reversed, creating a tail at the bottom of the bar. There are, however, ways to trade this type of market profitably.

In general, all trading ranges are continuation patterns, meaning that they more often than not break out in the direction of the trend that preceded them. They also tend to break out away from the EMA. If they are below the EMA, they usually break to the downside, and if they are above it, they tend to break out to the upside. This is especially true if the trading range is adjacent to the EMA. If they are far from the EMA, they may be setting up a test back to the EMA. If a bull swing pauses in a trading range, the odds favor the ultimate breakout taking place to the upside. However, there may be several failed breakouts of the top and bottom before the final breakout, and sometimes the market breaks out Countertrend. Also, the longer a trading range continues, the greater are the odds that it will become a reversal pattern (accumulation in a bear trading range, distribution in a bull trading range). Because of these uncertainties, traders need to be careful and look for risk price action setups. Trading ranges on a 5-minute chart that last for hours with many big, hard-to-read swings can be small, clean, and easy to read trading ranges on a 15- or 60-minute chart, so it sometimes is helpful to look at higher time frames.

TIGHT TRADING RANGES

A Tight Trading Range is a common pattern that has been called many different things, but none of the terms is adequately descriptive. It is any sideways movement of two or more bars with lots of overlap in the bars. The bulls and bears are in balance, and traders are waiting for a breakout and the market's reaction after the breakout. Will the pullback reverse through the opposite side or just test the breakout and then continue?

When a Tight Trading Range slopes slightly up or down, it is still a Tight Trading Range, and it should be treated the same way. The bulls and bears are in close balance, and in general it is best to wait for failed breakouts and Breakout Pullbacks. In general, they are continuation patterns, like the small one that ended at Bar 1.

The range that started at Bar 2 in Figure 5.1 was after two sharp bear legs and should be expected to be protracted and likely to lead to two up

FIGURE 5.1   Tight Trading Range That Is Sloping Upward

legs (the move to Bar 3 became the first of the two legs). These patterns are difficult to trade and often have false breakouts. It is wise to trade them minimally if at all, and simply wait for the inevitable clarity that will reappear.

A Tight Trading Range is usually a continuation pattern, but after a climax (usually a trend channel overshoot and reversal), even a small one, the market can break out in either direction. This is because the climax has generated momentum in the opposite direction and you will not know whether this opposite momentum will be continued and lead to a breakout, or if the momentum of the prior trend will be continued.

Horizontal flags and Barb Wire are small forms of Tight Trading Ranges and, like most Tight Trading Ranges, usually break out in the direction of the prior trend. Sometimes the pattern can extend to 20 or more bars with tiny tails, and it then truly becomes a setup with no predictive value. Since guessing is never a sensible approach to trading, price action traders have to wait for the breakout before deciding what to do. In the majority of cases, there is a failure within a bar or two of the breakout, and the odds of a profitable trade are higher if you base your entry on the failure rather than on the breakout. In most cases, the failure fails and becomes a Breakout Pullback. Enter in the direction of the breakout on a stop once the bar after the pullback takes out the extreme of the Pullback Bar. In a bull breakout, you would enter on a buy stop at one tick above the Pullback Bar. If the Pullback Bar instead plunges through the opposite side of the Tight Trading Range or if it does so in one of the next couple of bars, you enter short on a stop at one tick below the Tight Trading.

Because the move after the breakout is often not strong, the market remains largely trendless for the rest of the day, resulting in this frequently being not a particularly profitable trading pattern. The pattern is more reliable with stocks, and it occurs frequently and sometimes results in an extended trend, so it is worth understanding. It often has other types of setups (small trendline breaks, High/Low 2s, and so on) within it, and those are often tradable and have a much higher chance of resulting in a profitable trade than a Tight Trading Range breakout. Only enter if the setup bar is a small bar near the top or bottom of the range, and only fade the move (for instance, sell below the low of a small bar near the top of the trading range). In fact, it is usually better to focus on them than to wait for the breakout.

By Bar 4 in Figure 5.2, it was clear that the market had entered a Tight Trading Range. Both Bars 5 and 6 failed to break out of the top, and the Tight Trading Range evolved into a triangle, which is also usually a With Trend pattern. Since the last trend was up from the low of the day, an upside breakout was likely, especially since all of the bars are holding above the EMA. After two failed breakouts, the odds were much higher that a

FIGURE 5.2 Tight Trading Range

third breakout would succeed. Also, Bar 7 was a High 2 pullback from the Bar 5 high, which had some momentum. An aggressive trader would have bought the High 2. The next logical buy is a breakout above the high of Bar 5, the first failed breakout. You could also buy at one or two cents above the high of the day. The highest probability entry was the First Pullback at Bar 9, which reversed up after taking out the bear reversal bar's low by only one tick, trapping shorts. Another high-probability buy is the M2B at Bar 10. Both of these high-probability trades resulted in smaller gains but with a much higher chance of success.

LEH formed a Tight Trading Range starting at Bar 6 in Figure 5.3, which could be part of a two-legged pullback forming a Higher Low in a new bull. The bear trendline is broken, and the market has held up for a long time (about 30 bars). You could enter on a stop at the breakout of any prior swing high, such as Bars 7, 5, or 4.

Bar 3 reversed up from yesterday's low, and it was the third push down on the day, which often leads to a rally. The sideways move went well past the bear trendline, indicating that the bears had given up to the point that they were in balance with the bulls.

Bar 6 formed a Higher Low after the trendline break. The odds were high that there would be a rally that would extend to at least the top of Bar 2, the first bull signal bar in the bear leg. The First Pullback after the

FIGURE 5.3 Tight Trading Range That Is Also a Higher Low

breakout was the small bull inside bar at Bar 9, so buying at one tick above its high was a high-probability long.

Bar 10 was a false breakout of a small flag that was also a three bar Tight Trading Range and about a 65 percent retracement of the bear down from Bar 1. The 65 percent is significant only because it means that the rally had retraced a lot of the selloff from the Bar 1 high, and if the rally extended much further, the market would likely be in a new bull phase. Fibonacci traders would call the rally to Bar 10 a 61.8 percent pullback and say that it was close enough, but every pullback is "close enough" to some Fibonacci number, making the Fibonacci numbers essentially meaningless most of the time.

By Bar 3 in Figure 5.4, Barb Wire was present because of three sideways bars with at least one being a doji. This means that you should only look to fade failed trend bar breakouts or small bars near the top or bottom. Bar 6 was a bear trend bar breakout followed by an ii setup that led to a long scalp.

Bar 7 was a failed bull trend bar breakout following the first failed breakout to the downside, and Failed Failures are second entries and therefore especially reliable. The short after Bar 7 is also a small Expanding Triangle (as was Bar 5, but it was too tight to expect much movement), which is a good reversal pattern.

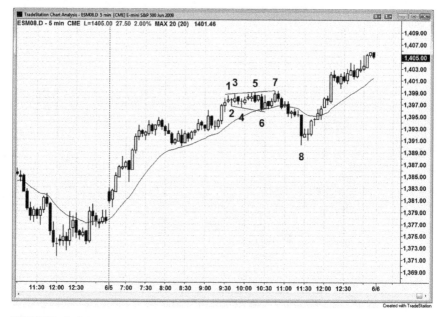

FIGURE 5.4   Barb Wire Type of Tight Trading Range

BARB WIRE

Read this carefully because it is the most important piece of information in this book. It helps you to avoid one of the biggest sources of losses in trading. An important version usually occurs in the middle of the day and in the middle of the day's range, almost always near the EMA. It is a type of a Tight Trading Range called "Barb Wire," where there are three or more bars that largely overlap and one or more of them have a tiny body (doji). Don't touch Barb Wire, or you will be hurt. The small body indicates that the market moved away from the bar's open but traders with an opposite opinion moved it back by the close of the bar. Also, sideways bars where one bar overlaps much of the prior bar mean that no one is in control of the bar. As with all trading ranges, the odds favor a With Trend breakout (a breakout in the direction of the trend that led to the trading range), but Barb Wire is notorious for sharp whipsaws and repeated losses for break-out traders. One good way to trade Barb Wire is to wait for a trend bar to break out of the pattern. The trend bar is the first sign of conviction but since the market has been two-sided, the odds are high that it will fail so be ready to fade it. For example, if there is a bull trend bar that breaks out to the upside by more than a couple of ticks, as soon as the bull trend bar closes, place an order to go short at one tick below the low of that breakout bar. Sometimes this short entry will fail, so once short and once the entry bar closes, place an order to reverse to long at one tick above the high of the entry bar, which would become a Breakout Pullback entry. It is unusual for the second entry to fail. Once the market begins to form trend bars, either the bulls or bears will soon be in control.

You can also fade small bars near the top and bottom of Barb Wire, if there in an entry. For example, if there is a small bar near the high, look to scalp a short with an entry order to sell at one tick below the low of that bar on a stop. Finally, you can also look for 3-minute small bars to fade as well. You should rarely if ever fade off 1-minute bars because the 3- and 5-minute bars provide better winning percentages.

Whenever you are not certain, the best course always is to wait, which is difficult to do when you feel like an entry is overdue. However, that is what a smart trader always does because it simply does not make sense to trade low-probability setups. One very good rule is that if there is a trading range setting up and it is near the EMA, never look to buy if the bars are mostly below the EMA, and never look to sell if the bars are mostly above the EMA. This one rule will save you an enormous amount of money over the years. The move will most likely be some form of M2 entry in the direction of the EMA (if the pattern is below the EMA, an M2S is often a good trade, and if the pattern is above the EMA, consider buying an M2B setup), and the breakout from the M2 can run far.

Bar 1 in Figure 5.5 was a large outside bar followed by a doji inside bar. When there are three sideways bars and one or more of them is a doji, no one is in control, and the best trade is to wait for one side to gain control, as evidenced by a trend bar that clearly breaks out, and then look for a fade. Most trend bars coming out of these patterns fail and become setups in the opposite direction (but some breakouts lead to very strong trends and there will not be a failure). This entry also frequently fails, which is a signal for a second trade. It is unusual for this second entry to fail.

Bar 2 is a bull trend bar, but it did not break out of the pattern (it only extended one tick above the Bar 1 outside bar, and a reliable breakout must extend about three or more ticks beyond the trading range). Also, this bar is too big to fade because you would be shorting in the lower half of a sideways pattern, which is never a good idea.

Bar 3 is a large bear trend bar that broke out of the bottom of the outside bar by two ticks. Many traders would be short here, thinking that the market failed on its upside breakout attempt and is now breaking out of the bottom, running the stops on the last remaining longs who bought Bar 2 (realistically, virtually none of even the weakest traders bought there, so no one is trapped). However, the rule is to fade the first clear breakout trend bar, and Bar 2 was not a breakout. Clearly, Bar 3 is also not a great

FIGURE 5.5 Barb Wire: Three or More Sideways Bars with at Least One Being a Doji

downside breakout, but you have to assume that there are now shorts who think that they outsmarted the Bar 2 longs. You could look to fade by buying Bar 4, but when the market lacks clarity, it is always best to wait for a second entry. Bar 5 was a good long because it was a second entry and a High 2 above the EMA in a bull.

So are these new longs the same as the Bar 2 longs? Almost certainly not. The Bar 2 longs were weak hands that could not move the market up, just like the Bar 3 shorts who could not drive it down. The Bar 5 longs were institutional traders who bought with conviction, as evidenced by the large bull trend bars that followed. Some of the Bar 2 and Bar 3 traders also became longs, but this was almost certainly an institutional move, and it is the move that made the most sense based on price action.

When Barb Wire forms in the middle of the day's range, almost invariably next to the 20-bar EMA, it is best to enter on a failed breakout. Here in Figure 5.6, the market broke out of the top in a High 2 and immediately reversed to break out of the bottom in a failed High 2, where you would short at one tick below the low of the prior bar. Remember, this pattern is below the EMA so the best entry will be some kind of short below the

FIGURE 5.6 Barb Wire Entries Are Best in the Direction of the EMA and after a Failed Countertrend Breakout through the EMA

EMA, and it will usually be an M2S, preferably after a failed H2 long setup (which you should not buy). However, you have to be thinking about the possibility of a failed upside breakout to be able to place the sell order. Remember, that upside breakout was a strong bull trend bar at some point in the first minute or two, and that bullish strength made lots of traders think exclusively about getting long. Those traders let themselves get trapped out of the short trade. You must constantly be thinking, especially when the market is starting to move. Not only must you look for a way to get in, you must also always think about what happens if the initial move fails and then quickly goes the other way. Otherwise, you will miss great trades, and traps are among the best.

Barb Wire can also form at the high or low of the day, after a breakout. These are usually With Trend setups so watch carefully for a With Trend entry, like a High 2 in a bull, a Low 2 in a bear, or a failed breakout, or a failed failure, which is a Breakout Pullback, and a strong setup. If a second entry also fails, it is best to wait for more clarity before entering again.

The cardinal rule for trading in Bar Wire is never enter on a breakout. Instead, always be looking to fade, especially if there is a relatively small bar near the top or bottom of the trading range. Sell at one tick below the low of a small bar near the high of the range, especially if that bar broke out of the pattern by a tick or two, and look to buy at one tick above a small bar near the low of the range, again, especially if it was a small breakout bar. A trader could actually sell on a limit order at one tick above the high of the prior bar if the prior bar is near the top of the range, and look to buy a down-side breakout. Clearly, institutions do that all the time because that is why most breakouts fail. However, it is better to enter on stops, so that the market's momentum is sweeping you along with it. It is simply against the nature of many traders and can cause too much stress to be trading in the opposite direction of the momentum, even if it is a sensible trade. It is preferable to miss a few signals than to experience the anxiety that comes from trading outside of your comfort zone. There will be plenty of other trades that will suit your personality and it makes more sense to wait for those.

When Barb Wire or a protracted Tight Trading Range forms at an extreme of the day after a breakout, it often becomes a continuation pattern. Look for a With Trend entry, which often happens after a false breakout. Here in Figure 5.7, there was a small bear reversal bar that was a failed bull

FIGURE 5.7 Barb Wire in a Bull Trend: Look for an H2 Long

breakout of the top of the trading range, but this top failed on the bar after entry. A Failed Failure that results in a With Trend entry is a perfect entry. It essentially is a resumed breakout (a Breakout Pullback), even though the breakout initially appeared to have failed.

FIGURE 5.8 Bear Barb Wire: Look for Some Type of M2S to Sell

There were Bar Wire patterns in Figure 5.8 that each formed a Low 2 providing a good entry in a strong bear. The second pattern is long enough to think of it more as a simple Tight Trading Range rather than a Barb Wire version, which usually is only about 5 to 10 bars long and contains relatively large bars and tails. Also, Bar 2 was a small bear reversal bar at the top of the pattern near the EMA, making it a great setup with little risk (the height of the bar plus two ticks, one for the entry stop and the other for the exit stop). This was clearly a trend day (Trending Trading Ranges at a minimum, but the minimal pullbacks make it even a stronger bear) so you should swing part of every short.

Barb wire formed in Figure 5.9 after a breakout to a new low of the day, but it is also the second leg down, and two legs commonly lead to a reversal. Also, it took out yesterday's low, so again there is an increased chance of a reversal upward.

FIGURE 5.9 Barb Wire Reversal Pattern

Bar 2 was the end of an upside breakout that reversed down from the EMA in a Low 2 (the Low 1 was on Bar 1, even though the low of Bar 1 was at and not above the low of three bars earlier). The failed breakout failed on Bar 3, meaning that the failed upside breakout was just setting up a Breakout Pullback and not a reversal.

Bar 3 was also a Double Bottom Pullback buy setup (a Double Bottom followed by a deep pullback that formed a Higher Low).

MIDDLE OF THE DAY, MIDDLE OF THE RANGE

The middle third of the day, from around 8:30 A.M. until 10:30 A.M. PST can be difficult for traders on days that are not clearly trending (in other words, most days). If the market is trading in the approximate middle of the day's range and it is now in the middle of the day's trading hours, the chance of Barb Wire type of trading is significant, and most traders would be wise to trade sparingly. Most trading should be confined to Barb Wire type of entries. It is usually better to forgo any less than perfect entry under these circumstances and instead wait for a test of the high or low of the day. A trader who is not yet successful should not trade when the market is in the middle of the day while it is also in the middle of the day's range. This change to her trading alone can be the difference between being a loser and a winner.

Sometimes there will be an extremely great-looking pattern setting up in midday in the Emini, and you will get one tick of slippage on the entry. If the market does not race to your profit target within seconds, the chances are high that you have been trapped. It is almost always better to place a limit order to get out at breakeven. Whenever something looks too good to be true, so obvious that everyone will look to enter, the odds are high that it is exactly as it appears to be ... not true.

When the day is not a clear trend day, traders should be very careful during the middle third of the day when the market is around the middle third of the day's range. There are lots of overlapping bars in Figure 5.10, small dojis and tiny failed breakouts, making the price action difficult to read. With experience, a trader can be successful trading under these circumstances, but the vast majority of traders would more likely give back most or all of the profit that they made in the first couple of hours. The goal is to make money, and sometimes your account is much better served by your not placing trades and instead waiting for strong setups. In the above chart, the sideways action lasted until 11:45, which is relatively late in the

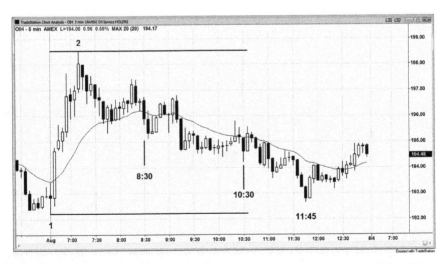

FIGURE 5.10 The Middle Is Bad: Middle Two Hours of the Day, Middle of the Day's Range

day. The time parameters are only guidelines. The overriding factor is the price action, and on trading range days the best trades are fades of the highs and lows of the day, but this takes patience.

BIG UP, BIG DOWN

When the market has a big up move and then a big down move that retraces about the entire up move, it is likely forming a trading range, but it may be the beginning of a new trend. The key is whether or not there is a reversal pattern at the end of the second move. If there is, there should be at least a reversal scalp. If not, the second leg may just keep trending, and an approximate first target is twice the height of the first leg.

LLY's daily chart in Figure 5.11 shows a sharp up move that ended at Bar 2 (a Failed Final Flag, and two legs up to a new high of the day) and was followed by a sharp down move. There was no clear buy pattern on the way down and instead there was a Low 2 Breakout Pullback short entry at Bar 4, below the EMA.

Bars 6 and 7 were short signal bars following brief bear Micro Trendline breaks (Bar 6 was an EMA Gap Bar).

The Bar 8 low of this Spike and Channel bear was not quite a Measured Move and was followed by a test of the Bar 4 start of the bear channel.

FIGURE 5.11 Big Up, Big down Often Means Indecision and Is Often Followed by a Trading Range

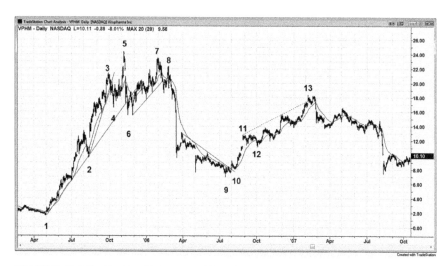

FIGURE 5.12 Big Up, Big Down Followed by a Trading Range

The daily chart of VPHM in Figure 5.12 had a strong breakout after the Bar 1 low, presumably based on a news event. At some point, the momentum traders controlled the market and drove it much higher than the fundamentals warranted. There was then a sharp move down to Bar 9, where there was a Three Push pattern (a Wedge variant) that resulted in the up move to Bar 13, effectively creating a large trading range.

Bar 10 was a Breakout Pullback Higher Low second chance to get long.

After many momentum players dumped their longs on the rally up from the Bar 4 trendline break, the bulls were able to drive the market to a new high at Bar 5, but this found aggressive sellers who were able to break the major bull trendline as they pushed the market down to the Bar 6 low, setting up a large reversal down from the Bar 7 Lower High test of the Bar 5 trend high. The reversal down came off of the Three Pushes Up to Bar 7. At this point, the momentum players were out and looking for another stock.

The market continued to selloff until value traders thought that the fundamentals were strong enough to make the stock a bargain around Bar 9. Bar 9 was also a Three Push Down buy. It could also be near some Fibonacci retracement level, but that is irrelevant. You can just look and see that the pullback is deep, but not so deep that the force of the rally from Bar 1 is totally erased. The bulls still have enough force left to rally the stock, especially since the value traders are back in play. They feel that the stock is cheap, based on fundamentals, and they will keep buying as the stock continues to drop (unless it drops too far).

Incidentally, the Bar 11 spike up led to a channel that ended at the Bar 13 overshoot and reversal of the trend channel line. Spike and Channel bulls, no matter how strong they appear, are usually followed by a test of the beginning of the channel, which was the Bar 12 low.

TRADING RANGES SETTING UP TREND REVERSALS

These are common in Trending Trading Range days, where there usually is a reversal of at least the final trading range in the final hour or two and rarely even a reversal of the entire day.

Sometimes the low of a bear trend day, especially a climactic one, can come from a small trading range that has large bars, often with large tails or large reversal bodies. These reversals are less common at tops, which may be less climactic than bottoms (if this is true, it is meaningless because it does not factor into decisions about trading). These trading ranges are often other signals as well, such as Double Bottom Pullbacks or Double Top Bear Flags.

FIGURE 5.13 A Trading Range Can Lead to a Trend Reversal: Double Bottom Pullback Bottom

Sideways price action after a sharp selloff in Figure 5.13, with large trend bars and large tails, often leads to a reversal. This is also a Double Bottom Pullback bottom.

The FOMC report was released at 11:15 A.M. PST and the 5-minute Emini in Figure 5.14 formed a large bull outside bar at Bar 1, but its high was never exceeded. Even though reports can be volatile, the price action is reliable. Don't get caught in the emotion, and just look for sensible entries.

In general, when there are a pair of big range bars of opposite direction or one or more big range dojis at an extreme of the day, it is usually better to look for a reversal entry because the big bars indicate two-sided trading and when there is two-sided trading, it is not prudent to be buying at the high of the day or selling at the low.

Bar 2 formed a bullish M2B (a High 2 at the EMA), but the bars were large so the long entry would be at the high of a trading range and the risk would be great because of the size of the bars. It is far wiser to wait for small bars or for a trap. Bar 3 was a failed High 2, so there are trapped bulls at the high of the day creating a great short entry. It was also a Low 2, again near the high of the day, which is a good place to be looking for

FIGURE 5.14 A Trading Range Can Lead to a Trend Reversal: Failed M2B

shorts. Finally, it was a Double Top Bear Flag after a large bear trend bar, and a Spike and Trading Range Top.

Bar 6 was a Low 1 short. There was not a good reversal bar at the low so the bulls had not gained control and traders should still be looking for With Trend (short) entries. The inside bar after Bar 5 was too big to be a bull setup, especially since the huge Bar 4 outside down bar would probably be followed by two legs down. Instead, always look to fade small bars that occur after big bars, since a trading range is likely forming and you should only be selling near the high or buying near low.

After scalping out of the Bar 6 short, traders would now be faced with a High 2 buy setup. However, the bars are too large and overlapping (that is, a trading range), and it is far better to be fading small bars at the high and low of the pattern and to be looking for trapped traders. Bar 8 trapped bulls into their longs, and they would exit on Bar 9, one tick below Bar 8. The smartest traders would have waited for the trap and shorted the Low 2 breakout below the small Bar 8 bar that was at the top of the trading range. It was a bonus to have bulls trapped.

Bar 10 was another bull trap that was bought by weak bulls at the top of a big tempting doji. Again, smart bears would look for a small setup bar for a short entry because the bulls would be forced to sell and there would be no buyers left, making the market quickly reach the short scalp profit target. This is a trading range, so there is nothing for reversal patterns to reverse, and they all become traps.

This trading range became a Failed Final Flag that reversed up on the open of the next day with a High 2 entry on the third bar of the day. This bar reversed the bear flag and the low of that day as well.

CHAPTER 6

Breakouts

A Breakout is simply a move beyond some prior point of significance such as a trendline or a prior high or low, including the high or low of the previous bar. To a trader, it implies strength and a possible new trend. For example, if a bull breakout bar has a strong close and the next several bars also have strong closes and trending highs and lows (no bar pullbacks), then the market will likely be higher than it is at the current moment at some point before the market reverses back beyond the start of the breakout move.

The breakout can be of anything, such as a trendline, a trading range, or the high or low of the day or yesterday. It does not matter because they are all traded the same. Fade it if it fails, as most breakouts do, and re-enter in the direction of the breakout if the failed breakout fails and therefore becomes a Breakout Pullback. Only rarely is it best to enter on the breakout and it is almost always better to wait for a failure or a Breakout Pullback. On most days, traders look at new swing highs and lows as possible fade setups. On a strong trend day, however, the breakouts are usually on huge volume, and there is very little pullback even on a 1-minute chart. It is clear that the trend traders are in control. When a trend is that strong, a price action trader will be entering With Trend on a High/Low 1 or 2 pullback before and after the breakout and usually not on the breakout. She is always trying to minimize the risk of the trade. However, once you recognize that a strong trend is underway, entering With Trend for *any* reason is a good trade. In a strong trend, every tick is a With Trend entry, so you can simply enter at the market at any point using your swing size and use a reasonable swing stop.

BREAKOUT ENTRIES IN STRONG TREND

When a trend is strong, every breakout beyond a prior extreme is a With Trend entry, as can be seen by the huge volume, the large size of the breakout bar (a strong trend bar), and the follow-though over the next several bars. Smart money is clearly entering on the breakout. However, that is rarely the best way to trade a breakout, and price action traders almost always find an earlier price action entry like a High 1 or 2 in a bull. It is important to recognize that when a trend is strong, you can enter at any time and make a profit if you use an adequate stop.

If you miss the earliest entry of a breakout and you are waiting for a pullback, you can enter at the market or on a 1-minute pullback. It is best to wait for at least two strong trend bars (good-size ranges with small tails), or three or four moderate-size trend bars, and enter the 1- or 3-minute pullback using half of your normal size or whatever your swing size is. Allow a Pullback Test of the breakout and use the stop that you would use had you entered early and were now swinging a portion. Scalp out half, and then move your stop to breakeven. Since there is now a strong trend, you should add on or re-enter when there is a pullback.

The rally from the Bar 4 Higher Low in Figure 6.1 became a strong bull (Higher Low after a trendline break), with seven bull trend bars in a row as the market reversed through the Bar 1 high of the day. With that much momentum, everyone was in agreement that Bar 5 would be exceeded before there was a selloff below the start of the bull at Bar 4. Breakout traders

FIGURE 6.1 Breakouts: It Is Better to Take Price Action Entries on Pullbacks than Breakout Entries

would buy above every prior swing high, such as on Bars 5, 6, 8, 11, 13, and 16. Price Action traders would have entered earlier in every instance, on the Breakout Pullbacks, which were bull flags. For example, at the Bar 6 High 1, the Bar 8 High 2, the Bar 10 failed reversal, the Bar 12 High 2 and trendline break (not shown), and the Bar 15 High 2 test below the EMA (the High 2 was based on the two clear, larger legs down from Bar 14). Breakout traders are initiating their longs in the exact area where price action traders are selling their longs for a profit. In general, it is not wise to be buying where a lot of smart traders are selling. However, when the market is strong, you can buy anywhere, including above the high and still make a profit, but the risk reward ratio is much better on buying pullbacks than it is on buying breakouts.

Blindly buying breakouts is foolish, and smart money would not have bought the Bar 13 breakout because it was a third push and near a trend channel line. Also, they would not have bought the Bar 16 breakout, which was a Higher High test of the old high (Bar 14) after a trendline break (too much risk of a trend reversal). It is far better to fade breakouts when they fail or enter in the direction of the breakout after it pulls back.

Yesterday (not shown) in Figure 6.2 was a Trend from the Open Bull, which is one of the strongest trend patterns, so the odds were high that there would be a pullback and then a test of the high of the open and likely a bull close. Traders are all watching for a buy setup, expecting follow-through buying from the strong trend of yesterday. Bar 2 was a small Higher Low and an EMA Gap Bar second entry. The signal bar had a bear close,

FIGURE 6.2 Anticipate a Breakout and Look for a Price Action Entry Before the Breakout

but at least its close was above its open. If you did not buy there, you could watch the breakout and decide how to enter.

There were two large bull trend bars on the trendline breakout, each with strong closes and small tails. Had you gone long at Bar 3, you would be swinging a portion of your trade at this point, so you can enter that same position size at the market, using the stop that you would have used had you entered earlier. That stop would now be around the trendline, maybe below the breakout bar.

Bar 4 was a pause bar just below yesterday's high, and buying one tick above its high is another good entry. A pause bar is a possible reversal setup so buying above its high will be going long where the early bears are buying back their shorts and where the longs who exited early would also be buying back their longs.

At this point, the trend is clear and strong, and you should be buying every pullback.

Bar 8 is the only reasonable Countertrend scalp (a failed breakout to a new high after a trendline break) since it is a strong bear reversal bar and an Expanding Triangle top, but the trend is still up. Note that there has not yet been a close below the EMA and the market has been above the EMA for more than two hours.

Bar 9 is an inside bar after the first close below the EMA, so a test of the high is the minimum target.

BREAKOUT PULLBACKS ANDS BREAKOUT TESTS

After a breakout, eventually there will be a pullback. If the Breakout Pullback comes back to within a few ticks of the entry price, it is a Breakout Test. The test can occur on the bar after the breakout or even 20 or more bars later, or both. This test bar is a potential signal bar, and look to place an entry order at one tick beyond it, in case the test is successful and the trend resumes. It is a particularly reliable Breakout Pullback setup.

If there is a pullback within a bar or two of the breakout, the breakout has failed. However, even the strongest breakouts will have a one- or two-bar failure that in fact becomes just a Breakout Pullback instead of a reversal. Once the trend resumes, the failed breakout will have failed, which is the case in all Breakout Pullbacks. Since they are Failed Failures, they are second entries and therefore have an excellent chance of setting up a profitable trade. A Breakout Pullback is also referred to as a cup and handle.

Breakout Pullbacks can happen in the absence of an actual breakout. If the market strongly runs close to the breakout but does not exceed the old extreme, and then quietly pulls back for one to four bars or so, this will likely function exactly like a Breakout Pullback, and it should be traded as if the pullback followed an actual breakout. Remember that when something is close to a textbook pattern, it will usually behave like a textbook pattern.

If there was a strong move or a first leg of a trend earlier in the day, then a With Trend breakout later in the day is more likely to be successful, and a failure will likely fail and become a Breakout Pullback. However, if most of the day has been trendless with one- or two-bar breakouts in both directions, the odds of a failure leading to a reversal are increased.

After an initial run, many traders will take partial profits and then place a breakeven stop on the balance. The breakeven stop is not necessarily exact on every trade. Depending on the stock, a trader might be willing to risk 10 or even 30 or more cents, and it is still basically a breakeven stop, even though the trader will be losing money. For example, if GOOG is trading at $750 and a trader just took partial profits on half and wants to protect the rest, but GOOG recently has been running breakeven stops by 10 to 20 cents but rarely by 30 cents, the trader might place his breakeven stop at 30 cents beyond the breakout, even though it would result in at least a 30 cent loss and not a breakeven trade.

In the past year or so, AAPL and RIMM have been very respectful of exact breakeven stops, and most Breakout Pullback tests in fact end about five cents shy of the entry price. GS, on the other hand, routinely runs the stops before the pullback ends, so a trader would have to be willing to risk a little if he is trying to hold on to his position. Alternatively, he could exit at breakeven and then re-enter on a stop at one tick beyond the test bar, but he will invariably be getting back in at 60 or more cents worse than his initial entry. If the price action is still good, it makes more sense to hold through the Breakout Test and risk maybe 10 cents than getting out and then back in at 60 cents worse.

Bar 1 in Figure 6.3 is a potential Breakout Failure, but the breakout was strong and was made of three bear trend bars that covered most of the day's range. The market pulled back to the EMA and led to an M2S short. The second bear trend bar was the start of the reversal down from the second leg of the pullback to the EMA (a bull trend bar followed by a bear trend bar and then by a second bull trend bar is a two-legged move up).

Bar 3 again was a potential failed breakout to a new low of the day. This is the second attempt to rally after breaking below the low of the open, and second attempts have a much higher success rate. Also, there was a small reversal bar. Even though it was a doji and not a bull trend bar, it had a

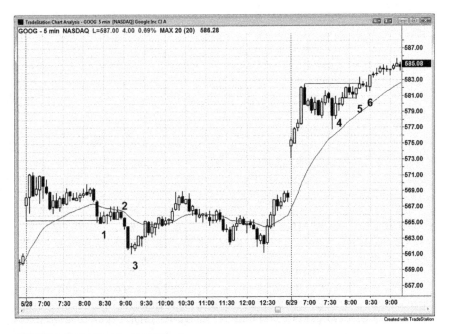

FIGURE 6.3 Breakout Pullbacks

bigger bull tail than bear tail, indicating some buying and some weakening
of the bears. Also, Bars 1 through 2 could be setting up a Failed Final Flag
since they are overlapping and largely sideways. Also, the entry bar was
a bull trend bar that was almost inside the doji, so this is similar to an ii
pattern, and the bull close of the second bar is a sign of strength.

Bar 5 is a pullback from a small rally that broke above a minor swing
high and almost broke to a new high of the day. When the market almost
breaks out and then pulls back, it will trade as if it had actually broken
out and is therefore a variant of a Breakout Pullback. This Bar 5 Breakout
Pullback traded down to only two cents below the top of the Bar 4 signal
bar, and when a stock is trading at $580, it is just about a perfect Breakout
Test and therefore a reliable long setup. Once the actual breakout to the
new high for the day occurred, there was a Breakout Pullback long entry
at Bar 6, one cent above the high of the prior bar.

Many stocks are often well behaved and will come back to test the
breakout to the exact tick, as LEH did four times today in Figure 6.4. Since
many traders will enter a breakout on a stop at one tick beyond the signal
bar, an exact pullback like these will run any breakeven stop by one tick.
However, re-entering at one tick beyond the test bar is usually a good trade
(for example, shorting at one penny below the low of Bar 2).

FIGURE 6.4 Breakout Tests (an Especially Reliable Type of Breakout Pullback)

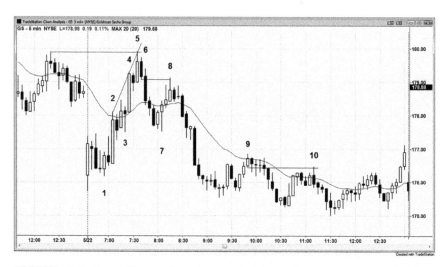

FIGURE 6.5 Some Markets Overshoot on Breakout Tests

GS has been notorious for running breakeven stops over the past year.

Bar 8 in Figure 6.5 extended six cents above the low of the Bar 6 signal bar.

Bar 10 hit two cents above the Bar 9 signal bar low, running an exact breakeven stop by three cents.

The Bar 5 high exceeded the swing high of the final hour of yesterday by two cents before reversing down. It also overshot the trend channel line drawn across Bars 2 and 4, and the trendline break down to Bar 7 was followed by the Bar 8 Lower High test of the bull extreme (Bar 5), leading to a bear swing.

GOOG formed a series of Breakout Pullback entries in Figure 6.6. The sharp rally off the open broke above the swing high of yesterday (Bar 1), and the pullback at Bar 5 could not even reach the EMA or the breakout point. When there is strong momentum, buying a High 1 pullback is a good trade. The signal bar is a small doji inside bar, indicating a loss of selling power following the large bear trend bar. The bears did not follow through. There was a second long entry at Bar 6, which was a High 2 (even though it is higher than the High 1 of three bars earlier).

Bar 8 was a Breakout Test that missed the low of the signal bar by two cents.

FIGURE 6.6 Breakout Pullbacks

Bar 9 was a Breakout Test that missed the signal bar low for the Bar 8 short by four cents. These are just observations and not needed to take the Breakout Pullback shorts at Bars 8 and 9.

The one-bar selloff at the Bar 9 M2S (a Low 2 at the EMA) was followed by an inside bar signal bar, creating another Breakout Pullback short entry on Bar 10.

Bar 11 broke below the Bar 5 pullback and resulted in a Breakout Pullback short at the EMA at Bar 12. This pullback also was a failed breakout of the trendline from Bars 7 to 9 (not shown).

Bar 13 only broke five cents below Bar 11 but quickly gave a Breakout Pullback short entry at the Bar 14 Low 1. Since Bar 14 had a bull body, a more cautious trader would have waited for a second entry. The doji bar following Bar 14 was an acceptable entry bar, but selling the outside bar that followed this doji bar was even better because it was a Low 2. Why was it a Low 2? Because it followed two small legs up. Bar 14 was the first leg up, and the outside bar two bars later traded above that small doji bar, creating a second leg up (and the Low 2 short entry).

Bar 15 was also an outside bar short entry for the pullback following the breakout below Bars 11 and 13. It was especially good because there are trapped longs who bought above the bull trend bar, thinking that it was a good false downside breakout reversal. However, there were four bear trend bars down from Bar 14, and smart traders would have wanted a second entry before going long.

Bar 16 was a Barb Wire Low 2 pullback after the breakout below the swing low at yesterday's close (Bar 2).

Many of these trades are tiny scalps and should not be the focus of the majority of traders. Their significance is that they illustrate a common behavior. Traders should concentrate on trading the bigger turning points, like Bars 4, 7, 9, and 12.

CHAPTER 7

Magnets

T his chapter has very little to do with trading and is included for completeness because it illustrates some price action tendencies, but these tendencies are not reliable enough to be the basis for trading. If you want to learn how to make money, do not spend much time here and instead focus on the best trades in Chapter 15.

Some prices act as magnets, drawing the market toward them. When you become aware of a magnet, trade the market as if it is trending toward the magnet, and do not trade Countertrend until after the magnet is tested, unless there is a clear trendline break and then a test of the extreme. Usually the market will overshoot the magnet and reverse, but after the test of the magnet, the market can continue to trend, form a trading range, or reverse, and you must wait for more price action before placing your next trade.

MEASURED MOVES BASED ON THE FIRST PULLBACK (AB = CD)

When a market makes a sharp move and then has a pullback, it will likely have a second leg, and the second leg is frequently approximately the same size as the first. This is sometimes called an ABC move or an AB = CD (a type of ABC but the B, C, and D correspond to the A, B, and C of the ABC). This is of minor importance because you should not be fading the move with a limit order based on Fibonacci extensions or Measured Moves or any other magnet. They just provide a guide to keep you trading With Trend until they are approached, and at that point you can consider Countertrend setups as well.

In addition to clear pullback entries that set up Measured Moves, sometimes there is a more subtle situation that is equally valid. When a market has a strong trend move and then a fairly strong pullback, which then begins to form a trading range, traders can use the approximate middle of the range to project where the second leg of the pullback might reach. As the trading range unfolds, keep adjusting the line where you estimate the midpoint to be, and that will usually be around the midpoint of the pullback once the move has finally completed its second leg. This just serves as a reminder of where you should be anticipating setups for a resumption of the trend.

XOM had a strong move from Bars A to B in Figure 7.1. After the Bar C Higher Low, a trader should be only on the long side to ride the second leg. Bar D slightly undershot the target (the top of the dashed line). Once in the area of the target, traders can consider Countertrend trades. If you were to use ABC labeling, Bar B is point A, Bar C is point B, and Bar D is point C.

Once there was a Higher Low at Bar E and the rally broke above bar D, a trader could look at AD as a first leg that contains two smaller legs (AB and CD), and then stay long until there was a Measured Move up (AD = EF, and the target is the top of the solid line).

Fibonacci traders also look to other extensions (62 percent, 150 percent, 162 percent, and so on) as valid areas to look for reversals, but this is too complicated and approximate. It is just as easy to make a best

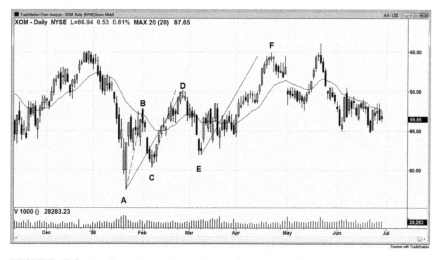

FIGURE 7.1   Trade with Trend Until Near the Area of the Measured Move

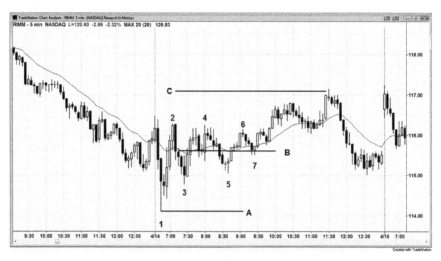

FIGURE 7.2 Measured Move from the Middle of a Trading Range

guess and then begin to consider Countertrend setups in addition to With Trend.

RIMM had a sharp move up to Bar 2 in Figure 7.2 after an Opening Reversal reversed yesterday's low (a trend channel line overshoot and reversal), and then there was a pullback. Since a second leg up was likely, if a trader was interested in knowing where it might end, he could keep adjusting Line B to be in the middle of the developing range and then after the market breaks out, make a parallel and drag it equidistant up from Line A for a Measured Move. This is just an observation and has nothing to do with trading. It is simply a reminder that the market is likely to go up for a second leg, and you should have a slight bias toward long entries until it is in the area of the Measured Move. However, you already have that bias since you are expecting the move and most of the bars are bull trend bars.

The pullback to Bar 3 was so deep that a trading range was likely, and until the market broke out of the triangle (above Bar 6) traders could trade in both directions, as with any trading range.

MEASURED MOVES ON BREAKOUTS BASED ON THIN AREAS AND ON FLAGS

This is a minor point but an interesting observation that can help you to be trading on the correct side of the market. However, if you are spending more than a second thinking about it while trading, you are likely missing good setups. This section is simply here because it is a common price action phenomenon and it is not a basis for trading.

A breakout often forms either a thin area, where there are no overlapping bars or minimal overlap as the strong momentum carries the market quickly well beyond the breakout, or a fat area, where there is a small trading range. The midpoint of both often becomes the midpoint of the move. The fat area is a trading range, which is an area of agreement on price, and its middle is the middle of what bulls and bears think is fair. A thin area is an area of agreement as well. It is an area where the bulls and bears agree that no trading should take place, and its middle is the midpoint of that area. In both cases, on a simplistic level, if those prices are a midpoint of agreement between bulls and bears, they are a rough guide to the midpoint of the leg that contains them. Once they form, swing part or all of the With Trend entries. Once the target is approached, consider Countertrend entries if there is a good setup. Most traders use the height of the prior trading range for measuring, which is fine because the exact distance is only approximate no matter how you do it (unless you are a Fibonacci or Elliott Wave trader and have the uncanny ability to convince yourself that the market almost always creates perfect patterns, despite the overwhelming evidence to the contrary). The key is to trade only With Trend, but once the market is in the area of the Measured Move, you can begin to look for Countertrend entries. However, the best ones always follow a trendline break.

If the market pauses again after the Measured Move has occurred, look at these two strong trend legs as a possible end of a higher timeframe correction instead of the end of a 5-minute bar chart trend, and then plan to swing part of any Countertrend entry. Two legs often complete a move and usually result in at least a protracted Countertrend move of at least two smaller legs, and sometimes a new, opposite trend. The Countertrend move will likely test the trading range that was at the middle of the Measured Move.

Sometimes the projections are exact to the tick, but most of the time the market undershoots or overshoots the target. This approach is only a guideline to keep you trading on the correct side of the market.

Two days with Measured Moves in Figure 7.3 form thin areas on the chart. A thin area is a breakout area where there is essentially no overlap of the bars.

The market had a sharp move up from Bar 3 on the FOMC report at 11:15 A.M. PST and broke above the Bar 2 high of the day. The flag at Bar 4 tested the breakout with a two-legged sideways correction, but after the High 2 long from this flag the market was left with a thin area between the top of Bar 2 and the bottom of Bar 4. The Bar 4 trading range is also a small fat area that could be used for the Measured Move. You could use either the low of Bar 1 or Bar 3 to calculate the Measured Move. The market reached

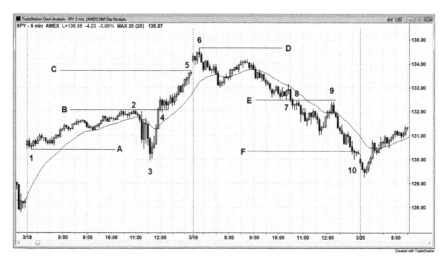

FIGURE 7.3 Measured Moves Based on Thin Areas

the Line C target from the Line A (Bar 1) to the Line B Measured Move exactly on the last bar of the day and poked above the Line D target using the Bar 3 to Line B projection on the open of the next day. Even though Bar 1 is higher than Bar 3, it can still be considered the bottom of the Measured Move by thinking of the selloff to Bar 3 as just an overshoot of the Bar 1 actual low of the leg.

On the second day, there was a thin area below Bar 7 and above Bar 8, and the Line F target was exceeded just before the close.

Incidentally, there was also a Double Top Bear Flag (Bars 8 and 9).

The move down to the Breakout Pullback flag around Bar 3 in Figure 7.4 was steep, and a reasonable target for a Measured Move down is from the top of the leg (Bar 2) to the approximate middle of the flag (Line C). This projected to Line D, which was overshot and led to an EMA test. You could also have used the Bar 1 high for a measurement, but you should generally look at the start of the current leg for your first target. After the Line D target was reached, the Line E target based on the Bar 1 starting point was hit soon afterwards. Note that the move down to Bar 4 from Bar 2 was a strong bear with no significant trendline break, so it was best to stick to With Trend setups.

The three-bar rally from Bar 4 broke a minor trendline and setup a minor possible Final Failed Flag, but since there has yet to be a sharp rally (like a gap bar above the EMA), Countertrend trades have to be scalps if you take them at all. You should only take them if you are a good enough trader to then switch to With Trend trades as soon as one develops. If you

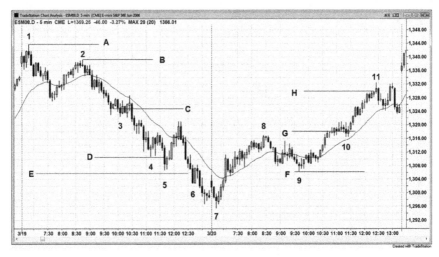

FIGURE 7.4   Measured Move Based on a Breakout Pullback Flag

cannot, you should not be trading Countertrend, and instead you should be working hard to take With Trend entries. Just being in the area of a Measured Move is not enough reason for a Countertrend entry. You need some earlier Countertrend strength.

On the second day, there was a flag around Bar 10 after the breakout, and this projected up to Line H (using Bar 9 as the starting point). If instead you used the Bar 7 low of the day, the target would have been reached shortly after the gap up on the following day.

Once there is a breakout flag, it is wise to swing part of your With Trend trade until the Measured Move is reached. At that point, consider a Countertrend trade if there is a good setup.

Line B in Figure 7.5 is the midpoint of the thin area in between the breakout (the high of Bar 2) and the low of the First Pullback (the low of Bar 5) and the Measured Move was hit to the exact tick at Bar 8.

Line E was the midpoint of a thin area, and the market greatly overshot its line F projection. The breakout from the Bar 12 bear flag had a huge thin area down to Bar 13, but it was so late in the day that a Measured Move from its midpoint was unlikely. However, at that point the day was clearly a bear trend day, and traders should only be shorting unless there is a clear and strong long scalp (there were a couple in the final hour).

The move to Bar 7 broke a trendline, indicating that the bears were getting stronger, and the move to Bar 9 broke a major trendline, setting up the Bar 10 Lower High test of the trend extreme (Bar 8), and the subsequent bear that followed.

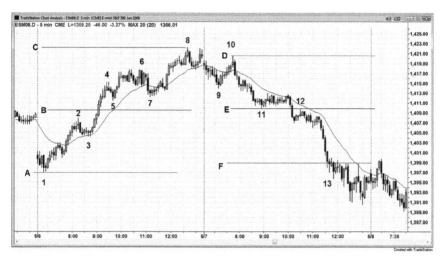

FIGURE 7.5 Measured Moves Based on the Middle of Breakouts

REVERSALS OFTEN END AT SIGNAL BARS FROM PRIOR FAILED REVERSALS

Prior failed reversals often provide targets for the successful reversal when it finally comes. For example, if there is a bear and there have been several bull entries that failed as the market continued to sell off, each of these entry prices (the high of each signal bar) will be targets once the reversal up finally succeeds. The market will often rally all the way to the highest signal bar's high before having a significant pullback.

It is not important to understand why this happens. The key is to realize that the market will tend to pullback after it tests those earlier signal bars. It is likely that some traders who entered on those signals scaled in as the market went against them and they then used their initial entry as their final profit target, exiting breakeven on their worst entry and taking profits on all of the other entries.

For many traders, it is something of a "Thank you, God, I will never do this again!" price. You did not exit a loser and your loss keeps growing and you keep hoping for the market to come back to your entry. When it finally does, you exit and swear that you will never make that mistake again. It might just be that smart traders believe this to be the case and will dump their longs at those targets, or it might simply be one of the many secret handshakes that great traders all know, and they exit there simply because they know that it is a reliable recurring pattern for pullbacks to end near

FIGURE 7.6   Failed Prior Reversals Are Often Targets after the Reversal Finally Takes Hold

earlier entry points. Also, since the market failed at these points earlier, traders will position themselves believing that the market might again fail, causing the correction to end at these prices.

The monthly chart of the SPY in Figure 7.6 had a strong bull that ended in 2000, but it had several attempts to reverse on the way up. Each of the bear signal bar lows becomes a target for any correction on the way down.

Likewise, the bear that ended in 2003 had several failed bull reversal attempts, and the high of each signal bar becomes a target for any subsequent rally.

Finally, the rally since 2003 had several failed bear attempts, and each one is a target in the current downswing.

None of the targets ever has to be reached, but each is a strong magnet that frequently draws the market back to its level.

OTHER PRICE MAGNETS

There are many other price magnets that will tend to draw the market toward them for a test. Here is a list of some of them, and many of these have been discussed earlier in the book. When a market is trending toward a magnet, it is prudent to trade With Trend until the magnet is tested and preferably overshot. Do not trade Countertrend at the magnet unless there has been some prior Countertrend strength, like a trendline break.

- Trendlines.
- Trend Channel Lines.
- Fibonacci retracements and extensions.
- AB = CD.
- Spike and Channel: the start of the channel is usually tested within a couple days. This is often followed by a period of consolidation within the area of the channel (as the trading range unfolds, its top and bottom are about the same as the top and bottom of the channel).
- Failed Final Flags: after the breakout from the flag, the market comes back to the flag and usually breaks out of the other side.
- High and Low of yesterday.
- Swing highs and lows of the past few days.
- Breakout points.
- The extreme of a trend after every type of pullback (see the chapter on the First Pullback Sequence).
- Trading ranges, including Tight Trading Ranges and Barb Wire: the extremes and the middle often get tested.
- Entry bar and signal bar protective stops.
- Entry price (Breakout Test).
- Huge trend bar opposite extreme (the low of a huge bull trend bar and the high of a huge bear trend bar).
- Common targets for scalp and swing positions: in AAPL, 50 cents and a dollar; in the Emini, 5–6 ticks for a 4-tick scalp, and 3 or 4 points for a 2-legged Countertrend move.
- Double the required stop (if an Emini trade required you to use a 12-tick stop to avoid getting stopped out, expect the move to extend about 12 ticks from your entry.
- Daily, Weekly, and Monthly swing highs and lows, bar highs and lows, moving averages, gaps, Fibonacci retracements and extensions, and trendlines.
- Emotional numbers like hundreds in stocks (such as AAPL at 100) and thousands in the Dow (Dow 12,000). If a stock quickly moves from 50 to 88, it will likely try to test 100.

When there is a huge trend bar with small tails, traders who enter on the bar or soon afterwards will often put their protective stops beyond the bar. It is fairly common for the market to work its way to those stops and then reverse back in the direction of the trend bar.

FIGURE 7.7   Stops Beyond Large Trend Bars Often Get Hit

Bar 1 in Figure 7.7 is a huge bull trend bar with a shaved bottom. The market reversed down off the bear inside bar that followed and formed a Higher Low, but not before running the protective stops below the low of the trend bar. Smart traders would have shorted the inside bar, but they were ready to go long above the Bar 2 bull reversal bar that hit the stops and then turned the market back up.

Bars 3 and 4 were also huge trend bars with small tails, but neither was followed by an immediate pullback that ran stops.

Incidentally, Bar 2 is the start of a channel in a small Spike and Channel rally, and is a likely magnet on any pullback. The first pullback after any surge commonly gets tested as the market consolidates into a trading range after the move. Here, however, Bar 3 tried to form a trading range in the area of the Bar 2 low, but it failed, and this resulted in close to a measured move down.

CHAPTER 8

Trend Reversals

The single most important rule in this book is that you should never even be thinking about trading against a trend until after there has been a break of a significant trendline. And even then, you should still be looking for With Trend trades because after this first countertrend surge, the market almost always goes back in the direction of the trend to test the old trend extreme. Only rarely is the trendline break on such strong momentum that the test won't be tradable for at least a scalp. If the market fails again at the price of the old extreme, then it has made two attempts to push through that level and failed, and whenever the market tries twice to do something and fails, it usually tries the opposite. It is after this test of the old extreme that you should look for countertrend trades and only if there is a good setup on the reversal away from the old extreme.

A Trend Reversal, or simply a reversal, is not necessarily an actual reversal. It can be a change from a bull trend to a bear trend or vice versa, or from a bull or bear trend to a trading range, or from a trading range to either a bull or bear trend. It can be as simple as a trendline break. The new trend may be protracted or limited to a single bar. The market may also simply drift sideways after a bar or two, and then trend again later either up or down. Many technicians will not use the term "reversal" except in hindsight, after a series of trending highs and lows has formed. However, this is not useful in trading because waiting for that to occur will result in a worse risk-reward ratio, since a significant pullback becomes more likely the longer a trend has been in effect. Once a trader is initiating trades in the opposite direction to the trend, that trader believes that the trend has reversed even thought the strict criteria have not yet been met. For example, if he is buying in a bear, he believes that the market will likely not even trade a single tick lower, otherwise he would wait to buy. Since he is buying with the belief that the market will go higher, he believes the trend is now up and therefore a reversal has taken place.

Many technicians will not accept this definition, because it does not require some basic components of a trend to exist. Most would agree on two requirements for a trend reversal. The first is an absolute requirement: the move has to break a trendline from the prior trend. The second requirement happens most of the time but is not required: after the trendline break, the market comes back and successfully tests the extreme of the old trend. Rarely, there can be a climactic reversal that has a protracted initial move and never comes close to testing the old extreme.

Everyone agrees that a new trend is present once there is then a series of trending Higher Highs and Lows in a bull and Lower Lows and Highs in a bear. Typically, the initial move will break the trendline and then form a pullback that tests the end of the old trend, and traders will look to initiate Countertrend (actually With Trend, in the direction of the new trend) positions after this test. The test may fall short of the prior extreme, or it may exceed it, but not by too much. For example, if there is a bear trend and then a sharp move upward that extends well beyond the bear trendline, traders will look to buy on the First Pullback, hoping for the first of many Higher Lows. However, sometimes the pullback extends below the low of the bear trend, running stops on the new longs. If this Lower Low reverses back up within a few bars, it can lead to a strong swing up. If, however, the Lower Low extends too far below the prior low, it is best to wait for another trendline break, upward momentum surge, and then a Higher or Lower Low pullback before going long again.

Although traders love to buy the first Higher Low in a new bull or sell the first Lower High in a new bear (there first must have been a break of a significant bear trendline), if the trend is good, there will be a series of pullbacks with trending swings (Higher Highs and Lows in a bull and Lower Highs and Lows in a bear), and each pullback can provide an excellent entry. The first pullback, for example, the first Higher Low in a new bull, can be a test of the bear low or a test of a breakout (of a key point like a trendline, prior swing point, trading range, or the moving average) and may not get very close to the bear low.

Most trends end with a breakout of a trend channel. For example, a bull typically ends in one of two ways. Either there is an overshoot of the bull trend channel line that fails and is followed by a reversal down and then a break below the bull trendline, or the market can fall through the bull trendline without first overshooting the trend channel line. If the bull ends with a failed breakout of the trend channel line, there will typically be two legs down, and the first pullback will almost always form a Lower

High (and only rarely a Higher High) as its test of the bull high. On the other hand, if the bull ends with a trendline break, the test of the bull high can either be a Higher High or a Lower High and each occurs about equally frequently. Since at least two legs down are to be expected, a Higher High should be followed by two legs down, and a Lower High may be followed by a single leg, since the first leg down already occurred just before the Lower High formed. If the market forms a Higher High in its test of the old extreme, one of the best trades is to sell the first Lower High, which is a test of the Higher High. In a bear after a Lower Low reversal (obviously after an upward momentum surge that broke a major trendline), it is imperative to buy the first Higher Low because this reinforces the premise that a major bottom is in.

An important point is that trends last much longer than most traders would ever imagine. Because of that, most reversal patterns fail (and some become continuation setups), and most continuation patterns succeed. Traders have to be very careful when trading Countertrend based on a reversal pattern, but there are Price Action setups that greatly increase the chances of a profitable trade.

If you find yourself drawing many trend channel lines, then you are too eager to find a reversal and are likely missing lots of great With Trend trades. Also, since most trend channel line overshoots and reversals are minor in a strong trend and fail, you will be trading lots of losers and wondering why these patterns are failing when they are supposed to be so good. Wait for a trendline break before looking for a countertrend trade and look at all those minor trend channel line overshoots as With Trend setups, and enter where the losers are exiting on their protective stops. You will be much happier, relaxed, and richer, and you will be entertained by how well they work when intuitively they should not.

In a bull trend, buyers continue to buy until they decide that the risk-reward ratio is no longer as favorable as they would like it to be, and at that point they will begin to take partial profits. As the market continues to rise, they will continue to take more profits and will not be eager to buy again until there is a pullback. Also, shorts are being squeezed out of the market as the market continues upward, and they are being forced to buy back their short positions. At some point, they will have covered all that they wish to cover, and their buying will stop. There will also be momentum traders who will continue to buy as long as there is good momentum, but these traders will be quick to take profits once the momentum slows.

So who is buying that last tick in a bull or selling the low of a bear? Is it the cumulative effect of countless small traders who are getting caught up in the panic and are being squeezed out or instead are impulsively buying a rapidly rising bull? If only we could be so influential! That might have been the case long ago, but not in today's market. If there is so much volume at the high and low of the day and the institutions make up most of that volume, why would they buy the high tick of the day if they are so smart? A large percentage and possibly the majority of the day's volume is driven by mathematical models, and some of those models will continue to buy until there is a clear trend change, and only then will they reverse to the short side. They will buy right up to the last tick of a bull and short to the very low of a bear because the designers of the systems have determined that this approach maximizes their profit. Because they trade such huge volume, there is an ample supply of buying at the high to take the other side of the huge volume of shorts that is coming in at the top (and vice versa at the bottom). Just because they are very smart and trade huge volume does not mean that they are making a 5 percent profit a day. In fact, the best of them are netting a fraction of a percent each day, and some of them have determined that that their profit is maximized by continuing to buy, even including the high tick of the day. Many also have complex strategies involving options and other products, and it is impossible to know what all the factors are at play at the extremes of the day. For example, they might be expecting a reversal down and be entering a delta neutral spread where they would buy one Emini and buy two Emini at-the-money puts. They only lose if the market goes sideways in a very tight range for several days. If the market goes up, the puts will lose money at a slower rate than the rate at which the Emini gains in value. If the market falls, the puts will increase in value faster than the long Emini will fall in value, and their neutral spread becomes increasingly more of a bear play. This will allow them to profit, even though they bought the Emini at the high of the day. All that you need to know is that there is huge volume at the extremes, and it is coming from institutions, some of which are buying the high while others are selling it.

Incidentally, there is one other common sign of just how active mathematical, computer-generated trading is. Just look at correlated markets, like the Emini and all of the related ETFs like the SPY, and you will see that they basically move tick for tick. This is also true for other related markets. This could not be taking place so perfectly all day long if it was being done manually. Also, chart patterns would not be as perfect as they are on all time frames, even down to tick charts, unless a huge volume of the trading was computer generated. People simply cannot analyze and place orders that quickly in so many markets simultaneously, so the perfection has to be the result of computer-generated trades, and they must make up a large part, if not a majority, of the trading.

When there is a strong trend with no significant pullbacks, it is common to start looking for a small reversal because common sense dictates that the market will eventually have to pullback as traders begin to take partial profits and enough Countertrend traders take new positions. A trader will have to decide if it is better to look for a Countertrend scalp or wait for the pullback to end and then enter in the direction of the trend. If the trend is strong, it is usually best to only trade Countertrend if there are clear signs of a trend reversal, such as a prior trendline breakout and then a test that ends with a strong reversal bar. However, the temptation is great to do something and many traders will begin to look at smaller time frame charts, like 1- and 3-minute, or 100 tick charts. Smaller time frame charts continue to form reversals as the trend progresses, and the vast majority of the reversals fail. A trader can rationalize taking the Countertrend trade by thinking that a 1-minute chart has small bars so the risk is only about 4 ticks, and if this turns out to be the very top of the market, the potential gain is huge. Therefore, taking a few small losses is worth it. Invariably, the few small losses turn into six or seven and their combined effect is a loss that cannot be recovered later in the day. Invariably, when they get lucky and pick the exact end of a trend, they will scalp out with a few ticks profit instead of riding the trade for a long way, as they originally had planned. Death by mathematics.

If a trader is becoming agitated because he is not in the market during an extended trend and he feels like he needs to trade and he begins to look at 1-minute charts, 1-minute reversals offer a very profitable way to make money. However, it is by doing the opposite of the obvious. Wait for a 1-minute reversal to trigger a Countertrend entry, which you do not take, and then determine where you would place a protective stop if you had taken the trade. Then, place a With Trend entry stop at that price. You will be stopped into a With Trend position just as the Countertrend traders are getting stopped out. No one will be looking to enter Countertrend at that point and likely not until the trend has moved further along and another Countertrend setup begins to form. This is a very high probability With Trend scalp.

The single most reliable Countertrend trade is entering Countertrend to a pullback, which is a small trend in the opposite direction of the major trend. Once the pullback traders have exhausted themselves and the trend traders have again demonstrated their resolve by breaking the trendline that contained the pullback, any small pullback to test this breakout is a great Breakout Pullback entry. This entry is counter to the trend of the pullback, but in the direction of the major trend, and will usually lead to at least a test of the major trend's extreme. The more momentum that is present in the trendline break, the more likely it is that trade will be profitable.

Momentum in a reversal can be in the form of a few large trend bars or a trending series of average-looking bars. The more signs of strength, the more reliable is the reversal. Ideally, the first leg of the reversal will extend for many bars, break well beyond the EMA, have the majority of the bars be trend bars in the direction of the new trend, and extend beyond swing points in the prior trend (if the prior trend was a bull, then it is a sign of strength if the first leg of the new bear drops below one or more of the Higher Lows of that prior bull).

Although the best reversals have strong momentum and go a long way, they often are very slow to start and can have several small bars before the sharp moves begin. The market is trying to trap you out of the trade so that you will have to chase the move and add fuel to it. It is common at the very start of a trend to find pullbacks on 1- and 3-minute charts, which trap traders out. Occasionally there will be one on the 5-minute chart and it will often turn into an outside bar, trapping you out and forcing you to re-enter the new trend at a much worse price. Some of the strongest trends come from these traps because they tell traders that the last trend trader just got burned and there is no one left from the old trend. Also, they tell us that weak traders just got out and now will be chasing the new trend, adding orders in our direction. This gives traders confidence. When this kind of agitated reversal happens after a trendline break and on the test of the trend's extreme, the new trend will usually last for at least an hour or two and will run for many points.

If a trader enters early but the move is hesitant (overlapping bars) for a few bars, this should not be a concern, especially if those bars are mostly trend bars in the right direction. This is a sign of strength, and everyone is watching and waiting for the momentum to begin before entering. A good price action trader can often get in before that happens and then is able to move her stop to breakeven soon after the momentum starts, allowing her to make a lot of money with minimal risk. If you are confident in your read, take your trade, and don't worry that no one else sees what you see yet. They eventually will. Make sure to swing part or even all of your position even though you sometimes will get stopped out on your breakeven stop once or twice before the trend begins its run.

When a reversal is gradual, it is traditionally called an area of distribution at the end of a bull or an area of accumulation at the end of a bear. In Price Action terms, a distribution top can be a Double Top Bull Flag, a Spike and Trading Range, or a Spike and Channel where the channel takes a while to form. An accumulation bottom has corresponding Price Action patterns.

Typically, entries in trend pullbacks look bad but are profitable, and entries in reversals look good but are losers. If you are looking to buy a reversal in a bear or sell a top of a bull, make sure that it is perfect. Trends constantly form reversals that somehow don't look quite right. Maybe there is too much overlap with the prior bars or too many dojis or the reversal bar is too small or pulls back several ticks just before it closes, or there is no prior break of a significant trendline or failed breakout of a trend channel line. These almost perfect reversals sucker you in and trap you, so you should never take a reversal trade unless it is clear and strong.

There is a rhythm to the market as it forms alternating trends. One trend will often end with a Trend Channel Line overshoot and reversal followed by a two-legged move that breaks the trendline. The two legs then allow for the drawing of a channel for the new trend. Some trends end with simply a trendline break and then a test, followed by a second leg. Again, these two legs form a new trend channel that may or may not be the start of a new trend. If the new trend is weak, it will usually just result in a pullback and then a resumption of the old trend. Traders should always be drawing or at least visualizing trendlines and trend channel lines and watching how the market reacts when it tests these lines.

Major reversals from bear markets often are volatile with large bars and several pushes up and down. People think that the worst is over and then realize "Oops, I'm too early," and they are quick to sell out. This can happen several times before the final bottom is in and accounts for why so many major reversal end with large range bars and either a Failed Flag or a Three Push pattern.

Bar 2 in Figure 8.1 was a Failed Final Flag reversal leading to a strong move up to Bar 3, which exceeded the last Lower High of the bear.

Bar 4 formed a Higher Low, which allowed for the drawing of a trendline.

FIGURE 8.1 The Daily Emini Had Many Trend Changes, All of Which Followed Standard Price Action Principles, as Would Be Expected

Bar 5 pulled back below the trendline and immediately reversed up. However, this now generated a flatter trendline.

Bar 6 was a small Wedge and the pullback to Bar 7 created a new trendline.

Bar 8 was a reversal after a Wedge top, and that usually leads to two legs down. It was also a Third Push up.

The Bar 9 leg fell below the last Higher Low (Bar 7) of the bull, indicating bear strength. Bar 9 broke the bull trendline so two legs down are expected. Bar 9 ended the first leg, and it should be followed by a Lower High or a Higher High. Here, there was a Lower High, and the second leg down ended at Bar 11.

Bar 10 was a strong rally, and this strength could only be negated by a strong move below Bar 9, the first leg down.

Bar 11 reversed back up after falling just a little below Bar 9, so this was likely the end of a two-legged correction in the prior bull. However, this correction broke a major trendline from the Bar 2 low, so the market could reverse down after a test of the Bar 8 high.

Bar 12 formed a two-legged Higher High, and the new bear should have at least two legs down. It was also a small Expanding Triangle (Bar 6, 7, 8, 11, and 12).

The first leg down to Bar 13 was very strong, dropping well below the Bars 8 to 11 bull flag.

Once the Bar 14 Lower High formed, it could be used to create a trendline and then a trend channel line.

Bar 15 reversed up from its breakout of the trend channel line, so it should be followed by two legs up and a break above the bear trendline, which it was.

Bar 16 broke below the first bull trendline and reversed up.

Bar 17 was a Breakout Pullback from the breakout above the bull trend channel line.

This rally ended in a small Wedge at Bar 18, which formed a nominal Higher High and an Expanding Triangle (Bars 8, 11, 12, 15, and 18). A Wedge is a form of a trend channel line overshoot, and two legs down are likely. Bar 18 was a Double Top with Bar 12.

Bar 19 fell below the bull trendline.

Bar 20 formed a Lower High, and it allowed for the creation of a trendline and trend channel line.

Bar 21 fell below that Bar 18–20 trend channel line (not shown) and formed a Wedge that began at Bar 19.

The rally up to Bar 22 broke above the last small high of the bear, and it broke above the bear trendline, but formed the second Lower High in the leg down from the Bar 18 high. The test of the Bar 22 high failed at Bar 23 (it did not go above Bar 22), so another down leg will form.

Bar 24 reversed up after falling below a trend channel line.

The rally to Bar 25 broke the bear trendline.

Bar 26 failed to go above the Bar 25 first leg up, and this Lower High should have led to a leg down and formed either a new low (which it did) or a two-legged pullback bull flag. It was a Double Top Bear Flag.

Bar 27 was a two-legged Lower Low after the Bar 25 breaking of the bear trendline. At least two legs up should follow.

Bar 28 was a pullback from the two legs up, but it formed a second Higher Low, so at least two more legs up should form.

Bar 30 was a new high after the small Bar 29 Wedge, so at least two legs down should follow.

Bar 31 formed a Double Top Bear Flag (a Lower High) that followed the break of the bull trendline. It is the end of the pullback from the first leg down and should be followed by at least one more leg down.

Bar 32 tested the Wedge bear trend channel line. The market should either reverse up or collapse. Traders would sell on a stop at one tick below the low of the Wedge.

Bar 33 was a reversal up from a bear trend channel line overshoot, and it led to a small rally above the trendline.

Bar 1 in Figure 8.2 was about 10 percent above yesterday's low, capping off a huge two-day bull in GS.

Bar 3 broke the bear trendline in the pullback and then ran protective sell stops on the two-legged Lower Low move down to the Bar 4 reversal

FIGURE 8.2 When There Is a Strong Trend, Look for a With Trend Price Action Entry During a Pullback

bar. This was a great buy setup. You don't have to check, but the first big pullback in a strong trend usually tests the 15-minute EMA (and this one was an almost exact test, but that information was not needed to place the trade). As great a price action buy setup as this was, notice how the entry bar was a small bull trend bar. The market had not yet realized how good this was. It is natural to become nervous when you take what you thought was a great trade in a major stock, but no one else saw it as great yet. Sometimes this happens, and the market can have several small bars (usually With Trend) before the bull reversal is perceived as having taken place. That realization occurred during the big bull trend bar, Bar 6. It had great momentum and a shaved top and bottom, meaning that the bulls were extremely aggressive, and higher prices should follow. By the close of Bar 6, your stop is breakeven, and you are holding for a test of the Bar 1 high. It would be wise to scalp some of your shares out after about the first one dollar of profit.

Once there has been a strong Countertrend move, there will be a pullback that will be a test for both the bulls and the bears. For example, if there was a strong downward move in a bull market and the move broke through a trendline that has held for 20 to 40 bars, and the down move continued for 20 bars and carried well below the 20-bar EMA and even below the low of the last Higher Low of the bull, then the bears have demonstrated considerable strength. Once this first leg down exhausts itself, bears will begin to take partial profits, and bulls will begin to reinstate their longs. Both will cause the market to move higher, and both bulls and bears will watch this move very carefully. Because the down leg was so strong, both the bulls and bears believe that its low will likely be tested before the market breaks out into a new high. Therefore, as the market rallies, if there is not strong momentum, the new bulls will start to take profits, and the bears will become aggressive and add to their shorts. The rally will likely have many bear bars and tails, both of which indicate that the bulls are weak. The selloff down from this rally creates the first Lower High in a potential new bear. In any case, the odds are high that there will be a second leg down, since both the bulls and bears expect it and will be trading accordingly.

TRENDLINE BREAK

The single most important concept in this book is that you should only be trading in the direction of trendlines and you must wait for the break of a significant trendline before taking a Countertrend position.

Virtually all reversals begin with either a trendline break or trend channel line overshoot and reversal, and all of those eventually break the trendline when there is a reversal. The trendline break is what traders need to see before they feel confident about Countertrend positions. Until there is one, most will scalp out of any Countertrend trade. In the absence of a trendline break, there is still a strong trend in effect, and traders should make sure that they take every With Trend entry and don't worry about missing an occasional Countertrend scalp. The best odds and the most money are in the With Trend trades. True V bottoms and tops in the absence of trend channel line overshoots and reversals are so rare that they are not worth considering. Traders should focus on common patterns, and if they miss an occasional rare event, there will always be a pullback where they can start trading with the new trend.

Strong trend channel line reversals are from greatly overextended trends and often run far after they break the trendline. The First Pullback after the reversal is often shallow because the market is emotional and everyone quickly agrees that the trend has reversed. Because of the confidence, traders will be much more aggressive and will add on during the smallest pause and not take profits, keeping the pullbacks small.

When there is a strong break of a trendline, there will usually be a second leg after a pullback. The pullback often retraces and tests the old trendline, but there are almost always more reliable Price Action reasons for entering there in the attempt to catch the second leg of the pullback (or new trend). The stronger the move through the trendline, the more likely it is that there will be a second leg after a pullback. The pullback that tests the trend's extreme can overshoot (a Higher High in a reversal down from a bull or a Lower Low at the end of a bear) or undershoot (a Lower High in a new bear or a Higher Low in a new bull). If there is an overshoot but it extends well beyond the old extreme, the reversal is nullified, and the old trend has resumed. Traders need to look for another trendline break or trend channel line overshoot before taking a Countertrend trade.

Signs of strength of a trendline break (the first leg of a possible reversal) include:

- The move covers many points.
- It goes well past the EMA.
- In a bear reversal, it extends below the final Higher Low of the bull, and in a bull reversal, it extends above the final Lower High of the bear.
- It lasts many bars (10 to 20 or so).
- There were other strong prior trendline breaks (this isn't the first sign of Countertrend strength).

- The reversal back to test the old trend's extreme lacks momentum, as evidenced by its having many overlapping bars with many being trend bars in the direction of the new trend.
- The reversal back to test the old trend's extreme fails at the EMA or the old trendline and does not get close to the extreme.

The weak bear leg to Bar 4 in Figure 8.3 barely broke the trendline, and it did not come close to falling below the last Higher Low in the bull (Bar 2), and it could not break through the EMA. However, Bar 6 is still an acceptable Higher High test of the Bar 3 bull extreme, especially since it is a reversal on the open from a breakout of the prior day's high.

The bear leg to Bar 9 broke below a longer trendline, the EMA, and the last Higher Low of the bull (Bar 5), and it followed a previous sharp attempt at a trend reversal (the selloff to Bar 4). Also, the small rally that followed it did not come close to testing the underside of the trendline or the Bar 8 first pullback in the first leg down. All of these are signs of strength of the trendline break and increase the chances for at least a second leg down or an actual trend reversal. The pattern was also a Head and Shoulders Top, but it is not worth looking at price action with that in mind; it is better to pay much more attention to the bars closer to where you are thinking of entering. Also, most Head and Shoulder patterns fail and are not nearly as reliable as the bar-by-bar price action.

Bar 10 is a Low 4 short in a low momentum Lower High test of the trend extreme (Bar 6).

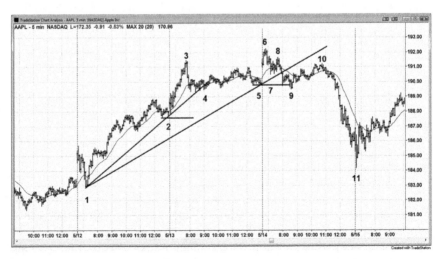

FIGURE 8.3 Don't Trade Countertrend Until after There Has Been a Trendline Break

After the break of a bull trendline, traders would start to draw bear trendlines (not shown) and these become increasingly important as the market transforms into a bear trend with a series of Lower Highs and Lows.

TREND CHANNEL LINE FAILED BREAKOUTS: CLIMAXES, PARABOLAS, AND V TOPS AND BOTTOMS

All of these moves have one thing in common: their slope. Instead of being linear (a straight line), it is curved and increasing. At some point, the market quickly reverses direction and usually at the very least there will be a protracted sideways move and possibly a trend reversal. All of these patterns are simply trend channel line overshoots and reversals, and therefore they should be traded as such; giving them special names adds nothing to your trading success. The trend channel line might not be obvious at the moment of the reversal, but once a parabolic move is underway, price action traders are constantly drawing and redrawing trend channel lines and then watching for an overshoot and reversal. The best reversals have large reversal bars and preferably a second entry. The first leg of the reversal will almost always break the trendline, and if it does not, then the reversal is suspect, and a trading range or continuation pattern becomes much more likely. If a second reversal entry fails, the trend will likely resume and run for at least two more legs.

Countertrend traders are always drawing trend channel lines, hoping for an overshoot and a reversal that will allow for at least a scalp and preferably a two-legged Countertrend move.

Bar 2 in Figure 8.4 broke a small trend channel line, but there was no earlier Countertrend strength, and the setup bar had only a small bull body. Smart traders would wait for a second entry, and if one did not develop, they would view this as a With Trend setup, which it turned out to be (it is a channel in a steep Spike and Channel bear trend). Notice how the breakout below Bar 2 was in the form of a strong bear trend bar. This is because many longs were tempted to enter early on this Wedge, and most would not concede that the reversal failed until there was a move below the Bar 2 low of the Wedge. That is where their protective stops were. Also, many bears will have entry stops there as well because a failed Wedge usually runs about the height of the Wedge as a minimum, creating a great short entry.

Bar 3 overshot another trend channel line, but there was no entry signal so there were very few trapped bulls. Also, there was no prior bull strength

FIGURE 8.4 Trend Channel Line Failed Breakouts Can Be Reliable Countertrend Setups

in the form of a break of a bear trendline, so smart traders would only be looking to short.

Bar 5 opened well above the bear trendline, but it was essentially a first EMA Gap Bar (close enough . . . its body was large and entirely above the EMA, even though its low was below the EMA), creating a Trend from Open move down.

Bar 6 did not reach the trend channel line, so although it tried to reverse yesterday's low, the move was suspect. When a move approaches a magnet like a trend channel line, most traders would wait for the overshoot, and in its absence, would want at least a second entry. Also, the signal bar was a doji with only a tiny body, which means that the bulls were not strong.

Bar 8 overshot the bear trend channel line, and the signal bar was an inside bar with a good-size bull body. This setup was also a second attempt to reverse yesterday's low (a Failed Final Flag buy setup after the breakout of the Bar 7 flag), creating a dependable Opening Reversal setup.

SIGNS OF STRENGTH IN THE FIRST LEG OF A REVERSAL

Some reversals result in trend reversals, and others simply in small Countertrend swings. Carefully analyzing the price action before and after the reversal helps a trader gauge how much if any of his position he should swing and how big a move to anticipate. When there is a strong trend, traders should not be taking Countertrend trades until there has been a trendline break or at least a climactic reversal from a trend channel line overshoot. In a trading range market, however, traders can trade reversals in both directions.

There are many characteristics of strong reversals, and the more that are present, the more likely it is that a Countertrend trade will be profitable and the more aggressive the trader should be in her decision over how much of her position she should swing. The stronger the prior trendline break in a trend reversal, the more likely the reversal will gain more points and last longer and have two or more legs. The strongest trendline breaks have strong momentum and surge well past the EMA and usually beyond swing points in the prior trend.

Here are many characteristics of strong reversals:

- Strong reversal bar.
- Second entry signal.
- Trap Bar (trapping traders out) forming a small Higher Low in a new Bull or Lower High in a new Bear.
- Began as a reversal from an overshoot of a trend channel line from the old trend.
- Reverse a significant swing high or low (such as breaking below a strong prior swing low and reversing up).
- Break well beyond the trendline of the old trend.
- Break the EMA by many ticks and close beyond it for many bars.
- Break above the last Lower High of the prior bear or Higher Low of the prior bull.
- The pullback from the first Countertrend leg forms an M2B or an M2S.
- The first leg lasts many bars and reverses many bars of the prior trend.
- Trending anything: closes, highs, lows, or bodies.
- Small pullbacks, especially if only sideways.
- Bars with tiny or no tails in either direction.

If you do get stopped out, be aware of the possibility that you were trapped out of a great trade and look to re-enter quickly. Here are several examples of Trap Bars that trapped traders out of new trends.

Bar 1 in Figure 8.5 is a strong bear trend bar and a Low 1 after a strong bear into the prior day's close. There was a big gap down on the open followed by three bull trend bars. With this much bull strength on an overdone open, smart traders would not be shorting a Low 1 far from the EMA. The failed Low 1 was a great long entry (a small Higher Low) because it trapped bulls out and bears in, and both will chase the market up.

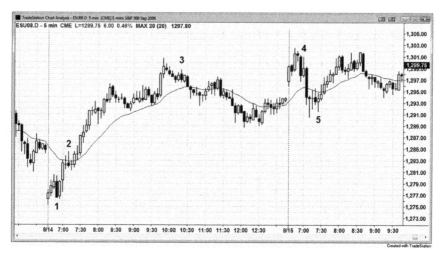

FIGURE 8.5 Don't Get Trapped Out of a New Trend

Bar 3 was an outside bar down. Smart traders would not be buying in here since the market was attempting to reverse from a Final Bull Flag and they are expecting two legs down. Also, small bars after a climax (a large bull trend bar breakout from that flag) almost always lead to a protracted move. The market is not in a hurry, as indicated by the small size of the bars.

Bar 4 tried to form a large bull trend bar after a big bear trend bar, possibly setting up a Trend from the Open Bull day. It had a close below its midpoint, and it became an inside bar. This bar trapped longs and set up a bear leg.

Bar 5 was a failed Low 1, and it became a small Higher Low that was also a second EMA Gap Bar with a flat EMA, which is always a good setup for at least a scalp on the long side.

TRENDS REVERSE WITH A TEST: EITHER AN UNDERSHOOT OR AN OVERSHOOT

Trends end with a reversal (a Countertrend move that breaks a trendline) and then a test of the final trend extreme. The test may overshoot the old extreme, as in the case of a Lower Low in a new bull or a Higher High in a new bear, or it may undershoot it with a Higher Low in a new bull or a Lower High in a new bear. Rarely, the test will form a Double Top or

Double Bottom to the exact tick. Overshoots are strictly speaking the final leg of the old trend because they form the most extreme price in the trend. An undershoot is the pullback from the first leg in the new trend. Tests themselves are frequently made of two legs.

For example, at a market top, after the trendline break the market will almost always rally one more time in a second attempt to drive the market to higher prices. If instead the sellers again overwhelm the buyers around the price level that they did earlier, the bulls will have made two attempts to drive the market higher and both failed. When the market tries to do something twice and it fails both times, it usually then tries to do the opposite.

Since a Countertrend move after a trendline break usually has at least two legs, if a bull reversal has a Higher Low for the test of the bear low, it will also be the start of the second leg. On the other hand, if it forms a Lower Low for the test, that low will be the start of the first leg, and after that first leg it is likely that there will be a pullback and then a second leg. Likewise in a bear reversal, a Lower High is the start of the second leg, but a Higher High test is the start of the first leg.

A very common pattern is where there is a strong Countertrend move (a spike) without any pullbacks, and this spike could be a trend reversal, but there is then a resumption of the trend. If this resumption has enough bars and retraces enough of the spike it will make traders wonder if it represents a failed reversal rather than a pullback after a successful reversal. However, the extremes of most of those sharp momentum spikes that have deep, lengthy retracements still end up being tested, and most are exceeded. For example, a large spike down that is followed by a slow rally that retraces most of the spike will usually be followed by a second selloff that tests the low of the initial spike. At that point, the original trend can continue (Double Bottom Bull Flag), the reversal can continue down, or the market can enter a trading range. The test is much more likely if the spike is in a trading range or in the direction of the trend (like a spike up in a bull), and it is not likely if it is the first Countertrend move in a strong trend. For example, a sharp bear spike in a strong bull will usually just trap bears and not get tested.

A climax reversal (usually an overshoot and reversal of a trend channel line, or a climactic Failed Final Flag) does not have to have a pullback that tests the extreme. Climaxes are much more common on smaller time frame charts. For example, a 1-minute chart often has several each day, whereas a 5-minute chart might only have a couple each month. Perfect V top and bottom patterns are rare, and there is nothing to be gained by a trader thinking of these patterns as anything other than a reversal after a failed trend channel line overshoot, and it should be traded as such.

FIGURE 8.6 A Pullback in a Strong Trend Is Usually Followed by a Test of the Extreme of the Trend

Any series of strong trend bars (big bodies, small tails, and very little overlap) that is followed by a pullback almost always has a test of its extreme. Bar 3 in Figure 8.6 tested and exceeded the Bar 1 spike low, but there was no reversal, and the bear continued for several more bars, forming a Wedge bottom.

Today's open formed a Higher Low in its test of the Wedge at yesterday's low. It was also a Double Bottom Bull Flag (with the last swing low of yesterday) and a failed breakout of the large two-legged bear flag of the final two hours of yesterday.

Bar 5 was the top of a protracted, big rally off the Bar 4 bear spike, but the Bar 4 spike low was tested at the close of the day.

The Bar 1 bear spike in Figure 8.7 was tested and exceeded later in the day by a much larger bear spike (the Bar 3 low). This second bear spike was tested with the Bar 5 Higher Low.

The Bar 1, 3, and 6 bear spikes and the Bar 4 and 8 bull spikes in Figure 8.8 all were tested on this 60-minute AAPL chart.

Bar 4 is a bull spike in a bear and does not have to be tested, but it was about 10 bars later.

Bar 8 is a bull spike in a trading range and a break of a major trendline, so it was likely to be tested.

Bar 7 was a new swing low (a Lower Low and possible bear bottom after a trendline break) but not a spike, so it does not have to be fully tested. Bar 9 formed a Higher Low test of Bar 7 and was a bull reversal.

FIGURE 8.7 The Extreme of a Strong Momentum Reversal Usually Gets Tested

FIGURE 8.8 Strong Moves Usually Get Tested after a Pullback

Bar 1 in Figure 8.9 was a bear spike in a strong bull and was unlikely to be tested. It was simply the first EMA Gap Bar, and it trapped bears.

Bar 2 was a bear spike that followed a Wedge top, making it likely to be tested since at least two legs down should be expected.

Bar 3 was a bear spike in a bear and was tested with a Higher Low that led to resumption of the higher time frame bull.

FIGURE 8.9 Countertrend Spikes Usually Do Not Get Tested

FIGURE 8.10 Test of a Strong Bull Spike Up

RIMM closed yesterday with a strong bull spike in Figure 8.10, so the odds were excellent that today was going to try to exceed it. Although today's rally was sloppy and did not look particularly bullish, note that the market could not put two consecutive closes below the EMA. This chart was going up, but its strength was deceptive.

The rally to Bar 1 in Figure 8.11 broke a bear trendline and the Bar 3 test of the bear low was a two-legged Lower Low. A Lower Low test usually

FIGURE 8.11 A Reversal after a Test Usually Leads to at Least Two Countertrend Legs

results in at least two Countertrend legs, and that is what happened here (the up moves from Bars 3 and 9).

Bar 9 was a Higher Low after the break of yesterday's major bear trendline (broken by the rally to Bar 1), and as a Higher Low it is the start of the second leg, and the completed second leg can be the end of the move up. Bar 3 was a Lower Low after a bear trendline break so it was a possible major trend reversal. You now need to be looking to buy the first Higher Low, which occurred at Bar 7. It is common for the market to run the breakeven stops once or twice before it takes off so you need to look to buy again and again swing part of your position and Bar 9 offered a great opportunity.

This Bar 2 climactic Opening Reversal (inverted V top) in the SKF UltraShort Financials ETF in Figure 8.12 was simply a reversal of yesterday's high after breaking out of the top of a bear trend channel line. It was also a second entry after breaking above yesterday's high.

Incidentally, it was a Measured Move up from yesterday's trading range, but this is only a minor consideration when contemplating a trade. When a strong trend reaches an area of a Measured Move, traders can then begin to consider Countertrend trades but only if there is a good setup. Measured Moves are of minor importance and not terribly reliable and in general should be ignored.

The 5-minute OIH in Figure 8.13 had a climactic Opening Reversal below yesterday's low, and it was also a reversal of three trend channel line overshoots. A trader should buy above the large reversal Bar 1, and again

FIGURE 8.12 A Test of a Prior High Can Be a Very Strong (Climactic) Up Move That Leads to a Reversal Down

FIGURE 8.13 A Test of a Prior Low Can Be a Strong Climactic Move That Leads to a Reversal

at the High 2 First Pullback at Bar 2, expecting at least two legs up. Always swing part of your position when two legs are likely because sometimes there will be a protracted new trend rather than just a two-legged pullback.

When there is a strong trend, there will be many reversal attempts on the 3-minute chart and far more on the 1-minute. Until there is a clear reversal on the 5-minute, if you choose to look at the 1- or 3-minute charts, you should treat each reversal attempt as a With Trend setup. In Figure 8.14 each of the five attempts on this 3-minute chart to reverse attracted eager bulls who thought they were risking little and they might be gaining a lot if they were catching the bottom of a climactic V bottom reversal, a very rare event. Rather than joining them, think about where they will have to sell out of their longs and place an entry sell stop at that very location. You will consistently succeed in transferring money from their accounts into yours, which is the primary objective of trading. For example, as soon as the bulls went long at the Bar 1 bull reversal bar (there was not a prior trendline

FIGURE 8.14 Never Trade Countertrend off the 3-minute Chart (Unless There Is Also a 5-Minute Setup)

break in this steep selloff so no longs should be considered), smart traders would place orders to go short on a stop at one tick below the signal bar.

The short at Bar 4 was below the entry bar, since the bulls would have tightened their stops once the entry bar closed. Since this is a trend, you should swing a large part of your position.

Bar 5 was an ii pattern, which often is a reversal pattern (but it needs an earlier trendline break), and it is commonly the final flag before a two-legged Countertrend move (as was the case here). It represents balance between the bulls and bears, and the breakout is reaching outside of the balance. There is often a strong force pulling it back to the pattern, and usually through the other side. Since there was no prior trendline break, the only breakout that was a valid entry was a bear breakout. However, an ii is just wide enough to break a small trendline so any reversal up within a few bars afterwards is a valid long entry of a small Failed Final Flag.

This is the 1-minute chart of the same bear move, and the numbered bars are the same as on the prior chart. Bars C, D, and E in Figure 8.15 were

FIGURE 8.15 Trading Countertrend off the 1- and 3-Minute Charts Is a Tempting but Losing Strategy and Will Cause You to Miss Much More Profitable With Trend Entries

valid Countertrend setups that followed two legs down and small trend-line breaks; each was a tradable long scalp. Although these are possible to trade, it is usually too difficult to read a second chart and place orders this quickly, and you would likely make more money if you just traded with the 5-minute trend. It looks very easy on a chart printed at the end of the day but is much more difficult in real time. If you were to sell based on the 1-minute chart, all five of the numbered bars provided With Trend (on both the 1 and 5-minute trend) short entries that would allow for swinging part of the position.

Here in Figure 8.16 is a 1-minute chart of a 5-minute strong bull (not shown). Trading shorts profitably is difficult (none of the six shorts above yielded a four-tick profit). It is far more profitable and less stressful to simply look for With Trend entries on the 5-minute chart and never look at the 1-minute. The only valid reason to look at 1-minute short signals is to find long (With Trend) entries. Once a short triggers, look for where the protective stops are and place buy orders there, since the trapped shorts will push the market to your long profit target as they buy back their losers.

Some news must have been released that led to a sharp selloff at 10:30 PST in Figure 8.17. You should never pay attention to the news because it creates a distance between you and what you have to do. It requires thought that you then have to reconcile with the chart, which can only reduce your profit. The chart tells you all that you need to know. Something happened that made the institutions sell aggressively, and that is all the information that a trader needs. It is time to look for short setups.

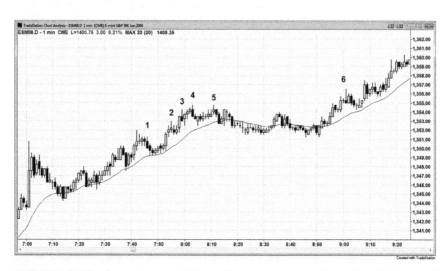

FIGURE 8.16 Countertrend 1-Minute Setups Are Better Viewed as With Trend Setups (Enter on Their Failures)

FIGURE 8.17 Ignore the News and Just Trade the Price Action That It Generates

Bar 1 in Figure 8.17 was a strong bull trend bar that trapped early buy-ers who bought the candle pattern or a smaller time frame reversal. A buy was not even triggered on this 5-minute chart, since the next bar did not go above the Bar 1 high. These bulls would exit below the low of Bar 1 and won't look to buy again until more price action unfolds. Place an order to short on a stop at one tick below the low of Bar 1, which is where those longs will have their protective stops, and as they cover they will provide plenty of downside fuel. If it gets hit, you know the trapped longs will get out and not want to buy again soon, and the smart bears will be adding to their shorts. With no one left to buy, the market will almost certainly provide a scalper's profit and likely much more.

Incidentally, Bar 5 is the third overlapping bar, and at least one of the bars was a doji (all three were) ... this is Barb Wire, which is usually a continuation pattern, and you should never buy at its high or sell at its low. You fade small bars at its extremes, and you wait for a trend bar breakout to fail (which it did at Bar 7, after the two prior trend bars broke out of the pattern).

Bars 3 and 5 were classic candle pattern traps. Traders who memorize candle reversal patterns will be eager to buy these very large candles with long bull tails because they will see the long tails and the closes near the highs as evidence that the bulls were gaining control. Remember, a doji bar is a one-bar trading range and you cannot buy above a trading range in a bear. Since the doji is a trading range, it is a bear flag and not a reversal pattern. When you see a big bar with a long tail and a small body in a bear, it tells you that if you buy above its high, you are paying way too much. In a bear, you want to buy low, not at the top of a huge bar with a small body and no prior trendline break. These two bars again were perfect candle pattern traps. Bar 5 was even better than Bar 3 since it was a gravestone doji, which candle novices worship. Also, the market traded above the high of the bar, "confirming" the strength of the bulls, and it was a second attempt at a bottom (a Double Bottom with Bar 3). But what went wrong? When you see these small-bodied big candles in a strong trend where there has yet to be a trendline break, you should get excited because they are great traps and therefore perfect short setups. Just wait for the small bar that always follows, and its lack of upside follow-through makes these early bulls very scared. Everyone knows where those bulls are putting their protective stops, so that is exactly where you will be putting your entry stop to go short. When you see those big doji candles, you, too, see bullish strength, but then assume that since the price was hovering at the high of those bars and the bulls were now in balance with the bears, the highs of those bars are likely to be in the middle or top of a trading range and not at a bottom.

The two-legged rally to Bar 6 broke a trendline, and you now know that the bulls are eager to buy, so a perfect long setup would be a failed breakout to new lows. Smart traders will just wait for a one- or two-bar break below Bars 3 and 5 and then starting placing buy orders at one tick above the high of the prior bar. They will keep moving the orders down if they don't get filled, but if the move continues too far down, they will wait for another trendline break before looking to buy again. The earlier bulls with two or three losses by now will wait for confirmation this time and will enter late, providing additional fuel for the up move after the Price Action longs get in.

Even though Bar 7 had a bear body, at least it closed above its midpoint, indicating some strength. Presumably bulls are a little cautious after losing on entries from Bars 1, 3, and 5. Also, it was a failed breakout from Barb Wire. The odds were high that this would be a profitable long, and smart traders would have been anticipating it, so there was no excuse to miss it.

The entry bar had a bull body, albeit small, which is constructive. Also, it was an inside body variant (its body was inside the body of the signal bar and is a weaker version of an inside bar), which means that the bears did not take control. At this point, you are feeling confident because your protective stop was not hit on the bar after entry, as was the case for the earlier bulls.

The next three bars all were bull trend bars with closes above the prior close, so the closes are in a bull trend. Some of the best swings begin with several overlapping bars that make you impatient and worried. It is reasonable to assume that there will be two legs up, but almost certainly there will be a stop run down before the second leg. The breakeven stop was not hit on the violent move down in Bar 8, which turned into a bullish outside bar and the start of the second leg up (a Higher Low).

The targets for the rally are the bull signal bar highs in the bear (the highs of Bars 3 and 5 and possibly Bar 2). Bar 9 exceeded the final target by one tick. The momentum was so strong that the Bar 8 low was likely just part of the first leg up and not the start of the second leg up, and there instead should be a bigger pullback and then a second leg up (it ended at Bar 11).

Bar 11 set up a Low 2 short from the rally up from the Bar 8 low.

DOUBLE TOP AND BOTTOM PULLBACKS

If a market forms a Double Bottom after a selloff, but before the bull takes off, and it then has a pullback that tests just above the Double Bottom low, this is a Double Bottom Pullback long setup. The market made two attempts to go down, and both times the buyers overwhelmed the sellers around the same price level. The Double Bottom does not have to be exact and usually the second bottom is slightly lower than the first, making the pattern sometimes look like a Head and Shoulders pattern. If the second bottom does not at least reach the first, there is a risk that the bottom is only forming a two-legged sideways to up correction, and it would be better to look for a scalp long rather than a swing. A Double Bottom (or Top) Pullback pattern can be thought of as a Three Push Bottom (or a Triple Bottom) where the third push down did not have strong enough sellers to create a new low. It also can be thought of as two failed attempts to exceed the prior extreme (often a Low 2), and two failed attempts usually lead to a reversal. Some technicians say that Triple Bottoms and Tops always fail and always become continuation patterns, but they require that the three extremes be identical to the tick. With that strict definition, the pattern is so rare that it is not worth mentioning. Traders will make much more money by using loose definitions. When something resembles a reliable pattern, it will likely trade like the reliable pattern.

This is a reversal pattern and not a continuation pattern, like the Double Bottom Bull Flag. Both are long entry setups, but one is the beginning of the trend (a reversal pattern), and the other takes place in an established trend (a continuation pattern), or at least after there has been one strong leg.

Likewise, if there is a Double Top in a bull and there is then a pullback that reaches close to the high, this Double Top Pullback is a good short setup.

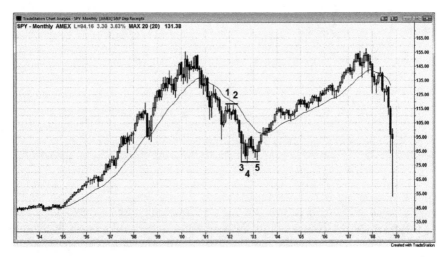

FIGURE 8.18 Double Bottom Pullback Buy

The monthly SPY in Figure 8.18 had a Double Bottom Pullback buy at the Bar 5 outside bar, one tick above the high of the prior bar. Bar 4 was slightly below Bar 3, but this is common and actually preferable in Double Bottom Pullback buy patterns. These often are Head and Shoulders patterns.

Bars 1 and 2 formed a Double Top Bear Flag (a continuation pattern and not a Double Top, which is a reversal pattern at the end of a bull).

Although pundits are saying that since Warren Buffett is buying the collapse in the last bar on the chart and therefore the bottom is in, there is no price action evidence yet of a bottom and the tremendous value that Buffett is seeing might become an even far greater value in the months to come. Don't buy just because Buffett is buying. Wait for a break of a bear trendline on the daily chart and then for a test of the low that reverses back up. The momentum down is too strong to be looking to buy at this point. Wait for a price action bottom, which will eventually come. The huge bar might be a sign of exhausted sellers, but until there is price action evidence for a bottom, smart traders who are trading the daily chart are only looking to sell.

FIGURE 8.19 Double Bottom Bull Flag

Bar 1 in Figure 8.19 was the end of a large second leg down and therefore a possible reversal setup. Although the move up to Bar 2 was small, neither Bars 3 nor 4 could take out the low and therefore formed a Double Bottom Bull Flag.

Bar 6 made an exact test of the Bar 3 low and was unable to drop below it (or below the Bar 1 low), so this was a broader Double Bottom Bull Flag, with Bar 3 (or Bars 3 and 4) forming the first bottom. This is also referred to as accumulation. The institutions were defending the Bar 1 low instead of attempting to run the stops, indicating that they believe that the market is going up.

Bar 5 was an EMA Gap Bar, which often provides the necessary Countertrend momentum to lead to a trend reversal. It broke a major trendline, and Bar 6 was a Higher Low test of the Bar 1 trend extreme.

Bar 4 in Figure 8.20 looked like a setup for a Double Bottom Pullback long but Bar 3 was five cents above the Bar 2 low in a very strong bear. This slightly Higher Low usually negates the pattern and makes a two-legged bear rally much more likely than a new bull. Also, the First Pullback (whatever minor rally that would follow Bar 2) in a strong trend almost always sets up a With Trend entry so it is not wise to be looking for bottoms here. However, the market rallied over $1 from the long entry, if a trader took the trade. With the big tails on Bars 2, 3, and 4, and with the market still in the first 90 minutes and therefore prone to Opening Reversals, it was a reasonable trade. However, the smartest traders would be shorting the EMA test, and if you instead scalped that long, it could be difficult to quickly switch to a shorting mentality.

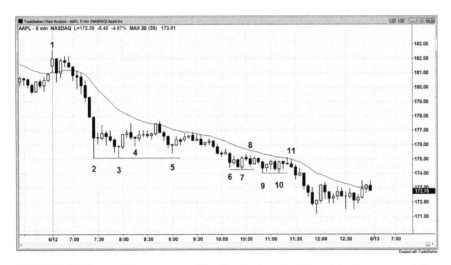

FIGURE 8.20 Double Bottom Pullbacks Need to Be Viewed in Context and Are Not Automatic Reversal Setups

Bar 8 was a Double Bottom Pullback setup, with Bar 7 being 13 cents below the Bar 6 low, but the entry never triggered (the bar after Bar 8 was unable to take out the high of Bar 8). Again, bottom picking in a strong bear without a prior strong trendline-breaking up leg is not a good approach. This is a Trend from the Open bear, which is one of the strongest types of bear trends and you should only be looking to short. You should only be looking for reversals after there has been a strong break of the bear trendline.

Bar 11 was a third attempt at the bottom formation. Bar 10, was above the low of the first bar (Bar 6) by two cents, making the pattern weak at best.

In a bear, the smartest traders enter on With Trend shorts off the EMA, like the M2s following Bar 8 and the Bar 11 M2S.

Bars 1 and 2 in Figure 8.21 formed a Double Bottom, although at first glance, Bar 1 might be easy to overlook. The bottom of an entry bar has protective stops below it, and it will often be tested, as it was with Bar 2, and two moves down to the same level is a Double Bottom, even if the first one is not a swing low. With the big tail on the bottom of Bar 1, there was almost certainly a 1-minute Higher Low (and there was). Bar 3 was a deep pullback that tested the Double Bottom, so it was a second attempt to run the stops, but it could not even get as close as the first attempt (the Bar 2 low) before the bears pulled out and the bulls took control.

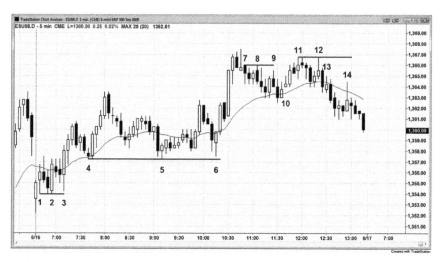

FIGURE 8.21   Double Bottom and Top Pullback Reversals

Bars 4 and 5 created a Double Bottom Bull Flag on this Trending Trading Range day, and this Double Bottom was tested by the Bar 6 pullback, forming a large Double Bottom Pullback. You could call it a Triple Bottom as well, but that term does not add any trading benefit here, and so it is not worth using.

Bar 7 is similar to Bar 1, in that it is also an entry bar. It and Bar 8 formed a subtle Double Top. Bar 8 tried to run the protective stops above the Bar 7 short entry bar but failed. Bar 9 was a second attempt and failed at an even lower price, creating a Double Top Pullback short setup with an entry on a stop at one tick below the low of Bar 9. With all of the dojis and overlapping bars in this pattern, this was likely to result only in a scalp, which it did. When you have to look this hard for a pattern, it is usually better to not trade until a clear and strong pattern develops.

This selloff tested into the top of the middle trading range of this Trending Trading Range Day but reversed back up.

Bars 11 and 12 formed a Double Top, alerting traders to look for a Double Top Pullback short setup. The Bar 13 bull trend bar was an attempt to rally and test the Double Top and an attempt to form a High 2 (an M2B), and it failed, but it is not wise to short near the bottom of a trading range unless there is a strong setup, and this is not.

Bar 14 was a better pullback, but it still did not retrace close enough to the Double Top for it to be reliable, and again you would be shorting the low of a trading range on a day composed of bull Trending Trading Ranges.

CLIMAX: SPIKE AND TRADING RANGE REVERSALS

A climax is simply any market that has gone too far, too fast in the eyes of traders, and then reverses. A climactic reversal is a strong momentum move (a "spike") with a series of big trend bars that often overshoot a trend channel line and then reverse. The word "spike" implies that there was a strong move in one direction and then immediately afterwards, a strong move in the opposite direction. The reversal move is smaller; otherwise instead of a Spike and Trading Range, there would be a clear and strong reversal without the hesitation that takes place in the trading range. In a Spike and Trading Range reversal, instead of quickly moving through the EMA in a strong Countertrend move, the market reverses for only a bar or two and then goes sideways and forms a Tight Trading Range that can break out in either direction. It is as if it the market tried to form a reversal but couldn't quite complete it, and on a higher time frame, instead of a strong reversal bar, there would be a big bar with a big tail and a close somewhere in the middle.

Sometimes a Countertrend Double Top/Bottom flag forms within the trading range, providing an additional reason to enter into a trend reversal trade (if a With Trend Double Top/Bottom flag forms, it is a With Trend setup). The reversal leg that leads to the trading range is often relatively small compared to the prior trend, but it usually breaks the trendline, and it can be the first leg of an opposite trend. Despite that, it is still easy to overlook, so whenever there is a climactic move, it is something that you should try to find. It may have a low momentum drift toward the old extreme, which leads to a failed test (a Lower High in a bull top or a Higher Low at a bottom), or it could continue to a new extreme and not be a reversal. If instead it does reverse, the new, opposite trend sometimes becomes very strong very fast and often forms a Spike and Channel trend pattern.

An inside bar after a breakout bar can be thought of as a possible miniature Spike and Trading Range reversal setup. The distance from the extreme of the breakout bar to the other extreme of the inside bar is the spike, representing a possible small climax reversal, and the inside bar is the trading range. As with all Spike and Trading Range patterns, the breakout can go either way, and the important thing is to be aware of both possibilities. Once the trend begins, look for With Trend setups.

Sometimes there can be an impressive spike, then a pullback, and then the start of a channel, only for the channel to fail and reverse directions. In hindsight, that pullback was the spike in the opposite direction and led to the channel. However, once you recognize it, then you know there is a trend, and you should try to take every With Trend entry.

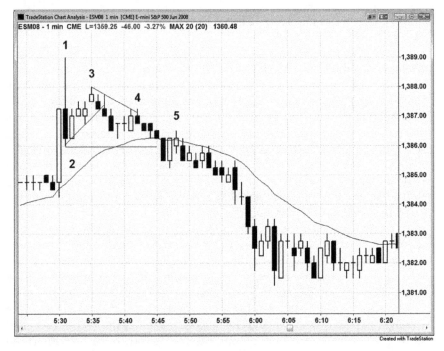

FIGURE 8.22 Bear Spike and Trading Range Top

The Globex 1-minute Emini in Figure 8.22 spiked up on a 5:30 A.M. PST report but formed a strong reversal bar down at Bar 1. Bar 1 was a 3-point tall bar, which is big on a 1-minute chart and therefore qualifies as a possible spike down. Bar 3 was a two-legged move up, forming a Low 2 in the possible new bear. Also, Bar 2 was an ii variation if you only look at the bodies (the body of Bar 2 was inside that of Bar 1, which was inside that of the prior bull breakout bar, and an ii indicates indecision), and the move up to Bar 3 was a false breakout of the top of the ii. The market went sideways for about 10 bars, which qualifies as a trading range after the down spike. Bar 4 had a minimal break above a minor trendline, and then the market resumed its downtrend. Bar 5 is a second-chance entry (a Breakout Pullback).

There was a strong reversal on the first bar of the day (Bar 5 in Figure 8.23) that overshot a bull trend channel line and then reversed back to the area of the line. The market went sideways for five bars and then formed a Lower High at Bar 7, completing a small trading range after the Bar 5 spike down (it spiked up and reversed down in what had to be a spike down on a 1-minute chart). Bar 9 can be viewed as an expansion of the trading range, a

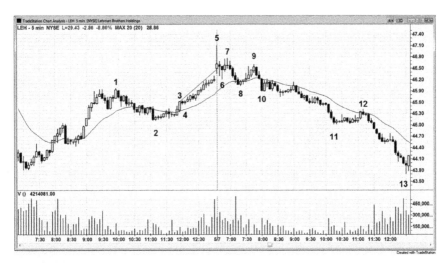

FIGURE 8.23 Bear Spike and Trading Range Top

Lower High, or a Double Top Bear Flag (it is approximately the same level as Bar 7, and at least a second attempt to rally to the Bar 5 high). The name is irrelevant, but it is a good short setup. The market then trended lower for the rest of the day and accelerated as it fell. Bar 10 is a spike, and the move down to Bar 11 is a channel. Yesterday, Bar 3 was a spike followed by a channel that began at Bar 4. The start of the channel usually gets tested within a day or two (the Bar 4 low was taken out with the bear following the Spike and Trading Range top that began with Bar 5, but the Bar 10 high beginning of the channel down was not tested during the following two weeks).

Both charts in Figure 8.24 are of the same time period of the 5-minute SPY. The run up to Bar 2 was a strong bull spike. After the sharp EMA pullback to Bar 3 that broke a trendline, the bull channel began. However, it failed in a two-legged Lower High at Bar 4. Once the market broke out of the bull channel with the Bar 5 pullback, which also broke the major bull trendline, it became obvious that this was not a bull Spike and Channel day and that the market was forming a trading range. This became a triangle top and then a Spike and Channel down. When the EMA Gap 2 long failed at Bar 8, it was clear that the bears were in control and that a bear channel was under way, with the push down to Bar 5 being the bear spike. At this point, you should try to take all short entries and consider any longs to be scalps (in general, it is better to ignore the long setups and just trade With Trend when there is a strong trend like this) until there is a climactic

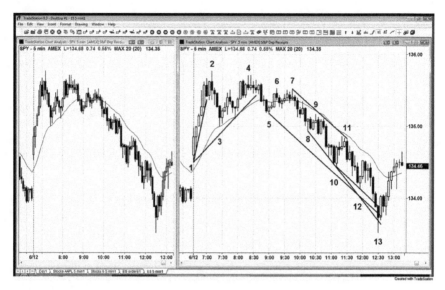

FIGURE 8.24 Spike and Channel Top After a Failed Bull Spike and Channel

overshoot of the bear trend channel line and reversal up. Bar 13 reversed up from breaking three such lines.

CLIMAX: THREE PUSHES AND WEDGES (TREND CHANNEL LINE OVERSHOOTS AND REVERSALS)

Trends often end with a test of the extreme, and the test often has two legs, each reaching a greater extreme (a Higher High in a bull or a Lower Low in a bear). The first extreme and then the two legs make Three Pushes, which is a well recognized reversal setup with many names. Very frequently it takes a Wedge shape, but sometimes the Wedge is only based on the candle bodies instead of the tails. It is not useful for a trader to draw subtle distinctions among the variations because there are enough similarities that they trade the same. For simplicity, think of these Three Push patterns as Wedges since most of them end in a climatic Wedge-like point. A trendline and trend channel line in a Three Push pattern can be parallel as in a Stair pattern, convergent as in a Wedge, or divergent as in an Expanding Triangle. It does not matter because they all behave similarly and you trade them the same.

The majority of Three Push patterns reverse after overshooting a trend channel line, and that alone is a reason to enter, even if the actual shape is not a Wedge. However, the Three Pushes are often easier to see than the trend channel line overshoot, and that makes the distinction from other trend channel line failures worthwhile. These patterns rarely have a perfect shape, and often trendlines and trend channel lines have to be manipulated to highlight the pattern. For example, the Wedge might be only with the candle bodies, so to draw the trendline and trend channel line with a Wedge shape, you have to ignore the tails. Other times, the end point of the Wedge won't reach the trend channel line. Be flexible, and if there is a Three Push pattern at the end of a big move, even if the pattern is not perfect, trade it as if it were a Wedge. However, if it overshoots the trend channel line, the odds of success with the Countertrend trade are higher. Also, most trend channel line overshoots have a Wedge shape, but it is often so stretched out that it is not worth looking it. The reversal from the overshoot is reason enough to enter.

If a Wedge triggers an entry but then it fails and the market extends one or more ticks beyond the Wedge extreme, it will often run quickly to a Measured Move (about the same height of the Wedge). Sometimes, just after failing, it reverses back and creates a second attempt at reversing the trend, and when this happens, the new trend is usually protracted (lasting at least an hour), and it usually has at least two legs.

Sometimes the second push has more momentum than the first, and if it does, ignore the first and assume that the second is actually the first push. The second and third pushes that follow are two attempts to extend the trend, and both failed. Two legs are always expected after any strong move.

When a Wedge occurs as a pullback after the first leg of a reversal, it usually does not exceed the start of the trend but sometimes does. In either case, a trader should be looking for the second entry into the possible new trend, expecting the test to hold (for example, in a new bull, as a Higher Low or Lower Low).

Three Push, low momentum, Countertrend moves that last for a couple of hours in the middle of the day are common and setup a thrust into the close, resuming the trend from the open. View this as a type of Wedge for the following reasons: it has Three Pushes; there is often a trend channel line overshoot; it often has the shape of a Wedge; and it has the same behavior as a Wedge. Remember, if you see everything in shades of gray, you will be a much better trader.

When there are three or more pushes and each breakout is smaller, then this is called Shrinking Stairs. For example, if there are Three Pushes up in a bull and the second push was 10 ticks above the first and the third was only 7 ticks above the second, then this is a Shrinking Stair pattern.

It is a sign of waning momentum and increases the odds that there will be a two-legged reversal. Sometimes there will be a fourth or fifth step in a strong trend, but since the momentum is waning, Countertrend trades can usually be taken. On the other hand, if the third step is significantly beyond the second and then reverses, this is likely a Trend Channel Line overshoot and reversal entry.

Sometimes the third push undershoots the second one and forms more of a double top, but the meaning is the same, and it is still a reversal setup. When the third push greatly undershoots the second, a Head and Shoulders reversal pattern forms.

Remember that sometimes a Failed Final Flag grows into a Wedge flag that often becomes a second, larger Failed Final Flag. For example, in a bear Failed Final Flag, the highest point of the bear flag becomes the first point of the Wedge and the failed breakout becomes the second. The two or more legged rally that follows becomes the rest of the Wedge, which is a large bear flag. It might become a Failed Final Flag and then reverse the market up, or it can be a continuation pattern in a larger bear, or the market can go sideways.

The shorts enter on a stop at one tick below the failure bar near the top of the range, and the longs buy on a stop at one tick above the failed breakout bar near the low of the range. Breaking out beyond any swing high or low, even if it was part of an earlier and opposite trend, is a sign of strength and a potential trade setup. Notice that Bar 12 in Figure 8.25

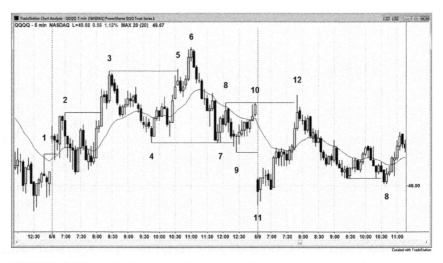

FIGURE 8.25   In Trading Range Markets, Fading Breakouts Is a Good Strategy

rallied above a swing high in the prior downtrend and then failed after the pause bar that followed (Bar 12 was also Three Pushes up and a failed trend channel line breakout created by using the highs of the first two minor swing highs on the day, but this is not shown). Several trades were also failed trendline and failed trend channel line breakouts as well.

Bars 2, 3, and 6 also represent a Shrinking Stair pattern, which often leads to a good reversal. With Shrinking Stairs, the second breakout is smaller than the first, indicating loss of momentum. Here, Bar 3 is 19 cents above Bar 2, but Bar 6 is only 12 cents above Bar 3. Whenever Shrinking Stairs are present, the trade becomes more likely to be successful and usually signals an imminent two-legged pullback in a strong trend.

Bar 3 is an example of a Failed Final Flag that expanded into a Wedge, or sorts. The first leg of the Wedge (the first push down) is the low of the Final Flag, on the bar before Bar 3. Bar 3 is the second leg. The two legs down to Bar 4 make up the rest of the Three Pushes Down. This became a larger bull flag that ultimately was the last one in the bull swing.

Shrinking Stairs, with each breakout extending less than the prior one, signal waning momentum and increase the odds that a profitable Countertrend trade is near. After the Bar 4 step in Figure 8.26, the move to Bar 5 broke the trendline, setting the stage for a test of the Bar 4 low and a likely two-legged rally (which occurred after the Bar 6 Lower Low).

Bars 3–5 show a Failed Final Flag growing into a Wedge bear flag, which became a larger Failed Final Flag.

FIGURE 8.26 Shrinking Stairs

FIGURE 8.27 Wedge Pullback

The daily SPY topped in March 2000, and then there was a Three Push rally to Bar 8 in Figure 8.27. Bar 8 also formed a Double Top Bear Flag with Bar 2 (it slightly exceeded the Bar 2 high). Bar 8 did not quite reach the bear trend channel line. This Wedge Lower High was followed by a huge bear.

The daily Dow in Figure 8.28 broke a major trendline in a two-legged move down to Bar 6, well below the EMA. There was then a small Three

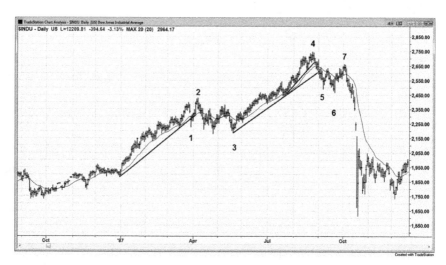

FIGURE 8.28 Three Pushes Up to a Lower High

Push up move that formed the Lower High at Bar 7 that led to the 1987 crash.

Bars 3, 4, and 5 in Figure 8.29 formed a Wedge, but Bar 5 did not overshoot the trend channel line. The Bar 5 inside bar with a bear close was a reasonable Low 2 short setup.

Bar 6 was a second entry on the failed High 2. This was a small Spike and Trading Range top as well.

Bars 7, 8, and 9 created a Three Push long setup with an entry above the Bar 9 bull reversal bar, even though the close was midrange. The day was clearly not a trend day so a weaker reversal bar is acceptable. This pattern had diverging lines, although it was not an Expanding Triangle since the high after Bar 8 was below the high after Bar 7. Bar 9 did not overshoot the trend channel line, but it was still a good long setup on a trading range day.

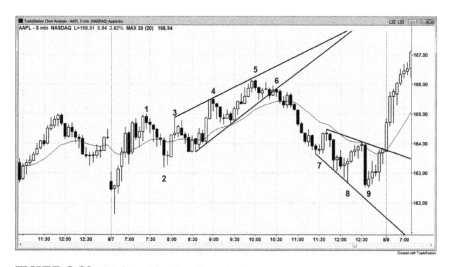

FIGURE 8.29 Wedge without an Overshoot

EXPANDING TRIANGLES

An Expanding Triangle is a type of Three Push pattern and can be either a reversal or a continuation pattern and is made of at least five swings (sometimes seven, and rarely nine), each one greater than the prior. Part of its strength comes from its trapping traders. In a bullish reversal, it has enough strength to rally above the last Lower High, trapping longs in, and then collapsing to a new low, trapping longs out and bears in, and then reversing up, forcing both sides to chase the market up. In a bear reversal, it does the opposite. Bears are trapped in by a Lower Low, then they are forced out and bulls get trapped in by a Higher High, and both then have to chase the market down as the market reverses down for the final time. The initial target is extending beyond the opposite side of the triangle, where the market often then sets up an Expanding Triangle flag (a continuation pattern) in the opposite direction. The term "triangle" is misleading because the pattern often does not look anything like a triangle. The salient point is that it is a series of progressively greater Higher Highs and Lower Lows that continue to trap breakout traders, and at some point they capitulate, and then all of the traders are on the same side, creating a trend. It has three pushes and can be viewed as a variation of a Three Push Reversal pattern, but with deep pullbacks. For example, in a reversal of a bear swing, both pullbacks form Higher Highs but in a conventional Three Push pattern like a Wedge, both pullbacks would form Lower Highs (i.e., not an expanding pattern).

The Emini in Figure 8.30 ran up off an Opening Reversal from the Bar 6 gap pullback test of the EMA and yesterday's close. Yesterday's low at Bar 5 formed an Expanding Triangle bottom (a reversal pattern, since the trend was down prior to the triangle), which often runs to a new swing high and then forms an Expanding Triangle bear flag (continuation pattern). It did that at the Bar 7 overshoot of the bull trend channel line (the triangle was formed by Bars 2, 3, 4, 5, and 7). After a trend channel line failed breakout, especially when there is an Expanding Triangle, there is usually a two-legged move down. Incidentally, Expanding Triangles don't have to

FIGURE 8.30 Expanding Triangle Bottom

have a perfect shape, and they do not have to touch the trend channel lines (Bar 5 fell short).

The rally up to Bar 7 was very strong, but the Low 2 short was worth taking under these circumstances (an Expanding Triangle and a small Failed Final Flag). Bar 8 was the second doji in a row, and dojis represent an equilibrium between bears and bulls. Since they are in balance, that balance point is often the midpoint of the move down and is a rough guide for how much further down the market might go in its search for enough buying power to swing the market back up. The target was hit at Bar 9, but the market did not rally until after overshooting the bear trend channel line and reversing up at Bar 10. Bar 10 also tested the original long entry above the Bar 6 signal bar to the exact tick (a perfect Breakout Test).

In an Expanding Triangle reversal pattern, the lows keep getting lower, and the highs keep getting higher. Typically, there are five turns before the reversal but sometimes seven, as in the 5-minute SPY above. There are usually valid reasons to scalp each leg (for example, each leg is a new swing high or low), but once the fifth leg is complete, a larger trend can develop, and it is wise to swing part of the position. Also, once the pattern completes, it usually sets up an Expanding Triangle pattern in the opposite direction. If the first was a reversal pattern, then the next part of this pattern (which will be in the opposite direction), if it develops, will be a continuation pattern and vice versa.

Bar 5 in Figure 8.31 was then the fifth leg (Bar 1 was the first) and therefore a buy setup for at least two legs up. However, Bar 6 was a failed

FIGURE 8.31 Expanding Triangle Bottom

breakout short setup and a small Wedge, creating an Expanding Triangle bear flag (the first of its five swings is Bar 2).

The seventh leg had a second entry at Bar 8 (Bar 7 was the first setup at a new low, but it failed, as expected since the entry was above a Barb Wire pattern and should not be taken).

Bar 10 tested the Bar 8, but its low was one tick higher. However, as a test of yesterday's low and a High 2 and EMA Gap 2 Bar, it was a good Opening Reversal. It was also similar to a ninth leg of an Expanding Triangle, and in trading, similar is usually good enough.

Bar 11 was a Breakout Pullback from taking out the high of the open, even though it did not break above the Bar 9 high of the triangle.

Bar 12 was a Low 2 and a one-tick bear Breakout Failure on this SPY chart (it traded one tick below the prior bar but then traded above its high). The Emini chart, however, held above the reversal bar's low and did not trigger the short. The Emini gives fewer false signals because each tick is 25 cents and a false signal would have to be a 25 cent move, which is equivalent to 2.5 cents in the SPY. Since there was no significant bull trendline break (the up momentum was strong), this is not a short setup.

Bar 13 is a second entry for the Breakout Failure short above Bar 9, but again there was no trendline break earlier in the rally, so it would be unwise to short in the absence of some earlier bear strength. Instead of Breakout Failures, Bars 12 and 13 were Breakout Pullbacks.

Bars 1–5 in Figure 8.32 created the five legs of the Expanding Triangle bottom. The entry is one tick above the Bar 5 Lower Low. Bar 6 failed to

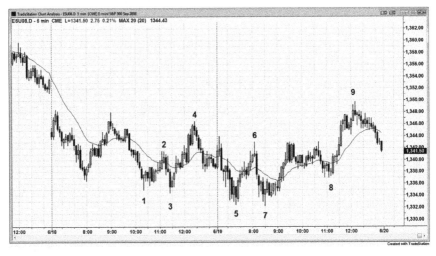

FIGURE 8.32 Expanding Triangle Bottom

take out the high of Bar 4 before dropping to a new low. Bar 7 is a second-chance entry at the Expanding Triangle bottom, but with this many bars between Bars 5 and 7, the triangle has lost its influence, and this is now just a reversal from a new low on the day.

Bar 8 formed a Higher Low that was also a Double Bottom (Bars 5 and 7) Pullback long.

After reaching the target of a new swing high, Bar 9 set up an Expanding Triangle bear flag (Bars 2, 3, 4, 7, and 9), and this short has a target of below the Bar 7 low. Eventually, however, one of these increasing larger triangles fails, and a trend begins. Incidentally, the market gapped below Bar 7 on the open of the next day, reaching the target.

CHAPTER 9

Minor Reversals: Failures

E very pattern fails some of the time, and traders should accept that as a normal occurrence, which sometimes offers other opportunities. Also, the failure can fail, resulting in a resumption of the original move. A failure is any trade that does not reach its goal, resulting in either a smaller profit or, more commonly, a loss. For a scalper, the goal is a scalper's profit. But if a trader was expecting more and the market failed to meet his expectation, even if it provided a scalper's profit, it is still a failure. Failures are often excellent setups for trades in the opposite direction, since the traders who were just forced out will be hesitant to re-enter in the same direction, making the market one-sided. In addition, as they exit with their losses, they drive the market even further in the opposite direction.

If a trade makes a scalper's profit (and therefore the trader exited some or all of his position) and then comes back and takes out the original signal or entry bar stops, there is much less fuel left in the market to drive the market in this new direction because there are far fewer traders who are trapped. Also, many of the scalpers would exit the balance of their positions at breakeven after taking partial profits, so their stops would be tighter than the original ones beyond the entry or signal bars.

Although a minor reversal might just be a reversal in a trading range that is good for only a scalp, it can sometimes turn into or be a part of a major reversal of a trend. The single most reliable minor reversal is one that takes place at the end of a pullback in a strong trend, especially near the EMA, because you are then entering in the direction of a larger trend and it is reasonable to expect at least a test of the prior extreme of the trend. Any reversal pattern, including major reversal patterns, can fail and result in the resumption of a trend.

FAILED SIGNAL AND ENTRY BARS AND ONE-TICK FAILED BREAKOUTS

When traders enter a trade, many place a protective stop at one tick beyond the signal bar. After the entry bar closes, many move it to one tick beyond the entry bar. How do you know this? By simply looking at charts. Look at any chart and find possible signal and entry bars, and see what happens when a bar reverses beyond them. So much of the time, the reversal will be in the form of a strong trend bar, and most of the time the move will be enough for at least a scalper's profit. This is because once traders get flushed out of a new position with a loss, they become more cautious and want more price action before re-entering in the same direction. This leaves the market in the hands of just one side, so the move is usually fast and big enough for a scalp.

Why is a one-tick failed breakout so common, especially in the Eminis? With stocks, failures often come on 1 to 10 cent breakouts, depending on the price of the stock and the personality of the stock. Every stock has distinct characteristics in its trading, presumably because many of the same people trade it every day, so a small group of traders trading sufficient volume can move the market enough to create recurring patterns. If the market is sideways to down in a weak bull, many traders will believe that if the current bar extends one tick above the prior bar, traders will buy there on a stop. Most smart traders will expect this. However, if enough other traders with enough volume feel that the correction has not extended deep enough or long enough (for example, if they believe that a two-legged move is likely), those traders might actually go short at one tick above the prior bar. If their volume overwhelms the new longs, and not enough new longs come to the rescue, the market will likely trade down for a tick or two.

At this point, the new longs are feeling nervous. If their entry was at such a great price, why didn't more buyers come in? Also, now that the market is even a tick or two cheaper, this should look like even better value to traders looking to get long, which should quickly drive the price up. But the longer the market stays down even just a couple ticks, the more new bulls will become concerned that they may be wrong. Some will start selling out at the market, adding to the offers, and others will place sell exit stop orders at one or two ticks lower, maybe basing these orders on a 1- or 3-minute chart, with the order one tick below the most recent bar.

Once these are hit, these new buyers will also become sellers, pushing the price further down. Also, the original shorts will sense that the new longs are trapped and many will increase their short positions. As price falls three, four, or five ticks, the stopped out buyers will switch from looking to buy to waiting for more price action to unfold. In the absence of buyers, price will continue to fall in search of enough bids to satisfy the sellers. At some point, sellers will begin to cover and take profits, slowing the price fall, and buyers will again begin to buy. Once the buying pressure overtakes the selling pressure, the price will then go up again.

A One-Tick Failure is a common source of losses for a new trader. The trader will see what he believes is a good setup, for example, a buy, and he confidently places a buy stop order at one tick above the high of the prior bar. As expected, the market ticks up and hits his entry stop, making him long. But the very next tick is one tick lower, then two, then three, and within 30 seconds, he loses two points as he watches his protective stop get hit. He wonders how anyone could be selling exactly where he was buying. It was such a great setup! Almost invariably, he was buying Countertrend before there was a sign of bullish strength, like a prior surge above a bear trendline. Or he was buying above a huge doji with a tiny body at the top of Barb Wire or a bear flag that he misread as a reversal, overcome by his eagerness to get in early in what he perceived as an overdone bear.

A third common situation is when there is a huge trend bar with a tiny tail or no tail. If it is a bull trend bar, lots of traders will put their protective stops at one tick below the bar. It is common for the market to work its way down and hit the stops, trapping traders out, and then reversing back up in the direction of the trend bar.

Finally, Breakout Tests often test the entry price to the exact tick, trapping out weak hands who will then have to chase the market and re-enter at a much worse price.

What that novice trader doesn't realize is that lots of big traders view these as great short setups and they are happy to short, knowing that only weak hands would be buying, and as they are flushed out, they will help drive the market down. A One-Tick Failure is a reliable sign that the market is going the other way, so look for setups that allow you to enter. All of the above is true for down markets as well, and all of the One-Tick Failures can sometimes be two ticks, and even five to ten ticks in a $200 stock.

Here in Figure 9.1 are six examples of one-tick false breakouts (the label for Bar 1 is well above the bar). Once the breakout traders enter on their stop and discover that the market is pulling back by a tick or two instead of immediately continuing in their direction, they start to place protective stops, and Countertrend traders smell the blood and will enter just where the trapped traders are taking their losses.

FIGURE 9.1 One- and Two-Tick False Breakouts Leading to Reversals Are Common in the 5-Minute Emini

There were many examples of One-Tick Traps in these two days in the Emini in Figure 9.2.

Bar 1 is a One-Tick failed Low 2 in Barb Wire.

Bar 2 is a One-Tick failed High 2 in Barb Wire that trapped traders who thought that they were being conservative by waiting to buy above the large outside bar only to be trapped buying at the top of a trading range below a flat EMA.

Bar 3 was a One-Tick Failed Reversal in a runaway bull where smart traders were eagerly waiting for any pullback to buy (here, a High 1).

FIGURE 9.2 One-Tick Traps

Bar 4 broke one tick below the small swing low of four bars earlier.

Bar 5 was a large bull trend bar, and there would therefore be stops at one tick below its low. These were run by one tick on Bar 7.

Bar 9 went one tick lower, trapping traders into what they thought was a Lower High short but actually was a sideways bull flag.

Bar 10 ran the breakeven protective stop for the Bar 6 shorts by two ticks.

Bar 14 is one of the most reliable One-Tick Failures . . . a failed High 2 in what novice traders erroneously assumed to be a bull pullback. This is a perfect trap and lead to a strong down move (not shown). They missed noticing the trendline break by the pullback to Bar 11 and then the Higher High test at Bar 12. Also, there were five bear trend bars and one doji down from the high and no trendline break after the Bar 13 High 1. This was not a good High 2 long setup since there was no prior strength. Remember, a High 2 alone is not a buy signal. There have to be signs of strength, and certainly not signs of a reversal (like a trendline break and reversal down off a Higher High).

The horizontal lines are one tick beyond signal and entry bars and are likely places where traders would place their protective stops.

Look what happened in Figure 9.3 when protective stops are hit beyond signal and entry bars. Most of the time, there is a trend bar, and the move is big enough for a scalper to make a profit. Many of the failures on this chart were for weak setups that smart Price Action traders would not have taken. However, enough traders took them so that they moved the

FIGURE 9.3 When Stops Are Hit, the Market Usually Continues to Move Far Enough for a Scalp

market in the opposite direction as they were forced out with a loss. For example, traders who went long off the Bar 4 reversal would have their stops either below the entry or signal bars. Both were run by the big Bar 5 bear trend bar, and smart shorts who had their entry stops at those exact locations made at least a scalper's profit.

As a corollary, if the extreme of the bar is tested but not exceeded, the stops are tested but not hit, and the trade will often be profitable. If it is a protective stop on a long entry that is missed by one tick, the test effectively forms a Double Bottom Bull Flag, with the first bottom being the bottom of the signal or entry bar and the second one being the bar that came back to that level but failed to reach the protective stops.

FAILED HIGH/LOW 2

A High or Low 2 is one of the most reliable With Trend setups. If a trade fails, there will usually be at least two more corrective legs before a High or Low 4 once again tries to end the correction. If a High or Low 4 fails, the pullback might have become a new trend, and further price action is needed before placing more trades.

The most common cause of a High or Low 2 failure is that the trader is in denial about a strong trend and is looking for a Countertrend entry before there has been a strong trendline break. This is common after a climax reversal and the trader is still looking to enter in the direction of the old trend, which no longer is in effect. These are not reversal patterns in strong trends and in fact are With Trend setups. When they fail, they almost always result in a With Trend entry. In a bull, a failed Low 2 will often be a High 2 long entry.

A Triple Bottom and a Double Bottom Pullback are both failed Low 2 long setups. In both cases, the market made two attempts to continue the bear downward, and both failed. Whenever the market tries to do something twice and it fails both times, it will usually do the opposite. The With Trend traders will wait for more price action, and the Countertrend traders know that they are in control, at least for a scalp.

A Low 2 setup is not enough reason to take a Countertrend trade in the absence of a prior strong trendline break. In fact, it will almost always fail and turn into a great With Trend entry, like a High 2 buy, as happened at Bars 4 and 6 in Figure 9.4. Before shorting a strong bull, you first need the bears to show that they have already been willing to be aggressive. You look to short their second attempt at pushing the market down, not their first, since the first usually fails.

Today in Figure 9.5 there was a gap down Double Top (at Bar 2) and then a new low. At this point, traders do not know if the two legs down

FIGURE 9.4   A Failed Low 2 Top in a Bull Is a Great With Trend Long

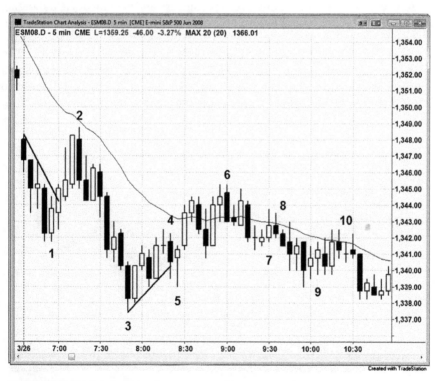

FIGURE 9.5   A Failed Low 2 in a Bear Pullback Is Usually a Buy Setup

to Bar 3 ended a move or if there is more to come (the first leg was from yesterday's close down to Bar 1). Although the Bar 4 Low 2 short reached its scalper's profit target and therefore could not technically be a failure, the break below the trendline and the reversal up made it likely that the market would behave like a failed Low 2 and have at least two more legs up and then attempt to form a Low 4 bear setup.

There were a couple of problems with the Low 2 short at Bar 4. First, it followed a trendline break (the rally up to Bar 2), which meant that Bar 3 could be the low of the day (a bad place to be shorting) since the high or low of the day usually develops in the first hour or so. Next, the Low 2 was too far from the EMA and therefore not a good EMA test. Normally, second tests of the EMA are closer to the EMA or penetrate it more than the first, and the first test at Bar 2 was clearly closer. Many traders won't feel comfortable entering With Trend unless the pullback touches or comes within a tick or so of the EMA. When the reversal begins before this happens, it will be missing the fuel that those shorts would have provided.

Bar 6 formed a Low 4 setup and was the second push above the EMA. However, this rally had many overlapping bars and several dojis, indicating that the bulls and bears were fairly balanced and a big, fast move down was unlikely. Therefore, trading at this point might not be worthwhile for traders who prefer high-probability trades with big profit potential. The solution? Either wait for more price action, knowing that good setups will always come if you can be patient, or take the short but be prepared to allow for a pullback, like the one on the bar after entry.

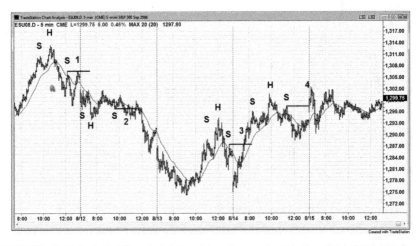

FIGURE 9.6 A Failed Head and Shoulders Pattern Is Usually a With Trend Setup

Bar 2 in Figure 9.6 took out the right shoulder of a Head and Shoulders Bottom (a failed attempt at a Higher Low), and this led to a strong resumption of the bear trend.

Bars 3 and 4 had strong breakouts above the right shoulder (Lower High) of Head and Shoulders tops.

Bar 1 attempted to rally above the Lower High (right shoulder) and failed, creating a Double Top Bear Flag setup.

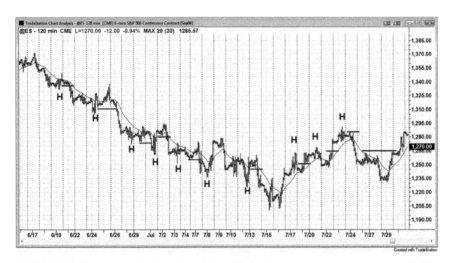

FIGURE 9.7 Many Failed Head and Shoulders Patterns

Most Reversal Patterns fail and become two-legged pullback continuation patterns. Note the large bars and strong momentum in Figure 9.7 when the right shoulders are taken out (the break beyond the line drawn across the right shoulder), forcing out reversal traders with a loss and also indicating strong With Trend traders entering on the failed Higher Lows (in the bear leg) and the failed Lower Highs (in the bull leg).

FAILED HIGHER HIGH AND LOWER LOW BREAKOUTS

Most days are trading range days and offer many entries on failed swing high and low breakouts. You can also fade new swing highs and lows on trend days after a minor trendline break and when there is a strong reversal bar.

When the price goes above a prior swing high and the momentum is not too strong, place an order to short the Higher High at one tick below the low of the prior bar on a stop. If the order is not filled by the time the bar closes, move the order up to one tick below the low of the bar that just closed. Continue to do this until the current leg gets so high and has so much momentum that you need more price action before shorting. That can be in the form of a second entry (a Low 2), a nominally Higher High, or a pullback that leads to a trendline break and then another Higher High. It is far more reliable if you wait for a signal bar with a strong bear close and beginners should restrict themselves to this type of fade setup.

Similarly, the first failed breakout below a prior swing low is a Lower Low buy setup, and you place an order to buy at one tick above the high of the prior bar on a stop. Again, the odds of success are greater if the setup bar is in the direction of your entry, so it is best to wait for a bull reversal bar before buying. If your order is not filled, keep lowering the order to one tick above the high of the prior bar, but if the market drops too far or too fast, wait for a second entry, a nominally Lower Low, or a pullback and another Lower Low setup.

The rally to Bar 1 in Figure 9.8 is strong, but since Opening Reversals are often sharp and it is a Higher High (above the swing high near yesterday's close) that broke above a bull trend channel line, it is a reasonable short. The short entry is either on the outside down bar or below the inside bar that followed it, which is a better choice since outside bars can be unreliable.

The Bar 2 pullback after the Bar 1 swing high is deep, and the bars today have been large with big tails. There is two-sided volatile trading,

FIGURE 9.8 A Failed Higher High Reversal Is Often a Buy Signal

and until a bull clearly develops, traders should assume that both bulls and bears are active. Since this has not proven itself yet to be a bull trend day, it should be traded as a trading range day. Bar 3 is a Higher High since it is a swing high that is above an earlier swing high. The momentum up to Bar 3 is too strong to consider a short without a second entry or a strong reversal bar, but if a trader shorted, the move down was 26 cents so it could have been minimally profitable.

Bar 5 is a Higher High and a reasonable short, especially since it has two small legs (there was a bear trend bar in the middle that represents the end of the first leg up from Bar 4). The market dropped only 18 cents before going back up. A nimble trader might have taken some off, but most would have just scratched the trade with a 4 cent loss.

Bar 7 is part of this same up move, so it was a second entry (a Low 2) short. Bar 7 was a Double Top with Bar 5 to the penny, and essentially a truncated Three Push Up pattern (Bars 3, 5, and 7), so two down legs should be expected.

Bar 10 was a Lower Low and the second leg down in a possible larger bull (its low was above the Bar 2 low, so the market might still be forming large bull trending swings). Two legs down in a bull or sideways market, especially two pushes below a flat EMA, is always a good long.

Bar 11 is a Higher High because it was above the Bar 9 swing high, even though Bar 9 was part of the prior down leg. There will still be traders who will trade there (there will be stops on shorts, stops to buy the breakout, and new shorts), because going above any prior swing high is a sign of strength and a potential fade on a trading range day (look for breakouts to fail and signs of strength to lack follow through).

Bar 13 was one tick below Bar 11 and was a Double Top Bear Flag and therefore a short setup. It was two legs up from Bar 10 and the second leg above a flat EMA (Bar 11 was the first).

Bar 14 is a Lower Low for both the swing lows at Bars 10 and 12.

Incidentally, the longs from Bars 10 and 14 are both failed overshoots of a bear trend channel line drawn from Bars 4 and 8, increasing the chances of successful long trades.

AMZN has been prone to having large one-bar failed breakouts on the 5-minute chart, but even for AMZN today was unusual. After the climactic run up on the open in Figure 9.9 and then the large reversal down, the bulls and bears both demonstrated strength and increased the odds that any move by one side would be reversed by the other throughout the day (a trading range was likely). All of the labeled bars are failed breakouts. The Tight Trading Range began after Bar 3 and turned into a small Expanding Triangle (that ended at Bar 7) in the middle of the day that ended up trendless. By midday it was clear that the day was small and sideways, which greatly increases the chances that all breakouts would likely fail.

FIGURE 9.9   Failed Breakouts

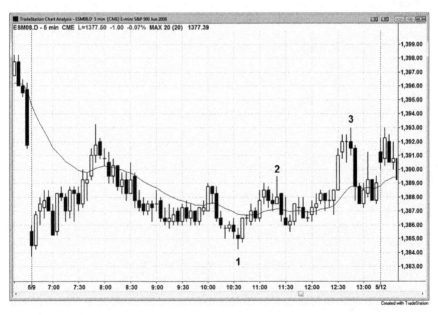

FIGURE 9.10   Second Entries on Breakout Fades

Bars 1, 2, and 3 in Figure 9.10 were second entries on breakout fades. The trend bar leading up to the Bar 3 top was very rapid and had big volume, sucking in lots of hopeful bulls who bet that there might finally be a trend. This is always a low-probability bet on a small day, and it is much better to fade the breakouts or look for strong Breakout Pullbacks. The breakouts to the Bar 1 low and the Bar 2 high were weak (tails, overlap) so it was likely both times that the breakouts would fail. The breakout that ended in Bar 3 never had a Breakout Pullback to give the bulls a low-risk long, so the only trade was the second entry short.

AAPL is one of the best behaved stocks for day traders. Like many other stocks, AAPL will sometimes trap traders out of great trades by running stops at the start of a reversal. Here in Figure 9.11, Bar 2 broke below Bar 1 by one tick before giving a second entry long on the next bar, after the Bar 2 test of the bear low after the trendline break. The first entry was two bars before Bar 2 at a High 2, but it followed five bear trend bars and was back into the Tight Trading Range. It made sense to wait for more price action, and the failed breakout below the tight range was perfect. What made it especially good was that it trapped new longs out and immediately reversed up on them, so psychologically it would be difficult for them to buy. They will then chase the market up, entering late, adding fuel to the upswing. This is also a Double Bottom Bull Flag (Bars 1 and 2).

FIGURE 9.11 Second Entry

FAILED TRENDLINES AND TREND CHANNEL LINES

Trendlines and trend channel lines should hold and lead to reversals away from the lines, indicating that they were successful in containing the trend. Sometimes one will fail to hold the price action, and the market will not stop and reverse on the test of the line. The breaking of a trendline has the opposite implication from the breaking of a trend channel line. The break of a trendline means that a possible trend reversal is underway, but breaking a trend channel line means that the trend has increased in strength and is now steeper.

A trendline break is the first step in a trend reversal, and if the break is on strength, the odds of a successful test of the trend's extreme increase. For example, after a bear trendline break, the test of the low would likely form a Higher Low and then at least a second leg up, or a Lower Low and then at least a two-legged up move.

Steep trendlines with one- or two-bar false breakouts are reliable With Trend patterns and therefore attract a lot of traders. However, whenever a reliable pattern fails, then there will be an unusually large number of trapped traders. The reverse move will likely be a profitable trade, and it can be sharp and result in a trend reversal. This is more common on 1-minute charts, but it is far better to not trade Countertrend off 1-minute charts since most reversals fail. You should almost always trade in the direction of the 5-minute chart.

Whenever a trend channel line fails (the market breaks through it instead of bouncing off it), you should assume that the trend is much stronger than you thought, and you should look for With Trend entries.

Bar 4 in Figure 9.12 was a strong breakout of the bear trendline after the Bar 3 Lower Low (Expanding Triangle bottom), so traders will look for a pullback and then a second leg up. A Higher Low can be followed by only a single up leg since that leg is already the second leg up from the low at the start of the move.

Bar 8 was the break of another bear trendline, so a test of the Bar 7 low should result in a long. A Lower Low usually is followed by two up legs.

Bar 9 is also a higher timeframe Higher Low compared to the Bar 3 low.

For example, Bar 1 in Figure 9.13 broke above a steep, three-bar Micro Trendline and then had a good short entry at one tick below its low.

Bar 3 was a strong bull reversal bar break above a steep Micro Trendline and therefore was a bear setup (any break above the trendline, even if it is by a strong bull reversal bar, is a setup for a short), and a short was triggered below the inside bar that followed. Bar 3 followed a

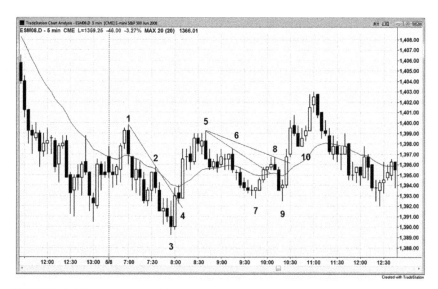

FIGURE 9.12 Breakout Pullbacks

break below an ii (a possible Failed Final Flag), but the ii did not break the trendline, and there was no other sign of bullish strength, so longs would want a second entry, which they got on Bar 4. Although a nimble scalper might have been able to make some profit on the 29 cent breakout to the Bar 4 low, it would have been difficult, so this is effectively a failed failure

FIGURE 9.13 One- or Two-Bar Failed Breakouts of Trendlines Are Usually Great With Trend Setups

(the market failed to make an easy short scalper's profit after it failed
to break above the bear trendline). Failed failures are usually good for a
two-legged move, and when it occurs with a Micro Trendline, it operates
like a breakout pullback long setup, even though it is a Lower Low. There
was a small two-legged rally after the entry on the Bar 4 outside bar. That
prior bar was the entry bar for the short from the failed Micro Trendline
break, and there are always stops above short entry bars, making the Bar
4 long even more certain.

Bar 6 broke above a steep Micro Trendline, setting up a short, which
failed on Bar 7. Bar 7 was also a High 2 in a trading range or weak bull and
arguably a Bull Flag Double Bottom (with Bar 5).

Bar 1 in Figure 9.14 broke above a steep Micro Trendline but there
was no pullback bar to setup a short . The general convention for trading
outside bars is to place entry stop orders at one tick above its high and one
tick below its low and enter on whichever is filled. However, in general, you
should wait for more price action, which is obviously what most traders
did, as seen by the sideways action.

Bar 2 was a second attempt to rally above that trendline and so was
a reasonable long entry, independent of the meaningless small sideways
outside Bar 1. It was effectively a Breakout Pullback long entry following
the Bar 1 breakout above the Micro Trendline. The next three bars tried to
pull back but failed (all had the same low and none was able to trade below
the prior bar), which is a sign that the bulls were taking a stand.

FIGURE 9.14   Failed Failure of Trendline Breakout

FIGURE 9.15 Failed Wedges Usually Result in at Least a Measured Move

Bar 4 in Figure 9.15 completed a Three Push down move from Bars 2 and 3, and also bounced off a bear trend channel line from Bars 1 and 3. However, the market went sideways rather than up. The bulls were not strong, so what appeared to be excess bearishness was not an excess at all. When a climax pattern fails to form any Countertrend momentum, then assume that you read the market wrong and are looking to trade in the wrong direction.

Bar 8 was a bull reversal bar until the final seconds when it quickly sold off into a bear trend bar. What overly eager bulls thought was going to be a bull reversal bar at the bottom of a Wedge and two bear trend channel lines turned into a bear breakout of the bear trend channel lines, which means that everyone now agrees that there is much more to go. This is confirmed by the series of bear trend bars that followed the Wedge reversal failure. If you watched the market action, you would have seen the bull reversal bar collapse into a bear trend bar, and you then would have shorted it, knowing that there were trapped early entry longs who bought what they thought was going to be a strong bull reversal bar off a bear trend channel line (don't front run the bars; always wait for them to close and the next bar to confirm the reversal). Even without knowing this, shorting one tick below the low of that bear trend channel line breakout is still a smart trade.

Bar 11 was another Three Push down pattern, but with all of those dojis and overlapping bars, a second signal was needed for any long, and traders should be looking for a small bar near the high of the Barb Wire to short (like Bar 12, which clearly trapped longs on the breakout from the bull reversal bar entry one bar earlier). Bar 12 was a bad bull reversal bar because it had too much overlap with the prior bars, forcing you to be buying near the high of a bear trading range (remember, buy low, sell high!). This has been a very strong bear trend day, and the best traders would not be looking for Wedges. Instead, they would be looking to short near the EMA. Since there were so few opportunities, the bears were very strong and smart shorts would be selling every failed buy signal as well as Low 1 and Low 2 entries.

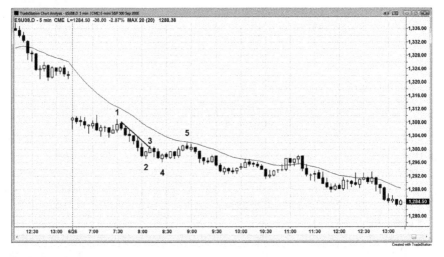

FIGURE 9.16   Failed Failure of a Trendline Breakout

Bar 3 in Figure 9.16 broke above a steep Micro Trendline, setting up a short. However, the failed trendline breakout failed two bars later at Bar 4 (technically, it did not fail because it reached a scalper's profit), and a failed failure is always a good setup (here, a Breakout Pullback long).

The trend is strong in Figure 9.17, and you are missing all of the With Trend shorts because all you are seeing are trend channel lines and potential reversals in what you believe is an overdone selloff in a trading range day (channels in Spike and Channel patterns always look that way). Be patient, and only trade With Trend until there is a reversal that is so clear and strong that you don't need to draw the line to see the excess, like the large Bar 6 that reversed yesterday's low and was a Three Push Down pattern (Bars 4, 5, and 6). Don't trade what you believe should be happening. Only trade what is happening, even if it seems impossible.

FIGURE 9.17 Whenever You Find Yourself Drawing Multiple-Trend Channel Lines, You Are Invariably Blinded to What Is in Front of You by Your Anxiety Over What You Can't Believe Is Happening

FAILED REVERSALS

All patterns fail, no matter how good they look. When they do, there will be trapped traders who will have to exit with a loss, usually at one tick beyond the entry or signal bars, and this is an opportunity for smart traders to enter for a low-risk scalp. Place your entry stop order at exactly the same place that these trapped traders are placing their protective stops, and you will get in where they will get out. They won't be eager to enter again in their original direction, and this makes the market one-sided in your direction and should lead to at least a scalp and usually a two-legged move.

Most are tradable, but always scalp out part of your position and move your stop to breakeven in case the pattern fails.

Bars 2 and 4 in Figure 9.18 formed a Double Top Bear Flag that failed, and the market then formed a Bars 3 and 5 Double Bottom Bull Flag.

You then had to reverse again at the Bar 4 and 6 Double Top Bear Flag, but you would have netted 70 cents from your long. At this point, you knew that the market was forming a trading range, likely a triangle.

Bar 7 was another failure but a good long since trading ranges following a strong move (the rally to Bar 1) are usually continuation patterns and Bars 3, 5, and 7 all found support at the EMA. When the prices are holding above a rising EMA, always look to buy above the high of the prior bar if that bar touches the EMA, especially if its close is in your direction.

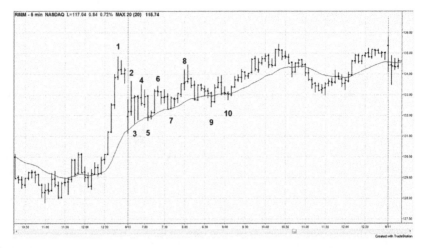

FIGURE 9.18 Stocks Commonly Form Double Top or Bottom Flags in the First Hour

The selloff to Bar 9 was seven bars long with no bullish strength so it would be better to wait for a second entry, despite Bar 9 being a Higher Low (compared to Bar 7).

The Breakout Pullback at Bar 10 was a perfect second entry long after the Micro Trendline breakout to the upside failed (it only gave the shorts a scalper's profit) and the failure failed at Bar 10.

Bar 4 in Figure 9.19 was a setup for a Double Bottom Bull Flag entry, but it failed with the Bar 5 M2S Breakout Pullback, which led to two legs

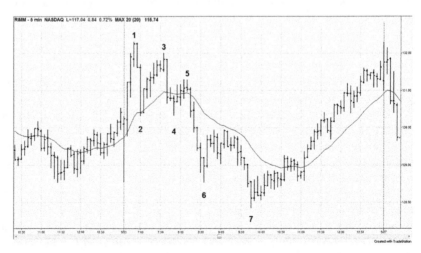

FIGURE 9.19 Failed Double Bottom Bull Flag

down. You could either short the M2S, or you could sell on a stop at one or two ticks below the Bar 4 low. When the market makes two attempts to do something (like rally off the price around the low of Bar 2) and fails, it usually will then do the opposite.

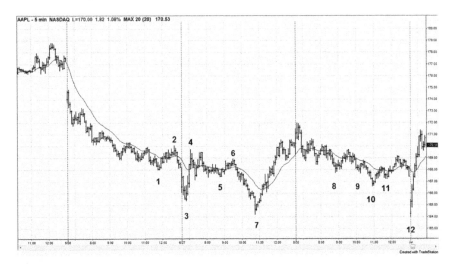

FIGURE 9.20 Most Head and Shoulder Patterns Fail and Become With Trend Setups

Bars 5 and 11 in Figure 9.20 were right shoulders of Head and Shoulder Bottoms, most of which fail, as they did here. The shape alone is not enough reason to place a Countertrend trade. You always want to see some prior Countertrend strength prior to the reversal pattern. Even then, there are no guarantees that the trade will be successful. Bar 2 broke a trendline, and the rally to Bar 4 was strong, although its failure to exceed the Bar 2 high was a sign of weakness. Although most smart traders would not have reversed to short at the Bar 6 failure after the Bar 5 Double Bottom Bull Flag long entry, they would have moved their stops to breakeven, thinking that if the stop was hit but the trade was still good, the stop run would set up a Breakout Pullback long setup. Here, the stop was hit, but the market kept selling off. The one-bar Breakout Pullback just after the breakout below Bar 5 was a great short.

The Bar 11 right shoulder was a buy, but again the breakeven stop would have been hit.

The selloffs to Bar 2 and to Bar 6 in Figure 9.21 broke major trendlines, so a two-legged test of the prior high should setup a good short. The Bar 3 Low 2 short was successful, either by shorting below Bar 3 or taking the second entry two bars later.

FIGURE 9.21 A Failed Reversal Is a With Trend Setup

The Bar 8 short is less certain because the test was a large bull trend outside bar (almost outside, since it had the same low as the prior bar). The traditional way to enter after an outside bar is on a stop at one tick beyond both extremes, getting filled in the direction of the breakout. However, outside bars are basically one-bar trading ranges, and most trading range breakout entries fail. You should only rarely enter on a breakout of an outside bar because the risk is too great (to the opposite side of the bar, which is large).

If you shorted at the Bar 8 breakout of the inside bar, you would be nervous by the bar's close (a doji bar, indicating no conviction). However, most traders would not have taken that short because three or more sideways bars where at least one is a doji usually create too much uncertainty (Barb Wire). The two small bars before the outside bar were small enough to act like dojis, so it is best to wait for more price action. However, if you did not short on Bar 8, you would have to believe that many did and the doji close of their entry bar has these traders feeling uncomfortable with their positions. They will be quick to exit and are therefore trapped. They will likely buy back their shorts at one tick above the Bar 8 entry bar and be reluctant to sell again until they see better price action. With the shorts out of the market and with them buying back their positions, going long exactly where they are exiting (Bar 9, one tick above the short entry bar) should be good for a scalp and likely two legs up. Either buy Bar 9 at one tick above the doji inside bar or above the Bar 9, relying on Bar 9 being a bull trend bar and therefore a good long signal bar.

FAILED FINAL FLAGS: TIGHT TRADING RANGE

A protracted trend often forms a horizontal flag that extends sideways for several bars, breaks a trendline, and then breaks out to a new extreme but quickly reverses in the next few bars. This Failed Final Flag breakout often marks the end of the trend and sometimes leads to a reversal. In most cases, there will be a tradable, extended Countertrend move that will have at least two legs. A key point is that the flag is usually mostly horizontal and often can be as simple as an ii pattern.

A horizontal area is an area of two-sided trading where the buyers and sellers are evenly balanced, and therefore this area acts as a magnet that pulls each little move up or down back to the center or opposite side. For example, after an extended bull move, if the bulls seize control and push the market up, they will likely be quick to take profits and the bears will be confident that the prior trading range (flag) was an area of balance and therefore likely to be tested. Usually, the bulls will be reluctant to be aggressive again until after at least a two-legged correction that extends well below the flag (the flag breakout failed).

A Micro Trendline Breakout Pullback is something of a Failed Final Flag. For example, when there is a break above a bear Micro Trendline and the market reverses down, but the selloff fails within a bar or two, the break above the trendline is effectively a Failed Final Bear Flag.

Sometimes a Failed Final Flag reversal just leads to the development of a larger flag with a Wedge shape. For example, in a Failed Final Flag in a bull, the first leg of that flag is the lowest bar of the Wedge. The second leg is the bar that reversed the market down below the flag. And the rest of the Wedge is the two or more legged selloff down. This is now a larger bull flag that usually leads to a bull breakout. The flag may become a larger Failed Final Flag or just a continuation pattern in a larger bull.

Bar 1 in Figure 9.22 ended two legs down from the open and was therefore a possible low of the day. It broke out of a sideways bear flag after a protracted move, so this could be a Failed Final Flag and a reversal up. Bar 1 was a good reversal bar, triggering the Failed Final Flag long, causing traders to expect at least two legs up.

The Bar 4 breakout above the open was on strength, and led to the formation of a Tight Trading Range in Figure 9.23. This often becomes the middle of the up move. Here, the strong breakout of the flag ended at Bar 7, which was a two-legged move up (Bar 5 was the first leg). Two-legged moves out of flags often set up a major reversal that typically has at least two legs. Instead of seeing Bar 6 as a Breakout Pullback long, you could read it as still part of the horizontal pattern and the end of the first leg

FIGURE 9.22 Failed Final Flag

FIGURE 9.23 Failed Final Flag

down from the Bar 5 high. The bear bar after Bar 6 becomes the second leg down and buying above its high is reasonable since you are buying after two attempts down in a bull failed. Always be thinking about what is taking place.

The move down to Bar 10 was in two legs, but it only had a single Countertrend bar (Bar 9), which means that it was likely going to be just the first leg of two larger legs.

The Bar 9 interruption was not strong enough to be considered the end of the first leg. In any case, if a short trader is unsure, he could move his stop to breakeven. Also, an outside bar at the start of trend should be considered as the true beginning of the trend and there will usually be at least two legs down following the outside bar, so the High 2 after Bar 10 is actually just a High 1. Also, it was a Micro Trendline short and therefore should be viewed as Low 1.

Bar 11 failed to run the stop, and the High 2 at the EMA (M2B) failed, as expected since it functionally was just a High 1, resulting in a strong bear. It was easy to anticipate that this High 2 would fail because smart traders would be regarding it as a High 1 and the Higher High at Bar 7 followed a trendline break so the trend should be considered down at this point. Smart traders would not be looking to buy a High 2, especially after an outside down bar, and especially since two clear down legs are likely. In hindsight, the Bar 4 trading range turned into a Failed Final Flag in the bull move up from Bar 1, but smart traders would have anticipated this possibility and swung part of their short.

FAILED FINAL FLAGS: HUGE TREND BAR

Sometimes a Final Flag can be only one or two bars long. This is common when the market is moving fast with unusually large trend bars. The breakout from that small flag often reverses after a bar or two, and this usually results in a two-legged pullback that lasts for an hour or more. This is a tradable Countertrend setup, but it does not reliably lead to a trend reversal. The strong momentum demonstrated by those large trend bars usually is followed by a test of the trend extreme.

Bar 3 in Figure 9.24 was a huge bear trend bar that followed four other strong bear trend bars after the market gapped above the bear trendline. The break of the bear trendline alerts traders to look for a test of the Bar 1 low of the bear to see if the sellers fail again around the same price level.

Bar 4 was the setup for a short off a small bear flag and the Micro Trendline Low 1. Given the climactic behavior of the market to this point

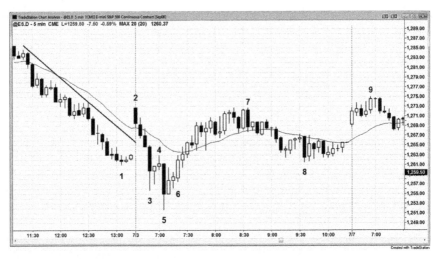

FIGURE 9.24 Failed Final Flag

and yesterday's trendline break, traders will be looking for this to be a Final Flag that will lead to a reversal up after a test of the Bar 1 Bear low.

Bar 5 was another huge bear trend bar, and Bar 6 was an ii long entry, with the expectation of a rally that will last at least an hour and have at least two legs up. Both ii bars had bull closes, which makes the chances for a successful long trade greater. The second leg occurred at Bar 9 on the following day. The strength of the downward momentum demonstrated by the large bear trend bars usually makes traders push the market down for a test of the low within a day or two. Although it is not shown, the Bar 9 high lead to a selloff later that day that went far below the Bar 5 low.

Bar 3 in Figure 9.25 was a two-bar pullback after a huge and possibly climactic bull trend bar, and therefore it is a possible Final Flag. Bar 4 was also a second leg up from yesterday's low (Bar 1 was the end of the first leg).

Bar 4 was an ii setup for a Failed Final Flag short that should be expected to lead to a two-legged, protracted correction, which it did. The Bar 3 bull flag turned out to be the Final Flag, and its breakout failed and reversed down after Bar 4. Note that the second bar of the ii pattern had a bear close, which is always desirable when a trader is looking to short. The first bar also had a bear close but the second bar is always more important because it is the more recent history.

The strong momentum up to the Bar 4 high made traders drive the market up to test the trend extreme later in the day.

FIGURE 9.25 Failed Final Flag

Bars 3–5 evolved into a larger Wedge-shaped bull flag. Bar 3 is the first push down and Bar 5 is the third. Three bars earlier was the second push down. The market then had a weak bull breakout of this downward sloping, Wedge-shaped bull flag, but failed in a Lower High at Bar 6. A Wedge flag can also lead to an extended bull move or become a larger Failed Final Flag.

FAILED WEDGES

Wedges most often fail when traders are overly eager to enter Countertrend, do not wait for a clear trendline break and countertrend strength, and fade the first small Three Push pattern that appears. Three Pushes alone, especially when small, will rarely reverse a trend in the absence of a prior trendline break or a major trend channel line overshoot and reversal. These Wedges should be viewed as With Trend setups, and smart traders will enter where the Countertrend traders will be taking their losses.

Sometimes after a Wedge reverses, the reversal fails, and the trend resumes only to be followed by a failed breakout to a new extreme. This is a failed failure, which is a second signal and therefore likely to result in at least a two-legged correction. For example, if there is a Wedge top in a bull and the market drops a little but then reverses strongly to a new high, and that new high fails, this can lead to a strong bear move since it is a second failure by the bulls to push beyond this price area. The move down from

FIGURE 9.26   A Failed Wedge Reversal Is a With Trend Setup

the original Wedge typically breaks the trendline, and the move to the new high is a Higher High test of the bull top and therefore a short setup.

The market tried to form a Wedge reversal in Figure 9.26 but Bar 3 was the third overlapping bar in a row in an area of dojis (Barb Wire). This is acceptance of the lower price and not rejection, so it made a reversal up unlikely. The Bar 3 entry bar was an outside up bar that trapped bulls who overlooked the absence of a significant overshoot of the bear trend channel line and only saw the Three Pushes. A Wedge is a type of climax reversal, so climactic behavior is needed for it to be effective. There needs to be a spike down and not a series of overlapping bars (a trading range or bear flag).

When a Wedge fails, the move will usually be an approximate Measured Move equal to the height of the Wedge (here, the move down below Bar 3 was about the same number of points as there were from the top of the Wedge just after Bar 1, to the bottom at the low of Bar 3).

The market was in a bear Trend from the First Bar on a gap down day in Figure 9.27. Overly eager bulls will rationalize buying the Bar 2 Wedge reversal by convincing themselves that it was the end of a two-legged move down and there was a trendline break at Bar 1. However, Bar 1 was a *failed* trendline break and did not represent the bulls' taking control of the market with any momentum. The Bar 2 Wedge long entry above the inside bar was a successful scalp but not a setup that would likely turn into anything more. The bear Micro Trendline from the open to Bar 2 is a sign of bearish strength. The move down to Bar 2 did not have a meaningful trendline

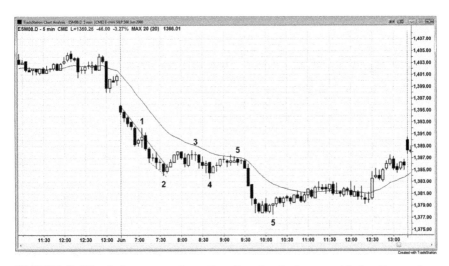

FIGURE 9.27 If There Is No Prior Trendline Break, Expect a Wedge Reversal to Fail, So Don't Fade the Trend

break or upward momentum in the middle and therefore looked more like a single leg down made up of two smaller legs. There should be a second leg down after a break of the bear trendline before any meaningful rally could be likely.

There was then a Low 2 short at Bar 3. This little rally did break a trendline so buyers could look for a scalp on a failed new low, which occurred at Bar 4. However, in the absence of a strong bull reversal bar, this long was likely to fail, which it did at the Bar 5 M2S short, and the market then broke down into the second bear leg that ended at the Bar 5 Failed Final Flag one-tick false breakout.

This was a Trend from the Open bear, which is one of the strongest types of bears and smart traders would be forcing themselves to take every short and would not be taking longs.

Bar 9 in Figure 9.28 was a bear trend channel line overshoot reversal and a Third Push Down (Wedge). However, it was not a strong bull signal bar because it overlapped the prior bar too much and had a weak close (small bull body). There is no clear rejection of excessive selling. At best, you should wait for a second entry before buying. Also, there was no prior bullish strength in the move down from Bar 5 so you should not be looking for longs.

Bar 10 was a One-Tick Failure for any traders who bought the Wedge. It was the third sideways bar, so now smart traders are seeing a trading range in a bear, which is usually a continuation pattern. Overlapping bars mean that the market is accepting these lower prices, not rejecting them.

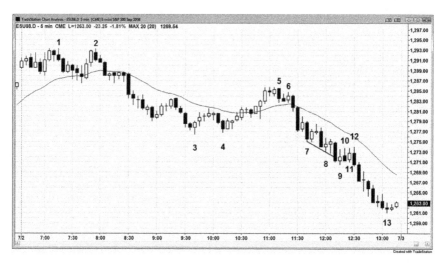

FIGURE 9.28 A Wedge without an Earlier Trendline Break Is Not a Reversal Setup

You need a sign of rejection before you buy in a bear. Basing a trade on a belief that the market is overdue for a correction is a losing approach to trading. Trends can go much further than most traders could ever imagine.

A trader could short the Low 1 at Bar 11, but this is a trading range, and smart traders will not short at its low without a stronger bull trap. It was a second One-Tick Failed Breakout. Also, a Wedge usually makes two attempts to rally (two legs up) so you should only short if the Wedge failed (that is, fell below the Bar 9 low), or if the second attempt to rally fails as it did at the Bar 12 Low 2 Short.

Bar 12 was a third One-Tick Failed Breakout in a row, but this time, it followed two legs up (Bars 9 and 11) and was Low 2 short. This is the first trade that smart traders would take, because it is a Low 2 in a bear flag. What made it especially good was that there were two failed attempts to make the Wedge reverse upward (Bars 10 and 12), and both failed. These represent the two legs up from the Wedge, and they are clearly weak. Also, three One-Tick Failures in a row is very rare, so it is likely that the next move would run, especially since it was With Trend in a trend day.

A trader could also have waited to short below the low of Bar 9 because it was only then that the Wedge definitively failed. The heavy volume on the breakout (14,000 contracts on the 1-minute chart) confirmed that many smart traders waited until that point to short.

Traders would have recognized this day as a Trending Trading Range day shortly after the breakout from the Double Top. It is usually safe to trade in both directions on this type of bear trend day, but the longs are

Countertrend so the setups must be strong, like those at Bar 3 and two bars after Bar 4 (second entry long).

To buy, you first need a trendline break, and it is better to have a reversal bar. Since Bar 9 was a weak reversal bar and you are inclined to buy after a trend channel line overshoot and reversal, you could wait for a second long entry. Bar 12 was a second entry, but it was a purchase at the top of a four-bar trading range, and you can never buy at the top of a bear flag. Once that weak second entry failed, the bears took control, and that was the trade that you needed to take instead of spending too much energy convincing yourself that the long setups were adequate.

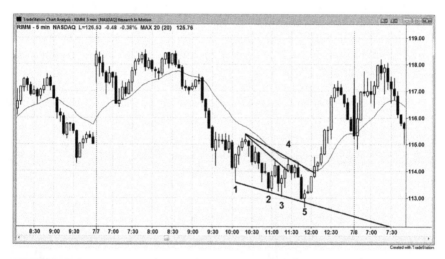

FIGURE 9.29 A Failed Failed Wedge (a Failure That Failed)

Bars 1, 2, and 3 in Figure 9.29 formed a Wedge reversal. Bar 4 broke above the trendline, but there was a Lower Low test of the Bar 3 low. Sometimes Wedges fail, and the failure fails, resulting in a Lower Low. This Lower low is a reversal because it followed a trendline break at Bar 4. Bar 5 also completed a larger Wedge bottom.

FAILED SCALPS: FIVE-TICK FAILED BREAKOUTS AND FAILURE TO REACH A SCALPER'S PROFIT TARGET

In the Emini, a very popular trade is a scalp for four ticks. In a trend, there may be a series of successful scalps, but when one hits the limit order and does not get filled, this Five-Tick Failure is a sign of a loss of momentum.

These are also common on 1- and 3-minute charts. Since a six-tick breakout is needed to make a four-tick scalp (one-tick for the stop entry, four-ticks profit, and usually one more tick to be sure the profit target limit order is filled), a move that goes only five ticks and then reverses often indicates that the trend traders have lost control and a pullback or reversal is imminent. There are comparable failures in other markets that have many scalpers, like the SPY and the QQQQ. For both, a common profit target is 10 ticks, which usually requires a 12-tick move beyond the signal bar. If the move only reaches 10 or 11 ticks (or even 8 or 9) and then reverses, it usually leads to at least a profitable scalp in the opposite direction, since the scalpers are trapped and will get out on the reversal of the signal or entry bars and add fuel to your trade.

If a stock reliably reaches more than a dollar on a scalp but then falls just short on two attempts at the one dollar target, then this is a good scalp in the opposite direction.

Scalping short for four ticks was a successful strategy for almost two hours. However, the short from the Bar 4 inside bar in Figure 9.30 dropped only five ticks and reversed up. This means that many shorts did not get

FIGURE 9.30 Five-Tick Failure in the Emini

filled on their profit target limit order and that the shorts were quick to exit at breakeven and certainly above Bar 5. The market was testing yesterday's low, and it was the second probe below the trend channel line (based on the trendline from Bars 1 to 3). The bulls were looking for reasons to buy, and the failed short scalp was the final thing that they were hoping to find.

Each of these 5-minute QQQQ trades in Figure 9.31 reached between 8 and 11 ticks before failing. The protective stops would get scalpers out

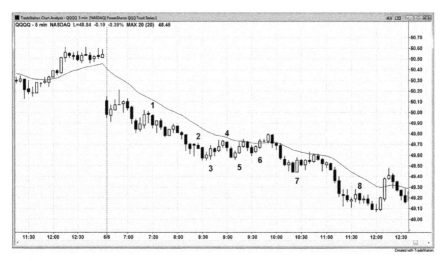

FIGURE 9.31 Failed Scalps Often Become Setups in the Opposite Direction

FIGURE 9.32 A Scalp That Just Misses Its Profit Target Is Often a Reversal Setup

at around breakeven in all of them, but it still was a lot of work with little to show. Clearly, however, there were many other profitable scalps, but it is tiring to scalp if there are too many unsuccessful trades, often making a trader lose focus and then miss profitable trades. On a clear Bear Trend from the Open day, the best approach is to only trade With Trend and look to sell M2S setups or simple Low 2s. Your winning percentage will be high, allowing you to have a healthy attitude and continue to take entries.

AAPL usually yields one-dollar scalps (the moves are usually more than one dollar, allowing a scalper to take partial profits on a one-dollar limit order). Bar 2 in Figure 9.32 extended only 93 cents above the entry above Bar 1, and then set up a Low 2 short. This Low 2 means that the market failed twice to reach the target. With the market largely sideways and just missing a one-dollar scalp, a trader would likely reduce his profit target to about 50 cents. He would have been able to take partial profits on this 61-cent drop.

CHAPTER 10

Day Trading

The first consideration in day trading is the selection of the market and type of chart that you want to use. It is best to trade stocks that are popular with institutions because you want to reduce the chance of manipulation by a specialist or market maker, and you want minimal slippage. There are so many great trades every day on any basket of 5 to 10 stocks that you won't have to resort to stocks with small volume that might carry additional risks.

The more bars in your day, the more trades you will make, and the risk per trade will be less. However, you might not be able to read the charts fast enough to see the setups, and you might not have time to place your orders without an unacceptable level of mistakes. There is a mathematical sweet spot that you will have to determine based on your personality and trading abilities. Most successful traders can trade a 5-minute chart. Reading a 3-minute chart is very similar and offers more trades and smaller stops, but in general it has a lower winning percentage. If you find that you are missing too many trades, especially the most profitable trades of the day, you should consider moving to a slower timeframe, like a 15-minute chart.

You can also use charts based on volume (like each bar representing 1,000 contracts) or ticks (for example, each bar representing 500 price changes or ticks) or simple bar charts. Line charts are also tradable, but a Price Action trader is giving up too much information when she cannot see bars or candles.

In general, since your risk per trade is smallest when you day trade, you should be trading your maximum number of contracts once you are consistently profitable (until then, you should trade only a single Emini or even only 100 SPY shares). Warren Buffet was quoted as saying, "If it's worth a penny, then it's worth a dime." Once you have decided that you have a valid entry, you need to be prepared to trade a reasonable number of contracts.

Traders are always thinking about the best way to maximize their profitability and the two most important considerations are trade selection and position size. A trader should focus primarily on taking only the best two to five entries each day, which are usually second entries in the form of reversals at new swing highs and lows on non-trending days (maybe 80 percent of days), and pullbacks on trend days. Once a trader is consistently profitable, the next goal should be to increase the position size rather than adding lower probability entries. If a trader consistently nets only one point a day in the Eminis but trades 25 contracts, this comes out to over $1,000 per day. If the trader can get up to 100 contracts, he will make $1,000,000 per year. If he nets four points a day, that is $4,000,000 per year. The Emini and Treasury Bond and Note markets can easily handle this size of trading. For very liquid stocks with prices over $100, an experienced trader can net 50 cents to a dollar on most days and these stocks can handle 1,000 to 3,000 share orders with minimal slippage. ETFs like the QQQQ can handle 10,000 share orders, but the daily range is smaller and a more realistic daily net would be about 10 to 20 cents for a good trader, or a couple hundred thousand dollars a year.

If a trader is managing a fund of $50,000,000 and he was trading 1,000 Emini contracts per trade (he might have to split his orders into 200 to 400 lot pieces), and he only netted a point per day, this would generate $10,000,000 for his clients before fees. Concentrate on taking the best trades and then increasing your volume.

SELECTING A MARKET

Price action techniques work in all markets but most day traders prefer markets that have many entries a day on the 5-minute chart and can handle large position sizes without slippage. The 5-minute S&P Emini futures contract can handle any order size that an individual trader can place; you will never outgrow it. The Russell, however, is popular with some individual traders because they feel that it trends well intraday and the margin is relatively small for the size of the average swing. Most successful individual traders eventually want to trade more contracts than the Russell can handle without the worry of slippage.

When starting out, you should consider trading the SPY instead of the Emini. If the Emini is trading around 1,100, the SPY will be around 110.00

and a four-tick scalp for one point in the Emini is a 10 cent scalp in the SPY (i.e., each Emini tick is two and a half times larger than an SPY tick). One Emini contract is identical to 500 SPY shares and if you trade 300 to 500 SPY, you can scale out of your swing position and not incur too much risk. One advantage of the SPY is that the 10 cent scalp value feels so small and comes so quickly that it will be easier to place orders for swing trades than for scalps, which is a better approach when just starting out.

Once you have increased your position size to 1,000 to 1,500 SPY, if you plan to continue to increase your size, switch to the Emini, which can handle huge volume without slippage being a significant problem. When just starting out, you can scalp 100 SPY and a 2-point Emini stop is the equivalent of a 20 cent SPY stop, so your risk is just $20 plus commissions. However, you cannot scalp and make money in the SPY unless your commissions are minimal, like one dollar for 100 shares. Also, you need an order entry system that allows you to quickly place orders. Otherwise, just swing trade until you are consistently successful, and then look to add some scalping.

Also, until you are profitable, you should only watch a single market because if you are not yet able to juggle one ball, it is foolish and expensive to try to juggle many more. Almost every major stock is well-behaved and tradable and it does not matter which you choose. What does matter is that you limit yourself to a single 5-minute chart of a single stock until you are consistently profitable. Even then, you will likely make more money if you stick to a single market. I trade stocks in addition to Eminis because it entertains me and makes me feel more a part of the trading world, which is good for my mental health because I am such a trading recluse. However, I would make more money if I just traded the Emini.

Currency futures and the Forex, and Treasury Bond and Note Futures can handle huge volume but give fewer entries than the Eminis on most days. Bonds and Notes can have protracted trends intraday so when a trade sets up, you can often enter and let it swing for hours. The Forex market usually doesn't offer many great trades during the Emini day session and since you don't want any distractions it is best to avoid it during the day. The DIA and Dow futures are a little thin so slippage can be a problem for scalpers. Just as the SPY is identical to the Eminis, the QQQQ is identical to the NASDAQ futures. Both can handle huge volume. The QQQQ is also very popular with day traders and can accommodate large orders.

Many stocks trade very well intraday and it is easiest to only trade those with an average daily range of several dollars and an average volume of 5 million shares or more. You want to be able to scalp 50 cents to a dollar with minimal slippage, and you want the possibility that the swing portion can run several dollars. Currently, AAPL, RIMM, GOOG, AMZN, GS, OIH,

DUG, UYG, and SKS are all good but there are many others and you can add or subtract from your list as needed. UYG's price is only around $10 but it can easily handle 3,000 share orders, so a 30-cent swing is about $900.

Later in the book in the Detailed Day Trading Examples chapter, there are charts of many markets that demonstrate possible price action trading.

TIME FRAMES AND CHART TYPES

For a scalper, it is easiest to use a 5-minute candle chart for the Emini. However, for intraday swing trading of the Emini or stocks, a simple 5-minute bar chart works well. This is because on a laptop or a single monitor you can fit six bar charts on your screen (Figure 10.1), each with a different stock, and each chart will contain a full day's worth of bars. If you use candles, which are wider than bars, your charts will only show about a half day of price action. An important reason for mentioning this is to remind traders that this approach works well with simple bar charts, especially when you are only trying to swing trade the best entries. The advantage of candle charts on the Emini for scalpers is that is it easy to quickly see who owns the bars, especially the setup bar. Also, a lot of High and Low 2 variants are not easy to see on bar charts.

Do you think that you can trade smaller time frames like the 3-minute or even 1-minute? If so, try it with 100 SPY shares for a couple of hours. Then look at the chart and honestly ask yourself if you read the price action correctly and correctly placed your entry, stop, and profit orders on at least four of the past five most recent setups. If you did, you might be able to do it, especially with the 3-minute, but I have yet to meet anyone who can do it on the 1-minute, especially for the 40 to 50 trades that occur every day on that time frame, and then do it year after year. Be realistic. If this is a job, you have to be able to do it for the long haul and it has to have minimal stress and you have to be satisfied that you are doing it really well. The 5-minute is the sweet spot and it offers at least 10 trades a day and gives you time to think about the setups and to place your orders. It can also handle whatever volume that you will ever trade. The 3-minute also works well but it is likely that you will end up cherry-picking too often and your winning percentage will be less.

When there is a trend, look to enter With Trend on a pullback, like an M2B in a bull or an M2S in a bear. Also, after a strong trendline break, look to enter Countertrend on a test, like a Higher Low or Lower Low in a possible new bull, if there is a strong reversal bar.

Price action trading techniques work in all market and all time frames, so a trader has to make the obvious basic decision of which markets and time frames he should trade. The objective of most traders is to maximize

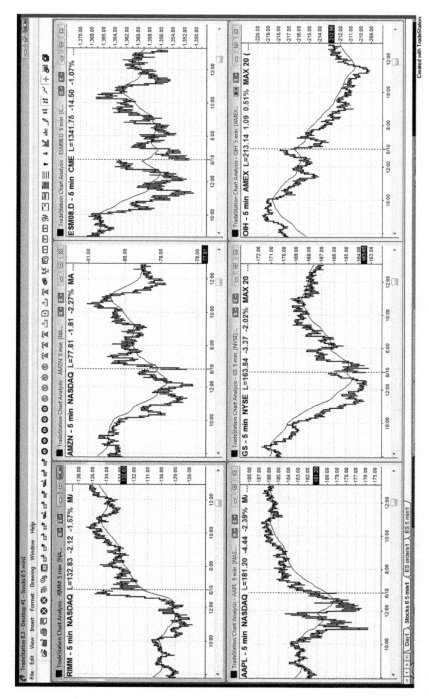

FIGURE 10.1 A Simple Bar Chart Is All That Is Necessary to Swing Trade Using Price Action

Created with TradeStation

profitability over the long run, and implicit in that is finding an approach that suits his personality.

If a 5-minute Emini chart offers a dozen good entries on average every day, and the 3-minute offers 20, and the 1-minute offers 30, and the risk (size of the protective stop) is eight ticks on the 5-minute, and six ticks on the 3-minute, and four ticks on the 1-minute, why not trade the shorter time frames? More trades, smaller risk, more money . . . right? Right, if you can read the charts correctly fast enough in real time to be able to place your entry, stop, and profit target orders at the exact prices correctly, and do this constantly for 7 hours a day, year in, year out. For many traders, the smaller the time frame, the more good trades they miss and their winning percentage goes down. They simply cannot scalp with this method fast enough on the 1 and 3-minute charts to be as profitable as they are on the 5-minute chart, so that should be their focus and they should continually work on increasing their position size. The best trades often come as a surprise and the setups can be hard to trust and most traders simply cannot process the information fast enough. Invariably, they will cherry pick and tend not to pick the very best setups, which are the most important ones to their bottom lines.

The average size of a move on a higher timeframe chart is greater than that on a smaller timeframe chart. However, almost every higher timeframe swing starts with a reversal on the 1- and 3-minute charts. It is just hard to know which ones will work and it can be draining trying to take 30 or more trades a day, hoping for a big move. The very best trades on 1- and 3-minute charts lead to strong entries on 5- and 15-minute charts and for most traders, it is much more profitable to focus on the best 5-minute trades and work on increasing their position size. Once they can trade successfully, they can make an incredible amount of money and have a very high winning percentage, which results in much less stress and a better ability to maintain the performance over time.

Also, as your position size increases, at some point the volume will affect the market on too many trades on a 1-minute chart. As an extreme example, if you had a limit profit target order to sell 5,000 contracts at two ticks above the market, anyone with a price ladder would see the aberration and you would have a difficult time getting filled on 10 to 15 trades a day. Also, entering that size on a stop would result in a tick or two of slippage, which ruins the risk-reward ratio of scalping. A trader can trade even 5,000 contracts per trade using price action, but not with the entry and exit scalping techniques needed for most of trades. May you someday have the problem of having to rethink your approach because your volume is adversely affecting your fills!

The 1-minute chart can be helpful in two situations, but this is in theory and not in practice and I strongly recommend against trading off of it. If the 5-minute chart is in a runaway trend and you are flat but want to get in, you can look at a 1-minute chart for High/Low 2 pullbacks to enter With Trend. The second situation where 1-minute charts are helpful is in swing trading trending stocks off the 5-minute chart. When stocks are trending, they are very respectful of the EMA and With Trend trades can be made off High/Low 1 or 2 setups at the EMA, risking the height of the signal bar. Traders can reduce that risk somewhat by entering on the 1-minute chart on the first reversal after an EMA touch or penetration on the 5-minute chart. If you plot a 5-minute 20 bar EMA plotted on the 1-minute chart, you can quickly see the touches and then place the order. You actually need to plot a 90-bar EMA on the 1-minute as a surrogate for the 5-minute 20 bar EMA. Why 90 and not 100 bars? Because the EMA on the 1-minute averages every 1-minute close and not every fifth close, and the weighting of the more recent bars tends to make a 100-bar EMA a tiny bit too flat. To correct for this, use a 90-bar EMA, which is very close to the 5-minute 20-bar EMA. In actual practice, you will rarely have time to look at a 1-minute stock chart because of your focus on the Emini. However, when a stock is strongly trending, you might occasionally take quick entries off the 1-minute. Let me again stress that I strongly recommend against ever looking at the 1-minute chart because it looks so easy that you will constantly keep trying to do it successfully and you will constantly wear down your account over time. *Don't do it!*

The thumbnail of the 5-minute Emini in Figure 10.2 shows that it went 11.75 points up off the open without a pullback. If a trader missed the Trend

FIGURE 10.2 The 1-minute Chart Can Get You into 5-minute with Trend Trades

from the First Bar long, he would have missed the entire swing because there were no pullbacks. However, if instead he looked at the 1-minute chart, there were three High 1 setups (Bars A, B, and C) where he could have entered. However, never look at the 1-minute and suddenly realize that those are reversals that can be shorted. You looked at the 1-minute for one reason only ... to find High 1 and 2 long entries because there were no pullbacks on the 5-minute. Trading Countertrend on the 1-minute will cost you money. In fact, those three long setups are at exactly the price that the 1-minute shorts would cover, and as they cover, they will become additional buyers, helping to drive the market up.

FIGURE 10.3   Only Consider Trading the 1-minute Chart in the Direction of the 5-minute Trend

This 1-minute chart in Figure 10.3 of AAPL during a strong bear trend day offered three good shorts at the 90-bar EMA (equivalent to the 5-minute 20 bar EMA) with low risk (the height of the bar). The thumbnail shows the strong 5-minute bear trend.

The top chart in Figure 10.4 is a 5-minute chart, the middle has 1500 ticks per bar (1,500 trades per bar), and the bottom had 20,000 contracts per bar (the bar closes on the first trade that makes the volume 20,000 or more contracts since the start of the bar). They have similar price action and all are tradable but since the highest volume takes place in the first hour or so, the tick and volume charts are skewed, with many more bars per hour earlier in the day and in the final hour.

FIGURE 10.4 Three Charts of the Emini Day Session

Reports can lead to very emotional moves with big bars, outside bars, and several reversals. However, despite the emotion that the rapid moves and big bars generate in all traders, price action setups are still very reliable. In general, always swing part of the position with a breakeven stop because sometimes a swing will go much farther than you could ever imagine.

The FOMC report was released at 11:15 A.M. PST and caused emotional trading as evidenced by large bars in Figure 10.5, outside bars and several reversals within the next thirty minutes. However, price action traders who remember the basic rules did well. Bar 2 was a large bull reversal bar but whenever there is a lot of overlap with the prior bar, a trading range might be forming and you should never be looking to buy at the top of a range. Instead, look for trapped traders, small bars, and second entries. Bar 3 was a great short scalp because there were trapped overly eager bulls who mistook the large reversal bar as a sensible long setup.

FIGURE 10.5 Follow Price Action Rules Even When There Is a Volatile Reaction with Huge Bars after a Report

Bar 4 was the second attempt to reverse the breakout below the low of the day formed at the open. Second entries are always worth taking and a bull trend inside bar is as good as you are likely to get on an emotional day. Since this should result in at least two legs up, you need to swing part of your position. The initial stop is around the middle of the signal bar, and then one tick below the Bar 4 entry bar once that bar closed. Then trail the stop below the low of the prior bar and eventually move it to breakeven. Emotional days often lead to trends that carry much further than you would ever imagine and catching one like this is much more profitable than the combined profit from many, many scalps. Here, the bull continued for almost 30 points, or about $1,500 per contract.

Bar 1 in Figure 10.6 was a false upside breakout on a gap up day.

Bar 2 setup a High 2 at the EMA and a trend channel line reversal.

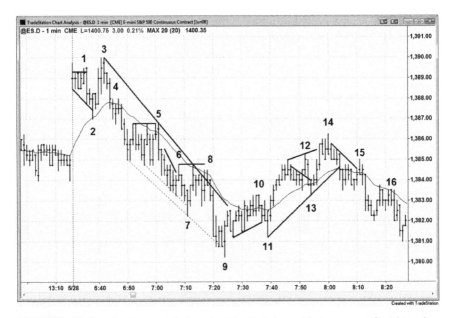

FIGURE 10.6 The first couple hours of the Emini provided many profitable scalps on the 1-minute chart for someone who can read price action and place orders very quickly. It is very difficult to do in actual practice.

Bar 3 was a short on a failed breakout to a new high on a gap up day that could lead to a test of the gap (the market usually tries to test gaps so traders should look for opportunities to trade in that direction).

Bar 5 was a Low 2 at the EMA.

Bar 6 was failed Micro Trendline breakout.

Bar 7 reversed two bear trend channel lines but was not a profitable long, leading you to believe that the bears are strong.

Bar 8 was a failed trendline breakout, a Double Top Pullback, a bear M2S, and a Five Tick Failure long from Bar 7. With so many factors favoring the shorts, it is no surprise that the market fell quickly.

Bar 9 was a second attempt to reverse up from the bear trend channel line overshoot. Expect at least two legs up.

Bar 10 is a questionable short because you are expecting a Higher Low and a second leg up. It turned into a 5 Tick Failure at Bar 11, which is a reversal pattern. Bar 11 was also a failed trendline breakout and a Higher Low and it followed a break of the bear trendline.

Bar 12 was a failed bull flag breakout but the short resulted in a one tick loss.

Bar 13 was a failed failure and therefore a bull breakout long. It was also a High 2.

Bar 14 was a Low 2 at a swing high, and a trend channel line reversal and a Double Top Bear Flag (with Bar 5).

Bar 15 was a Low 2 at the EMA (a M2S), a failed trendline breakout (from the Bar 14 high), and a Lower High after the Bars 11 to 13 trendline breakout.

Bar 16 was a M2S short.

Bar 1 in Figure 10.7 is a Wedge long and a Double Bottom but it would have resulted in a one tick loss for most traders. In general, a Wedge bottom (or Three Pushes Down, or any of many other names for this pattern) will lead to two legs up.

Bar 2 is a Higher Low and a Micro Trendline reversal.

Bar 3 was an M2B.

Bar 4 was a report that resulted in a false breakout to the upside (Failed Final Flag) and then an outside down bar. Traders would short below Bar 3, where the longs would have their stops.

Bar 5 was a Breakout Pullback.

FIGURE 10.7 The premarket is tradable but there are usually not many entries in the hour or two before the NYSE opens at 6:30 A.M. PST. There are often reports at 5:30 A.M. that result is quick trends and reversals.

Bar 6 was a second attempt to reverse up from a new swing low (Bar 5 was the first), and it gave a second entry.

GLOBEX, PRE-MARKET, POST-MARKET, AND OVERNIGHT MARKET

The same price action techniques apply in all markets, including overnight trading. The premarket extremes are often targets that get tested during the day session, but it is not necessary to look at Globex prices when trading the day session, since very little is gained and the signals will be based on the day session price action.

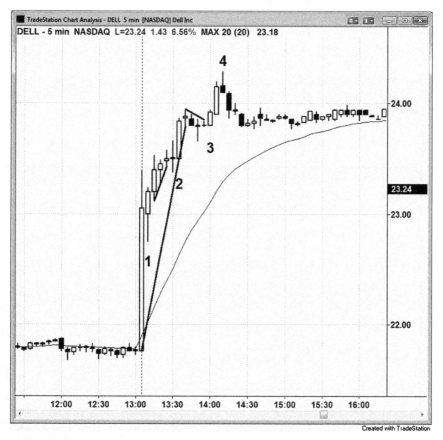

FIGURE 10.8 Dell Had an Earnings Report after the Close and Offered Some Post Market Trading Opportunities

Bar 1 in Figure 10.8 was a bull inside bar after the upside breakout and setup a long at one penny above its high (High 1).

Bar 2 was a long at one cent above the high of the outside bar, which also broke below a bull Micro Trendline and reversed up.

Bar 3 was a High 1 breakout long after a major trendline break.

Bar 4 was a short. It had a reversal bar and was a failed breakout of the Bar 3 bull flag (Failed Final Flag). Also, the Bar 3 flag broke a big bull trendline, indicating that the bears were gaining a little strength. Only fade a strong trend if there was first a trendline break. Also, a Countertrend trade in a strong trend needs a 5-minute (not a 3 or 1-minute) reversal bar. The market went sideways for the rest of the post market session.

The Emini in Figure 10.9 reacted poorly to the 5:30 A.M. PST unemployment report. Note that the thirty bars between Bars 1 and 5 all occurred within one minute due to the fast action off the report. These bars were forming so rapidly that it would have been impossible to trade anything other than market orders. It was theoretically possible to make many profitable scalps based on the price action but traders should never attempt to trade this. The only purpose of showing it is to demonstrate that standard patterns are present throughout.

The thumbnail charts are the 1 and 5-minute for the same 30 minutes of trading.

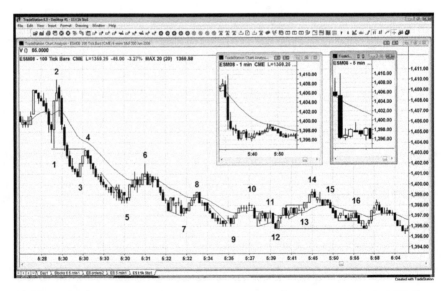

FIGURE 10.9 This Is a 100 Tick Chart Where Each Bar Represents 100 Trades, Independent of the Volume of the Trades or the Time

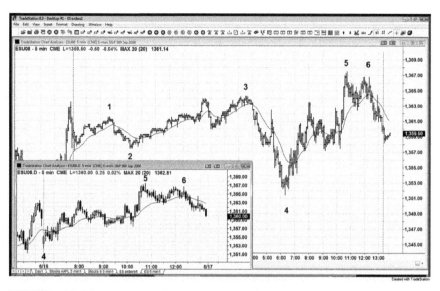

FIGURE 10.10 Globex 24 Hour Session

This Globex bar chart shows an Expanding Triangle ending at the Bar 5 high in Figure 10.10, and the thumbnail is the day session with the same numbering. A day session trader did not need to see the Globex Expanding Triangle to go short at Bar 5. Bar 5 took out yesterday's high and reversed down to the EMA, bounced to a Low 2 Lower High short, and then again to the Bar 6 Double Top Bear Flag (the first top was six bars earlier).

SCALPING, SWINGING, TRADING, AND INVESTING

An investor is someone who buys stocks based on fundamentals and plans to hold the stocks for six months to many years, allowing time for the beneficial fundamentals to be reflected in the price of the stock. He will often add to his position if the stock goes against him, since his belief is that the stock is a value at the current price. A trader is someone who trades off daily charts and short term fundamental events like earnings reports and product announcements with the intention of capturing a quick move, lasting from one to several days. He will take partial profits at the first pause and then move his stop to breakeven on the balance. He is not willing to have a profit turn into a loss. Traders are sometimes referred to scalpers, but that term more commonly is used to refer to a type of day trader.

In the eyes of a trader or investor using daily to monthly time frames, all day trading is scalping. However, to a day trader, scalping is holding a position for one to fifteen minutes or so and usually exiting on a limit order at a profit target in an attempt to capture one small leg on whatever time frame he is using for his trades. He does not want any pullbacks and will quickly exit at breakeven if the trade comes back before his target is reached, and he is therefore comparable to a trader on the daily charts. An intraday swing trader will hold a trade through pullbacks and he tries to capture the two to four larger swings of the day, holding each position from fifteen minutes to an entire day. He is comparable to an investor on the daily charts, who is willing to hold a position through pullbacks.

To scalp the 5-minute Emini chart effectively, you usually have to risk about two points and your profit target is one point or more. This means that you have to win on over 67 percent of your trades just to breakeven. However, if you read the charts correctly, this is achievable. Also, if you swing part of your trade using a breakeven stop after taking partial profits, this reduces the required winning percentage. Finally, if you move your stop from the signal bar extreme to the entry bar extreme (one tick beyond both) after the entry bar closes, and then to breakeven after a five tick move, this further reduces the required winning percentage to be profitable on the day. Finally, some scalpers use a wider stop of three to five points and add on as the market moves against them, and then use a wider profit target, and this again further reduces the required winning percentage.

Swing traders use the same setups and stops as the scalpers, but focus on the few trades each day that are likely to have at least a two legged move. They can usually net three or more points on part of their position on each trade and then move their stop to breakeven on the balance. Many will let the trade go against them and add on at a better price. However, they always have at least a mental stop and if the market gets to that point, they conclude that their idea can no longer be valid and they will exit with a loss. Always look for where scalpers will have their stops and look to add on to your position at that location, if the pattern is still valid. If you bought what you perceived to be a reversal, consider allowing the market to put in a lower low and then add on at the second entry. For example, with a reliable stock like AAPL, if you are buying what you perceive to be near the low of the move and the overall market is not in a bear trend day, consider risking two to three dollars on the trade and add on at a one to two dollar open loss. However, only an experienced trader who is very comfortable in his ability to read and in his ability to accept a large loss if his read is wrong should attempt this. On most days, the market should go your way immediately so this is not an issue.

Most swing traders will scalp out if the trade is not unfolding as desired and most scalpers will swing part of their position when they are entering on the best setups, so there is a lot of overlap in what both do. The fundamental difference is that the scalper will take far more trades and most of those trades are not likely to yield more than a scalper's profit, and a swing trader tries to only take the trades that are likely to have at least two legs. Neither way is superior and traders choose the method that best suits their personalities and both yield about the same profit.

It is reasonable to be primarily a scalper when trading Eminis and a swing trader when trading stocks. For the Eminis, exit part or all of your trade on a limit order after four ticks of profit, which usually requires the move to extend six ticks beyond the signal bar (the entry is on a stop at one tick beyond the signal bar, then you need four more ticks for your profit, and your limit exit order usually is not filled until the price moves one tick beyond your target). Four ticks in the Emini is one point, which is equivalent to a ten cent (ten tick) move in the SPY (ETF contract).

When it comes to stocks, there is much more variability in the size of the profit targets. For a $500 dollar stock with an average daily range of $10, it would be foolish to scalp for 10 cents because you would likely have to risk about two dollars and your winning percentage would have to be over 95 percent. However, scalping for 10 cents might be worthwhile in QQQQ, especially if you are trading 10,000 shares.

It is relatively easy to look for swings in high-volume stocks (at least three million shares per day but prefer seven million or more) that have an average range of several dollars. You want minimal slippage, reliable patterns, and at least one dollar profit per trade. Try to scalp for one dollar and then use a breakeven stop on the balance and hold until the close or until a clear and strong opposite setup develops. You might be able to watch about five stocks regularly throughout the day and sometimes check on up to another five or so at different times during the day, but you will rarely ever trade them.

An Emini scalper will likely only be able to enter a couple stock trades a day since Emini day trading takes so much attention. Also, only use bar charts for stocks, which allows you to put six charts on one screen. Just pick the one stock that is trending the best and then look for a pullback near the EMA. You can also trade reversals if you see a trend channel overshoot and reversal after there was a prior strong trend line break. If the Emini market is active, consider only trading 15-minute stock charts, which require less attention. If you are missing too many good Emini trades, it might be that you are getting distracted by the additional charts and it is far better then to stop looking at them and only trade the Emini.

Although all stocks trade basically the same way, there are subtle personality differences between them. For example, AAPL is very respectful when it comes to testing breakouts, whereas GS tends to run stops, requiring a wider stop.

FIGURE 10.11 After a Strong Break of a Bear Trendline, Expect Two Legs Up

Baidu broke above the 15-minute trendline in Figure 10.11 late yesterday and therefore was likely to have at least two legs up. It was possible that the second up leg ended at Bar 5, but today's open was so strong that there likely would be an attempt to exceed it after a pullback. The drop to Bar 7 was sharp but Bar 7 was a strong bull reversal bar that reversed the EMA Gap, the gap up open, and the test of the Bar 3 high (it ran the stops below that high and turned up sharply). For a $300 stock, you need a wider stop so trade fewer shares to keep the risk the same, but use a larger profit target on the scalp portion of the trade. Two dollars is a reasonable initial target and then move the stop to breakeven and exit by the close.

When you are anticipating a significant move or a new trend, or when you are entering on a pullback in a strong trend, exit 25 to 75 percent of your contracts at a scalper's profit and then scale out of the remaining contracts as the market continues to go your way. Move your protective stop to around breakeven (sometimes you will want to risk as many as four ticks in the Eminis if you feel strongly that the trade will remain good, and an exit and then a re-entry approach will be at a worse price) after you exit the scalp portion of your trade. A good trade should not come back to let late comers in at the same price as the smart traders who got in at the perfect time. If the trade is great, all of the traders who missed the initial entry are now so eager to get in that they will be willing to enter at a worse price and will place limit entry orders at a tick or two worse than the original entry, keeping the breakeven stop of the original traders from being hit. However, sometimes the best trades come back to beyond the breakeven stop to trap traders out of what will become a huge, fast trend. When that seems like a possibility, risk a few extra ticks. Also, if it comes back and runs those stops and then immediately resumes the new trend, re-enter or add to your swing position at one tick beyond the prior bar (in a new bull, this is one tick above the prior bar's high).

If the market touches the profit target limit order but does not go through it and the order is still filled, that means that there might be more trend pressure than is evident on the chart and the chances increase that the market will go beyond the profit target within the next several bars. If you were long and the market was willing to buy your position back from you (you were selling on a limit to take profits) at the very highest tick of the leg, the buyers are aggressive and will likely reemerge on any pullback. Look for opportunities to get long again.

Similarly, if the market touches your profit target (five ticks beyond the signal bar) but you do not get filled, this can be a failure. Consider placing an order to reverse at one tick beyond the opposite end of the current bar once it closes. If you were long and the market hit five ticks above the signal bar and you were not filled, consider moving your stop to breakeven. Once this bar closes, consider placing an order to go short at one tick below this bar because that is likely where most of the remaining long scalpers will get out, providing selling pressure. Also, they will not want to buy again until more price action unfolds, thus removing buyers from the market and increasing the odds that the sellers will push the market down enough for you to scalp out of your short. A Five-Tick Failed Breakout is common at the end of a protracted trend and is often the first sign of a reversal.

ALWAYS IN THE MARKET

A good alternative to scalping and occasionally swinging a portion of the trade is to try to stay in the market most of the day, exiting on the close. Traders should focus on major swing points and reversals for entries and either swing the entire position or trade at least two contracts, scalp one, and then move the stop to breakeven on the other. For Eminis, there are often stop runs and deep pullbacks so it is preferable to scalp half and swing half, making sure that you get something out of every trade that reached at least a scalper's profit.

For stocks, breakeven stops have much less chance of being hit so it is more profitable to look to swing trade. Typically, look to scalp out a third to a half after about a one dollar move and then swing the balance. If the market appears to be reversing but has not yet reversed, like at a test of a high of the day, take off another quarter to a third, but always let at least a quarter run until your breakeven stop is hit, or until there is a clear and strong opposite signal, or until the close. Trends often go much further than you could ever imagine.

Hold the position through repeated pullbacks unless the protective stop is hit, even if the pullbacks are violent. If it is hit, stay out of the market until there is another clear and strong setup in either direction. If there is a clear and strong setup, repeat the process. If your trading size is two contracts and you are long one when a reversal pattern triggers, sell three. One gets you out of your remaining long position and the other two start the process in this new, opposite direction. Scalp the first and swing the second.

The key to this approach is to only enter or reverse when there is a clear and strong setup. If not, rely on your breakeven stop, even though you may give back all of the gains on your swing portion. If you watch a small basket of stocks, almost every day at least one will setup with a reliable entry that will allow you to put on a swing trade.

AAPL had a gap test at Bar 1 in Figure 10.12, which was a strong reversal Bar that reversed up after hitting a new low on the day and after

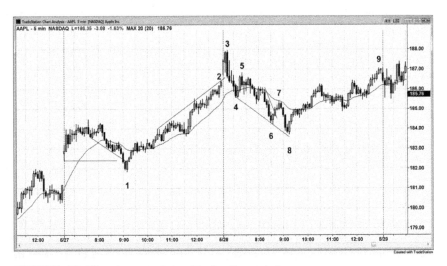

FIGURE 10.12 Always in Swing Trades Example 1

breaking below a bear trend channel line. This was a great entry for a swing long that would have netted almost $4 by the close.

Bar 3 was a strong bear reversal down from the prior day's high and a bull trend channel line overshoot. There was a large bear trend bar, and this setup offered a highly probable trade for at least a two-legged move down.

Bar 8 was a Lower Low test of the Bar 6 low and it followed a trendline break. It also tested a bear trend channel line, and was a good reversal trade. If you simply exited your short instead of reversing to long, the trade would have netted about $2.40.

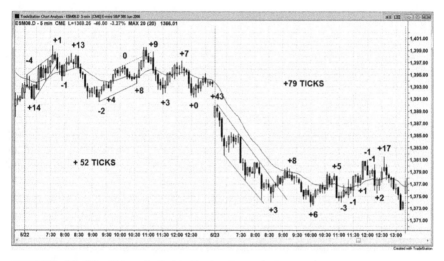

FIGURE 10.13 Always in Swing Trades Example 2

The first day in Figure 10.13 is a trading range day and the Always In approach could have netted 52 ticks, or about $600 per contract. The second day began as a Trend from the Open and then entered a trading range. An Always In trader could have netted 79 ticks or about $950 per contract. If a trader traded two lots and scalped one and swung one, he could have had ten successful scalps each day, yielding an additional $450 per contract per day. It sounds and looks easy but is very difficult to do.

HAVE AT LEAST TWO REASONS TO ENTER A TRADE

Some basic rules make trading much easier because once a rule is satisfied, you can act without hesitation. One of the most important rules is that you need two reasons to take a With Trend trade or any trade in a trading range day, and any two reasons are good enough. Once you have them, place your order to enter, and once in, just follow basic profit target and protective stop loss rules, and trust that you will be profitable by the end of the day. One important note is that if there is a steep trend, never trade Countertrend, even if there is a High or Low 2 or 4, unless there was first a prior significant trendline break or trend channel overshoot and reversal. Also, it is far better if the trendline break had strong momentum instead of just a sideways drift.

Learn to anticipate trades so that you will be ready to place your orders. For example, if after a bear trendline break there is a two-legged break below a major swing low, or an overshoot of a trend channel line, look for a reversal, or if there is a ii break out, look for a reversal. Once you see an outside bar or a Barb Wire pattern, look for a small bar at the extreme for a possible fade trade. If there is a strong trend, be ready for the first EMA pullback and any two legged pullbacks to the EMA and for the first EMA Gap pullback.

There are only a few situations when you only need one reason to enter a trade. First, anytime there is a strong trend, you must enter on every pullback that does not follow a climax or failed flag breakout, even if the pullback is just a High or Low 1. Also, if there was a trend channel line overshoot and a good reversal bar, you can fade the move. The only other time that only one reason is needed to enter a trade, whether in a trading range or a trend, is when there is a second entry. By definition, there was a first entry, so the second entry is the second reason.

Here are some possible reasons for entering a trade (remember, you need two or more):

- Reversal bar
- Good signal bar pattern
- EMA pullback in a trend, especially if two legged
- Breakout Pullback
- Breakout Test
- High/Low 2 or 4 (there must have been a prior trendline break if fading a strong trend)
- Failure of anything: Prior High or Low, flag breakout, reversal from an overshoot of a trendline or a trend channel line, 5 tick failure

Bar 2 in Figure 10.14 is an M2B in a strong bull and is reason enough to go long. It was the first EMA touch in more than two and a half hours in a Trend from the First Bar bull with a big gap up. It was also the first good trendline break, so a test of the high is expected.

FIGURE 10.14 Any Two Reasons to Enter Will Do

Bar 3 was a Lower High after a trendline break and it followed the second failed attempt to break above Bar 1. There was an ii setup with the second bar having a bear close.

Bar 5 was an M2S in a bear swing (there was a Lower High at Bar 3 and a Lower Low at Bar 4).

Bar 6 was a bear trend channel line overshoot and reversal but there the setup bar was a bear trend bar, so one more reason was needed to enter. That came at the Bar 7 Higher Low, which was a Breakout Pullback after breaking the Micro Trendline down from Bar 5 (not shown).

Yesterday closed with a surge to Bar 4 in Figure 10.15, completing four legs of an Expanding Triangle. If you noticed that, you would look for a long entry after a break below Bar 3. Bar 5 dropped below Bar 3, completing the Expanding Triangle bottom, and now you just had to wait for an entry setup. There was a High 2 at Bar 6 and Bar 6 completed a Down Up Twin reversal, with an entry on the next bar at one tick above Bar 6 on a stop.

ENTERING ON STOPS

A price action trader is looking for a reason to enter and the bar that completes the setup is called a signal bar. The bar when you actually enter is called the entry bar. One of the best ways to trade using price action is to enter on a stop because you are being carried into the trade by the market's momentum and therefore are trading in the direction of at least

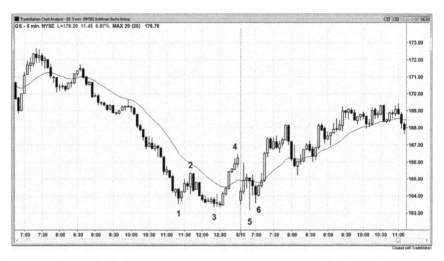

FIGURE 10.15   If There Are Two Reasons to Enter, Then Take the Trade

a tiny trend (at least one tick long). For example, if you are shorting a bear, you can place an order to sell short at one tick below the low of the prior bar, which becomes your signal bar after your order is filled. A reasonable location for a protective stop is at one tick above the high of the signal bar. After the entry bar closes, tighten the stop to one tick above the entry bar.

A scalper in the Eminis usually needs a six-tick move beyond the signal bar to scalp four ticks of profit. This is because the entry stop is one tick beyond the bar, and then you need four more ticks for your profit, and your profit target limit order usually won't get filled unless the market moves one tick beyond your order. Sometimes your order will get filled without the market moving through it, but when that happens, the market is usually strong and will likely move beyond that price within a few minutes of your fill. Similarly, to scalp 10 ticks in the QQQQ, you usually need a 12-tick move.

When a setup looks weak, it is best to not take it and wait for another opportunity. If it is weak, it will likely fail and you cannot take needless risk. Often a weak setup will have a second entry, in which case it becomes a strong setup.

Although most trades should be entered on stops, when there is a strong trend, it is safe to enter anytime, and entering at the EMA on a limit order or on a 1-minute chart on a stop is particularly good in stocks, which tend to be well-behaved. This allows for a smaller risk and greater reward and essentially no change in the winning percentage.

FIGURE 10.16 It Usually Takes a Six-Tick Move Beyond the Signal Bar to Net a Four-Tick Scalp in the Eminis

The entry stop is one tick above the Bar 2 signal bar's high at line A in Figure 10.16, where you will be filled. Your limit order to take four ticks profit on your scalp is four ticks above that, at line B. Your limit order usually won't get filled unless the market moves one tick beyond it to line C, which is six ticks above the high of the signal bar.

Bar 1 in Figure 10.17 was a second entry short (a Low 2 on the outside down bar) following a test of yesterday's high. The run up was strong and therefore it was better to wait for the second entry.

Bar 2 was a High 2 following a large inside doji bar but the down momentum was strong. It is better to wait for a trendline break before buying. Likewise, Bar 3 was a bad second long entry because it followed a strong bear trend bar and you should still be waiting for a bear trendline break before looking to buy. The top of the day was a Higher High after a trendline break and the market has been below the EMA for many bars so you

FIGURE 10.17 Enter on a Stop but Only If There Is a Good Setup

should only be looking for shorts because the bull leg is now over. Trade what is there now, not what was there earlier in the day.

Bar 4 was an M2S but it followed four bars that almost entirely overlapped. In a Tight Trading Range like this, you should never enter in either direction until after there is a large trend bar that breaks out of the pattern by at least 3 or 4 ticks, and then wait for that bar to fail, or unless there is a small bar that you can fade near the top or bottom of the trading range.

Many of One-Tick False Breakouts like those at Bars 2 and 3 occur in the first minute or two of a Countertrend 5-minute entry bar. Breakouts that occur in the final minute of the bar tend to be more reliable because you then have momentum right at the end of the bar. The chance of it continuing into the next bar is greater than if it occurred four minutes earlier and has since pulled back.

Trading low probability trades will wipe out more than all of your gains.

When a stock is in a strong trend like the Trend from the Open bear in Figure 10.18, it is safe to enter on a limit order on the first couple tests of the EMA, or you can enter on the 1-minute chart with a price action stop entry at the EMA. At Bars 1 and 2 in AAPL, a second entry off the 1-minute chart at the 5-minute EMA plotted on the 1-minute chart had about a 25-cent risk, and the price action entry off the 5-minute chart

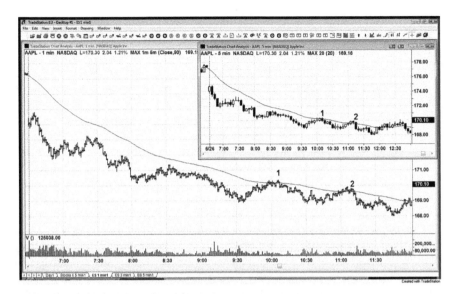

FIGURE 10.18 When the Trend Is Strong, You Can Consider Entering on a Limit Order at the EMA (but It Is Better to Wait for a Stop Entry)

(insert) had about a 45-cent risk. You could also short at the market on the first 5-minute close beyond the EMA and use about a 20-cent stop. Here, at Bars 1 and 2, the market went only four cents above the close before reversing down. In general, it is better to either wait for the second 1-minute entry or use the traditional 5-minute price action entry (on a stop below the bar that tests the EMA) because there is very little gained by the other methods and they just involve more thought, which can distract you from your Emini trading.

PROTECTIVE STOPS AND GETTING TRAPPED IN OR OUT OF A TRADE

The initial stop is one tick beyond the signal bar until the entry bar closes when it is tightened to one or two ticks beyond the entry bar. If the bars are too large, it is wiser to use a price stop, like eight ticks on the Emini 5-minute chart, or a 60 percent pullback. For example, in a long off a large signal bar, you would place the protective stop about 40 percent of the distance up from the bottom of the signal bar to the entry price. The size of the money stop is in proportion to the size of the bars. For example, in the October 2008 bear, several days had ranges of over 40 points and required an 8-point stop, but this allowed you to use a 4-point profit target. You need to reduce your position size by 75 percent to keep your risk the same, but if you follow basic price action principles, you could make the same or even more than on a typical day. After the market reaches the first profit target and partial profits are secured, move the protective stop to about breakeven (the entry price, which is one tick from the signal bar extreme). The best trades will not hit a breakeven stop, and the majority don't go more than four ticks beyond the entry price on the 5-minute Emini (for example, three ticks below the signal bar high after getting long). If the trade is good, the market won't come back to let timid traders come in at a better price. If it does come back, that is a sign that the trade might not be strong.

If you are uncertain if today will be a huge range day and will require large stops, trade just one contract for the first one or two trades and see how large a stop would have been needed to keep you in the trade. Rely only on a stop beyond the signal bar and once it closes, rely on a stop just beyond the entry bar. Once your one point profit limit order is filled, see how many ticks the stop would have had to be for it not to have been hit and you can use this as your stop for the day. If the market would have hit a 14-tick stop but not a 16-tick stop, you could use a 4-point stop for the rest of the day, but reduce your position size by 50 percent and increase your profit target to 2 points. If after an hour or two, the 2-point targets are not getting filled, you will likely notice that a 2- or 3-point stop is now working. If so, just go back to using a smaller stop and a smaller target and increase your position size back to normal.

When a protective stop is hit before making a scalper's profit, you were trapped, so reversing on the stop is occasionally a good strategy. This depends on the context. For example, a failed Low 2 short in a pullback in a bear is usually a good reversal into a long trade. However, a stop run in a Tight Trading Range is not a reversal. Take time to make sure that you read the chart correctly before considering a trade in the opposite direction. If you don't have time to get right back in, wait for the next setup, which will always come before too long.

After studying a market, you will see what a reasonable stop is. For the Emini 5-minute chart, eight ticks works well on most days. However, pay close attention to the maximum size stop required in the first hour because this often becomes the best stop to use for the rest of the day. If the stop is more than eight ticks, you will likely be able to increase the size of your profit target as well. However, this provides a modest advantage at best unless the bars are exceptionally big.

For example, if you are confident that a low will hold but a long trade would require a much greater money stop than you typically use, you can use the larger stop and then wait. If you are concerned enough about the extra risk that you can't take the trade, cut your position size in half and place the order. If the market hits your profit target without much of a pullback, take your profit. However, if it only goes a tick or so beyond your entry and pulls back almost to your stop and then starts up again above your entry price, raise your profit target. As a general rule, the market will rally enough to equal the size of the stop that it required you to have to stay in the trade. So if the market dipped eleven ticks below your entry before reversing back up, only a twelve tick stop would have work and therefore the market will likely go about twelve ticks above your entry price. It would be wise to place a limit order to exit at a tick or two below and when it approaches the target, move your stop to breakeven and wait to see if your profit target order gets filled.

There is one situation where you can often enter on a limit and not a stop. This occurs when you see a second entry after a trendline break and a strong reversal bar. For example, if you just bought and the market tests the exact low of the entry bar several times over the one or two bars, consider placing a limit buy order to double your position at one tick above the low of the entry bar and risk just two ticks (to the original stop, just below the entry bar). You would likely not get filled if you tried to buy the low of the entry bar on a limit order since usually the market has to trade through the limit price for the order to get filled. Everyone knows that there are many protective stops just one tick below that entry bar low . . . why isn't the smart money gunning for it? Because if those stops are hit, the character of the market will have changed. Instead of being a strong second entry, the chart now has a failed second entry, and that is a With Trend setup and will likely result in two further legs down. If smart money had loaded up on the bottom, they do not want to see the market drop for another two legs, so they will do exactly as you did. They will continue to accumulate longs to defend the bottom. Eventually, sellers will give up and start to cover and as they do, the market will rise well beyond the scalper's target. Do not place this kind of trade until you have been consistently profitable for a long time because until then, you should keep your trading style simple and you should not be thinking this hard.

Once the entry bar closes, move the stop to one tick beyond the entry bar. If risk is too great, use a money stop or risk about 60% of the height of the signal bar.

If you shorted on Bar 1 in Figure 10.19 below the Double Bottom Twin (the two prior bars had the same low), the initial stop would be above the signal bar. Incidentally, this is not a good short since it is a pullback to the EMA on the open and has a high chance or rallying back up. The Bar 1 entry bar reversed up immediately after entry but did not exceed the top of the signal bar, so this would have eventually ended up as a profitable short scalp. Once the entry bar closed, move the stop up to one tick above its

FIGURE 10.19   the Initial Protective Stop Is One Tick Beyond the Signal Bar

high. In this example, the signal and entry bars had the same high, so the stop would not have to be tightened.

The Bar 3 entry bar immediately sold off but did not fall below the low of the signal bar, or below 60 percent of its height (if you used a money stop, thinking that this signal bar was too big to use a price action stop below its low). Once the entry bar closed, move the protective stop up to one tick below its low. Two bars later, there was a Pullback Bar but it did not hit the stop. If tested the entry bar low to the tick, creating a Double Bottom and a great trap, trapping weak longs out.

The stop for the short at the Bar 4 M2S was not hit, despite a Pullback Bar two bars after entry. Given the large size of the bars, it would have been better to short below the low of the bear trend bar rather than simply on the Low 2 below a bull trend bar. The stop is above the entry bar and does not get tightened to above the high of the most recent bar until after the market has moved about four ticks in your direction. Give the trade time to work. Also, when the entry bar is a doji, it is usually safe to allow a one tick pullback. A doji bar is a one bar trading range and it is foolish to buy above a trading range, so don't buy back your short there. Rely on your original stop until the market has moved at least several ticks in your direction.

The Bar 5 High 2 long immediately sold off to test the signal bar low (this is evident on the 1-minute chart, not shown) forming a two bar Double Bottom and then a successful long scalp. Rely on your stop and ignore the 1-minute chart. When taking a 5-minute entry, rely on a 5-minute stop, else you will lose too often and be stopped out of a great many trades in your attempt to risk less per trade.

The Bar 7 M2B long tested the stop below the signal bar but missed by one tick, and then tested the tightened stop below the entry bar, but neither stop was hit. The dojis prior to entry increase the risk of the trade (Barb Wire), but with six closes above the EMA after the surge from a new low of the day, you had to be expecting a second leg up and the M2B was a reasonable entry. An even better one was four bars later, above the small bear bar, because this was essentially a High 4 long (a second attempt at a High 2 out of the Barb Wire)

If a trader bought above the Bar 8 ii, the stop was hit on the entry bar and this would have been a good reversal, as are most failed ii patterns. The buy was bad because a Double Top Bear Flag was setting up (with Bar 4) and you should not be buying near the high except in a bull trend. Also, most of the previous twenty bars overlapped several of the bars before them, giving the market a strong trading range quality (the move up from Bar 7 was a small channel in a Spike and Channel bull). Therefore, you would not want to be buying at the top of the second leg up when that might be the end of the rally.

If you shorted the Bar 11 swing high, you could either have reversed on the Bar 12 reversal bar that tested the EMA or you could have reversed on a buy stop at one tick above the entry bar that followed the Bar 11 short.

The short from the Bar 13 swing high, Low 2 became a 5 Tick Failure and a failed Low 2. You should reverse to long on Bar 14 at one tick above the entry bar (the bar after the Bar 13 signal bar), since there are trapped shorts and you should expect at least two more legs up.

The selloff to Bar 1 in Figure 10.20 was climactic and bounced up on a Down Up Twin bottom after breaking out of an inside bar Failed Final Flag three bars earlier. If a trader bought above Bar 1 (not wise since it was a bear trend bar), he would expect a two legged move up and that the low of Bar 1 would hold. In this strong a bear, it would make more sense to wait for a second signal, especially since there was not even a small prior trendline break.

The Bar 3 pullback dipped one tick below the entry Bar 2 low but bounced back up in a second Down Up Twin reversal that missed the signal Bar 1 low by one tick. If a trader then bought above Bar 3, he would know that Bar 1 was an acceptable but risky long and that the dip at Bar 3 was 17 ticks, so an 18 tick stop would have been needed to stay long. Therefore, the trader could raise his target from four ticks to about 16 ticks. The

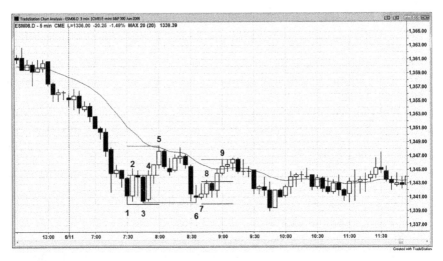

FIGURE 10.20 Protective Stop Placement

second leg up ended at exactly 18 ticks above the entry price. When the
risk is about twice normal, a trader should trade half as many contracts to
keep the dollar risk the same. A sensible long entry would be to wait for
Bar 4 to close and once you see that it was a strong bull trend bar, and you
know that it was the second strong bull trend bar in four bars, and there
is room to the EMA (an obvious magnet), enter on a buy stop at one tick
above its high. Yes, this is buying the top of a bear flag, but here was good
bullish strength and room to run to the EMA.

A similar situation was present on the Bar 6 low. Here the market was
trying to form a Double Bottom Bull Flag with the Bar 3 low but Bar 6 has a
weak close. Conservative traders would not have bought at one tick above
the high and instead would have waited for a second signal. After Bar 7
closed, an acceptable second signal would be to buy at one tick above Bar
7, which would be a second attempt to rally, but it also had a weak close so
this is not ideal. This Bar 8 entry bar again would require a stop below the
Bar 6 Double Bottom Bull Flag low, which was also the initial signal bar,
and it was only a couple ticks below the entry bar so the added risk was
worth it, given the likelihood of two legs up. Once long in Bar 8, the stop
would be twelve ticks, so it was likely that the move would extend about
twelve ticks up. A target of ten ticks was worth trying (and proved to be
successful). The market tested the Bar 8 low in each of the next two bars,
so the institutions were defending the stop, making a rally more likely. Bar
9 reached twelve ticks, and the market went one tick higher two bars later.
A safer entry would be to buy above the bear inside bar that followed the
Bar 8 bull trend bar because the strength of Bar 8 showed that the bulls are
willing to defend the bottom.

FIGURE 10.21 The Largest Stop Needed in the First Hour Is Usually a Good Stop for the Rest of the Day

A short off the Bar 1 signal bar that poked above yesterday's high in Figure 10.21 would have required nine ticks, since after the entry bar closed, the stop would be one tick above its high. Bar 2 tested the entry bar high, and it would have hit an eight tick stop but not a nine tick stop. Remember that for the rest of the day.

If you bought the failed Low 2 at Bar 3 and placed the initial stop at one tick below the signal bar's low, you would risk eight ticks. One tick stop runs are common when there are dojis and you know that a nine tick stop was needed earlier in the day, so it would have been wise to risk the extra tick. This was not a great buy because it followed a tiny breakout and the last seven bars were largely sideways with several dojis (Barb Wire). A second entry would be better.

Today had a big gap in Figure 10.22 down so the day was likely to trend up or down. Following Bar 3, the market sold off strong into a lower range, and by the time Bar 6 formed, the day was a Trending Trading Range Day or a Trend from the Open bear. It is usually safe to buy near the bottom of every range in Trending Trading Ranges and short near the top.

Bar 5 broke above a Micro Trendline. Bars 4 and 6 were strong bull reversal bars, with Bar 6 setting up Breakout Pullback long. The entry bar became a bear trend bar, which is a sign of weakness. If the market traded one tick below its low, this would have been a failure and the market would likely have dropped quickly down in two more legs. Since smart money

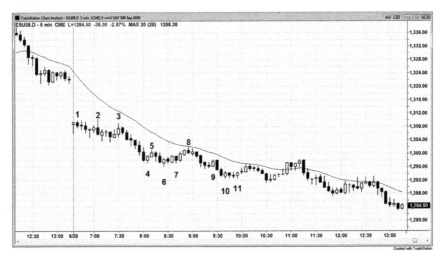

FIGURE 10.22   Institutions Defending their Stops

believed that this was a Trending Trading Range Day and they bought the second entry (Bar 5 being the first), they will defend it by continuing to buy down to the low of the entry bar. They do not want the market to go one tick lower because they will then have a losing trade. The market missed those protective stops by one tick many times over the next fifteen minutes and patient longs were rewarded.

CHAPTER 11

The First Hour

The best trades initially are usually related to patterns from yesterday and you first need to look for failed breakouts, breakout pullbacks, Trends from the Open and their first pullbacks, and then common price action patterns. Although there is a tendency to think that the patterns are different in the first hour, the reality is that from a Price Action perspective, they are not. The setups are the same as during any other time of the day and on any time frame. What is different is that the volatility is often greater, and therefore the patterns run further, and the reversals are often unexpectedly abrupt. It is common for reversals to look weak and have two or three doji bars before the trend breaks out. Realize that this is common, and if you entered and see this weakness, don't scratch out. Rely on your read because you will likely be right, and you stand to make a large swing profit.

If the bars are larger, to keep his risk the same, a trader needs to trade fewer contracts. The market is moving quickly, and it is difficult to spend time doing exact math while trying to read the charts and place orders. Just quickly cut the position size in half or two-thirds. It doesn't matter what you do; what matters is that you do it quickly, stop thinking about it, and concentrate on what is much more important: reading correctly and placing your orders.

One other difference about the open is that many trades set up based on yesterday's price action. There will often be a large flag that develops in the final couple of hours of yesterday and then a breakout occurs on today's open, or the market gaps well beyond the flag. In either case, watch for reversals and continuations.

A final important difference is that the high or low of the day occurs in the first hour on most days, so it is critical to swing part of any trade that could be a major high or low, and use a breakeven stop to allow yourself to collect the windfall profits that often happen off the open.

The first hour or two of the day is often rich in reliable trades. On most days, there are one or more tradable reversals, usually with several opportunities to re-enter after scalping out with a profit. Occasionally a trend will develop from the first bar or two and run for an hour or more without a pullback (a Trend from the Open or Trend from the First Bar), but traders should always be looking for a reversal in the first hour or so because they are the rule and not the exception, and they commonly lead to a protracted trend.

On most days, there are one or more tradable reversals in the first couple hours of the day. Why does the market open and then make a big move over the next several bars and then reverse? Why doesn't it simply open at the low or high of the day? The location of the open of the day is not set by any firm or group of firms and instead represents a brief equilibrium between buyers and sellers at the instant of the open. If the institutions have a large amount of buying planned for the day, why would the market ever open above yesterday's close and then selloff before rallying to a new high? If you were an institutional trader and had a lot of buy orders to fill today, you would love the market to open above where you wanted to buy and then have a sharp move down into your buy zone where you could aggressively buy along with all the other institutions who likely also have lots of similar buy orders from their clients, and then hope to see a small sell climax that will form a convincing low of the day.

If the reversal back up is strong enough, very few traders will be looking to short because there will be a general feeling that the upward momentum is sufficiently strong to warrant at least a second leg up before the low is tested, if it gets tested. Would there be anything that you, if you were an institutional trader, could do to make this happen? Yes! You could buy into the close of the premarket to push the price up and fill some of your orders. Not as much volume is needed in futures or stocks to move the price before the 6:30 A.M. PST open. Then, once the market opens, you could liquidate some or all of your longs and even do some shorting. Since you want to buy lower, you will not start buying until the market falls to an area that you consider to represent value. Price action is very important. You would like to see how the market responds once it gets down to some key price, like the EMA or a prior swing high or low or the low of yesterday. If the downward momentum begins to wane and if the market starts to reverse up from the key price, you will liquidate any shorts and aggressively buy to fill your orders. Since most firms will have similar orders, the market will start to rally. If you believe that the low of the day might be in, you will continue to buy as the market rallies, and you will aggressively buy any pullback. Since your order size is huge, you don't want to buy all at once and risk causing a spike up and then a buy climax. Instead, you would rather just keep buying in an orderly fashion all day long until all of your orders get filled.

Is this what actually happens? Traders at institutions know if this is what they do, but no one ever knows for certain why the market reverses on any given day. Also, reasons are irrelevant. All that matters is price action. Reversals often happen seconds after a report is released, but an individual trader is unlikely to understand how the market will respond to a report by simply watching CNBC. The market can rally or selloff in response to either a bullish or bearish report, and a trader is simply not qualified to reliably interpret a report in the absence of price action. The best way to know how the market will respond is simply to watch it respond and place your trades as the price action unfolds. Very often, the bar before the report is a great setup that gets triggered on the report. Place your order and then your stop, and trust your read.

Opening Reversals often happen quickly, and the sharpness of the reversal makes it difficult to understand the fundamentals. If the market was so bearish a couple of minutes ago, how can it be so bullish now? Don't give it any thought. Instead, just look for standard price action setups, and trade them mindlessly without giving any consideration to the reasons why the reversal is taking place. All that you need to know is that it is in fact taking place and you must enter.

Although the 5-minute chart is the easiest to read and the most reliable, the 3-minute chart trades well, particularly in the first hour. However, it is prone to more losers, and if you like the highest winning percentage and don't want the negative emotion that comes from losing, you should stick to trading the 5-minute chart and work on increasing your position size.

As a trader, it is best to keep your analysis simple, especially in the first hour when the market is moving quickly. The vast majority of opens are related to the price action of the final hour or so of the prior day and take the form of a breakout, a failed breakout, a breakout pullback, or a trend from the open, and any of these can move very fast.

PATTERNS RELATED TO THE PREMARKET

When looking at tick or volume charts of the Globex, the open is not easy to spot because it is just part of the 24-hour trading day and appears indistinguishable from the rest to the chart. There is a tendency for Globex highs and lows often to get tested in the day session, and there are patterns in the Globex that get completed during the first many bars of the day session. The first hour or so usually moves quickly, and the day session alone provides great price action. Since most traders are not capable of trading two charts well, especially in a fast market such as after the open, just watch the 5-minute day session. Most trades that setup on the Globex chart will have price action reasons for the same trade based on the day session alone. You should be willing to miss an occasional trade rather than risk losing money while being confused as you quickly try to analyze two charts while you place entry, stop, and profit target orders.

FIGURE 11.1   Nothing Is Gained by Watching Both the Day and Globex Sessions

Bar 1 in Figure 11.1 on both the Globex chart on the left and on the day session chart on the right is the 6:40 A.M. PST bar. The Globex had a Failed Flag reversal buy signal, and the day session had a strong bull reversal bar that was a Breakout Pullback above the two-legged up move into yesterday's close and a possible bull Trend from the Open. Remember that if the first bar of the day is a trend bar, it is usually a setup for a scalp. If it fails, especially with an opposite trend bar, it is a setup in the opposite direction.

Nothing was gained by watching both charts, and trying to do so increases the chances that you will not be quick enough to take all of the available trades and make mistakes in your order placement.

PATTERNS RELATED TO YESTERDAY

Breakouts, Failed Breakouts, and Breakout Pullbacks from yesterday's swing highs and lows, large flags, trendlines, or trading ranges are the most reliable patterns in the first hour. These setups usually lead to one extreme of the day and therefore are important swing setups for at least part of the position. Try to anticipate setups before the market opens, based on yesterday's price action. As you can see from the huge volume, the best traders in the world are taking them, and so should you.

Many trades in the first hour are related to patterns from the prior day, and lots of large traders base their entries off daily charts and the high, low, and close of the prior day. Before the open, look at the final hour or two of yesterday, and see if there was a strong trend or a trading range and therefore a trendline, or if there was a trendline break and a test of the extreme is now likely, or if there is a possible Three Push pattern or a trend channel line test setting up. The market often tests yesterday's high or low in the first hour, resulting in a tradable breakout pullback or a reversal.

The 5-minute OIH chart yesterday in Figure 11.2 had a three-hour, two-legged rally that broke the major bear trendline (not shown) after morning selling, and the rally overshot a bear trend channel line twice, reversing down both times (Bars 4 and 5), showing that the bulls were losing control. The length of the rally is evidence of bullish strength. A two-legged Countertrend move in the final hour or two that breaks a major trendline is a common pattern. It alerts you to look for a trend reversal on the open in the form of a Higher Low or a Lower Low.

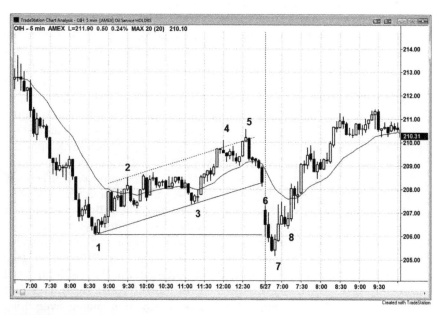

FIGURE 11.2 Failed Breakout

Today the market gapped down and quickly traded below yesterday's low where it formed a strong bull reversal bar. This large bear flag failed breakout occurred over two days and provided an excellent long entry at one tick above the high of the Bar 7 signal bar. Opening Reversals that reverse the high or low of the prior day often form the high or low of the day so traders should swing some or most of their contracts.

Since one extreme of the day usually occurs in the first hour or so, it is important to swing some or all of your shares. Here, a breakeven stop would have allowed a trader to make as much as five dollars on a swing to a new swing high above Bar 5.

When the open forms a breakout of a pattern from the prior day's close, traders should enter on a failed breakout setup (like Bar 7) and then enter in the opposite direction if the failed breakout fails and becomes a Breakout Pullback. Here, there was no good Breakout Pullback short because the move up from the Bar 7 low was strong (a second entry short would be worth taking, but there was only a Low 1 and not a Low 2, and the Low 1 led to the Bar 8 High 1 long), but on a smaller scale, Bar 8 was a Breakout Pullback long on the pullback from a new high on the day.

Obviously, the EMA in the first hour can be misleading when the market opens far from it but then reverses strongly. For example, the EMA is falling yet the market is rising strongly. Although the EMA is often helpful in the first hour, the price action is more important so do what the market is telling you and not what the indicator is saying.

The market gapped up into a bull trend bar at Bar 5 in Figure 11.3, creating the possibility of a bull Trend from the Open. Instead of breaking above Bar 5, the market broke below its low, creating a Double Top Twin and a bear trend bar. When either of the first bar or two of the day is a strong trend bar, it usually leads to at least a tradable scalp and often a good swing. The early longs who bought Bar 5 were stopped out below its low, and when the second bar closed as a strong bear trend bar, the longs would likely wait before looking to buy again, and the odds of a profitable short were therefore high. It would be very unusual for back-to-back opposite trend bars on the open to both fail to yield at least a scalp.

Yesterday closed with Three Pushes Up after a sharp rally (effectively a Wedge), and this commonly leads to a deep pullback that tests the lows and then rallies to a new high above the Wedge. The selloff down to Bar 4 had enough momentum so that a failed test of the prior Bar 3 high was likely (normally, a Lower High), and it would have been a good short for a second leg down, which is common after a Wedge top. The market gave a Higher High test on the open at Bar 5. Although the Wedge did not sell off much (just down to Bar 4), Bar 5 can be looked at as a second attempt to get down to the beginning of yesterday's rally. Remember, everything is gray, and although a Wedge does not typically fail (the upside breakout

FIGURE 11.3 Failed Test of Yesterday's High and Then a Successful Test of Yesterday's Low Followed by a Higher Low

to Bar 5 was the failure because it extended above the top of the Wedge), here the failure failed, and failed failures are usually good entries. Always think about what is going on. Wedges usually don't fail before having at least a two-legged correction, so when the market gapped up and formed a bull trend bar, the bulls were excited. However, on the very next bar, they were stopped out, and smart traders saw this as a failed failure and shorted.

Bar 6 was a failed Micro Trendline break in a steep bear, so was a short. Bar 7 set up a bear M2S short.

Bar 8 was the deep correction that price action traders were looking for since the Bar 3 Wedge. It was also two legs down on the day and a test of yesterday's low. Bar 8 was a great second entry long. Bar 9 was another chance to buy since it was a failed Low 2, which usually results in at least two more legs up (to form a possible Low 4). This was a great trade because it trapped bulls out of a strong up move and they would then have to chase the market up. A trap like this is common at the start of a strong trend and is a sign that the trend will likely go far. Bar 10 was a strong up leg that broke the trendline and broke above the EMA and had many bull trend bars, so a Higher Low was likely to follow. Bar 10 was also an EMA Gap Bar (gap above the EMA) with a bear signal bar and it is reasonable to assume that it would be good for at least a short scalp. However, at this point you would be looking to buy a pullback, since the trend is up until proven otherwise.

Bar 11 was a failed breakout from a Tight Trading Range, and it broke a trendline. Bar 12 was a failed failure ... after the failed breakout of the top of the Tight Trading Range, the market now appeared to be failing on its breakout of the bottom.

The market formed two small bear trend bars en route to Bar 13, and this is effectively a two-legged correction from the Bar 12 reversal up. You could buy on Bar 13, above the second bear trend bar, or you could buy on Bar 14 after the inside bar that acted as a Breakout Pullback.

There was no pullback when the market broke above Bar 10, indicating that the bulls were strong. You could look for a High 2 on the 1-minute chart to go long or wait for a 5-minute pause or pullback.

Bar 15 is not a good long because it was after a small bear trend channel line breakout and reversal. Also, the setup bar was too big, and its high was too high (buy low, sell high!). Bar 16 was a High 2 long on the breakout above the small inside bar, which allowed for a tight stop.

AAPL closed yesterday with a Tight Trading Range in Figure 11.4, which could be a setup for a Failed Final Flag. On Bar 3, AAPL quickly tested below the bull flag from yesterday's close and then broke out of the top. However, it reversed back down on the next bar. Although this is a decent Failed Final Flag short entry, the momentum was strong, and the original failed breakout through the downside means that it might be better to wait for more price action before entering. At this point, a Failed Flag breakout and a reversal of yesterday's high make a bear case more likely.

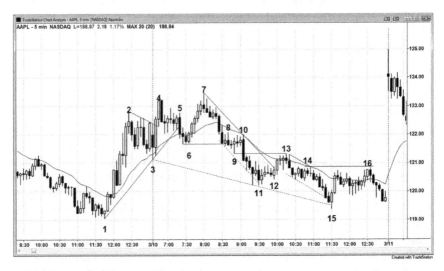

FIGURE 11.4 Failed Final Flag Followed by a Test (Forming Three Pushes up and a Double Top)

Bar 5 came at the end of a Barb Wire pattern that trapped bulls into buying a High 2, and was a great short entry at one tick below the low of the High 2 signal bar (the prior bar). This one bar would trap the bulls long and force them out. Barb Wire often has a second reversal so you have to be prepared to reverse. Bar 6 was a signal to reverse to long, because it was a failed breakout and a second leg down to the EMA in a bull (most bars are above a rising EMA).

Note that the selloff to Bar 6 broke a trendline, indicating that the bears are willing to become aggressive, so you need to be prepared for a failed test of the Bar 4 top of the bull.

Bar 7 was a reversal bar that failed in its breakout to a new high, and it was the second failed attempt to breakout above yesterday's high (Bar 4 was the first). Since the range of the day so far had been only about half of that of a typical recent day, there was a good chance that a breakout in either direction would double the range and likely have at least two legs (the trend traders would likely be confident enough to make at least a second run after any pullback). The Bar 7 Double Top (and third push up in the bull) was the top of the day.

Bar 9 broke below the Bar 6 swing low but not the low of the day, so the odds were very high that there would be at least one more push down to test that low, which was a magnet and very close. Bar 10 completed a Barb Wire pattern, but since everyone was confident of a second leg down and a test to a new low of the day, it offered a great M2S short below the small inside bar. It was also a Breakout Pullback from the breakout below Bar 6.

The Barb Wire pullback to Bar 10 broke a minor trendline (not shown), so it might be the correction that ended the first leg down, but the momentum down has been so strong that the bulls would not be confident enough to buy aggressively yet. They would need more price action.

The break to the Bar 11 new low of the day was essentially straight down and therefore likely not the end of the move (traders will look for a second leg down to at least test the Bar 11 low). Since it was a failed breakout of a bear trend channel line, two legs up were likely first.

Bar 12 was a Double Bottom Pullback long and a failed Low 2, but in the absence of a prior good trendline break or a strong reversal bar, it would only be a scalp. Also, since a second leg down is likely, it would be much wiser to focus on getting short again or adding to shorts than allowing yourself to be distracted by a small bull scalp after seven sideways bars with big tails.

Bar 13 was another M2S opportunity for the bears, but the rally to the EMA broke a good bear trendline. This is a signal to both the bulls and bears that the next reversal up from a new swing low has a good chance of having two legs up, if the reversal is strong enough.

Bar 14 was another M2S short.

Bar 15 was a break to a new low, and it had a strong bull reversal bar off the new low, and it overshot two bear trend channel lines. Since it was a Spike and Channel down, a test of the Bar 14 start of the channel was likely. It was also the second leg down from the first trendline breaking pullback to Bar 13. Finally, it was the second leg down from the high of the day. All of these are signs of strength and increase the odds that the rally will have two legs. The second leg ended at Bar 16, which broke above the high of the first leg and reversed, and it failed to break above the Bar 14 high, forming a Double Top Bear Flag with Bar 14.

Incidentally, when there is a strong move that ends in Three Pushes and then sells off with less momentum (shallower slope, smaller trend bars, more tails), the odds are high that the high of the Three Pushes will be exceeded shortly because this is likely a higher time frame Higher Low. The market fulfilled its Bar 7 objective on the open of the next day.

Yesterday in Figure 11.5 was a bull Trending Trading Range day or a Trending Stairs day but had Three Pushes up and walked up a trendline, which usually means that a trendline break is imminent. The market broke the trendline with the gap opening, and Bar 1 was a Breakout Pullback short, and it might be the start of a bear Trend from the Open.

Bar 3 tried to form a failed breakout, but there were too many overlapping bars on the way down and no climax bottom. There were Three

FIGURE 11.5 Small Breakout Pullback and Possible Bear Trend from the Open

Pushes down to Bar 3, but the pushes were small, and there was no prior bear trendline break.

Bar 5 tried to form a Double Bottom with yesterday's low (to the penny) and instead led to a small Wedge rally that formed a Double Top Bear Flag at Bar 6. A Double Top Bear Flag is a common setup after an initial down move off the open, especially in stocks, and is often followed by a protracted bear trend that is often a Trending Trading Range bear. The Bar 6 signal bar was an EMA Gap Bar.

Bar 7 was a Breakout Pullback short even though the breakout had not yet developed. Close enough. It was also a failed Double Bottom Pullback, a successful Double Top Pullback setup, and a Micro Trendline short.

Bar 9 was a two-legged Breakout Pullback from breaking below yesterday's and today's lows.

Yesterday's day-long bull trend was actually just a large bear flag, and today was the bear trend that came from its breakout.

Yesterday in Figure 11.6 was a strong bear, but Bar 4 broke above a major trendline, indicating that the market might try to reverse after a test of the Bar 3 low (usually a two-legged drop). Instead, the market sold off in two legs into the close.

Bar 8 broke above the new, flatter major trendline generated by the Bar 4 rally and then had a small two-legged Breakout Pullback to the EMA at Bar 9 (two bear trend bars separated by a bull trend bar). This Breakout Pullback led to a Trend from the Open Bull. It was also a Higher Low and the start of the second leg up from the Bar 7 trend channel line overshoot.

Bar 10 was the third push up (three Trending Trading Ranges), so a two-legged pullback was expected.

FIGURE 11.6 Breakout Pullback and Possible Bull Trend from the Open

Bar 11 tested the low of the prior trading range and was an 11:45 A.M. PST sharp move down to trap bulls out of the market. It formed an EMA Gap Bar long that was also a High 2, and this final bull leg broke out of the top of the third trading range and extended to almost a measured move up into the close (twice the height of the Bar 10 to Bar 11 selloff).

Bar 1 in Figure 11.7 was a sharp pullback to test yesterday's strong close, and it quickly reversed up, creating a buy entry at one tick above the high of Bar 1.

Bar 4 is a Breakout Pullback short setup. The open generated a Lower Low after the Bar 3 Lower High, and Bar 4 set up a Low 2 short.

Bar 5 followed the Lower Low test of the bear low that formed yesterday after the bear trendline break. Today opened up and traded down to test that Lower Low. The Breakout Pullback entry above Bar 5 was effectively a High 2 since Bar 5 was the second leg down (yesterday's close was the first leg).

The small Bar 6 Lower High and then trendline break resulted in a Breakout Pullback short. The entire prior day was a large bear flag and a Double Top Bear Flag with the high of the day before.

Bar 7 was a Wedge long setup (a failed breakout below the bear trend channel line and below yesterday's low), and the Wedge followed a break of a major bear trendline.

Bar 8 was a two-legged Breakout Pullback from the strong rally up from Bar 7 that broke a bear trendline. Since a second up leg was likely, traders would look to buy. The easiest entry was the High 2 at Bar 9.

FIGURE 11.7 Patterns from the Prior Day Almost Always Influence the First Hour

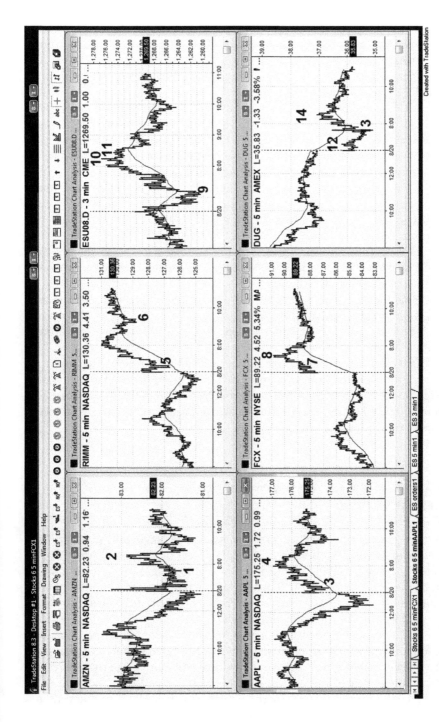

FIGURE 11.8 Swing Trade Stocks off 5-minute Bar Charts

AMZN, Breakout Pullback long. Bar 1 in Figure 11.8 is a Double Bottom Pullback in a large Breakout Pullback after the market broke above the bear trendline from yesterday's close. This is a good entry into the Higher Low that followed the trendline break. Bar 2 is a Wedge short, a Failed Final Flag, and a Lower High.

AAPL, Breakout Pullback long. Bar 3 is a High 2 long on a second test of the EMA after the market gapped above yesterday's bear trendline and then pulled back to the EMA. Whenever there are three or more overlapping bars, it is better to wait for a second entry, like a High 2. Bar 4 is a Wedge short and a failed breakout of yesterday's high.

RIMM, Breakout Pullback long. The market broke above yesterday's high, and then Bar 5 formed a High 2 Breakout Pullback long at the EMA and a possible bull Trend from the Open. Bar 6 was a two-legged EMA gap pullback long.

FCX, Trend from the Open. The market had a large gap up and then went sideways for several bars, setting up a High 2 long entry above the Bar 7 ii. Bar 8 was a Wedge short.

Emini, Failed Breakout. The Emini broke below yesterday's large bear flag but then reversed up at the Bar 9 second entry, which was also a small Failed Final Flag. Bar 10 was a Failed Final Flag short above yesterday's high.

DUG, Failed Breakout. Bar 12 was a Double Top Bear Flag, and with the large gap and no immediate pullback the day was a possible Bear Trend from the open. The market strongly reversed up on a report and formed a small Higher Low at Bar 13. Bar 14 was a Wedge short near yesterday's close.

TREND BAR ON GAP OPEN: FIRST OR SECOND BAR

If there is a gap open and the first bar is a strong (small tail, good-size bar) trend bar, trading its breakout in either direction is a good trade. If you enter and your protective stop is hit on the next bar, reverse for a swing trade because the market will usually move more than the number of ticks that you lost on the first entry, and there is always the possibility that it could develop into a Trend from the Open day.

Even if there is not a gap open, a trend bar for the first bar is a good setup for a trade, but the chance for success is higher if there is a gap, since the market is more overdone and any move will tend to be stronger.

The first bar of the gap down day is a bull trend bar. The long entry in Figure 11.9 on the next bar turned into a One-Tick Failure and then a

FIGURE 11.9   Reverse on a Failed Entry on the Open

reversal down. You had to reverse at your stop, one tick below the low of the bull trend bar. Usually the second entry will more than make up for the loss on the first trade.

GAP OPENINGS: REVERSALS AND CONTINUATIONS

A large gap opening from yesterday's close represents extreme behavior and often results in a trend day in either direction. It does not matter whether or not there is also a gap on the daily chart since the trading will be the same. The only thing that matters is how the market responds to this relatively extreme behavior ... will it accept it or reject it? The larger a gap is, the more likely it will be the start of a trend day away from yesterday's close. The size, direction, and number of trend bars in the first few bars of the day often reveal the direction of the trend day that is likely to follow. Sometimes the market will trend from the first bar or two, but more commonly it will test in the wrong direction and then reverse into a trend that will last all day. Whenever you see a large gap opening, it is wise to assume that there will be a strong trend. However, sometimes it might take an hour to begin. Make sure to swing part of every trade, even if you get stopped out of your swing portion on a few trades. One good swing trade can be as profitable as 10 scalps, so don't give up until it is clear that the day will not trend.

The gap should be looked at as if it were one huge, invisible trend bar. For example, if there is a large gap up and it is followed by a minor pullback and then a channel type of rally for the rest of the day, this is likely a Gap Spike and Channel Bull, with the gap being the spike.

These three days in Figure 11.10 each had large gap openings (gaps from the close of the prior day), and Bars 1 and 9 were also gap openings on the daily chart.

Bar 1 had a shaved top (no tail at the top) and became a large bear trend bar, which is a good scalp setup (if the first bar of the day is a strong trend bar, as seen in the thumbnail, especially on a gap opening, there will usually be follow through), and it was followed by a second large bear trend bar. On most days, this would lead to a bear trend day, and it did here as well (a bear Trend from the Open). There was a sharp rally to Bar 3 that tested the open but this failed Breakout Pullback (the attempted bull reversal up from Bar 2 failed) resulted in a Lower High or a Double Top and then a lengthy down move.

FIGURE 11.10 Gap Openings

Bar 6 was an EMA Gap Bar, a Failed Breakout of large bear flag that formed in the final two hours, and a failed bear trend bar from the open. A short based on that bear trend bar would be risky, since it is in the area of the trading range of the final hour of the day before. It would make more sense to wait for a second entry, which did not come, or a failure, which happened after the Bar 6 signal bar.

The sharp rally up to Bar 7 tested the close of the prior day, formed a Lower High and failed, and became a Breakout Pullback and a Double Top Bear Flag (with the last bar of yesterday). Big Up (to Bar 7), Big Down usually ends in a trading range, as it did on this day.

Bar 9 gapped below the low of the prior day and formed a bear trend bar, but it had big tails. It could be the start of a Trend from the Open bear. The second bar was a second bear trend bar with a close on its low, indicating that the bears were strong. Most traders would short at one tick below that low. The very next bar was the entry bar for the short, but it became a bull reversal bar. However, the protective stop above its high was not hit (and a two-point protective money stop was also not hit), and a scalper would have taken partial profits on his short at Bar 10.

Bar 10 was also the second leg down (from the Bar 7 high), which can lead to a reversal. The first four bars of the day were largely overlapping, forming a Tight Trading Range, so trading breakouts is a risky proposition. A Tight Trading Range is like Barb Wire, and it acts as a magnet, drawing breakouts back toward its middle. The best thing to do is to fade small bars near its extreme, fade failed breakouts, and look for Breakout Pullbacks. This day had all three.

There was a small inside bar after the Bar 10 breakout to a new low and a High 2 variant buy setup, and this is an acceptable long, but with four of the first five bars of the day being bear bars, this was not ideal. At this point, it was a failed breakout below yesterday's low.

Bar 11 was a Breakout Pullback (the breakout below yesterday's trading range) and a bear M2S. This M2S broke a small bull trendline at Bar 12 and reversed back up, setting up a Breakout Pullback long above the inside bar that followed Bar 12. A market that turns up from a Low 2 often rallies for at least two more legs, and since big gap days often become trend days, this could be, and was, the start of a big move.

TREND FROM THE OPEN OR TREND FROM THE FIRST BAR

Sometimes the first bar of the day forms the high or low of the day, and the day begins a trend from the very first bar (a Trend from the First Bar version of a Trend from the Open). The trend can also start from the second bar (or even after a few sideways bars) and still qualify as a Trend from the Open. This often leads to a strong trend day, and if you miss the entry on the open, look to enter on the First Pullback.

The market gapped below yesterday's low in Figure 11.11 and broke out of a large trading range formed over the second half of yesterday (a Head and Shoulders Bear Flag). The first bar today was a bull trend bar, which usually leads to a partial gap closure. Many went long on a stop at one tick above the high of the bull trend bar. However, the market trapped those longs two bars later when it traded below the low of the bull trend signal bar (and the entry bar). Bar 1 provided a great opportunity to go short at one tick below the low of the bull trend bar because this is where most of those trapped longs will get out, driving the market down. It was a Breakout Pullback short. Also, any potential buyers will be waiting for more price action, so there are only sellers in the market, making for a high-probability short. Shorts added on at the bear flags along that way that trapped other early longs.

Bar 2 appeared to be a failed Low 2, but it did not hit the protective stops above the entry bar, and smart traders are holding short on a bear trend day. There was no strong reversal bar or good prior trendline break, and the down momentum from the open was strong. Also, this was a bear Barb Wire pattern and the odds favor a downside breakout. The presumption was that this is a Trend from the Open Bear day, which is a very strong trend, and therefore smart traders will try to stay short. Also, many

FIGURE 11.11 Trend from the Open

traders would hesitate to short the Low 2 because it followed a bull out-side bar. They would be happy to wait for the second entry, which came below Bar 2.

This Bar 3 flag is the second down leg of the day, and the market often tries to reverse after two legs, making the bears more cautious and the bulls more daring. However, once it failed, everyone expected at least two more legs down, which they got (the Bar 4 flag was the end of the first small leg down, and the second leg ended one bar later). This created a small Three Push Down pattern and then a small two-legged test of the EMA, but in strong bear trend days, it is often wise to ignore the buys to make sure that you catch the shorts.

Bars 4 through 5 formed a Failed Final Flag that grew into a Wedge bear flag. The first leg of the Wedge is the Bar 4 high and the second leg is the bottom of the reversal out of the Failed Final Flag. The other two pushes up are the two small legs up to Bar 5. This Wedge became a larger Failed Final Flag, as it often does.

Smart bulls would only begin to look to buy after the Bar 5 rally to the EMA broke the bear trendline.

Bar 6 was a two-legged drop to a new low, giving a High 2 Lower Low buy entry.

Bar 7 was a Higher Low entry, a High 2, and a failed Micro Trendline breakout, and was a good buy because even the bears are looking for at least a second leg up. The large bear trend bar three bars earlier was a great bear trap, making lots of traders believe that the bears had regained control. However, it was followed by two dojis, meaning that there was no conviction to the selling, and it simply trapped longs out of a great trade. This flush out to a Higher Low could be the start of a new bull or at least a two-legged Countertrend move up. Note that the second and fourth bars after entry were Pullback Bars (a Low 1 and a Low 2). That would be un-usual for a bull with conviction, and it told everyone that much more bullish price action will be needed before a protracted bull leg unfolds. However, a failed Low 2 in a bear usually results in two more legs up, which happened over the next several bars. This keeps bears on edge and will force them to take profits quickly. The first area where they will take partial or full profits is above a prior swing high.

After a second leg up to a new swing high, the market failed at a Low 4. The bulls took profits and were unwilling to buy again until there was significant bullish price action. The new shorts off the second failed swing high feel confident that the bulls won't overwhelm them soon on this bear trend day, and they will continue to sell as the market drops. This resulted in seven consecutive bars that the bulls could not own.

Bar 1 in Figure 11.12 is the breakout below the 5-minute Signal and Entry Bars. Bar 2 broke above a two-bar Micro Trendline, forming a High 2.

FIGURE 11.12   This Is a 1-minute Version of the Same Chart

This trapped eager bulls who covered on the next bar, one tick below the entry bar, and this created a Low 2. The Low 2 was a great entry for bears because not only was it a With Trend Low 2, but there were also clearly newly trapped longs who wouldn't be eager to buy once they sold to cover. This resulted in a large bear trend entry bar with several bear trend bars following it. There were only bears in the market at this point, after both the 5-minute bulls and then the 1-minute bulls were forced to liquidate. Bulls now would be waiting for much stronger price action evidence of a reversal before buying again and shorts would be adding on, believing that any blip up would be temporary and that there would be at least a new swing low that would allow them to get out around breakeven at worst.

The first bar in Figure 11.13 was a bear trend bar and a possible start of a bear Trend from the Open. The market failed to reverse the Bar 2 swing low from yesterday so it will likely now test yesterday's low at Bar 1, an obvious magnet. Place an order to go short at one tick below the low of Bar 3, even though the big tail at the bottom indicates that the bears are not in complete control. Once the market falls below yesterday's low at

FIGURE 11.13 The Market Opened with a Moderate Gap Down, Which Can Be Near the High or Low of the Day

Bar 1, it should try to reverse up again, so you need to place an order to go long on a stop at one tick above the first good signal bar. Bar 4 was a bear trend bar, but the next bar created a Down Up Twin buy setup, followed by a long entry. If the order wasn't filled and the next bar had a lower low, you would try to buy above its high, since you are looking for a failed breakout below yesterday's low to form an Opening Reversal up. However, if the market falls much further without a good entry setup, traders should only trade shorts until after a rally breaks a trendline.

The market made a small two-legged rally to the EMA and above the high of the day. The two legs were the bull trend bar followed by the bear trend bar, and then the second leg up was the Bar 5 bull trend bar. Countertrend moves are often made of two legs, and since this might be a bear trend day, this is a good short setup (two legs up to a new high, forming basically a Double Top Bear Flag at the EMA on a gap down day). Since you were not filled on your short entry order on the bar after Bar 5, you would move the stop to one tick below the low of the next bar, a bear inside bar, and you would be filled. This is also a Low 2 Breakout Pullback short (the Low 1 was on the bar after Bar 3).

Bar 6 is a setup for a High 2 long (the High 1 occurred after Bar 4) and a reversal from a new low of the day and a second test of yesterday's low. This long stalled at the EMA and formed a series of sideways bars and many dojis.

Bar 9 was a setup for a M2S short, and it was a decent setup, but it is often best to wait for a clear false breakout when there are sideways bars and dojis (Barb Wire).

Bar 10 was a High 2 breakout to the upside that quickly reversed back down, forming a Double Top Bear Flag with Bar 9 and trapping bulls who didn't have enough time to realize that they needed to reverse and not just exit. You should never buy a breakout from Barb Wire, especially below the EMA. All slow traders were trapped out of shorts by the quickness of the reversal and will be forced to chase the market down. The best trade would be to short once the market formed an outside bar or as it broke below Bar 8. The market tried to form a Higher Low at Bar 8, and instead it failed and formed Lower Highs at Bars 9 and 10. The bears are clearly in control, so you need to expect at least two legs down.

Bar 12 was a Breakout Pullback that might be the end of the first leg down. In any case, you need to short below Bar 12, expecting a second leg down. The Bar 12 high exactly tested the Bar 6 low (a Breakout Test) and then the bear resumed.

The Bar 5 new high converted this day from a Trend from the open type of bear, which is very strong, into a likely Trending Trading Range day, which is a less strong bear and often has a late rally that reverses at least the final trading range, making the day close above its low.

THIRD BAR OF THE DAY AND THE 15-MINUTE CLOSE

When trading the 5-minute chart it is easy to not be thinking about the many institutional traders who are also paying attention to 15-minute charts. The first 15-minute bar closes at the close of the third 5-minute bar, and therefore activity around this third bar will influence the appearance of the first 15-minute bar. For example, if the first two bars of the day move in one direction and then the third bar is a smaller pause bar, the breakout of the bar will determine if there is a 15-minute breakout or if there could be a failure, and therefore trading the breakout of the third bar of the day often leads to a big move. Do not place a trade on the third bar alone on most days, but be aware of its extra significance. If it is an important bar, there will usually be other price action to support the trade, and that additional information should be the basis for the trade. This is not an important point and can be ignored by most traders.

Similar logic can also be used for the last 5-minute bar of the 30- and 60-minute charts, but focusing on such longer time frames and their infrequent entries increases the chances of missing one or more profitable 5-minute trades and therefore is not worthwhile.

FIGURE 11.14 The Third Bar of the Day Is the Close of the 15-minute Bar

Bar 1 in Figure 11.14 is the third bar of the day, and it is a small bull reversal bar, and it reversed up from the EMA and a swing low from yesterday. This is a great Opening Reversal long entry, and it also prevented the first 15-minute bar from being a strong bear trend bar.

Bar 3 also reversed a swing low from yesterday and led to a scalper's profit, but the bull entry bar reversed down in an Up Down Twin reversal for a short entry. Note that Bar 3 was a bear trend bar and not a good reversal bar, so this is not a good Countertrend long setup.

The break below the Bar 3 low was also a break below the first 15-minute bar of the day on a day with a large gap down, increasing the odds of a tradable downswing.

STRONG TREND BARS IN THE FIRST HOUR OFTEN PREDICT STRENGTH LATER IN THE DAY IN THE SAME DIRECTION

Sometimes the market trends for the first bar or two of the day, and that first bar ends up as one of the extremes of the day. When the market Trends from the Open, it is important to enter early. This pattern is most common with gap openings, large or small, and although you should always scalp part of your trades in the first hour, when you enter a trade where you might be at the start of a huge trend, it is particularly important to swing some contracts. If the pattern is very strong, you should swing most of your contracts and then quickly move your stop to breakeven.

However, if the strong opening is reversed (a breakout to a new extreme of the day in the opposite direction), then the day might trend in the opposite direction, or it could turn into a trading range (Big Up Big Down day). A strong trend off the open, even if it is reversed, still means that there were traders willing to trade aggressively in that direction, and they will be quick to trade again in that direction later in the day if the reversal falters.

If there is a series of strong trend bars off the open and then a partial pullback that gets tested 5 to 10 bars later (the pullback is followed by a minor retracement and then a retest of the extreme of the pullback), this forms a Double Bottom or Top Flag entry and has a good chance of leading to a new extreme on the day and often leads to a trend.

The seven-bar run up to Bar 4 in Figure 11.15 had several large bull bars and only two small bear bars, showing that the bulls were willing to be aggressive. This is something to remember later in the day if another buy setup appears, making traders more willing to swing part of their longs.

Bar 8 was a successful second attempt to reverse the breakout to a new low of the day, so it should be expected to lead to a rally that had at least two legs. In fact, the two-legged rally only had a small pullback (Bar 10), making the rally to Bar 9 a possible first leg of a larger first leg (it ended at Bar 11).

Bar 12 was an M2B buy for a second larger leg up, which also had two smaller legs.

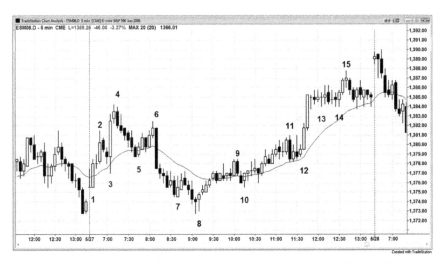

FIGURE 11.15 A Strong Move Off the Open Is Sometimes Repeated Later in the Day

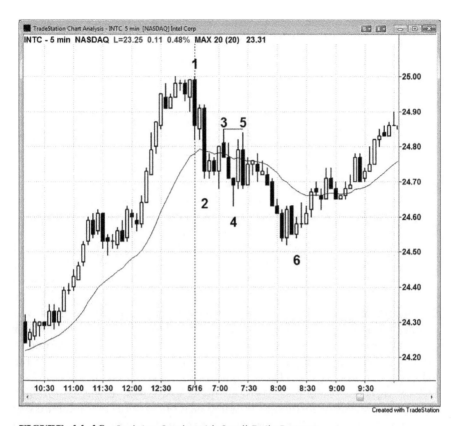

FIGURE 11.16 Scalping Stocks with Small Daily Ranges

In general, you should not often scalp stocks with average daily ranges under three dollars, but price action entries still work. You have to trade far more volume and even a $1 commission eats up too much of a 10 cent scalp. INTC had two large bear trend bars in the first 15 minutes and then formed a Double Top Bear Flag (Bars 3 and 5 in Figure 11.16). This is a reliable pattern that often leads to a bear trend day. Yesterday's bull was so strong that today's two-legged selling reversed back up at Bar 6 (likely at the EMA on the 15- or 60-minute charts), but it was good for at least a 10 cent scalp.

OPENING PATTERNS AND REVERSALS

Besides the Gap Opening Reversals and Trends from the Open discussed earlier, common reversal patterns and moves on the open are the same as patterns occurring at any other time of the day and include the following:

- Trading range breakouts
- Sharp pullbacks to the EMA
- Failed Breakouts of anything, including swing points, trendlines, trend channel lines, trading ranges, and yesterday's extremes
- Breakout Pullbacks (Failed Failed Breakouts: that is, a Failed Breakout that went on to fail)

On most days, either the high or low of the day is formed within the first hour or so. Once one of the day's extremes is formed, the market reverses toward what will become the other extreme of the day. (Obviously on a Trend from the Open day, there is no reversal, but the market still works toward the other extreme, which will usually be near the close of the day). This Opening Reversal is often recognizable and can be a great trading opportunity for a swing trade. The first move on the open is often fast and covers many points, and it is hard to believe that it could suddenly reverse directions, but this is a common occurrence. The turn is usually at some key point like a test of the high or low of yesterday, a swing high or low of yesterday or today, a breakout of a trading range of yesterday or today, a trendline or trend channel line, a moving average, or any of the above on a different time frame chart or on the Globex chart. Even if the best setup is on a 60-minute or daily chart, there will almost always be a price action reason to take the trade based entirely on the 5-minute day session chart, so a trader adept at chart reading only needs to watch the one chart that he is using for trading.

The patterns in the first hour are the same as those later in the day but the reversals are often more violent, and the trends tend to last longer. An important key to maximizing trading profits is to swing part of any position that could be a high or low of the day. If the trade looks particularly strong, swing all of the position and take partial profits on a third to a half after the trade has run two to three times your initial risk. If you had a price action stop that was three points (such as the distance to the other side of the signal bar) and a two point money stop in the Emini, your initial risk was two points so take a third to a half off at around four points. If there is a strong trendline break and then the market pauses and appears to be reversing into a trendline breakout test, look to take some more off, maybe a quarter, just in case the entire pattern fails. Hold the remaining contracts until there is a clear and strong opposite signal or until your breakeven stop is hit. Look to add to your position at every With Trend setup, like a two-legged pullback to the EMA in a strong trend. For these additional contracts, scalp most or all of the position, but continue to swing some contracts.

Some reversals start quietly and trend only slightly for many bars before forcefully breaking into a trend, whereas others have strong momentum from the entry bar. Be open to all possibilities, and make sure to take every signal, especially if it is strong. One of the difficulties is that reversals often are sharp and a trader might not have enough time to convince herself that a reversal setup could actually lead to a reversal. However, if there is a strong trend bar for the signal bar, the chances of success are good, and you must take the trade. If you feel that you need more time to assess the setup, at least take a half or a quarter position because the trade might suddenly move very far very fast, and you need to be involved, even if only in a small way. Then look to add on at the First Pullback.

FIGURE 11.17 GOOG 5-minute Opening Reversals

Bar 1 in Figure 11.17 is an M2S with a steep EMA, and it closed the gap below yesterday's low by six cents, setting up a Breakout Pullback reversal that formed the high of the day.

Bar 2 is an EMA pullback and then an ii bull breakout and a failed small trend channel line overshoot reversal.

Bar 3 was a Failed Breakout and reversal up from breaking the trendline from the rally into the prior day's close.

Bar 5 was a High 2 Double Bottom Bull Flag (the first bottom was two bars earlier) that also was the first pullback (a Breakout Pullback) after the breakout above yesterday's high. This could turn into a Trend from the Open Trend day.

Bar 1 in Figure 11.18 for AAPL was a second entry (Low 2) for an Opening Reversal off a trend channel line overshoot (a Failed Breakout of the trend channel line).

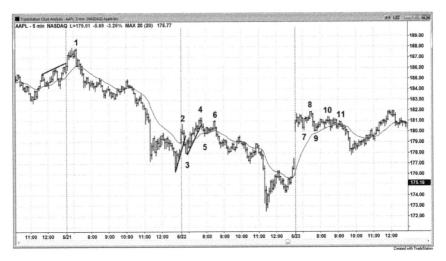

FIGURE 11.18 AAPL, Opening Trades

Bar 2 was a reversal down from a breakout (a Failed Breakout) above the trading range in the final hour of the day before and of the bear trendline going into the close of the prior day. The market then reversed up from the EMA, forming the Bar 3 Higher Low, which was also a Breakout Pullback.

Bar 4 was a reversal down from a Higher High on a day that was not yet a bull, and therefore a good short. It also had a Wedge shape and was two legs up after yesterday's strong bear.

Bar 6 was a Lower High after the Bar 5 break of the trendline.

Bar 7 was a High 2 Breakout Pullback in a day with a large gap up, but the market reversed back down at the Bar 8 Higher High and Failed Final Flag breakout. Since this was not a bull trend day at this point, this is a good short.

Bar 9 was a new low, but it came with strong momentum, making a second leg down likely.

Bar 10 was a Low 2 and a Lower High.

Bar 11 was a second entry into the short based on an M2S. It was also a possible Spike and Trading Range Top and then a possible Spike and Channel bear.

Bar 2 in Figure 11.19 was a strong bear reversal bar and an EMA test in a strong bear, forming a Failed Breakout above yesterday's bear trendline (not shown). However, it gapped above the trendline from yesterday's bear move and might have a second leg up (the first leg was the gap).

Bar 3 was not a reversal bar, but it was a High 2 variant (the High 1 was the bull trend bar that followed the Bar 2 down bar) that was a

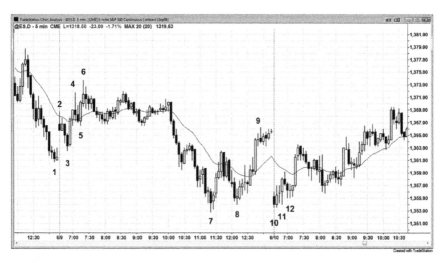

FIGURE 11.19 Emini Trades off the Open

Breakout Pullback (breakout of yesterday's bear trendline). This was a possible Higher Low after a climactic close, and after a climax (the strong bear into the close had virtually no pullbacks and since it was likely not sustainable, it was therefore climactic), there is often a two-legged Countertrend move.

Bar 6 was a Wedge top and a two-legged move up from the Bar 3 Higher Low.

Bar 10 was a Double Bottom Bull Flag and a Failed Breakout below the two-legged rally up from Bar 7. The first bottom was Bar 8 or the inside signal bar following Bar 7 low. It was also a reversal up from a test of yesterday's low.

Bar 12 was a Higher Low and led to a breakout an ii pattern. It was also a failed Low 2 in a bear, which trapped bears who saw the big gap down and shorted the second entry (Low 2 gap pullback).

DOUBLE BOTTOM AND DOUBLE TOP FLAGS

Unlike a Double Bottom Pullback that is a reversal pattern, a Double Bottom Bull Flag is a continuation pattern that develops after the bull has already begun. Functionally, it is the same as a Double Bottom Pullback, since both are buy setups.

The same is true for Double Top Bear Flags, which are continuation patterns in an ongoing bear and not a reversal pattern, like the Double Top Pullback. Both, however, are short setups. After a strong down move and a pullback, the bear will resume. If the market pulls back again to about the same level as the First Pullback and again finds sellers around the same price, this trading range is a Double Top Bear Flag, and it is a short entry setup. The market made two attempts to go above a price and failed both times and this usually results in the market doing the opposite, especially when the opposite is With Trend. More often than not, the second pullback will be slightly below the first, as would be expected in a bear trend (each swing high tends to be below the prior one). The entry is on a stop at one tick below the setup bar.

FIGURE 11.20 Double Top Bear Flag

Bars 2 and 3 in Figure 11.20 formed a Double Top Bear Flag on a big gap down day (the gap was the flag pole of the Bear Flag).

Bar 3 gave a M2S short entry and a minor Failed Final Flag.

Bars 3 and 4 in Figure 11.21 formed a large Double Bottom Bull Flag after the rally to Bar 2. Bars 6 and 7 formed a Double Top Bear Flag after the strong move down to Bar 5.

GS pullback had a strong move up to Bar 1 in Figure 11.22 and then formed a broad Double Bottom Bull Flag.

Bar 10 slightly undershot Bar 6 and formed a Double Top Bear Flag. It could have topped out at Bar 7 or at Bar 5 as well and still have been the same pattern.

Bars 8 and 9 formed a sloppy Double Bottom Bull Flag, but it had too much of a Barb Wire look to be a great setup.

FIGURE 11.21 Double Bottom Bull Flag

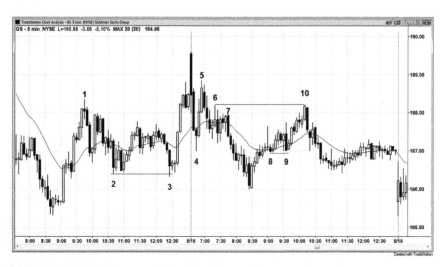

FIGURE 11.22 Double Bottom Bull Flag

TRADING RANGE BREAKOUTS

Sometimes the market forms a trading range in the first 3 to 10 bars or so with 2 or more reversals. If the range is small compared to the average daily range, a breakout is likely. A trader could enter on a breakout from the range, but the risk is smaller if you are able to fade small bars at the

FIGURE 11.23 Trading Range Breakout off the Open

top or bottom of the range, or wait until after the breakout and enter on a failed breakout or a Breakout Pullback, just as you would with any trading range.

GOOG went sideways in Figure 11.23 into a 7:00 A.M. PST report and then broke out of the trading range to the downside. A trader could enter on a stop below the trading range low, but it is less risky to short the Low 2 below Bar 5. This is a Low 2 because Bars 3 and 5 were two legs up (bull trend bars separated by one or more bear trend bars). It was also a failed High 2. It is basically Barb Wire below the EMA and therefore will likely have a downside breakout (bear flag).

Some days open with a flat EMA, big overlapping bars, and just no safe setups (no small bars near the top or bottom where a fade trade could be placed). This is Barb Wire in Figure 11.24, and it should be traded like all Barb Wire and requires patience. Wait for one side to be trapped with a trend bar breakout, and then look to fade the breakout.

Bar 7 was a reversal up after a breakout of the bottom of the Barb Wire, but it followed a series of bear trend bars, and there was no prior trendline break and no good signal bar. You need a second entry. Even though it was

FIGURE 11.24 Barb Wire on the Open

a High 2, the High 1 was an outside down bar that trapped longs, and that bar should be considered the start of the down move. That is, expect two legs after the outside down bull trap bar, making Bar 7 actually a High 1, since the down move began at the top of Bar 6 and not the top of Bar 5.

Bar 7 broke a Micro Trendline (across the three prior bars but not shown), and then Bar 9 formed a second attempt at reversing the break to a new low below the low of the day and yesterday. Second entries are always good, especially on nontrend days, and this alone was all the reason that a trader needed to go long, even with the weak reversal bar (a bear close, but at least the close was above the middle of the bar). The market then trended up through the other side of the opening range and gave a M2B Breakout Pullback long at Bar 10.

FIRST PULLBACK

Entering on the First Pullback after a strong first leg is simply capitalizing on the propensity for strong moves to test the extreme. Most strong moves have at least two legs so entering on the First Pullback through a trendline has a very good chance of leading to a profitable trade. This entry is especially important on Trend from the Open days if you missed the original entry. In strong trends, what constitutes the First Pullback is not always clear because trends frequently have two or three sideways bars that don't break a meaningful trendline and therefore really aren't significant enough to constitute a pullback. They are all great With Trend entries, and you can continue to enter With Trend with confidence even after the First Pullback that breaks a meaningful trendline. Only after a trendline is broken has there been a significant pullback, and the first leg has likely ended. Even then, the first break of the trendline has very high odds of setting up a With Trend entry that will lead to second trend leg and a new extreme in the trend. Consider the First Pullback trade to be the first one after a trendline break, and all the With Trend entries before then are simply part of the first leg of the trend. Look for High/Low 1 and 2 setups and enter on a stop at one tick beyond the setup bar (for a buy, buy on a stop at one tick above the setup bar).

The market in Figure 11.25 formed a bull Trend from the Open, and the Bar 2 break below the Micro Trendline was the First Pullback. Traders should buy on a stop at one tick above its high, even though it was a weak signal bar (bear close, but at least the close was above the midpoint).

FIGURE 11.25 First Pullback

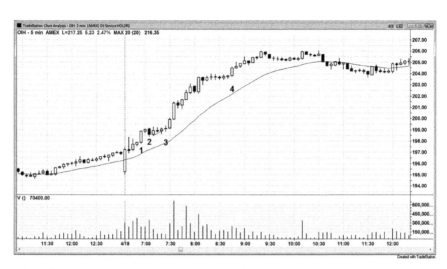

FIGURE 11.26   Bull Trend from the First Bar without a First Pullback

FIGURE 11.27   In Strong Trends, the First Pullback Often Is Unclear

The OIH in Figure 11.26 had a bull Trend from the First Bar and there really never was a First Pullback with enough Countertrend strength to break a meaningful trendline. The ii breakout at Bar 1 is a good entry, and the Bar 3 breakout of the two-legged sideways correction was another. Finally, there was the Tight Trading Range breakout at Bar 4. All of these entries should be considered to be part of the first up leg and not a first pullback, which comes after the first leg and sets up the second leg. Rarely, days just don't seem to pull back and traders are forced to enter on breakouts from even brief sideways pauses. The reality is that on strong days like this you can just buy your swing size position at the market at any point, trusting that even if there is a reversal, the odds are overwhelming that the market will make another high before the pullback retraces very far.

When that is the case, the odds are very high that your trade will be profitable because an unclear pullback means the Countertrend traders are very weak. Bars 2 and 3 in Figure 11.27 were tiny pullbacks that did not break a meaningful trendline. The First Pullback to break a trendline was Bar 4. The first trendline break has a very good chance of being followed by a second With Trend leg and is a great entry (like shorting Bar 4).

CHAPTER 12

Detailed Day Trading Examples

B ars 3, 4, and 5 in Figure 12.1 were shorts on testing the EMA in a bear.

Bar 6 was a second entry bear trend channel line overshoot and reversal up, but the signal bar was weak (a small doji). It was also a Wedge reversal. However, the rally from Bar 6 broke the trendline, setting up a long on a test of the low.

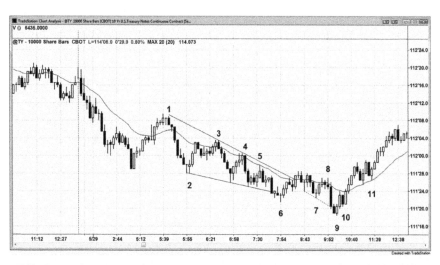

FIGURE 12.1 Shows a TY Futures, 10,000-Share Chart (Each Bar Is 10,000 Contracts and Not Based on Time)

Bar 9 was a Lower Low test of Bar 6 and a bear trend channel over-shoot and reversal, and it was a bull reversal bar. Also, it was a failed failed Wedge (the Wedge bottom at Bar 6 failed, and its upside breakout broke a trendline and then had a two-legged move to a Lower Low), which is a very strong buy signal, as can be seen by the powerful rally that followed.

Bar 10 was an inside bar that ended the first tiny pullback (bear trend bar), so traders could go long above it. After the Spike and Channel bear (Bar 2 ended the spike) and the Three Pushes Down (Bars 2, 6, and 9 ended them), it was likely that a protracted two-legged up move would develop, so the Bar 10 pause was likely to just be part of the first leg up and not the end of the first leg (that would make the leg too small for what should be expected based on the size of the pattern that created the reversal). Spike and Channels usually retrace to the start of the channel, which was the Bar 3 high.

Bar 11 was an M2B buy setup (the High 1 was two bars earlier) and the actual First Pullback since it broke a trendline.

The 5-minute EURUSD (Forex) in Figure 12.2 reversed down at Bar 2 after a new high. This bull leg had strong momentum, as evidenced by eight bars in a row without a bear trend bar, so the odds were high that there would be a Higher Low rally that tested the Bar 2 high before there was a breakout below the start of the leg (Bar 1). Bar 3 was an EMA Gap Bar that also was a Breakout Test of the Bar 1 beginning of the rally.

The market formed a triangle, which ended up as a Tight Trading Range.

FIGURE 12.2 5-Minute EURUSD (Forex)

Bar 8 was a failed upside breakout attempt (one tick below the Bar 4 high) that reversed through the bottom of the range in a bear outside bar. It formed a Double Top Bear Flag with Bar 6.

Bar 9 was a Breakout Pullback small bar above the middle of the outside bar, offering a low-risk short.

Bar 10 was another Breakout Pullback short. You would not be buying above that small doji because a doji is a one-bar trading range, and you don't buy above a trading range in a falling market.

Bar 11 was a M2S short and a second attempt to break out below the Bar 3 spike low.

Bar 12 was another M2S. Always keep placing your orders. A bear might become complacent because of the bull doji Higher Low, but you still need to be thinking that the market is in a bear swing and if it falls below this bar, it will form an M2S.

Bar 13 was a ii long setup with a strong bull bar for the second bar after the trend channel line overshoot.

Bar 15 was Three Pushes up and the first EMA Gap Bar.

Bar 16 was an ii setup (with bull ii bars) for a Higher Low long, since traders were expecting at least two legs up from the trend channel overshoot and reversal off the Bar 13 low entry. It formed a Double Bottom Bull Flag with Bar 14. The large bear trend bar trapped bears into shorts and trapped weak bulls out of longs.

Bar 2 in Figure 12.3 was a trading range after the Bar 1 spike up. Bar 3 was a second small leg up after the bar 1 spike down, and it broke out of

FIGURE 12.3 Soybeans, 5-Minute Chart

the top but failed (a Failed Final Flag), setting up a nice short below Bar 3 or below the trading range.

Bar 4 overshot a bear Micro trend channel line and reversed up. The entry was above the Bar 6 ii bar, which had a bull close.

Bar 9 was a Wedge and a four-legged move up from the Bar 4 low, making it a Low 4 variation. It was a test of the Bar 3 high but could not get up there to form a perfect Double Top Bear Flag.

Bar 10 was a Breakout Pullback from the trendline breakout.

Bar 11 was a huge bull reversal bar following a new low on the day, but Bar 12 could not trade above it, making a short below Bar 12 inside bear trend bar a great entry because of the trapped longs who entered early in Bar 11. It was also a Breakout Pullback, as was the Bar 13 short.

Bar 1 in Figure 12.4 was a High 1 Breakout Pullback from the breakout of the earlier trading range.

Bar 3 was a good High 2 long, despite the Barb Wire, because Bar 2 was not a climax and the momentum remained strong (as seen by the large bull trend bars leading up to Bar 2).

Bar 5 was a Three Push High short, so two down legs should follow (a climax usually is followed by at least two Countertrend legs). The move down to Bar 6 broke the trendline, and it broke below the Bar 3 Higher Low of the bull, indicating strong bears.

Bar 7 was a two-legged Breakout Test of the Bar 5 signal bar, and it was a Lower High and an Up Down Twin short setup and a sharp rejection of the poke above the EMA.

FIGURE 12.4 Crude Oil

The chart below is a close up of this area. It is virtually impossible for most traders to read a chart correctly fast enough to catch most of these trades in Figure 12.5 but the chart illustrates that price action analysis even works on the 1-minute level.

Bar 1 in Figure 12.6 was a failed Low 2, so effectively a High 2 long.

FIGURE 12.5 A 1-minute Chart Showing Many Price Action Scalps in the First 90 Minutes

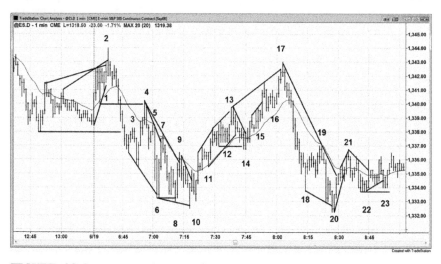

FIGURE 12.6 This Is a Close Up of the 1-minute Emini's First 90 Minutes Highlighting Price Action Scalp Setups

Bar 2 was a Wedge short and a failed breakout of a bull flag.

Bar 3 was a Breakout Pullback short.

Bar 4 was a Breakout Test short even though it was a Higher High (above the Bar 3 swing high), which is a sign of strength.

Bar 5 was a Lower High and an M2S below the EMA.

Bar 6 was a Wedge long and an Expanding Triangle bottom.

Bar 7 was a failed trendline breakout short.

Bar 8 was a two-legged Lower Low after the Bar 7 break of a trendline, and a Lower Low on a trading range day.

Bar 10 was a Wedge and a Lower Low on a trading range day.

Bar 11 was the First Pullback after a trendline break, and it was an M2B long.

Bar 12 was another bull M2B.

Bar 13 was a Wedge short and a possible Double Top bear Flag (with Bar 4).

Bar 14 was a failed trendline and trading range breakout failure, a Double Bottom Bull Flag, and a possible start of a second leg up.

Bar 15 was a High 2 that followed a Breakout Test two bars earlier.

Bar 16 was a High 2 in a bull.

Bar 17 was a Wedge and a failed test of the high of the day, and therefore a possible Lower High.

Bar 19 was a bear Low 2 (M2S) and a Five-Tick Failure for traders who bought Bar 18.

Bar 20 was two pushes to a new low of the day (Bar 18 was the first) in a trading range day (even though there was a strong bear leg from the Bar 17 high ... it is not a bear day at this point). It was also a reversal up after a one-tick new low of the day (a one-tick failed breakout). It was also a Wedge.

Bar 21 was a small second leg up and a possible Double Top Bear Flag (with Bar 19).

Bar 22 was a two-legged pullback to a Higher Low after a trendline break (Bars 17 to 19), and a Double Bottom (Bars 10 and 20) Pullback long.

Bar 23 was a failed trendline break and a Double Bottom (Bar 23 was one tick higher than Bar 22) Bull Flag.

CHAPTER 13

Daily, Weekly, and Monthly Charts

A lthough daily, weekly, and monthly charts can generate intraday signals, they occur so infrequently that they become a distraction for a day trader and should be ignored. The most common signals are those based on yesterday's high and low, and you can see them on a 5-minute chart. However, there are frequently price action entries on these longer time frames, but because the signal bars are so large, far fewer contracts can be traded if the risk is to be the same as for a day trade. Also, overnight risk may mean that you should reduce your contracts even further or consider trading option strategies that have a defined risk, like outright purchases or spreads. A day trader should only trade these charts if they do not occupy his thoughts during the trading day because it is easy to miss a few day trades using large volume while nursing a trade of far fewer contracts or shares based on the daily chart, and these misses can more than offset any gain from the daily signal.

The price action of the stock of the largest companies in the world usually behaves in a more predictable way than that for the stock of small companies. The risk of a huge, overnight adverse move, especially on the upside in a protracted bull, is much less. This means that a Countertrend trade in WMT has a smaller chance of failing than in CHK. However, the profit potential is also less.

When trading counter to a strong trend, the goal should be a scalp of 1 or 2 percent, since most Countertrend trades just result in pullbacks that become With Trend entries. Gaps complicate the entries, and in general, the risk is less if the market opens within yesterday's range and then trades through the entry stop at one tick beyond the range. If you cannot watch the stock intraday and there is a gap open, it is probably best to pass on the trade. If you can watch the stock and there is a gap opening, watch for a gap pullback, and then enter on the failed pullback into the gap, as the market resumes its move away from yesterday's range. In other words, if you were looking to buy, but today gapped up, look for a selloff on the open today, and then buy a Breakout Pullback reversal back up, placing your stop below the low of today. If the entry fails and your stop is hit, look elsewhere or give it only one more try if there is a second buy setup. Don't spend too much time on a stock that is not doing what you wanted it to do because you will lose money. There is a natural tendency to want to make back your money on the same stock after a loss, but this is a sign of your emotional weakness. If you feel a need to prove that you were right and are in fact a great chart reader, you might be right about that, but you are not a great trader. Great traders accept their losses and move on.

Pullbacks on daily charts rarely have classic reversal bars, leaving traders with more uncertainty than when trading 5-minute charts. Uncertainty means risk, and when there is more risk, position sizes need to be smaller, and a trader will have to consider taking a partial position and adding to the position as the price action unfolds. In a bull pullback, additions can be made at a lower price if the market sells off a little more but the bears have not yet demonstrated that they are in control. Additions can also be made at a higher price, after the trend has resumed and a small pullback forms a Higher Low, above your original entry.

When you scan your daily charts at the end of the day, you will frequently see setups to consider for the next day. Once the setup triggers, there will often be an intraday trend that will provide you with many good 5-minute With Trend entries. If the stock is not one that you normally trade intraday but its volume is about 5 million shares or more, it is worth considering adding it to your basket of day trading stocks for a day or two. Sometimes, however, even with very liquid stocks such as the OIH, your broker might not have an inventory available for selling short, and you might be only able to trade buy setups.

Price action is the cumulative result of a large number of traders acting independently for countless reasons to make as much money as they can. Because of that, its fingerprint has remained unchanged and will always provide a reliable tool for making money for those who can read it. Figure 13.1 is a daily chart of the Dow Industrials in 1933 and 1934, and it looks like any stock trading today on any time frame.

Bar 2 is a Low 2 that broke a trendline.

Bar 3 is a small Failed Final Flag reversal and a Lower Low test of the Bar 1 low after a trendline break (a trendline break followed by a test of the trend's extreme can be a major trend reversal).

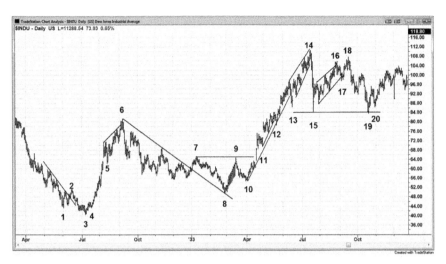

FIGURE 13.1   Price Action Remains Largely Unchanged Throughout History

Bar 4 is a Breakout Pullback and a small Higher Low.

Bar 5 is the First Pullback in a strong bull and a High 2.

Bar 6 is a Wedge that led to two large legs down, ending at Bar 8. A Wedge at the end of a strong surge usually results in a very deep pullback and then a new high.

Bar 7 was a trendline break and a two-legged pullback.

Bar 8 was a Lower Low after a trendline break and a Breakout Test of Bar 2.

Bar 10 is a Higher Low.

Bar 11 is a High 2 Breakout Pullback after the breakout above the failed Bars 7 and 9 Double Top Bear Flag.

Bars 12 and 13 are reversals up after a minor trendline breaks.

Bar 14 is a Wedge.

Bar 15 is a trendline break and a strong momentum Countertrend move that will likely be tested after a rally tests the Bar 14 high.

Bar 16 is a Wedge, and Bar 17 is a failed breakout of the Wedge.

Bar 18 is the Lower High test of the Bar 14 bull trend extreme, and it is a Low 2 entry for a short on the Wedge failed failure. There was a failed breakout below the Wedge, and now the Wedge is failing on its upside breakout. A failed failed Wedge often leads to a strong reversal. Bar 18 is also a Breakout Test of the Bar 14 signal bar low.

Bar 19 is the test of the Bar 15 low and is a Double Bottom Bull Flag.

Bar 20 is a Higher Low pullback in the reversal up and a Double Bottom Pullback.

FIGURE 13.2 AAPL, 5-Minute

AAPL was in a strong bull on the daily chart (thumbnail) and had a first EMA pullback at Bar 1 in Figure 13.2, which was a bear trend channel overshoot (the numbering is the same on both charts). Bar 2 on the daily had a strong intraday reversal up and closed near its high. It was reasonable to want to buy at one tick above the high of Day 2. However, the next day gapped above the Day 2 high. Rather than risk a possible reversal down day, it would be prudent to watch for a reversal up after a pullback test of the gap.

Bar 6 on the 5-minute chart closed the gap and was an EMA Gap Bar and a bear trend channel overshoot and reversal up. This was a great long entry with a protective stop below Bar 6. This 62 cent risk led to a several dollar gain.

After an extended bull run, the market broke out of a bull flag after the High 2 pullback at Bar 2 in Figure 13.3.

Bar 7 was a test of the trend channel line drawn across the highs of Bars 3 and 5, and it was also the signal bar of an Expanding Triangle, which setup a great short for at least a two leg pullback. Whenever a trade could be a major reversal, it is imperative to swing part with a breakeven stop after scalping out of some of the position.

Bar 11 broke above the bear trend line, but after this strong a down move the bulls would be reluctant to buy, expecting a second leg down from any rally. The market poked above the trend channel drawn from the highs of Bars 10 and 12 and formed two dojis at Bar 13, meaning the bulls

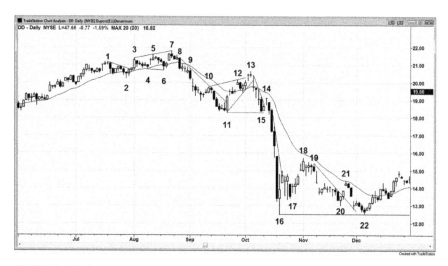

FIGURE 13.3 DuPont, the 1987 Crash

were no longer in control of the rally from Bar 11. This is a possible setup bar for an EMA Gap 2 Bar down (second attempt to close the gap to the EMA), so you must place an order to go short at one cent below the low of Bar 13. Since there are so many gap opens in stocks, resulting in terrible fills, it is better to place the order only after the open and only if there is no gap. If there is a gap down, as there was here, you would use the 5-minute chart to look for a price action justification for a short after the rally closed the gap.

Bar 14 broke above a Micro Trendline. You would place an order to short at one cent below the low of Bar 14. This is a variant of a Breakout Pullback, even though the breakout below the low of Bar 11 has not yet occurred. The four bars down to test the low of Bar 11 were very vertical, and you would expect it to behave the same as if in fact there was a small breakout. Therefore, the short below Bar 14 is a type of Breakout Pullback entry, and these trades often lead to protracted moves. The entry bar had a shaved top, which means that the bears were in control from the first minute.

Bar 11 ended the first leg down, and Bar 16 completed the second leg of the two legs down. Since the move down to Bar 16 was so steep, it is better to wait for a test of the low before going long, or some other indication that the sellers were going to wait for more price action before they short again. However, the steepness of the second leg and the size of the bear trend bars imply that there is a high probability of this being a sell climax, which usually is followed by at least a two-legged Countertrend rally that lasts for far more bars than most would expect.

The two-bar rally off the low broke a trendline, albeit a steep one, so it is sensible to buy the Bar 17 High 2 (Higher Low). You could then short the Low 2 near the EMA at Bar 18, or wait for more price action, since the pullback did not reach the EMA, and it is a bull trend bar, so more rally is possible.

Bar 19 was a signal bar for a Low 2 in a bear and a failed High 2, near the EMA, so it is a strong short. It was also a three-bar long Double Top Bear Flag.

Bar 20 poked below the Bar 17 low but immediately found buyers and the shorts covered. The market tried to form a Double Bottom Bull Flag. The longs from the Bar 20 signal bar only made it to the EMA, where they would take partial profits and move their stops to breakeven. They would have been stopped out, but they would buy again at the High 2 off the Bar 22 signal bar that tested the Bar 16 bear low, and it followed the Bar 21 break of the bear trendline. There was not a strong reversal bar, and although this could be the start of an extended bull and it must be bought, you would have to expect more two-sided trading to unfold before a strong trend in either direction begins.

GE rallied sharply in early 1987, but there was a small short based on the Bar 6 signal bar that was a reversal from a second overshoot of a bull trend channel line drawn from Bars 2 and 3 in Figure 13.4. The fill was one tick (one cent) below on a stop. Since there was not yet an earlier downward surge, this is likely going to fail on a two-legged down move to around the EMA, and be followed by a new high.

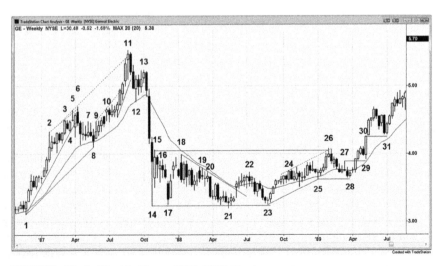

FIGURE 13.4 Weekly Chart of GE, 1987 Crash

The M2B (High 2 near the EMA) at Bar 9 was a good long entry for a test of the highs.

Bar 11 broke through the trend channel line attached to the high of Bar 5, which is a parallel of the trendline drawn from Bars 1 and 8. You would get a similar signal by drawing the trend channel line across the highs of Bars 2 and 5.

Bar 11 was a potential signal bar, but the next bar failed to take out its low. Instead, the next bar was an inside bar reinforced by a strong bear close. If you placed an order to short at one tick below its low, the order would be filled on the next bar (turning that bear inside bar into a signal bar for this short). After such a climactic move up through the trend channel line and following the earlier trendline break down to Bar 8, the shorts should expect at least two legs down to test the Bar 8 start of the channel up after the Bars 1 to 6 spike.

Bar 13 was the second small leg up in the pullback from the potential new bear. It is two legs up because there was a bull trend bar off the EMA, and then a bear trend bar (a down leg on a smaller time frame), and finally a second leg up, made of consecutive bull trend bars. Since the shorts are expecting a second leg down before any possible new high, place a stop order to go short at one cent below Bar 13 (which becomes the signal bar once the order is filled). The initial stop goes above the high of the signal bar. Once the entry bar closes, lower the stop to one cent above its high.

The market crashed in a large second leg down to Bar 14. Because this is two legs down and it did not take out the low of the prior bull, it could form a Higher Low in a longer time frame bull. Also, since the bear trend bars were so large, it is likely that there will be at least two legs up (and likely four legs), and the sideways to up action should last for a long time (at least 20 or 30 bars, as an approximation based on eyeballing the chart). The bears will likely relinquish control for an extended period and wait for more price action before being willing to short aggressively. They will, however, short every rally and take profits at every pause in the down move. Likewise, the bulls know that the market will probably go sideways to up for a long time, and they will start buying the dips but exiting quickly on stalled rallies, until there is price action that indicates that a trend up or down has begun.

Bar 16 is a potential signal bar for a Low 2, so the bears will place an order to short at one cent below its low.

Bar 17 tested the bear low and is a potential High 2 signal, so the bulls will place buy orders at one tick above its high (and the shorts will exit the remainder of their positions). It is a Failed Final Flag.

Bar 18 is a Double Top Bear Flag with Bar 15.

Bar 20 is a short entry bar based on a Low 2, especially after the market failed to hold above the Micro Trendline (not shown) over the six bars down from Bar 18. However, this is Barb Wire, and it is usually better and always less stressful to wait for a breakout to fail and then enter on the failure.

Bar 21 was another test of the bear low, forming a Double Bottom with Bar 14 (or, with Bars 14 and 17 both being considered as the first bottom). The rally to Bar 18 also broke a steep bear trendline from Bar 13 to any of the bars around Bars 15 and 16. A broken trendline and then a possible Double Bottom could be the start of a new bull trend. Bar 21 also reversed a break below a seven-bar bear trend channel line, drawn using a best fit of the bottom of the bodies of those immediately prior seven candles.

The rally to Bar 22 broke another bear trendline. Breaks of multiple bear trendlines is a strong indication that the bulls are asserting themselves and that a protracted swing up is becoming more likely. However, this was also the first test above the EMA so the Low 2 after Bar 22 is a good short, expecting two small legs down.

Bar 23 setup a High 2 long entry that was also a Higher Low (above Bar 21) and a Double Bottom Pullback and it followed a rally up to Bar 22 that contained seven consecutive, albeit small, bull candles. The nine-bar rally up to Bar 24 contained only one bear candle, and was followed by five consecutive bull bars that closed above the EMA, both indicating that the bulls are owing the market.

Bar 26 reversed after poking above a bull trend channel line (a parallel from the Bar 23 and 25 lows) and the Bar 15 initial up move off the climactic low. This is a potential Double Top Bear Flag. Since there was so much strength on the rally to Bar 26, it is likely that its high will be tested before the Bar 23 low is taken out, which would negate the expected two legs (minimum) down.

Bar 28 setup an M2B (a High 2 at the EMA). Also, it was second of two bear trend bars that tried to push back below the EMA (the first occurred three bars earlier) after 24 consecutive closes above the EMA. When two attempts at something fail, expect a big move in the opposite direction. It is also a Breakout Pullback from the Bar 26 rally above the trading range that has been in effect since Bar 15, and a large Double Bottom Pullback from the Bars 14 (or 17) and 23 (or 21) Double Bottom, and is sometimes called a cup and handle long setup.

Bar 29 tested the Bar 27 high, creating a Breakout Test, and then violently surged up in a large outside bar up trapping weak longs out of their positions and forcing them to chase the market up.

Bar 31 tested the gap that followed Bar 30, and it also setup a High 2 bull pullback long.

There was a two-legged move down from the 2000 high with the first leg ending at Bar B in Figure 13.5. The rally to Bar C broke the trendline,

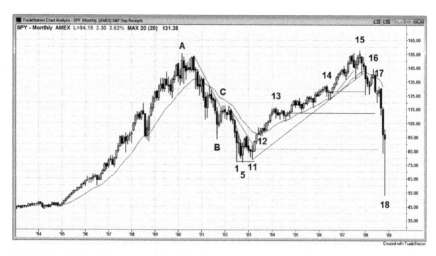

FIGURE 13.5 This Is the Monthly SPY Showing the Double Bottom Pullback Bottom in 2003

so traders were looking to buy a Higher Low or Lower Low test of the low of Bar B.

Bar 1 dropped too far below Bar B for traders to aggressively buy there in the absence of more price action.

Bar 5 was in Barb Wire (three or more overlapping bars with one or more being a doji), so you should only look to short a small bar near the high or buy a small bar near the low. Although Bars 1 and 5 did not have identical lows, they were close enough to be a possible Double Bottom, and in trading close is usually close enough. The rally from Bar 5 broke a bear trendline, so traders will look to buy a test of the Bar 5 low.

Bar 11 reversed up from a deep test of the Double Bottom low. This Double Bottom Pullback completed the two legs down from Bar A and an extended bull ensued. As is typical, the bull took out the highs of the bull signal bars that formed in the bear down from Bar A to Bar 5.

Bars 1, 5, and 11 correspond to those in the daily chart below.

The rally up to Bar 15 was very strong. It is interesting to note that any pullback would be expected to test the bear signal bars in the rally up from the Bar 11 low (see next chart). The selloff in fact fell through all of the earlier bear signals and became a major bear. However, nothing is ever surprising, and traders should just trade whatever patterns appear on the chart that they use for trading and not necessarily trade monthly patterns.

The Bar 15 top was a Three Push up Higher High test of Bar A (there obviously was a trendline break in the bear down from Bar A). Also, the third push up to Bar 15 followed a small trendline break.

Bar 16 was a M2S after the break of the major bull trendline.

Bar 17 was a Low 1 Breakout Pullback.

Although Bar 18 is a huge bar that might turn out to be a climactic test of the Bar 5 low, there is absolutely no price action evidence of a bottom at this point, despite what the pundits are saying on television. The climax might lead to a reversal or a trading range, but there has yet to be a break of the bear trendline and there has been no significant upward momentum. The trend is still down and although it is hard to imagine that the market could get much lower, it can. The market is not trading based on valuation at this point and when it is emotional like this, it will keep dropping until the last seller has sold. When he does, there will be a rally that will break a significant bear trendline and then a test of the low, but until then, the trend is still down.

Incidentally, although pundits have been attributing this 2008 crash to the housing bubble and the related banking crisis, the housing market began its crash almost three years earlier and the credit crisis has been simmering for at least a couple of years. What did happen was the world realized that Obama was going to become president and that he would increase business regulations and increase the cost of labor, both of which would reduce corporate profitability. When companies earn less, their stock is worth less. The worldwide market was just rapidly adjusting the value of stocks to reflect the reduced earnings that smart money anticipates under Obama. It is likely that the market has discounted this too much and that the market will rally back over the next many months as it waits to see what Obama does. This is similar to the huge stock market rally that began when the Republicans took over Congress in 1994 and it was never attributed to them (by the way, I am a very liberal Independent and not a Republican). The world adjusted its earnings expectations dramatically upward, significantly increasing the value of stocks. None of this is useful to a day trader, but it is an example of being willing to think differently from the experts and being comfortable holding a minority opinion. Never be afraid to see things differently from everyone else, especially the experts on television.

The strong rally up to Bar 3 in Figure 13.6 broke well above the EMA and broke the trendline. The end of the rally had a Wedge look to it and whenever there is a Wedge at the end of a strong surge, there is often a test of the start of the move (the Bar 1 low).

Bar 5 was a Lower Low test of Bar 1, forming a Double Bottom. Remember, traders live in a world of imperfection and if something looks reasonably similar to a reliable pattern, it will tend to act the same way. There was a bear trend channel break and reversal at the low, which was at the end of the big move down from Bar 3, and a test of Bar 3 is possible.

FIGURE 13.6 This Is the Daily Chart of the Double Bottom Pullback That Is on the Previous Monthly Chart

Bar 7 was a Lower High test of Bar 3, forming a Double Top Bear Flag, and it also ended in a small Wedge and therefore likely would have a deep retracement.

Bar 11 was a deep test of the Bar 5 low, and it reversed up, forming a Double Bottom (Bars 1 and 5) Pullback and then an extended rally. Bar 11 also was a failed break below a bear trend channel line, setting up for a test of the Bar 7 start of the leg down. However, the Double Bottom Pullback on the daily, weekly, and monthly charts made the test of Bar 7 turn into a breakout instead of a failed test followed by another selloff.

Many technicians would refer to this as a Head and Shoulders Bottom, but that does not tell anything about the price action. Most Double Bottom Pullbacks are Head and Shoulders Bottoms, but since most Head and Shoulder patterns fail (they usually just become continuation patterns instead of reversal patterns) and most Double Bottom Pullbacks succeed, you should distinguish them and never bother with the term "Head and Shoulders."

Bar 1 in Figure 13.7 was a spike, and it led to a channel that ended at Bar 6.

The Bars 2 to 3 rally was another spike, and it also led to a channel that also ended at Bar 6. The market has been so strong that it never attempted to retrace to the beginning of either channel (Bars 2 and 4).

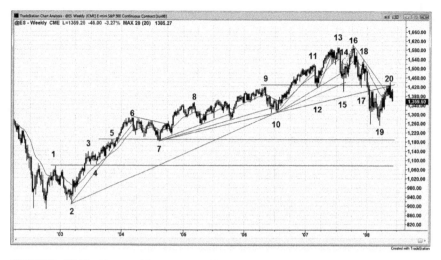

FIGURE 13.7 The Double Bottom Pullback Low at Bar 2 on the Weekly Eminis Led to a Major Rally That Contained Several Spike and Channel Bull Patterns

The Bars 2 to 6 rally also was a spike that led to a channel ending at Bar 9. Again, there was so much strength that the Bar 10 pullback did not come close to the Bar 7 start of the channel.

There was a thin area between Bars 1 and 4 on the breakout and then a trading range that ended around Bar 4. This was followed by close to a Measured Move up to the top of Bar 6 (from Bar 2 to the middle of the Bar 4 trading range).

There was another breakout thin area between Bars 5 and 7 followed by an approximate move from Bars 4 and 5 to around Bar 9.

The middle of the Bar 7 trading range was the pause after the spike, and it gave a Measured Move from the low of the chart to the top of the chart. There was a Breakout Pullback long shortly after the breakout from this flag. Remember, however, that Measured Moves are just observations and you should not consider them while trading.

The channel attempted to fail on the Bar 10 selloff but instead formed a Double Bottom of gap bars below the EMA. There were several other failed trendline breaks all of the way to the Bar 16 high that were also good long setups. The thin area between Bars 9 and 12 projected to around the Bar 13 high (from the Bar 7 low).

The Bar 15 plunge below the EMA and the major trendline was almost certainly going to be tested after a test of the high.

The high test was an overshoot (Higher High) that was a Wedge pattern (a spike up and then three small pushes up to Bar 16), and the end of an Expanding Triangle (Bars 11, 12, 13, 15, and 16).

Bar 18 was a Breakout Pullback (a variant, since the breakout below Bar 15 did not yet happen, but the momentum down to Bar 17 was enough to make the chart act like a breakout) and a Double Top Pullback.

Bar 20 was another Breakout Pullback and a test of the Bars 7 and 10 trendline from below.

As the market sells off to test the Bar 19 low, it will attempt to form a Double Bottom Pullback, but with the strength of the selling down to Bar 19, the market more likely will form a second leg down that ends below Bar 19, and it might ultimately test the Bar 7 channel low or even continue much lower. Whenever the market has so much strength that it does not come back to test the expected prices for several patterns as it did here with the Spike and Channel bottoms that go all the way back to the Bar 1 spike, when the correction finally comes, it will usually last longer and be much deeper than anyone anticipates.

Corrections after channels usually lead to trading ranges, and since this is a weekly chart, we may go largely sideways for several more years. Ultimately the market will break out in one direction or another, and since we are in a growing economy and the Emini is an average of the value of that economy, the market ultimately should break out of the upside but that could take a long, long time.

All of the pundits on CNBC have been saying that the bottom is in and that we are on the way to new highs, but the price action appears to be saying otherwise. However, any time the market is up a couple of percent, they round up bulls proclaiming evidence of the next great bull and every time it drops a couple of percent, they find the bears who claim that we are heading to a depression. You should look at them with amusement because you don't trade in their time frame, and the predictions have nothing to do with your income (and nothing to do with what the price action is telling you). These observations demonstrate that the same ideas that work for day trading also work for longer time frames.

HUGE VOLUME REVERSALS

When a stock is in a steep bear on the daily chart and then has a day with volume that is 5 to 10 times normal, the bulls may have capitulated and a tradable bottom may be present. The huge volume day is very often a gap down day, and if it has a strong bull close, the odds of a profitable long increase. Traders are not necessarily looking for a bull reversal, but after a climactic selloff the odds are good that there will be at least a two-legged move to at least the EMA that will allow them to place a profitable trade that will last from days to weeks.

Incidentally, on a 1-minute Emini chart that is in a strong bear, if there is a huge volume bar (about 25,000 contracts), it is unlikely to be the end of the bear, but often is a sign that a pullback will come soon, usually after one or two Lower Lows on less volume (volume divergence). You should rarely if ever look at volume on intraday charts because of its unreliable predictive value on the 5-minute chart, which is the chart that you should be using exclusively for trading.

Lehman Brothers opened with a huge gap down on Bar 3 and then ran below a bear trend channel line (from Bars 1 and 2 in Figure 13.8) but rallied strongly into the close. Volume was three times that of the prior day and about 10 times that of the average of the past month. With such a strong bull trend bar (seen more clearly on the candle chart thumbnail), it was safe to buy at the close, but a more cautious trader would wait until the market took out the high of this possible signal bar. The market gapped up on the next day. A trader could either buy the open, wait for a test down and then buy a new intraday high, or look for a selloff on the 5-minute chart and buy the reversal up after the attempt to close the gap failed. This kind of strength is almost always followed by at least two legs up (the second leg up to Bar 6 occurred after the successful Bar 5 gap test Higher Low) and a penetration of the EMA.

Bars 4 and 6 formed a Double Top Bear Flag.

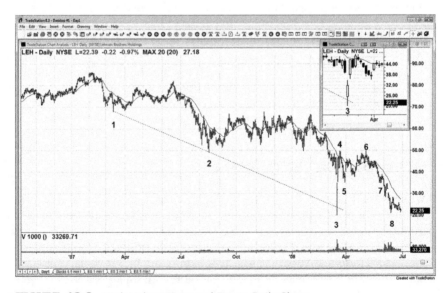

FIGURE 13.8 High Volume Reversal Bar on Daily Chart

Bar 7 attempted to form a Double Bottom Bull Flag with Bar 5, but instead it resulted in a Breakout Pullback short entry three bars later.

As of today, the market is currently testing the Bar 3 low, attempting to defend the stops below it and form a Double Bottom, but if it fails, there will likely be panic selling below the Bar 3 low that everyone was seeing as a strong, high-volume bottom.

Bear Stearns in Figure 13.9 had a huge bear trend day on a Friday with volume that was about 15 times that of a typical day, and the stock lost about 70 percent of its value over the prior two weeks. However, the volume was only about one and a half times that of the day before, and there was only a minimal bull tail. The price action was against the longs since there was no reversal from the break of the bear trend channel. In fact, the huge bear trend bar closed well below the line, confirming the strength of the trend channel line failure to contain the bear. The stock lost another 80 percent when it opened on Monday (Bar 3), but traded slightly less volume. Traders who bought the Friday close, thinking that a climactic bottom was in and that there was no way that the country's fifth-largest investment bank could fall any further, were devastated come Monday. Climactic volume in the absence of bullish price action is no reason to fade a strong bear trend. A television pundit might recommend the purchase, but without supporting price action, it was simply too risky.

This chart is during the same time as the above LEH chart. However, the LEH chart did not break the bear trend channel line (Bar 3) until

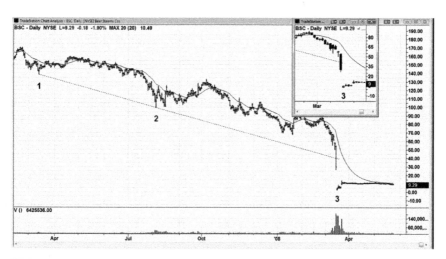

FIGURE 13.9 Huge Volume but No Reversal Bar

Monday, and it reversed up on that day on huge volume. Here, on the BSC chart, the huge volume day was a day earlier, and it also broke below the bear trend channel line, but the day closed near its low with no bullish price action. It gapped down on Bar 3, just like LEH (Bar 3 is the Monday for both stocks), but LEH rallied strongly whereas BSC could barely rally at all. Bar 3 for BSC was still a bull reversal bar following the break of a bear trend channel line, but any trader choosing between buying LEH and BSC on that day would obviously much rather buy LEH because of its very strong bull reversal bar. Even if a trader bought BSC at one tick above Bar 3, he would have made more than 100 percent over the next three days, but LEH was clearly a much more certain bull bet.

Since this chart was printed, BSC was bought out by JPM for a tiny fraction of its market capitalization of just a few months earlier. Within several months, LEH also went under.

CHAPTER 14

Options

A day trader will make more money if he does not trade off the daily charts because it is likely that his overall profit will be reduced by being unable to give his full attention to his day trades. Yes, it is fun to make money on options, but you will likely pay for that fun with income that you failed to make off day trades because you were distracted. There will be a couple of times a month when you might see a great opportunity for an options purchase, but if you are a day trader who is trading options more often than that, you are probably foregoing too much money on missed day trades to make it worthwhile.

Although there are many ways to trade options based on price action, if you are primarily a day trader, you want to limit your thoughts to the 5-minute Emini chart during the day. However you can use options sparingly when fading big moves on the daily chart. It is easiest to mostly buy puts or calls and sometimes sell spreads and look to hold the trades for one to several days. You can allow one new extreme against your position, and you can be willing to add on because your risk is exactly known and limited with these strategies. At a possible top, you could also simply sell short a small stock position, but you might tend to watch it too much during the day, and this would cause you to miss day trades in the Eminis and ultimately negate any gains from the stock trade.

There is one other rare occasion in which intraday options can be preferable to futures and stocks. That is when the market is in a huge freefall and it is close to limit down. If a reliable reversal pattern sets up, you might think that the risk of buying is small, even if a small position, but it can be substantial even with a reputable broker. How can that be?

Because their system can get overloaded and your orders might not get processed for 30 minutes or more. If you just bought what you thought was a bottom and then the market fell through your protective stop, your order might not get reported as filled for 30 minutes and you don't know when it will get filled. You could easily lose 10 points in the Emini. An alternative is to buy calls, so that you will be certain of your risk.

Chesapeake Energy in Figure 14.1 rallied 85 percent in the past four months but developed many small pullbacks after the sharp selloff in March, increasing the odds of a reversal from a new high. The market broke above the trend channel line drawn across Bars 1 and 3, and the line drawn across Bars 3 and 5. The final six days of the bull formed a Wedge when looking at a trendline drawn from Bar 6 and using just the bottoms of the bodies. There was a strong move up from Bar 4 followed by two more runs to new highs. Bar 8 was a small bar with a bear close. All of these are signs that the bulls were losing control of the market and there was now a very high likelihood of a pullback to the 20-day EMA, as at Bars 2 and 4, and a

FIGURE 14.1   Chesapeake Energy, Daily Chart

reasonable chance of a test of the trendline drawn using Bars 2 and 4, and possibly a major trend reversal. The ideal fade was to buy puts during the day of Bar 8 or wait until the next day when the market traded below the low of Bar 8, forming a Low 2, which is a second-chance short entry at a new high, a very high probability trade. You would buy at-the-money puts in the front month because they would have the least slippage (most liquid) and not worry about time decay since a fast move was likely. An alternative trade would be to sell an at-the-money call and buy the call one strike higher, but this is too complicated, and the down move should be sharp so long puts offered the best risk-reward ratio. There has yet to be an EMA Gap Bar pullback, and this selloff is likely to produce one. It would then setup a rally to test the Bar 8 high.

Apple in Figure 14.2 rallied over 300 percent in less than two years and then sold off 55 percent over two months down to Bar 6 on this weekly chart. Buying puts at the Low 2 at Bar 5 was a good trade since there was first a strong move down to Bar 3 that broke below a bull trendline from Bar 1. Also, this Low 2 entry bar was a second break of the bull trendline drawn from Bar 3, and a two-legged Higher High (two legs often end a move). Both the selloffs to Bars 1 and 3 tested the 20-week EMA, and the

FIGURE 14.2 AAPL, Weekly

odds were high for at least that much of a correction off the high at Bar 5 since the bears had already demonstrated good strength twice before in this bull.

Bar 7 was an EMA Gap 2 Bar, a second attempt to rally to close the gap below the 20-week EMA. It is also a Double Bottom Bull Flag with Bar 1. A minimum target is a rapid test of the moving average. Instead, the rally was so strong that more retracement up was likely, as was a second leg up. Since the move down from the high at Bar 5 was so strong, the odds are high that there will be at least an attempt to test the lows of Bar 6 before AAPL exceeds the Bar 5 high. A large trading range is forming, but the top might be in. Once there is a signal bar, a put purchase would be a reasonable trade.

When the moves are this violent, the market is less predictable, and risk is greater. A good way to have a defined risk is to buy options.

ANR in Figure 14.3 was in a strong bull on the daily chart (insert) and broke out of the top of a Wedge four days ago. Yesterday, it gapped above another trend channel line and above 100, a psychologically important number and therefore a magnet. As soon as the 5-minute chart started to come down, a test of 100 was likely. The July 100 puts could have been

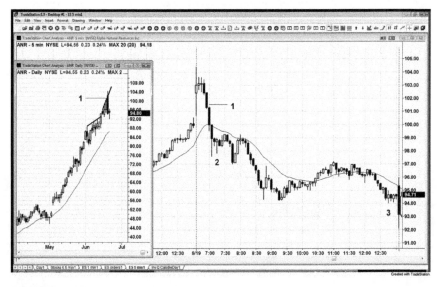

FIGURE 14.3 Runaway Markets Often Offer Profitable Fades Using Options, and This Type of Trading Does Not Cause Too Much Distraction for Day Traders Because the Risk Is Limited

bought for 7.20, and a reasonable protective exit would be a trade above the top of the trading range at the open, risking maybe a dollar or so on the puts. At Bar 2, those puts were 8.80. This first pause was a great place to take partial profits because there could be an opening reversal back up after testing below the EMA and below 100. However, the move down off the open was so strong that there would likely be at least two legs down. If a trader moved his stop to around 7.30, it would never have been hit, and the puts were worth over 10.00 by the close. On the daily chart, the day turned into an outside down day. In strong bulls, there is usually not much follow-through on the next day (here, there was a small doji day), because the large outside down bar will likely be the start of a small trading range. However, a test of the rising daily EMA is likely in the near term. When a day trader makes windfall profits off options, it is best to close the position and then look for other opportunities tomorrow. There was likely little left to be gained from this position, and holding it into the next day would be a distraction from day trading.

In Figure 14.4, when today gapped below yesterday's low and below a trend channel line and reversed up in an Opening Reversal, a trader could buy July 170 calls for 5.70, and the market's volume was so good that you could buy 50 at that price, and the bid ask spread was a dime (fairly tight). That is an advantage of trading stocks with large volumes. You could have sold half at the Bar 5 test of the Bar 3 high for 9.20 on a limit order. You

FIGURE 14.4 AAPL Had Three Pushes down on the Daily Chart (Left)

could have sold the balance on the Bar 6 Double Top and Lower High for the same price. That is a profit of $150 per call (less commissions). The initial purchase price of 5.70 was $570 per call. Since this is a great entry, you could risk about $200 per call (call price of 3.70) and double up on a $100 drawdown if there was a second long entry. This was not necessary since the first entry worked well.

The Bar A low of the day also indicates today's bar on the daily chart on the left.

CHAPTER 15

Best Trades

A ll of the trades in this chapter have already been discussed, and additional examples are included here for review. One or more of these setups occurs every day on the 5-minute Emini chart and on the 5-minute chart of just about every market. If a trader had the patience to wait possibly hours for one to develop and he restricted himself to only the trades in this chapter, he would be a very successful trader. However, learning to restrict yourself to the very best trades is perhaps the most difficult part of trading. If you are not making money yet, it is something that you seriously need to consider trying. One important component to making money is avoiding bad trades that invariably erase much more than what you will have earned from your good trades. The single most important trade to avoid until you are a skilled, profitable trader is Barb Wire, especially when it is in the middle of the day's range, near the EMA and on the wrong side of the EMA, and the day is not a clear and strong trend day.

Let's start by going back to the very first chart in the book, where there were a number of excellent entries on the daily chart of AAPL, all of which belong in this chapter. This chapter shows trendlines to make some of the trades easier to see and understand.

Bar 1 in Figure 15.1 was a two-legged pullback (flag, triangle, Tight Trading Range) to the EMA with a High 2 buy signal. It was the First Pullback after breaking a steep trendline.

Bar 2 was a Wedge short and also a small Expanding Triangle. It followed the Bar 1 break of a trendline and so was an acceptable Countertrend entry, and after a Wedge, it should have two legs down (and it did).

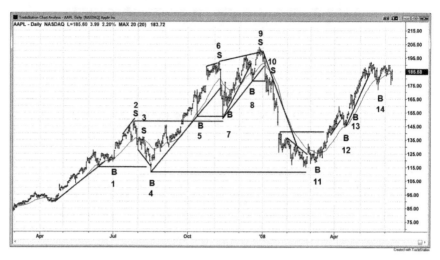

FIGURE 15.1   AAPL, Daily Chart through June 10, 2008

Bar 3 (the number is well above the bar) was an M2S and a Double Top Bear Flag after a sharp down move from a Wedge, so a second leg down was likely, and a Double Bottom Bull Flag with Bar 1.

Bar 4 was a Wedge and a Gap 2 long that reversed up after testing below the Bar 1 flag.

Bar 5 was a High 2 long Breakout Test (of the breakout above Bar 2).

Bar 6 was a Wedge short after the large trendline break at Bar 4. It normally would go through the EMA and likely have two legs. However, the down move was climactic, and it covered a reasonable distance down but did so in just one leg.

Bar 7 was a Gap 2 long and a Double Bottom Bull Flag (with Bar 5) and a second test of the Bar 2 breakout. It also reversed up from dipping below the Bar 5 spike. Although two legs down are to be expected, this setup made a tradable long worthwhile, with the plan to look to short a test of the Bar 6 high.

Bar 8 was a small two-legged drop following a Wedge (the line is not drawn, but the rally up from Bar 7 had Three Pushes Up) test of the Bar 6 high, but a two-legged test up of the Bar 6 high was more likely after such a big rally up from Bar 7. Bar 8 was the First Pullback through a steep trendline and a EMA reversal long. This was tricky in here as is often the case just before a major reversal. The choppy movement is a reflection of the emotion on both sides, and one side will soon win out. The bearish case is clearly stronger when there is a choppy rally after a major trendline break (down to Bar 7).

Bar 9 was a two-legged test of the Bar 6 high, forming a Higher High. It also followed the strong break of the trendline down to Bar 7 and the break of a smaller trendline down to Bar 8. At least two legs down are likely. Finally, it was a failed breakout above a Wedge, and therefore a second entry. The Wedge broke to the downside and failed at Bar 8. It then broke to the upside and failed at Bat 9 in the opposite direction.

Bar 10 is an M2S short after a sharp first leg down. It is also a Breakout Pullback after breaking below Bar 8 and below the EMA.

Bar 11 is a Double Bottom Pullback (in this case, a good-looking Head and Shoulders Bottom), forming a High 2 entry in a Higher Low after a trendline break. It also reversed up before falling below Bar 4, so it is a Higher Low, giving confidence to the bull. Finally, it was a Double Bottom Bull Flag (with Bar 4) and a Breakout Pullback after Three Pushes Down, and it should therefore have at least a second leg up.

Bar 12 is an M2B long on the First Pullback after a steep trendline break, and it is a Breakout Pullback after breaking above the January gap.

Bar 13 was a small two-legged correction and a failed Low 2, and therefore effectively a High 2 long (two failed attempts down is the same as a second attempt up).

Bar 14 is a Wedge pullback test of the EMA and the First Pullback after breaking a steep trendline. The market is close to the Bar 9 high and maybe the top of the first big pullback (Lower High) in a new bear. However, it could also be just testing the top of a big trading range, or a pause en route to a new high. This latter scenario is the least likely after such a sharp selloff down to Bar 11 and the relatively weaker current rally.

Remember that the channel up from Bar 4 was a target for a pullback, which occurred at Bar 11, forming the Double Bottom Bull Flag. A channel usually leads to a trading range so the rally up will likely fail in the area of the Bar 9 high and be followed by another move down. Eventually the market will break out in one direction or the other.

The first thing that any trader should do when trying a new approach is print out weeks of charts of the time frame and market he plans to trade and see if his setups appear to be valid. When he begins to trade, he should not trade more than two contracts, no matter how large his account is. Only after consistently making a profit for several weeks should he begin to increase his position size. However, most traders take many years to become consistently profitable.

The most difficult part of trading is deciding whether a setup is good enough to warrant placing a trade. It is especially difficult to do real time when you always feel like you need one more bar to be sure, but once that bar forms, you've missed the best entry. It takes many years of practice to be able to look at a chart and instantly see what is happening, and even then nothing is ever perfectly clear. However, some things are easier to recognize than others, and a beginner is wise to focus on just a couple of setups that are easy to anticipate. Fortunately, there are many setups that are easy to spot and have excellent odds for success.

If the chart starts near the lower left-hand corner and is near the upper right-hand corner and there have not been any bear legs that have dropped below the midpoint of the screen, or if there has been a number of swings with lots of bull trend bars and only small pullbacks, you should buy every High 2 where the setup bar touches or penetrates the EMA. Once long and once the entry bar closes, move your stop from one tick below the signal bar to one tick below the entry bar. Scalp out half (you can adjust this with experience), and then move your stop to breakeven or maybe a tick or two worse. Add on at every new opportunity. Most markets are in a strong trend maybe 20 percent of the time or less.

When the market is not clearly trending, look to fade second entries at new swing highs and lows. These days will have several swings lasting 5 to 10 or more bars, and then the trendline breaks, leading to an opposite swing. If the momentum on the move to the breakout is strong, wait for a second entry, which usually comes within five bars or so.

Once you are consistently netting a couple points every day in the Emini or 50 cents or a dollar in AAPL or some other major stock, you should focus on increasing your volume rather than adding lots of new setups. These are the very best setups, and if you trade 25 Emini contracts and net just two points a day, you will make $500,000 a year. If you trade 100 contracts and net four points, you will make $5 million a year. Many stocks like AAPL, GS, RIMM, and SKF can handle 3,000 or more shares without significant slippage most of the time. If you average 50 cents a day on 3,000 shares of just one stock, that is about $300,000 a year.

It is natural to get confident after some success, and most traders will start looking to add more setups to their arsenal. Also, they hate sitting for an hour or two while waiting for the best setups when they see lots of profitable scalps unfolding in front of them. The absolute worst thing to do is to start trading Barb Wire. These trading ranges typically occur in the middle of the day after you have been watching for an entry for a couple hours. They are usually in the middle of the range near the EMA, and they always look so simple. However, they will damage your account and your psyche. Unfortunately, most traders think that they can figure them out, and they trade them and wonder at the end of the month why they are down a couple of thousand dollars.

Another common mistake is to look at 1-minute charts. The trades are very easy to spot at the end of the day, but most are hard to trade real time. If your goal is to make money, and that should be your goal, only take the best trades, and avoid Barb Wire and 1-minute charts. If on the other hand this is just an exciting hobby for you, remember that hobbies cost money, and there may be another one out there for you that is just as much fun and much less expensive.

One of the best reversal patterns is a trendline break with strong momentum followed by a two-legged test that results in a new extreme. The two legs to the new extreme (a Higher High or Lower Low) are effectively two attempts to reestablish the old trend, despite the strong trendline break, and that failed second attempt has a high probability of leading to a strong reversal that should have at least two legs and often results in a new, opposite trend.

Finally, trading stocks in the first hour or so is one of easiest ways to make money trading. Focus on Failed Breakouts and Breakout Pullbacks from patterns from yesterday. If there is a strong reversal bar, take the first entry. If there are three or more largely overlapping bars, wait for a second entry. After you have about 50 cents to 1 dollar profit, move the protective stop to breakeven. Take one-half to one-third off at one dollar profit and maybe take another quarter off at two dollars. However, always let at least a quarter of your position run with a breakeven stop or until there is a clear and strong opposite signal because trends last much further than you would ever think possible.

MAJOR REVERSALS

Major reversals reverse a trend that has been in effect for at least a couple of hours and often for several days. The best trend reversal entries have a break of a significant trendline before the setup, because you do not want to enter countertrend unless the countertrend traders have already shown some ability to control the market. Enter on a pullback that tests the trend extreme. The pullback can undershoot (a Lower High in a new bear or a Higher Low in a new bull) or overshoot (a Higher High in a new bear or a Lower Low in a new bull) the old trend extreme, but if an overshoot goes much beyond the old extreme, the trend has resumed, and you should wait again for a new trendline break.

Lower Low (Bar 9) after a Trendline Break. GOOG gapped down in Figure 15.2, tested the gap and the steep EMA, and broke to a new low. Bar 1 was a good short (a Low 2 gap test near the EMA), but the trend was more certain after the breakout to a new low, as evidenced by the two large bear trend bars with small tails. The best trades were the Low 2 (M2S) entries at Bars 2 and 3.

Bar 4 was a second attempt at reversing the Wedge (the bear trend channel line), so it was likely to result in two up legs and did. The signal bar was a doji, which is a one-bar trading range, and in general it is unwise

FIGURE 15.2   GOOG, 5-Minute

to buy at the top of a bear trading range, but this was the second entry in a
Three Push pattern and also a Failed Final Flag reversal (of the two prior
small-bodied bars, which almost formed an ii).

Bar 5 barely broke a trendline from Bars 1 and 3, but Bar 7 clearly had
strong momentum up, breaking the trendline and the EMA, making traders
get ready for a long entry on a test of the Bar 4 low. Bar 7 was an acceptable
EMA Gap short, a Double Top Bear Flag with Bar 3, and two legs up in a
bear. Remember, breaking the trendline does not turn the trend into a bull.
It is still a bear until after the market tests the low so you should still be
looking for shorts.

Bar 8 reversed the low of the day, but the move down to Bar 8 was
strong, which would require a strong reversal like a strong reversal bar or
a second entry. Bar 8 was a bull outside bar, which can be an entry when
there are clearly trapped traders. When it is not clear, it is better to wait for
more price action.

Bar 9 was a second attempt to reverse the breakout to the new low
and was a great entry for an expected two-legged move up, and was the
best long setup of the day and easily anticipated after the strong trendline
break up to Bar 7.

Bar 10 reversed back up at eight cents (eight cents is tiny for a $500
stock) above the signal bar for the Bar 9 long and was an excellent Breakout Test, Micro Trendline long, and Higher Low, allowing traders to add
on above its high. It also trapped longs out, and they will now chase the

market higher. You always need to be looking to buy that first Higher Low after a possible major Lower Low.

Lower Low (Bar 13 in Figure 15.3) after a trendline break and then a Higher Low (Bar 17) after a bigger trendline break (not shown but across the highs of Bars 1 and 11). The Homebuilders SPDR was in a protracted bear. The first sign of bullish strength were the rebound from bear trend channel line overshoots at the Bar 10 low.

Bar 11 broke a major bear trendline (the trendline could also be started at Bars 2, 3, or 5, and all would be similar) and gapped above the EMA. At this point, traders would begin looking to go long on a test of the Bar 10 low either in the form of a Higher Low or a Lower Low, but the trend is still down until then.

Bar 13 formed a two-legged Lower Low, which is often how trends end.

Bar 12 was the first entry (it only went seven cents above the prior bar and is barely noticeable on this chart), but the down momentum was still strong, making most traders wait for more price action before buying.

Two bars later, Bar 13 set up the second long entry on the reversal from the new low below Bar 10, and it was two legs down from the Bar 11 surge. This is a perfect setup for at least a two-legged rally.

Bar 14 was the top of a very strong rally and therefore unlikely to be the end of the move up. The odds were very high that the market would test Bar 14 and likely surpass it before falling below the start of the rally (the Bar 13 low, if it ever gets there again).

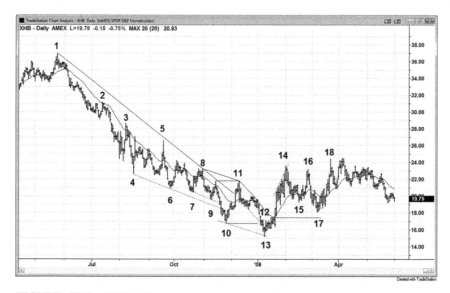

FIGURE 15.3 XHB, Daily

Bar 15 was a two-legged pullback but not a strong buy setup because Bar 14 was a small bull trend channel overshoot (based on the highs of the prior five bars) and would be likely to have a bigger, more proportional selloff.

Bar 17 was a second leg down and had a High 2 buy setup and was a test of the breakout that started the rally. It also went a little past a Fibonacci 62 percent retracement, but don't look at Fibonacci numbers when you trade because they are rarely any better than just an eyeball estimate of an acceptable level of retracement. It is a two-legged pullback to a Higher Low after a Lower Low and therefore a possible start of a major bull run.

Bar 18 fulfilled the goal of a high above Bar 14 and traders clearly took profits.

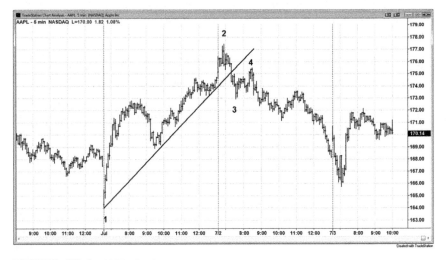

FIGURE 15.4   AAPL, 5-minute

Two-legged pullback to a Lower High (Bar 4 in Figure 15.4) after a trendline break. The trend was still up at Bar 3 because the trendline break is not yet a reversal. However, there was strong momentum on the move down to Bar 3 so smart traders would only buy a strong signal and instead would watch to see if the market failed again in its attempt to push above the 177 area where Bar 2 failed earlier.

Two-legged pullback to a Lower High (Bar 10 in Figure 15.5) after a trendline break. Bar 4 is not a misprint. It was a large gap up bull trend bar that closed on its high.

Amazon was in a strong daily bull but broke the major trendline on the move down to Bar 5. The bull is still in effect and traders will still be

FIGURE 15.5 AMZN, Daily

looking to buy for a test of the high if there is a good long setup (there was not). Because of the strength through the trendline and EMA, traders will look to short a test of the high, especially a second entry, whether it forms a Higher High or a Lower High.

The rally to Bar 6 was strong, but there was no clear second entry on this test of the high.

Bar 7 broke a smaller bull trendline, indicating more bearish strength, and then again tested the Bars 3 and 4 highs on the rally to Bar 10.

Bar 10 was Three Pushes Up from a sharp rally off Bar 7, and this always has to be considered a form of a Wedge reversal pattern. Bar 10 also formed an approximate Double Top Bear Flag with Bar 6 and a second test of the Bars 3 and 4 highs. This is as good a second entry short that a trader could hope to find: a Double Top Bear Flag made of a small Wedge in a two-legged rally to test the trend high (Bar 4) after a major trendline break (to Bar 5), all occurring at a time when traders were looking for a setup to allow them to go short with limited risk. Always make sure to swing part of your position after a major reversal, even if you get stopped out once or twice, because a single swing entry will usually make more money than many scalps.

Higher High (Bars 5 and 7 in Figure 15.6) after trendline breaks. Also, a Lower Low after a trendline break (Bar 11). The rally to Bar 5

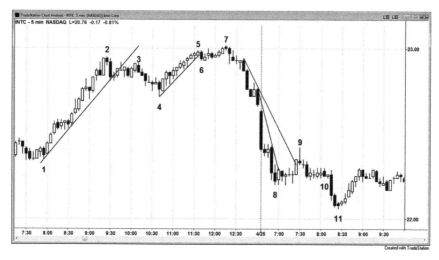

FIGURE 15.6 INTC, 5-Minute

was composed almost entirely of bull trend bars so a trader should wait
for more price action before shorting.

Bar 6 broke the Micro Trendline and then made a two-legged push to
a Higher High (higher than both Bar 2 and Bar 5) and was a strong short
setup and had a bear close.

There was also a Lower High (Bar 3) after a trendline break and Lower
Low (Bar 11) after a trendline break, which was a Failed Final Flag as well.

Bar 9 is a perfect example of why the break of the bear trendline does
not turn the market into a bull. It was a nice bear reversal, a Double Top
Bear Flag, two legs up, and a failed upside breakout of Barb Wire in a bear,
all setting up a good short trade. Even though Bar 9 was a doji, it is still a
good signal bar since it is setting up an entry in the direction of the trend
and there were several favorable factors that gave the trade an excellent
chance of success.

Higher High (Bar 7 in Figure 15.7) after a trendline break. It was
also a short entry on a large Expanding Triangle top (Bars 1, 2, 3, 4, and 7)

Bar 7 was a Failed Final Flag short after the trendline break down to
Bar 6. Since the Expanding Triangle Top formed over 10 months, traders
should expect that the bulls would not give up quickly. However, the Bar 7
high should hold if a major move down was to ensue, and that is where the
initial protective stop belongs.

Bar 8 was a Lower High after the sharp selloff below Bar 6 and a great
setup to trap the final bulls. It was a perfect Breakout Test of the short

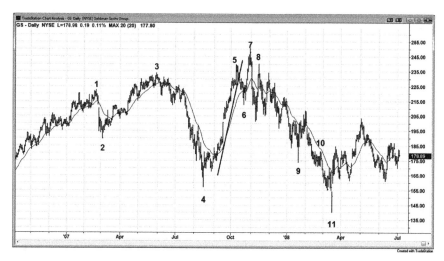

FIGURE 15.7 GS, Daily

below Bar 7. You always must look to short the first Lower High after a Higher High that could be a major reversal.

Once the market dropped below the Bar 6 spike down, the protective stop could be trailed above the most recent swing high.

Bar 11 was a long entry into an Expanding Triangle bull continuation pattern. Although that is a great trade, it is not as strong as the other reversals in this chapter.

There was also an acceptable short at the Lower High that followed Bar 3, and the Lower High at Bar 8, and a good long on the Higher Low that followed Bar 4 (there was a break of a steep trendline on the small rally up from Bar 4), and the pair of Higher Lows (Double Bottom Bull Flag) after Bar 11.

Three small pushes to a Lower Low (Bar 4 in Figure 15.8) after a trendline break.

Higher Low (Bar 6) after a trendline break (the bear trendline down from Bar 1). Bar 6 was the first Higher Low after a Lower Low that could be the end of a bear.

Higher High (Bar 9) after a trendline break.

The rally to Bar 3 broke the trendline but this alone does not create a new bull. The Wedge at Bar 3 was a strong short.

Three Pushes Up (Bar 4 in Figure 15.9), especially since it was near the top of a bear trading range. Also, Bar 1 was a Lower Low after the break of a steep trendline (not drawn).

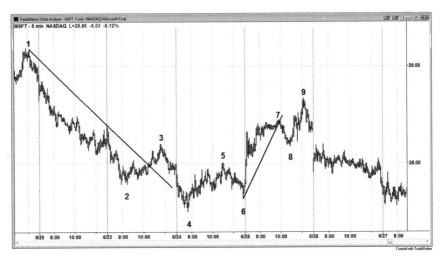

FIGURE 15.8 MSFT, 5-Minute

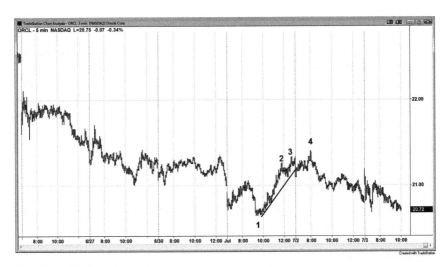

FIGURE 15.9 ORCL, 5-Minute

In Figure 15.10, there was a trend channel line overshoot and reversal (Bar 12).

Small Wedge top (Bar 2).

Lower High (Bar 4) after a trend line break.

Higher Low (Bars 6) after a trendline break. The rally from Bar 6 was a second leg up, but it ended in a Double Top Bear Flag.

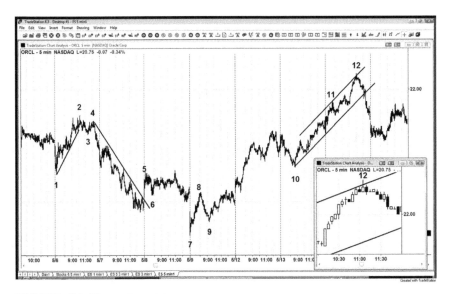

FIGURE 15.10 ORCL, 5-Minute

Lower Low (Bar 7) after a trendline break, followed by a Higher Low at Bar 9.

Bar 9 was the first Higher Low after a Lower Low that could be the bottom of the market (it followed a trendline break).

A broken channel in a Spike and Channel trend often corrects to near the start of the channel (here, Bar 10) as the market attempts to create a new range from which the next move will break out (in either direction).

Such a perfect day! If you look at the 5-minute chart on the right in Figure 15.11, the shape is unremarkable for a Higher Low bear trend reversal, but if you look at the price scale on the right, you can see that some of the bars were more than 30 points tall, in contrast to a normal day where the bars might have an average range of about 2 points. This is the market's attempt to put at least a temporary bottom in after the Dow lost 20 percent this week in the Obama Crash of 2008. The market tanked because of fear of Obama's policies, not the subprime mess, but that is irrelevant to trading. It's been clear for over a year that the market should fall below 10,000 in 2008 because it appeared that it might have entered a multiyear trading range. There may be a major top in place and the selling could lead to much lower prices, but a trading range is a more common and therefore more likely outcome. The worldwide fear that Obama's policies that will hurt businesses by increasing regulations and costs, and the fear that there would no longer be an economic leader of the free world, have just sped up the process.

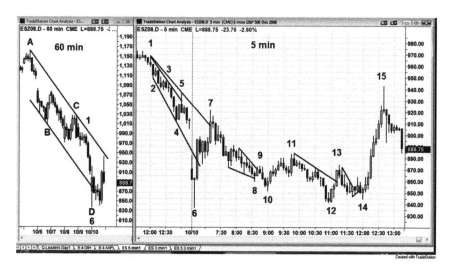

FIGURE 15.11 The Obama Crash of 2008

Even though the Dow had a range of 1,000 points today, it was still just another day at the office for a price action trader. If you cut your position size down to just 20 percent of normal because you had to risk about 10 points on each Emini trade, you could still end the day with more profit than on an average day by using a 4-point profit target. Also, on huge days like this, it is very important to swing part of your position and rely on a breakeven stop because there were many swings of 20 points or more. If there is an opposite signal before your breakeven stop is hit, exit, take a break, and marvel at the unbelievable profit you just made. Or, if you are an unusually good trader, reverse and repeat the process.

Today is Friday and the Dow had been down 200 to 700 points every day this week, so an attempt at a reversal was likely. However, you have to be patient and look for standard price action setups.

The chart on the left is a 60-minute chart and Bar D (it is also Bar 6 on the 5-minute chart on the right) fell through the trend channel line built off Bars A and C, and then reversed up.

On the 5-minute chart, Bar 6 formed a huge doji bar after the market fell below the Bar 2 to 4 trend channel line. Dojis are not great signal bars but the market was reversing trend channel line breakouts on both the 5- and 60-minute charts and the Dow was down 700 points, so a tradable rally was likely.

Bar 7 broke above the bear trendline but formed a Failed Final Flag top and two legs up, so a pullback was likely. However, the move up from the Bar 6 low was violent so it was likely that there would be a second leg up after a test of the bear trend low. Just patiently wait for a Higher Low (with that much upward momentum, a Lower Low was not expected). If your breakeven stop gets hit, enter again because there is an excellent chance of a very large move up under these circumstances and it is common for the market to hit breakeven stops a couple times before the trend accelerates upward.

Bar 10 was a possible bottom since it was a failure of a failed Wedge pullback and a Breakout Pullback (a Lower Low version) following the Bar 9 Micro trendline false breakout. However, the move down from Bar 7 lasted more than an hour or so and was very deep, so a second leg down was probable before the final bottom was in.

The move up to Bar 11 broke another bear trendline, so the bulls are gaining strength.

Bars 8 to 11 illustrate a common pattern in which a Failed Final Flag evolves into a Wedge. The flag breaks out and reverses up, as it did on Bar 10, and then there is a two-legged rally that is actually a third leg and therefore a Wedge. The first leg is the Bar 9 top of the Wedge. This type of larger pattern then often becomes a larger Failed Final Flag.

Bar 12 was a Lower Low compared to Bar 10 and therefore a possible Higher Low on the day, but the move down to Bar 12 had too much momentum and a test was likely.

The bull leg to Bar 13 had several bull trend bars and broke another bull trendline.

Bar 14 was a good-sized bull reversal bar and a Micro Trendline Breakout Pullback, and a Higher Low compared to Bar 12, so this could be the final low, which is was. This turned Bar 12 into the first strong Higher Low after Bar 6 and an excellent test of that bear low. This was the trade of the day and the one that you needed to be waiting for all day after the strong move up to Bar 7. There were many other trades today but this one was easy to anticipate and it unfolded perfectly. There were Trend Channel Line overshoots on the 5- and 60-minute charts, a huge move up to Bar 7, making a Higher Low likely, a two legged pullback to Bar 12 forming a possible 60-minute Higher Low, followed by a 5-minute Higher Low at Bar 14 that confirmed the Bar 12 Higher Low. You did not need the 60-minute chart to make this trade. It is here to show that there were longer time frame forces at work here as well and it is clear from the volume that institutions were paying attention to them.

Notice how the market has broken all four bear trendlines drawn on the chart (and longer ones that were not drawn). At some point, the developing bull trendlines (not drawn) become more important as the market transitions into a bull trend. Those bull trendlines include the ones drawn across the Bar 6 to Bar 10 lows, the Bar 6 to Bar 12 lows, and the Bar 12 to 14 lows.

Bar 15 was a doji but an excellent signal bar in this context. It was a trend channel line overshoot (not drawn but over the prior few bars) in a surge to a new high of the day. The runup was so sharp and the bar was so large that longs would be eager to take profits below Bar 15. Aggressive bears would know this and would be shorting, fully aware that no one on the other side would be eager to buy before seeing a pullback.

This is a perfect example of the importance of swinging part or all of your position at a major low. Your breakeven stop would have been hit on the long entry from Bar 12 but your long from Bar 14 would have made 60 points, and even if you increased your scalp size to 4 points, you still would have made as much as you did on 15 scalps!

Bar 15 reversed down after a new high on the day.

MINOR REVERSAL SCALPS DURING TRADING RANGE DAYS

If the swings are lasting for only a few bars to an hour or so, and the day is not a trend day, fading new swing highs and lows is an effective scalping technique, and it sometimes offers some reasonable swings as well. The very best of these minor reversals are second entries and Wedges at new extremes. One could question taking scalps when there are so many great swing trades, but the reason is simple. If there is a very high probability that you can make one point in the Emini by taking the trade, and the market can handle huge volume, you can make your entire day's profit off just one of these one-point scalps.

FIGURE 15.12   When a Day Is Not a Trend Day, It Is a Trading Range Day

Bar 2 in Figure 15.12 took out the high of the open so smart traders will be looking for a second entry short (if a Breakout Pullback long fails), which came after Bar 3. The up momentum at Bar 2 was strong enough that it is wiser to wait for a second entry to short.

Bar 9 was a second attempt up after breaking below the Bar 4 swing low and it was the second attempt to reverse the breakout to a new low (the first was the Bar 8 ii which became a Failed Final Flag).

FIGURE 15.13 On a Day That Is Not a Clear Trend Day, Traders Should Look to Fade New Extremes, Especially Second Entries and Wedges

Bar 1 in Figure 15.13 is a Wedge reversal with a strong reversal bar.

Bar 2 is a Wedge top.

Bar 4 is a doji in a steep decline and since it might just turn into a one- or two-bar bear flag, you need to wait for a second entry to buy.

Bar 5 is a reversal up from the second attempt to break out to a new low below Low 1. The inside bar that formed the signal bar had a bull close. It was also a Lower Low after the trendline break created by the move up from Bar 4, and a Failed Final Flag.

Bar 6 is a Low 4 short that reversed after breaking out above the Bar 3 swing high. It is also something of a Double Top Bear Flag (with Bar 3).

PULLBACKS IN A STRONG TREND

The sine qua non of this approach is that you believe that the chart is in a strong trend. Since most traders will not recognize that a day is trending on a 5-minute chart until after the first hour or two, these trades will usually not be in the first hour. The best setup is a two-legged pullback to the EMA. The pullback to the EMA usually looks as though it could never lead to much of a With Trend move, but invariably the move will take out the old trend extreme and carry much further than you would ever imagine. It is important to swing part of every With Trend entry on a strong trend day, even though that means that sometimes your breakeven stop will be hit on the swing portion of your trade. However, the big runs will more than make up for this. At every new setup, you can either simply add back your scalp portion or instead place a full position on top of your current open swing position. Once you scalp out of part, your swing portion is then twice the size of your normal swing (or three or four times, if you keep adding on at every new signal). Most traders would find it easier just to add their scalp contracts back because otherwise they will have ended up with too many contracts to be comfortable, and discomfort makes it hard to follow your rules.

Micro Trendline failed breakouts form High 1 long entries in a bull and Low 1 short entries in bear and are also excellent With Trend setups. If the entry fails within a bar or two, you then have a failure of a failed breakout, which is a Breakout Pullback and another reliable setup.

After the breakout below Bar 2 in Figure 15.14, traders would assume that today is a Trending Trading Range day or possibly even a stronger Trend from the Open Day. The Bar 4 Double Top Bear Flag began the bear Trend from the Open.

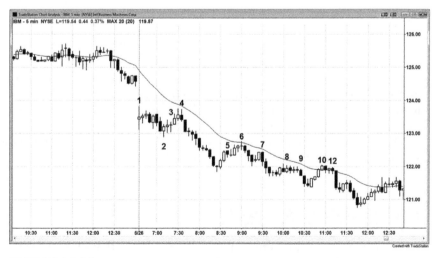

FIGURE 15.14   IBM, 5-Minute EMA Pullbacks in a Strong Trend

By Bar 6, traders should be shorting two-legged moves to the EMA and every Low 2 that they see.

Bar 6 is an M2S (Bar 5 was a small bear bar, ending the first leg up).

Bars 9 was a Low 2 short, and Bar 12 was a M2S (the small bull bar before it ended the second leg up). Neither look good, but you must trust that M2S entries have a very high probability of success during a strong bear trend day.

Almost every day, there will be stocks that are trending, and they will usually have one- or two-legged pullbacks to the EMA, offering great With Trend setups and limited risk.

By Bar 7 in Figure 15.15, traders would be looking at this as a likely Trending Trading Range Day, and they would buy the Bar 7 M2B and the Bar 8 Breakout Pullback (basically iii bodies).

Bar 14 was a Failed Breakout below the trading range at the close of yesterday and clearly a higher timeframe Higher Low, and the move up to Bar 15 might be leading to a Trend from the Open Day.

Bar 16 is a First Pullback long based on the Down Up Twin test of the EMA. It was also a Higher Low and an EMA Gap Bar long.

Bar 18 was not a good High 2 because the setup bar was a doji with a down close and it was setting up too close to the EMA magnet. Also, the move up to Bar 17 was parabolic and therefore climactic, and this usually makes a High 2 less reliable.

Bar 19 was a Three Push Down correction to the EMA.

Bar 21 was a High 2 with a Down Up Twin setup and a M2B.

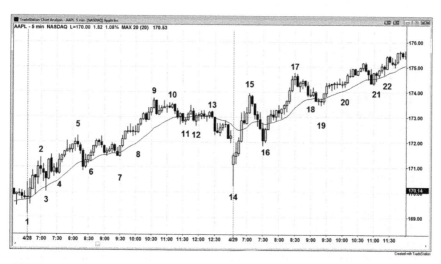

FIGURE 15.15 AAPL, 5-Minute, Trend Pullbacks

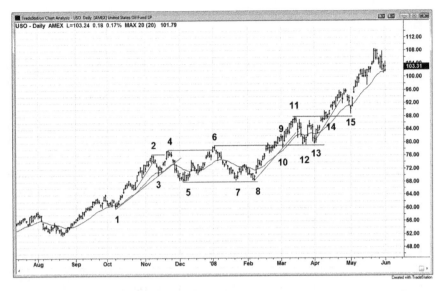

FIGURE 15.16 The Daily USO Was Clearly in a Bull Trend So the Best Trade Is a High 2, Especially Near the EMA

Bars 1, 5, and 12 in Figure 15.16 were clear buys.

Bars 8 and 13 were two-legged pullbacks below the EMA (Gap Bars).

Bar 8 was the second test of the Bar 5 trading range low, and Bar 13 was the second test of the Bar 6 trading range high breakout, and both formed a Double Bottom Bull Flags.

Bar 10 set up a second long entry on a Breakout Pullback (and a failed Expanding Triangle top from Bars 2, 3, 4, 5, 6, 8, and 9) and a Micro Trendline long.

Note that even though this is a clear bull, Bar 6 was a good short because there was first a trendline break down to Bar 5.

Bar 6 was a two-legged, Wedge- rally to a Higher High and the top of an Expanding Triangle (Bars 2, 3, 4, 5, and 6).

Bar 15 was a Breakout Test of Bar 11. Many With Trend setups will look terrible, but you have to trust your read and place your orders, or else you will be trapped out of great trades like so many other weak hands.

In a strong bull, you do not need setups to buy. You can buy at the market anywhere and make money, but setups allow you to use tighter stops.

This rally has a channel look so when the correction finally comes, the market will likely test the start of the channel in the area of the Bar 12 or even Bar 8 low (in fact, it fell all the way to 30 over the next 6 months).

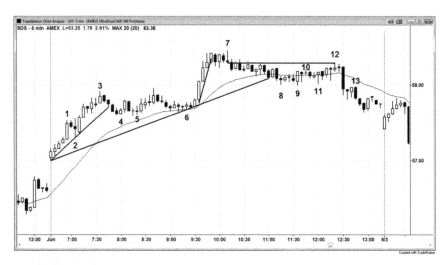

FIGURE 15.17 The 5-Minute SDS Had a Trend from the Open Day

There was strong up momentum with the first major leg ending at Bar 3 in Figure 15.17. When there is a strong bull, look to buy a High 2. Bars 5 and 6 were great High 2 long entries, and Bar 6 was also an M2B.

Bar 7 was the second leg up and a Failed Flag breakout that drifted down and broke the major trendline of the day.

When the market is no longer clearly trending, it no longer offers great trades. The remainder of this discussion is to remind traders of basic principles, and none of these trades belong in this chapter. The market was now sideways with lots of dojis, and smart traders would avoid this type of price action because there is too much risk of losing trades and not much chance of a big move.

Since there was no clear rally in the move down to Bar 8 and the bears have been in control for over an hour, it is reasonable to look for a second leg down (a possible Bear Spike and Trading Range top). Bar 10 was a small leg up, and Bar 12 was a second leg up, and it had a Low 2 on its rise from Bar 11. Also, Bar 12 was a small bar that gapped above the EMA. This is a good short for a second leg down.

Bar 13 was a Breakout Pullback of the Bar 9 breakout and a failed bull reversal bar, trapping longs.

So what were the high probability trades? Bars 5 and 6 in the strong trend were the best, and the Bar 12 short in the now sideways market was also a good trade. This short was a second leg up after breaking the bull trendline, a Low 4 and a Gap Bar in the second leg up from Bar 11 with a flat EMA, a Breakout Test of the short entry below the Bar 7 signal bar, and the second attempt to reverse the breakout above the Bar 10 swing high. However, only very experienced traders should be considering trades in Tight Trading Ranges and even most of them would look elsewhere. *Do not trade here!*

INTRADAY STOCKS

Trading stocks on a 5-minute chart is fairly easy if you limit yourself to three types of trades: EMA pullbacks in strong trends, clear and strong reversals after major trendline breaks, and first hour failed breakouts and breakout pullbacks of patterns from the prior day. The best trades are on strong trend days where most of the bars are on one side of the EMA and there are only a couple of EMA pullbacks during the day. Entering on those pullbacks, especially if they are M2B or M2S setups, is probably the single best stock day trade that you can make. If you follow a basket of about five stocks with large volume (over about 5 million shares traded each day) and an average daily range of three dollars or more, then you should be able to make one or two trades every day where you can net one dollar on the scalp portion of your trade and usually more on the swing portion. After entering, place a protective stop beyond the signal bar (you rarely will have to risk more than 1 dollar and usually under 60 cents) until the entry bar closes, and then move the stop to just beyond the entry bar. Once the stock moves about 60 to 80 cents in your direction, move the stop to breakeven and maybe a few pennies worse. For example, if you bought at 120.10 and the stock hit 120.80, move your stop to around 120.07. After you exit half or so of your trade on a limit order at 1 dollar of profit, rely on your breakeven stop. Trail your protective stop beyond swing points on the 5-minute chart and take a little more off at 2 dollars profit. Never exit the final portion until your stop is hit or unless a clear and strong opposite signal develops. There are several examples of this type of trade in the prior section.

The second type of trade is a trend reversal, but these are trickier for beginners because most reversals fail, and beginners tend to be overly eager and enter on weak setups. For a reversal, there has to be a strong break of a major trendline, with this first reversal leg showing a lot of momentum and having a strong reversal bar. You will then wait for a test of the trend's extreme and enter on a successful test (a Lower High or Higher High in a market top, or a Higher Low of a Lower Low in a market bottom). You want the signal bar to be a strong reversal bar. If the setup does not have every one of these components, do not take the trade. The stop management is the same as for the trend trades described above.

The final type of trade requires you to look for a pattern on yesterday's chart, like a flag, swing point, or trendline, and then today look to enter on a failed breakout or a breakout pullback. The high or low of the day commonly occurs on these opening reversals.

The market has been drifting down for several hours and has yet to pull back to the EMA, so this is a very strong bear trend. The best trades are the shorts on Bars 2 and 10 in Figure 15.18.

The Bar 2 entry price is 169.88, and the initial stop is above the entry bar at 170.38. The entry bar is an outside down bar, and you should place the stop above its high as soon as you enter, before the bar closes. This is reasonable because it defines your risk, and you would not want to be short if the market immediately reversed above the high of the bar. If it was not an outside bar, you would place your stop above the signal bar. The initial risk here is 50 cents.

Bar 5 was a High 1 that ran 7 cents above your short entry price, but you would not yet have moved your protective stop down because your largest open profit was only 38 cents, and you need to give your trade time to work. Typically, you should not move your stop to breakeven until there has been about 60 to 80 cents of open profit.

On Bar 6, you would have been able to exit half of your shares with one dollar profit using a limit order (the bottom of Bar 6 was 1.07 below your entry price). As you can see by the outside up nature of the bar, lots of traders likely covered part or all of their shorts as well. At this point, move your protective stop to breakeven or maybe a few pennies worse (170.91

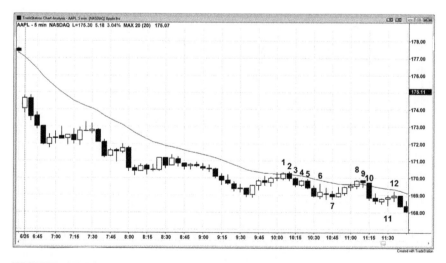

FIGURE 15.18 AAPL Is in a Trend from the Open Bear

is reasonable, since AAPL rarely runs stops by more than a penny), and do not exit unless there is a clear and strong reversal, which is unlikely on such a strong bear trend day. Expect pullbacks to scare weak shorts out. For example, the rally to Bar 9 hit breakeven stops to the penny (170.88) and then reversed back down.

If you were stopped out, you could short again on Bar 10, off the Bar 9 EMA test and Breakout Test. Bar 10 shows that the breakout test accomplished its goal of scaring traders out, because clearly lots of shorts came back in. If you let yourself be stopped out, you would now be short again, but at 41 cents worse!

However, in a Trend from the First Bar bear with only a couple of one bar rallies at the Bars 2 and 3 lows in Figure 15.19 (and those rallies never even got close to the EMA), there was no significant prior strong buying. Simply breaking a trend channel line is not a sufficient demonstration of bullish strength, and until that strength is present, any Countertrend trade is a scalp, which is a losing strategy against a strong trend.

If you think that the market fell too far, too fast and was due for a rally, look at the chart below (the bar numbering is the same). Once the Wedge bottom failed, the market fell another six dollars!

Never trade Countertrend unless the setup is perfect. It needs both a prior *strong* trendline break and a strong reversal bar.

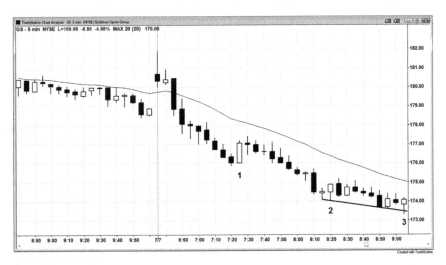

FIGURE 15.19   GS Sold off Hard but Formed a Wedge Bottom at the Bar 3 Strong Bull Reversal Bar

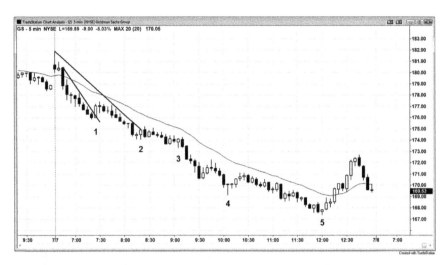

FIGURE 15.20 This is a perfect example of entries to avoid

Every day, you should be examining the chart throughout the day and especially in the first couple of hours to determine if the day is a trend day (the major types were described earlier). If it is, you should not be trading Countertrend. A Trend from the Open day like this in Figure 15.20 is the single easiest trend day to see. You would have suspected it by the third bar of the day (a large bear trend bar, dropping far from the open), and you would be very confident by the time the market broke below Bar 1.

The Bar 1 rally was a big bull trend bar, and it broke a trendline. An eager trader might then buy above the Bar 2, Bar 3, and Bar 4 reversal bars, thinking that the bulls showed adequate strength during that trendline break. However, the market has been below the EMA since the third bar of the day, and traders should remember that on Trend from the Open days like this, the first rally to the EMA usually fails and then tests the low. Don't convince yourself that the market has gone too far and is due for a rally. By definition, you are thinking Countertrend and looking for Countertrend scalps on a strong trend day. You are afraid to sell near the low and instead are hoping for a trend reversal, which is a low-probability bet. Do the math. Most long scalps will fail, and the amount you lose on each one will be too great to make up by the eventual winner or two.

On the other hand, GS did not have a tradable M2S all day, so most beginners eager to make a profit should look elsewhere for the best trades today. However, an experienced trader would be shorting even the tiniest pullbacks all day long, relying of the typical pullback sequence to bail him

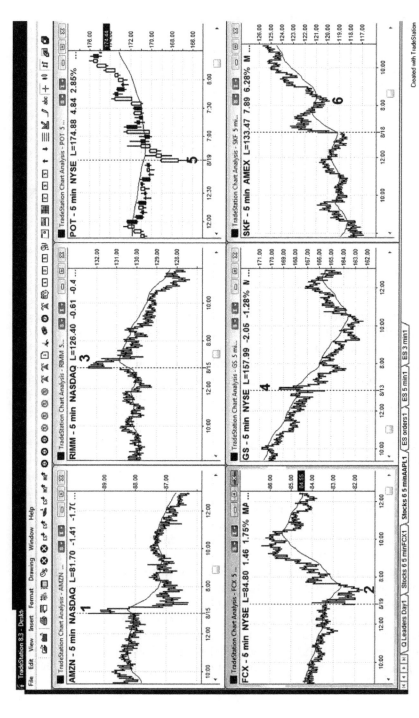

FIGURE 15.21 Stock Trades off the Open

out if a pullback went further up than he thought was likely. Every type of first pullback is usually followed by a test of the trend's extreme (here, the low of the day).

Always look for breakout pullbacks and failed breakouts.

Bar 1 in Figure 15.21 is a Failed Breakout short.

Bar 2 is a reversal up from a test of today's low, and it was a second attempt to sell off below yesterday's trading range (Failed Breakout). When two attempts at anything fail, it is likely that the market will do the opposite (here, rally). It is also a Wedge.

Bar 3 is a Failed Breakout above yesterday's high.

Bar 4 failed in its breakout above a bear trendline and above the EMA.

Bar 5 was a strong reversal bar up from a gap below yesterday's low (a Failed Breakout below yesterday's low).

Bar 6 was a Breakout Pullback from the opening rally that broke above yesterday's trading range. It was also a Higher Low at the EMA.

Trading Guidelines

Why guidelines and not rules? Because there are no rules.

1. Everything that you see is in a gray fog. Nothing is perfectly clear. Close is close enough. If something looks like a reliable pattern, it will likely trade like a reliable pattern.

2. Every bar is a signal bar for both directions and the market can begin a trend up or down on the next bar. Be open to all possibilities and when the surprise happens, don't question or deny it. Just read it and trade it.

3. Everything makes sense. If you know how to read price action, nothing will surprise you because you will understand what the market is doing. Beginners can see it on a printout at the end of the day. The goal is to learn how to read fast enough so that you can understand what is happening real time.

4. Simply understanding price action is not enough to make you profitable. You must learn how to take the best trades and follow your rules.

5. Trading is a job, and if you expect to make serious money, you need a business plan, just as you would have with any other business, and you must follow your plan. The plan can be simple, such as only taking two or three types of setups off a single 5-minute chart, scalping half and swinging the other half with a breakeven stop. However, you must follow your plan. The profit margin is tiny in this business so even a couple lapses in discipline a day can keep you in the red.

6. Don't turn the market into a casino, because that kind of math is relentless and unstoppable and will destroy you. Many strategies work often enough to make you believe that you will eventually be able to make a living off of them, but the math is against you. Trading off the 1-minute chart is the classic example. You win often enough to believe that you will eventually hone your skills to the point that you will make

a fortune. The reality is that many of the best trades happen too fast to catch and you will be left picking among the less profitable ones and make less than you would off the 5-minute, if you make anything at all.

7. There are no reliable Countertrend patterns, so never trade Countertrend unless there first has been a break of a *significant* trendline. And even then, first look for a With Trend trade that should lead to a test of the old trend's extreme. If the market once again reverses near the old extreme, then you should be entering in the direction of the new trend.

8. All patterns fail, and the failures often fail, but a failed failure is a second entry in the original direction and has a high probability of success.

9. When you see that one side is suddenly trapped, the reliability of a scalp in the opposite direction goes up. Trapped traders will be forced out as you are getting in, and they will likely wait for more price action before entering again in their original direction, so the only traders left will be in your direction.

10. Seeing traders getting trapped out of a trade on a stop run is as reliable a signal as seeing them getting trapped in a trade. If the market suddenly runs stops and then resumes its trend, this is a reliable setup for at least a scalper's profit.

11. Many beginners want excitement and tend to overtrade. Many great traders find trading to be lonely and boring, but very profitable.

12. Simple is better. You don't need indicators, and you should only look at one chart. If you can't make money off a single chart with no indicators, adding more things to analyze will only make it more difficult. Also, only trade the very best setups until you are consistently profitable.

13. Decide if this is a hobby or a job. If it is a hobby, find another one because this one will be too expensive and it is dangerously addictive. All great traders are likely trading addicts, but most trading addicts are or will likely end up broke.

14. If you can't juggle one ball, don't try to juggle two or three. If you are not yet making money, start with one chart, one market, one time frame (the 5-minute), and one concept (price action and not indicators).

15. Begin trading using a 5-minute chart and entering on a stop. Take some or all off on a limit order at a profit target, and then move the protective stop to breakeven on any remaining contracts.

16. Beginners should consider swing trading stocks instead of scalping or swinging Eminis because stock charts are usually easier to read and often trend well. The Eminis or bond futures become important

when your trading volume gets too large to allow for good fills in stocks.

17. When starting out, you should consider trading the SPY instead of the Emini. One Emini is identical to 500 SPY, and trading 300 to 500 SPY would allow you to scale out as you swing part of your trade, yet not incur much risk. Once you reach 1,000 to 1,500 SPY, if you are thinking that you will continue to increase your position size, then switch to the Emini. At that size, you can scale out of the Emini and you can increase your position size tremendously without slippage being a significant issue.

18. If you find that you did not take a couple Emini trades in a row and they worked, you are likely trading too large a position size. Switch to trading 100 to 300 shares of SPY and swing for at least 20 to 50 cents. Even though you won't get rich, at least you will make some money and build your confidence.

19. Buy low, sell high, except in a clear and strong trend (see chapter on trends). In a bull trend, buy High 2 setups even if they are at the high of the day, and in a bear, sell Low 2s. However, the market is in a trading range for the vast majority of the time. For example, if the market has been going up for a few bars and there is now a buy signal near the top of this leg up, ask yourself if you believe that the market is in one of the established clear and strong bull trend patterns described in this book. If you cannot convince yourself that it is, don't buy high, even if the momentum looks great, since the odds are great that you will be trapped.

20. Every segment of every chart commonly can be classified as more than one pattern, and almost always the patterns will point in the same direction. All you have to see is just one to place a trade. For example, a Failed Final Bear Flag long can also be a Double Bottom Bull Flag, and this might also be a Bull Spike and Trading Range Reversal that reversed up after overshooting a trend channel line and a larger bull trend line, and it can progress into a Spike and Channel Bull. If you recognize any of these, you can place a trade even if you do not see all of the others.

21. Good fill, bad trade. Always be suspicious if the market lets you in or out at a price that is better than you anticipated, but if the setup is good, take it. The corollary of bad fill, good trade is not as reliable.

22. Trends are always forming pullbacks that look like terrible entries but are profitable and reversals that look good but are losers. Most trend pullbacks follow just enough of a climax to make traders wonder if the trend has ended and trap traders out of entering on the pullback.

Also, the trend reversals are just good enough to attract and trap Countertrend traders. If you trade Countertrend, you are gambling, and although you will often win and have fun, the math is against you, and you will slowly but surely go broke. Countertrend setups in strong trends almost always fail and become great With Trend setups, especially on the 1 minute chart.

23. The easiest time to make money is in the first 90 minutes, and some of the easiest trades to spot are failed breakouts and breakout pullbacks of patterns from the prior day. Beginners should avoid trading in the middle of the day and in the middle of the day's range.

24. When you are about to take any trade, always ask yourself if the setup is one of the best of the day. Is this the one that the institutions have been waiting for all day? If the answer is "no" and you are not a consistently profitable trader, then you should not take the trade either. If you have two consecutive losers within 15-minutes or so, ask yourself if those were trades that the institutions have been waiting hours to take. If the answer is no, you are overtrading, and you need to become more patient.

25. Those who talk don't know and those who know don't talk. Don't watch TV or read any news. The traders who are making the most money trading are too busy to be on TV. Ask yourself, if you are netting even just two points in the Emini a day on large positions, do you really want to bother with going on TV? So why are you listening for trading ideas from someone who can't even make a couple points a day? Trading is a business, not a religion, so don't look for a trading savior.

26. Every bar and every series of bars is either a trend or a trading range. Pick one. Throughout the day and especially around 8:30 A.M. PST, you need to be deciding whether or not the day resembles any trend pattern described in this book. If it does and you are looking to take any trade, you must take every With Trend trade. Never consider taking a Countertrend trade if you haven't been taking all of the With Trend trades.

27. The best signal bars are trend bars in the direction of your trade. Doji bars are one bar trading ranges and therefore terrible signal bars. You will lose if you buy above a trading range in a bear or sell below one in a bull.

28. You will not make consistent money until you stop trading Countertrend scalps. You will win often enough to keep you trying to improve your technique, but over time your account will slowly disappear.

29. You will not make money until you start trading With Trend pullbacks.

30. You will not make money trading reversals until you wait for a break of a significant trendline and then for a strong reversal bar on a test of the trend's extreme.

31. You will not make money unless you know what you are doing. Print out the 5-minute Emini chart every day (and stock charts, if you trade stocks) and write on the chart every setup that you see. When you see several price action features, write them all on the chart. Do this every day for years until you can look at any part of any chart and instantly understand what is happening.

32. If you lost on two or three trades in a row or if you lost money on the day, you are overtrading and not being patient. You might be fooling yourself and looking for "low risk" early entries on the 1- or 3- minute charts, or you are trading Countertrend, or you are trading in Barb Wire. Bad habits always erase more than your winnings. You are on the path to a blown account, even though you might be moving slowly in that direction. But you will eventually get there.

33. You will not make money long term until you know enough about your personality to find a trading style that is compatible. You need to be able to follow your rules comfortably, allowing you to enter and exit trades with minimal or no uncertainty or anxiety. Once you have mastered a method of trading, if you feel stress while trading, then either you haven't yet found your style or yourself.

34. Always look for two legs. Also, when the market tries to do something twice and fails both times, that is a reliable signal that it will likely succeed in doing the opposite.

35. Never cherry pick because you will invariably pick enough rotten cherries to end up a loser. Either swing trade and look to take only the best two or three of the best setups of the day, or scalp and take every valid setup. That, however, is the more difficult alternative and is only for people with very unusual personalities (even more unusual than the rest of us traders!).

36. Beginners should only take the best trades and either scalp or swing. It is difficult to watch a screen for two or three hours at a time and not place a trade, but this is the best way for beginners to make money. If your overriding goal is to make money, this is what you must do. If you do not, then you have other goals that are interfering with what should really be your only goal.

37. Discipline is the single most important characteristic of winning traders. Trading is easy to understand but difficult to do. It is very difficult to follow simple rules, and even occasional self-indulgences

can be the difference between success and failure. Everyone can be as mentally tough as Tiger Woods for one shot, but few can be that tough for an entire round, and then be that way for a round every day of their lives. Everyone knows what mental toughness and discipline are, and everyone is mentally tough and disciplined in some activities every day, but few truly appreciate just how extreme and unrelenting you have to be to be a great trader. Develop the discipline to take only the best trades.

38. The second-most-important trait of great traders is the ability to do nothing for hours at a time. Don't succumb to boredom and let it convince you that it's been too long since the last trade.

39. Work on increasing your position size rather than on the number of trades or the variety of setups that you use. You only need to make one point in the Eminis a day to do well (100 contracts at 1 point a day is seven figures a year).

Glossary

All of these terms are defined in a practical way to be helpful to traders and not necessarily in the theoretical way often described by technicians.

2HM   The market has not touched the EMA for two or more hours. It is a sign of a strong trend, and it does not have to be the first two hours of the day.

Bar Pullback   In an upswing, it is a bar with a low below the low of the prior bar. In a downswing, it is a bar with a high above that of the prior bar.

Barb Wire   A trading range of three or more bars that largely overlap, and one or more is a doji. Only look to fade small bars near its extremes, especially if With Trend (for example, look to sell if the pattern is just below the EMA), and trend bar breakouts.

Bear Reversal   A change in trend from up to down (a bear trend).

Breakout   The high or low of the current bar extends beyond some prior price of significance such as a swing high or low, the high or low of any prior bar, a trendline, or a trend channel.

Breakout Bar (or Bar Breakout)   The current breaks out beyond the prior bar by having its high extend above the high of the prior bar or its low extend below the low of the prior bar.

Breakout Pullback   A small pullback of one to about five bars that occurs within a few bars after a breakout. It is a failed failure, since it is a breakout failure that failed. After two failures, the market usually produces a reliable trade.

Breakout Test   A Breakout Pullback that comes close to the original entry price. It may overshoot or undershoot by a few ticks. It can occur within a bar or two of entry or after an extended move (even several hours later on a 5-minute chart).

Bull Reversal   A change in trend from a down to up (a bull trend).

candle   The body is the area between the open and the close of the bar. If the close is above, it is a bull candle and shown as white in this book. If it is below, it is a bear candle and is black. The lines above and below are called tails, wicks, or shadows.

chart types   Line, bar, candle, volume, tick, and so on.

climax   A move that has gone too far too fast and has now reversed directions to either a trading range or an opposite trend. Most climaxes end with trend channel overshoots and reversals.

Countertrend   A trade or setup that is in the opposite direction from the current trend. In general, the direction of the most recent 5-minute signal should be assumed to be the trend's direction. Also, if most of the past 10 or 20 bars are below the EMA, With Trend is likely on the sell side.

day trade   A trade where the intent is to exit on the day of entry.

doji   A candle with a small body or no body at all. On a 5-minute chart, the body would be only 1 or 2 ticks, but on a daily chart, the body might be 10 or more ticks and still appear almost nonexistent. Neither the bulls nor the bears control the bar.

Double Bottom   The low of the current bar is about the same as the low of a prior swing low. That prior low can be just 1 bar earlier or 20 or more bars earlier. It does not have to be at the low of the day, and it commonly forms in bull flags (a Double Bottom Bull Flag).

Double Bottom Bull Flag   A pause or flag in a bull trend that has two spikes down to around the same price and then reverses back into a bull trend.

Double Bottom Pullback   A buy setup composed of a Double Bottom followed by a deep pullback that forms a Higher Low.

Double Bottom Twin   Two consecutive bars in a strong bear that have identical lows and small or nonexistent tails.

Double Top   The high of the current bar is about the same as the high of a prior swing high. That prior high can be just one bar earlier or 20 or more bars earlier. It does not have to be at the high of the day, and it commonly forms in a bear flag (Double Top Bear Flag).

Double Top Bear Flag   A pause or flag in a bear trend that has two spikes up to around the same price and then reverses back into a bear trend.

Double Top Pullback   A sell setup composed of a Double Top followed by a deep pullback that forms a Lower High.

Double Top Twin   Two consecutive bars in a strong bull that have identical highs and small or nonexistent tails.

Down Up Twin   A bull reversal setup where there are two overlapping bars that have bodies of similar size, and the first one is a bear trend bar, and the second is a bull trend bar.

early longs   Traders who buy as a bull reversal or trend bar is forming rather than waiting for it to close and then entering on a buy stop at one tick above its high.

early shorts   Traders who sell as a bear reversal or trend bar is forming rather than waiting for it to close and then entering on a sell stop at one tick below its low.

EMA The charts in this book use a 20-bar exponential moving average.

EMA Gap Bar In a flat or down market, it is a bar with a low above the EMA. In a flat or up market, it is a bar with a high below the EMA.

entry bar The bar during which a trade is entered.

fade Place a trade in the opposite direction of the trend (for example, selling a bull breakout that you expect to fail and reverse downward).

Failed Failure A failure that fails, resuming in the direction of the original breakout. Since it is a second signal, it is more reliable.

Failure A move where the protective stop is hit before a scalper's profit is secured or before the trader's objective is reached, usually leading to a move in the opposite direction as trapped traders are forced to exit at a loss. Currently, a scalper's target in the Emini of 4 ticks requires a 6-tick move, and a target in the QQQQ of ten ticks requires a 12 cent move.

Five-Tick Failure: A trade in the Emini that reaches five ticks beyond the signal bar and then reverses (for example, a breakout of a bull flag runs five ticks, and once the bar closes, the next bar has a low that is lower). It is usually a setup for a trade in the opposite direction.

gap A gap is a space between any two prices on the chart. An opening gap is a common occurrence and is present if the open of the first bar of today is beyond the high or low of the prior bar (the last bar of yesterday) or of the entire day. An EMA Gap is present when the low of a bar is above a flat or falling moving average, or the high of a bar is below a flat or rising moving average.

gap reversal A gap reversal attempt is present when the current bar extends one tick beyond the prior bar into the gap.

Gap 2 If the first gap reversal fails, and then a second attempt to close the gap develops, this second attempt is a Gap 2.

High 1, 2, 3, or 4 A High 1 is a bar with a high above the prior bar in a correction in an up or sideways market. If there is then a bar with a Lower High (it can occur one or several bars later), the next bar in this correction whose high is above the prior bar's high is a High 2. Third and fourth occurrences are a High 3 and 4. There are other variations as well.

High/Low 1 or 2 either a High 1 or 2, or a Low 1 or 2.

Higher High A swing high that is higher than a previous swing high.

Higher Low A swing low that is higher than a previous swing low.

Higher Time Frame A chart with each bar representing more time or trades than the bars on the current chart (for instance, a 60-minute chart is a higher time frame for all charts that have bars of 59 minutes or shorter; a monthly chart is the highest time frame).

ii Consecutive inside bars, with the second being inside the first. It is often a reversal signal in an overextended market. A less reliable version is when the second body is inside the first body, which is inside the body before it (ignore tails).

iii Three inside bars in a row and a somewhat more reliable pattern that an ii.

Inside Bar A bar with a high that is at or below the high of the prior bar and a low that is at or above the low of the prior bar.

ioi Outside bar with the bars before it and after it having highs below its high and lows above its low. It is often a breakout setup where a trader looks to buy above the inside bar or sell below it.

leg A small trend that breaks a trendline of any size, and the term is used only where there are at least two on the chart. It is any smaller trend that is part of a larger trend, and it can be a pullback (a Countertrend move), a swing in a trend or in a sideways market, or a With Trend move in a trend that occurs between any two pullbacks within the trend.

long A person who buys a position in a market or the actual position itself.

lot The smallest position size that can be traded in a market. It is a share when referring to stocks and a contract when referring to Eminis.

Low 1, 2, 3, or 4 A Low 1 is a bar with a low below the prior bar in a correction in a down or sideways market. If there is then a bar with a Higher Low (it can occur one or several bars later), the next bar in this correction whose low is below the prior bar's low is a Low 2. Third and fourth occurrences are a Low 3 and 4. There are other variations as well.

Lower High A swing high that is lower than a previous swing high.

Lower Low A swing low that is lower than a previous swing low.

M2B and M2S A second pullback to the EMA. An M2B is a High 2 in a bull and a buy setup or entry, and an M2S is a Low 2 in a bear and a sell setup or entry.

major trendline Any trendline that contains most of the price action on the screen, and it will typically be drawn using bars that are at least 10 or 20 bars apart.

micro trendline A trendline on any time frame that is drawn across from 2 to about 10 bars where most of the bars touch or are close to the trendline, and then one of the bars has a false breakout through the trendline. This false breakout sets up a With Trend High/Low 1 entry. If it fails within a bar or two, then there is usually a Countertrend trade (a Breakout Pullback from the break beyond the trendline).

Money Stop A stop based on a fixed dollar amount or number of points, like two points in the Eminis.

Opening Reversal A reversal in the first hour or so.

Opposite Twins An Up Down Twin or a Down Up Twin.

Outside Bar A bar with a high that is above (or, rarely, at) the high of the prior bar and a low that is below (or, rarely, at) the low of the prior bar.

overshoot The market surpasses a prior price of significance like a swing point or a trend channel line.

Pause Bar A bar that does not extend the trend. In a bull, a pause bar has a high that is at or below the prior bar, or a small bar with a high that is only a tick or so higher than the previous bar when the previous bar is a strong bull trend bar.

Price Action Any change in price on any chart type or time frame.

pullback A pullback is a temporary Countertrend move and is part of a trend, swing, or leg, and does not retrace beyond the start of the trend, swing, or leg. For example, a bull pullback is a sideways to downward move in a bull trend, swing, or leg that will be followed by at least a test of the prior high.

Pullback Bar A bar that reverses the prior bar by at least one tick. In an uptrend, it is a bar with a low below that of the prior bar.

Reversal: A reversal from a trend of any size to a trading range or an opposite trend.

Reversal Bar A trend bar in the opposite direction of the trend. In a bear, a bull trend bar has a tail at the bottom and a close above the open and near the top. A bear reversal bar has a tail at the top and a close below the open and near the bottom.

scalp A trade that is exited with a small profit, usually before there are any pullbacks. For the Eminis, the profit target might be four or eight ticks, or a test of the prior extreme. For the SPY or stocks, it might be 10 or 20 cents. For more expensive stocks, it can be $1 or $2.

scalper A trader who primarily scalps for small profit, usually using a tight stop.

scalper's profit A typical amount of profit that a scalper would be targeting.

scratch A trade that is close to breakeven with either a small profit or loss.

second entry The second time within a few bars of the first entry that there is an entry bar based on the same logic as the first entry (for example, a second signal within three or four bars).

setup A pattern of one or more bars used by traders as the basis to place entry orders. If an entry order is filled, the last bar of the setup becomes the signal bar. Most setups are just a single bar.

Shaved Body A candle with no tail at one or both ends. A Shaved Top has no tail at the top, and a Shaved Bottom has no tail at the bottom.

short As a verb, to sell a stock or future to initiate a new position (not to exit a prior purchase). As a noun, it is a person who sells something short, or the actual position itself.

Shrinking Stairs A series of three or more trending highs in a bull or lows in a bear where each breakout to a new extreme is by fewer ticks than the prior breakout, indicating waning momentum. It can be a Three Push pattern, but it does not have to resemble a Wedge and can be any broad swings in a trend.

Signal Bar   The bar immediately before the entry bar (the bar in which an entry order is filled). It is the final bar of a setup.

smaller time frame   A time frame that has more bars per hour than the current chart. If the chart is based on time, each bar contains less time (for instance, a 3-minute chart is a smaller time frame for all charts that have bars of four minutes or longer; a tick chart with each bar being only a single tick is the smallest time frame).

Stairs   A series of three or more trending swings that resembles a sloping trading range and is roughly contained in a channel. Two-way trade is taking place, but one side is in slightly more control, accounting for the slope.

swing   A smaller trend that breaks a trendline of any size; the term is used only when there are at least two on the chart. They can occur within a larger trend or in a sideways market.

Swing High   A bar that looks like a spike that extends up beyond the neighboring bars on the chart. Its high is at or above that of the bar before and the bar after it.

Swing High/Low   Either a swing high or a swing low.

Swing Low   A bar that looks like a spike that extends down beyond the neighboring bars on the chart. Its low is at or below that of the bar before and the bar after it.

Swing Point   Either a swing high or low.

Swing Trade   For a day trader using a short-term intraday chart like the 5-minute, it is any trade that lasts longer than a scalp and the trader will hold through one or more pullbacks. For a trader using higher time frame charts, it is a trade that lasts for hours to several days. Typically, at least part of the trade is held without a profit target, since the trader is hoping for an extended move.

test   The market approaches a prior price of significance, and it may break through it or fail and reverse. The failure can be an overshoot or an undershoot.

Three Pushes   Three swing highs where each swing high is higher or three swing lows where each swing low is lower. It trades the same as a Wedge and should be considered a variant.

tick   The smallest unit of price movement. For most stocks, it is one penny, for Ten Year Note futures, it is 1/64th of a point, and for Eminis, it is 0.25 points. On tick charts and on time and sales tables, a tick is every trade that takes place, no matter the size, and even if there is no price change. If you look at a time and sales table, every trade is counted as one tick when TradeStation charting software creates a tick chart.

Tight Trading Range   Any sideways movement of two or more bars with lots of overlap in the bars. The bulls and bears are in balance.

time frame The length of time contained in one bar on the chart (a five-minute time frame is made of bars that close every five minutes). It can also refer to bars not based on time, such as those based on volume or the number of ticks traded.

tradable The trade moved far enough to make at least a profitable scalp.

Trading Range Sideways movement, and neither the bulls nor the bears are in control.

trap An entry that immediately reverses to the opposite direction before a scalper's profit target is reached, trapping traders in their new position, ultimately forcing them to cover at a loss. It can also scare traders out of a good trade.

Trapped in a Trade A trader with an open loss on a trade that did not result in a scalper's profit, and if there is a pullback beyond the entry or signal bars, he will likely take his loss.

Trapped Out of a Trade A pullback that scares a trader into exiting a trade, but then the pullback fails. The market quickly resumes the move in the direction of the trade, making it difficult emotionally for the trader to get back in at the worse price that is now available. He will have to chase the market.

trend A series of price changes that are either mostly up (a bull trend or a bull) or down (a bear trend or a bear). There are three loosely defined smaller versions: swings, legs, and pullbacks. A chart will show only one or two major trends. If there are more, one of the other terms is more appropriate.

Trend Bar A bar with a body, which means that the close was above or below the open and is indicative of at least a minor price movement.

Trend Channel Line A line in the direction of the trend but drawn on the opposite side of the bars compared to a trendline. A bull trend channel line is above the highs and rising to the right and a bear trend channel line is a line that falls to the right and is below the lows.

Trend Channel Line Overshoot A bar penetrates a trend channel line.

Trend Channel Line Undershoot A bar approaches a trend channel line, but the market reverses away from the line without penetrating it.

Trend from the Open or First Bar A trend that begins at the first or second bar of the day and extends for many bars without a pullback, and the start of the trend remains as one of the extremes of the day for much if not all of the day.

Trending Closes Three or more bars where the closes are trending. In a bull, each close is above the prior close and in a bear, each close is lower. If the pattern extends for many bars, there can be one or two bars where the closes are not trending.

Trending Highs or Lows The same as trending closes except based on the highs or lows of the bars.

Trending Swings   Three or more swings where the swing highs and lows are both higher than the prior swing highs and lows (trending bull swings), or both lower (trending bear swings).

trendline   A line drawn in the direction of the trend. Most often, it is constructed from either swing highs or lows but can be based on linear regression or just a best fit (eyeballing).

Trend Reversal   A trend change from up to down or down to up, or from a trend to a trading range.

twin   Two consecutive bars that share some characteristic (like Up Down bars or Double Bottom bars).

undershoot   The market approaches but does not reach a prior price of significance like a swing point or a trendline.

Up Down Twin   A bear reversal setup where there are two overlapping bars that have similar size and the first one is a bull trend bar and the second is a bear trend bar.

Wedge   Traditionally it is a Three Push move with each push extending further, and the trendline and trend channel line are at least minimally convergent, creating a rising or descending triangle or Wedge-shaped pattern. For a trader, the Wedge shape increases the chances of a successful trade, but any Three Push pattern trades like a Wedge and can be considered one.

With Trend   A trade or a setup that is in the direction of the prevailing trend. In general, the direction of the most recent 5-minute signal should be assumed to be the trend's direction. Also, if most of the past 10 or 20 bars are above the EMA, trend setups and trades are likely on the buy side.

About the Author

A l Brooks, MD is 56 years old and has been trading full-time for his personal account for about 20 years. After growing up in a working-class family in New England and graduating with general honors and honors in math from Trinity College (Connecticut), he went to medical school at the University of Chicago where he also completed his ophthalmology residency. During his stay in Chicago, he always wondered if he should drop out and work on the floor of the Merc, but was too scared to take the chance. Upon completion of his residency, he was selected as a Heed Fellow, which is the most prestigious national award given to the top new ophthalmologists in the country. He then taught for a year at the Emory University School of Medicine and practiced in Los Angeles for about 10 years. During his academic years, he published more than 30 scientific papers and regularly presented his work at national ophthalmology meetings. In Los Angeles, he built one of the first Medicare-approved eye surgery centers in California and performed thousands of operations in his office OR.

Fifteen months after the birth of his first child in 1988, he had identical twin girls, and this gave him a great excuse to leave medicine (three girls under the age of 15 months). He sold his practice, moved to a small town outside of Sacramento, stayed home to raise his kids, and started trading. His girls are all in college now (two at Berkeley, one at Yale), and he is happy, living alone, and quietly trading his personal accounts. He is close to his family and has a couple fly fishing and tennis buddies and a girlfriend, but he spends most of his time alone, either trading, evaluating charts, watching news and political talk shows, or playing or watching sports (especially track and field and college football).

For the first 10 years of trading, he spent 10,000 hours writing and testing indicators and systems, making trading far more complicated than what logic told him it should be. About 10 years ago, he decided to start over again from the bottom up and trade off just price action, with the intention of adding indicators as needed over time. What he discovered was that simply reading price action alone off a single chart was all that was needed to be a successful trader, and he therefore decided to eschew indicators and adopted a minimalist perspective on trading.

As a scalper, he needs to focus intensely on every tick, and he doesn't want distractions. His room is dimly lit, all of the shades are fully drawn, and he trades off a single notebook computer screen. He has another computer on his desk with two 21″ monitors, but he keeps it off during the trading day and never uses it for trading. He trades best when he has minimal distractions and only a single chart with no indicators (other than a 20-bar EMA) and no additional monitors. He currently uses TradeStation for charting and places most of his trades through other brokers using price ladders without any front-end programs that automatically generate OCO profit limit orders and stop orders. He briefly tried a front-end program a few years ago, but using it violated his fundamental principle of keeping his life as simple as possible, so he stopped. He freely admits to being prone to making mistakes, and that costs him money, so the simpler he can structure his life, the less he gives back. He never watches TV while trading and has no interest in the results of economic reports or the opinions of experts. He also never reads newspapers, and he gets all of his news from the Internet. He just trades the price action that comes from those reports, rarely ever finding out what the actual numbers were. Although he has a high IQ, he feels that he simply is not fast enough to process all of the ramifications of a report, read the 5-minute chart, and place his orders correctly. He believes that he is far more profitable when he only trades off the 5-minute chart in front of him and ignores all other input and opinions. He also doesn't care where the market is going in the next year or even the next hour. All he wants to know is whether he has an 80 percent chance of making a profit in the next 1 to 10 minutes with little risk. Since all of his entries are on stops, he considers himself a trend trader because he gets swept into a trade by the market going in the direction he needs it to go to make a profit. He prefers fading moves because the least stressful trades for him are the ones where he strongly believes that traders are suddenly trapped on the wrong side and have to get out. However, he also enters on pullbacks in trends. If the trend is weak, there is a risk that he will be entering the pullback early. He finds this more stressful than a quick fade where he usually scalps out with a profit within a couple of minutes and the market does not hesitate at all on its path to his profit target.

He runs several days a week, lifts weights, plays tennis, and enjoys bike riding. He also likes to fly fish, hike, and ski, which is why he chose to live only 90 miles from Lake Tahoe (and he likes being only 75 miles from Napa and 100 miles from San Francisco).

Index